GENDER
AND
GOVERNANCE IN
RURAL SERVICES

GENDER
AND
GOVERNANCE IN
RURAL SERVICES

Insights from India, Ghana, and Ethiopia

THE WORLD BANK
Washington, D.C.

INTERNATIONAL FOOD POLICY
RESEARCH INSTITUTE

Supported by the CGIAR

© 2010 The International Bank for Reconstruction and Development / The World Bank
1818 H Street, NW
Washington, DC 20433
Telephone: 202-473-1000
Internet: www.worldbank.org
E-mail: feedback@worldbank.org

This volume is a product of the staff of the International Bank for Reconstruction and Development / The World Bank. The findings, interpretations, and conclusions expressed in this volume do not necessarily reflect the views of the Executive Directors of The World Bank or the governments they represent.

The World Bank does not guarantee the accuracy of the data included in this work. The boundaries, colors, denominations, and other information shown on any map in this work do not imply any judgment on the part of The World Bank concerning the legal status of any territory or the endorsement or acceptance of such boundaries.

Rights and Permissions

ISBN: 978-0-8213-7658-4
eISBN: 978-0-8213-8156-4
DOI: 10.1596/978-0-8213-7658-4

Library of Congress Cataloging-in-Publication Data

Gender and governance in rural services : insights from India, Ghana, and Ethiopia / the World Bank and International Food Policy Research Institute.
    p. cm.
    ISBN 978-0-8213-7658-4 — ISBN 978-0-8213-8156-4 (electronic)
    1. Rural development projects—India—Case studies. 2. Rural development projects—Ghana—Case studies. 3. Rural development projects—Ethiopia—Case studies. 4. Rural women—Services for—India—Case studies. 5. Rural women—Services for—Ghana—Case studies. 6. Rural women—Services for—Ethiopia—Case studies. 7. Rural women—India—Social conditions—Case studies. 8. Rural women—Ghana—Social conditions—Case studies. 9. Rural women—Ethiopia—Social conditions—Case studies. 10. Rural development—Government policy—India—Case studies. 11. Rural development—Government policy—Ghana—Case studies. 12. Rural development—Government policy—Ethiopia—Case studies. I. World Bank. II. International Food Policy Research Institute.
    HN49.C6G44 2009 2010
    307.1'412091724—dc22

                                                                        2009033126

Cover photo: Dominic Sansoni, World Bank (background);
Simone McCourtie, World Bank (foreground).
Cover design: Patricia Hord Graphik Design.

CONTENTS

BOXES, FIGURES, AND TABLES

Boxes

Figures

Tables

FOREWORD

Agricultural development throughout the developing world relies on the provision of economic services. Agricultural extension that enables farmers to increase their productivity and income and to link their production to markets is among the most vital of these services. Other, nonagricultural services, such as the delivery of safe drinking water, are similarly important for rural households.

A variety of factors makes provision of these rural services challenging: they have to be delivered every day throughout the country, even in remote areas, and service providers have often limited incentives to provide them efficiently.

An extensive body of literature has grown around the question of how to make demand for rural services more effective and how to improve the responsiveness of providers to this demand. If this body of literature conveys any consistent message, it is that no one-size-fits-all solution applies to the diverse settings in which services are to be delivered. Prevailing institutional structures and social norms impinge on the effectiveness of service provision in many ways. Context matters, particularly when designing services to reach women. And services that lack specific provision to reach women often bypass them altogether. Women make up the majority of the poorest 1.3 billion people in the world, and the global community formally recognized gender inequality as one of the major hurdles to development when it set gender equality and the empowerment of women as the third Millennium Development Goal.

Gender and Governance in Rural Services: Insights from India, Ghana, and Ethiopia hits at the center of these issues. Focusing on agricultural extension and rural drinking water supply, it provides an excellent description of the realities on the ground and explores approaches and strategies that work—and those that do not—in several contexts. The research project, which applies an accountability framework based on the *World Development Report 2004: Making Services Work for Poor People,* provides a useful and adaptable reference for analyzing the relations among citizens, public officials, and service providers in a variety of development settings.

In low-income agriculture-based countries such as Ethiopia and Ghana, where agriculture is a major engine of economic growth, the *World Development Report 2008: Agriculture for Development* emphasized the need for a productivity revolution in smallholder farming as a prerequisite for fulfilling the sector's tremendous potential both to contribute to macroeconomic development and to reduce poverty. In transforming countries such as India, where agriculture's share of economic activity is declining but the poor are nevertheless overwhelmingly concentrated in rural areas, a comprehensive approach is needed that pursues multiple pathways out of poverty: shifting to high-value agriculture, expanding nonfarm economic activity to rural areas, and enabling people to move out of agriculture. In both types of settings, women emerge in two lights. They often belong to the most constrained and vulnerable segments of the population. At the same time, their potential as agents of development is unparalleled. As gender research of the International Food Policy Research Institute has shown, increasing women's resources has particularly strong effects on household welfare, nutrition, and agricultural productivity. A productivity revolution in smallholder farming and mass poverty reduction through the proliferation of rural livelihoods will not be possible without women. Reaching rural women with resources and services is therefore a cardinal priority for agricultural and rural development. This book provides a wealth of important insights on how to achieve this challenging goal.

Juergen Voegele
Director
Agriculture and Rural Development
World Bank

Joachim von Braun
Director General
International Food Policy Research Institute

ACKNOWLEDGMENTS

This report was produced by a team from the International Food Policy Research Institute (IFPRI) and its partner institutions: the Institute of Social and Economic Change (ISEC) and the Tata Institute of Social Sciences (TISS) in India; the Institute of Statistical Social and Economic Research (ISSER) of the University of Ghana, Legon; and the Ethiopian Economic Policy Research Institute (EEPRI). Team members included Felix Asante, Afua B. Banful, Regina Birner, Marc J. Cohen, Peter Gaff, K. G. Gayathridevi, Leah Horowitz, Mamusha Lemma, Tewodaj Mogues, Nethra Palaniswamy, Zelekawork Paulos, Katharina Raabe, Josee Randriamamonjy, Madhushree Sekher, Yan Sun, and Fanaye Tadesse. The specific roles of the author team members are described below.

Felix Asante	■ Ghana survey implementation (lead)
	■ Analysis of Ghana survey data
Afua B. Banful	■ Analysis of Ghana survey data
Regina Birner	■ Overall management of project
	■ Karnataka surveys I and II implementation
	■ Bihar case studies
	■ Ghana survey implementation
Marc J. Cohen	■ Ethiopia case studies
Peter Gaff	■ Analysis of Karnataka II survey data
	■ Editorial assistance

K. G. Gayathridevi	■ Karnataka survey II implementation (lead)
	■ Bihar case studies
Leah Horowitz	■ Ghana case studies
Mamusha Lemma	■ Ethiopia case studies
Tewodaj Mogues	■ Ethiopia survey implementation
	■ Analysis of Ethiopia survey data
Nethra Palaniswamy	■ Karnataka I survey implementation
	■ Analysis of Karnataka I survey data
	■ Ghana survey implementation
Zelekawork Paulos	■ Ethiopia survey implementation
	■ Analysis of Ethiopia survey data
Katharina Raabe	■ Karnataka II survey implementation
	■ Analysis of Karnataka I and II survey data
	■ Bihar case studies
Josee Randriamamonjy	■ Analysis of Ethiopia survey data
Madhushree Sekher	■ Karnataka I survey implementation (lead)
	■ Karnataka II survey implementation
	■ Bihar case studies
Yan Sun	■ Analysis of Ghana survey data
Fanaye Tadesse	■ Ethiopia survey implementation
	■ Analysis of Ethiopia survey data

Data for the report were collected under the Gender and Governance in Rural Services project. In Ghana and Ethiopia, quantitative data were collected through surveys of household heads and their spouses, local political representatives, service providers, community leaders, and representatives of community-based organizations. Case studies were also conducted in the two countries. In India, two data sources were combined: a survey of households, communities, and local political representatives conducted in Karnataka under an earlier project and a survey of service providers and community-based organizations conducted under this project. Case studies were conducted in Bihar.

The Gender and Governance in Rural Services project was funded by the World Bank under the Bank Netherlands Partnership Program (BNPP) Trust Fund. The project was managed by Eija Pehu (task team leader, Agriculture and Rural Development Department [ARD]) and coordinated by Catherine Ragasa (ARD). Guidance for the project was provided by a World Bank task force comprising the following members: Nilufar Ahmad (South Asia Region–Social Development [SASDS]), Isabelle Bleas (World Bank Institute), Maria Correia (Africa Region Fragile States, Conflicts and Social Development [AFTCS]), Nora Dudwick (Poverty Reduction and Economic Management–Poverty Reduction [PRMPR]), Meena Munshi (SASDA), Nicolas Perrin (Social Development

Department [SDV]), Biju Rao (Development Economics [DEC]), and Sarosh Sattar (ECSPE [Europe and Central Region Poverty Reduction and Economic Management]). The peer reviewers for the project were Meheret Ayenew (Addis Ababa University); Radu Ban (DEC); Anne-Marie Goetz (United Nations Development Fund for Women [UNIFEM]); Reena Gupta (World Bank India Country Office); Jeannette Gurung (Women Organizing for Change in Agriculture and Natural Resources); Severin Kodderitzsch (World Bank India Country Office); Dr. S. S. Meenakshisundaram (National Institute of Advanced Studies, India); Smita Misra (World Bank India Country Office); Abena Oduro (University of Ghana); Nicolas Perrin (SDV); Giovanna Prennushi (World Bank India Country Office); Agnes Quisumbing (IFPRI); Aruna Rao (Gender at Work); Parmesh Shah (Agricultural and Rural Development, South Asia Region); and Melissa Williams (ARD, South Asia Region). Additional funding for the surveys drawn on in this report was provided by Irish Aid, under the Food and Livelihood Security Programme; by the World Bank, under the multidonor Trust Fund supporting the Productive Safety Net Programme; and by IFPRI, under its Ghana and Ethiopia Strategy Support Programs, funded by the Canadian International Development Agency (CIDA), the U.K. Department for International Development (DFID), the Embassy of Ireland in Ethiopia, the German Technical Cooperation Agency (GTZ), the Netherlands, and the U.S. Agency for International Development (USAID).

The author team would like to thank the following organizations and people who contributed in various ways to the project. In India, the Department of Rural Development, and Panchayati Raj of Karnataka provided support throughout the project. S. Srikanth, V. P. Baligar, and M. R. Srinivasa Murthy facilitated the surveys in their function as secretaries of the Department of Rural Development and Panchayati Raj. K. V. Raju, formerly with the Institute for Social and Economic Change and currently economic advisor to the chief minister of Karnataka, also supported the study. The field supervisors of the survey team for the Karnataka I survey were R. Bettappa, S. Chandrahasa, and Badrinarayan Rath. The Karnataka II survey team comprised Priyanka Das, Channabasavana Gouda, Veeresh Hugar, S. Kavitha, S. Parimala, M. N. Radha, and Subhash. Neeru Sharma and Amrita Shilphi contributed to the case studies in Bihar. Neeru Sharma also contributed to the Karnataka II survey. Thanks are also due to the TISS director, S. Parasuraman, for his support of the study.

In Ghana, Kamiljon Akramov and Shashi Kolavilli contributed to the sampling design and the development of the questionnaires. Joe Green cleaned the Ghana survey data set. Emelia Guo and Cynthia Tagoe contributed to the case studies, and Fatahi Abdullai and Sala Sulemana provided field assistance. Kipo Jimah provided advice on the local government system and logistical support to the team. Dzodzi Tsikata provided advice on the gender aspects of the project.

In Ethiopia, Degnet Abebaw managed the survey. Degnet Abebaw and Naod Mekonnen contributed to the design of the household and extension agent questionnaires. Leilina Abate and Zewdu Tadessa provided research assistance on the case studies. Gudina Bulte provided field assistance and translation services.

This study would not have been possible without the collaboration of the many people in India, Ghana, and Ethiopia who were interviewed, including members of the public administration, elected representatives, community leaders, representatives of nongovernmental organizations, and household members. The author team would like to express its thanks for their time and commitment.

The author team acknowledges the assistance of Patricia Katayama, Nora Ridolfi, and Dina Towbin in the Office of the Publisher at the World Bank in coordinating the production of this book, as well as Mike Donaldson and Barbara Karni in editing the text.

Leah Horowitz, a member of the author team, was killed in an accident in Ghana on May 23, 2009. It was her wish that this research contribute to improving the livelihoods of rural women. This report is dedicated to her memory.

ABBREVIATIONS

ATMA	Agricultural Technology Management Agency
ATVET	Agricultural Technology Vocational Education and Training (Ethiopia)
BJP	Bharatiya Janata Party (India)
BNPP	Bank Netherlands Partnership Program (World Bank)
BoARD	(Regional) Bureau of Agriculture and Rural Development (Ethiopia)
BPL	Below Poverty Line (India)
CBDSD	Capacity Building for Decentralized Service Delivery Project (Ethiopia)
CCDI	Comprehensive Composite Development Index (India)
CWSA	Community Water and Sanitation Agency (Ghana)
CWST	Community Water and Sanitation Team
DANIDA	Danish International Development Agency
DFID	Department for International Development (U.K.)
DISCAP	District Capacity Building Project (Ghana)
DLDP	District Level Decentralization Program
DWST	District Water and Sanitation Team (Ghana)
EEPRI	Ethiopian Economic Policy Research Institute
EPRDF	Ethiopian People's Revolutionary Democratic Front
EWLA	Ethiopian Women's Lawyer Association
FBO	farmer-based organization
GDP	gross domestic product

GIDI	Gender, Institutions, and Development Index
GTZ	German Technical Cooperation Agency
IFAD	International Fund for Agricultural Development
IFPRI	International Food Policy Research Institute
ISEC	Institute for Social and Economic Change
ISSER	Institute of Statistical Social and Economic Research
KVK	Krishi Vigyan Kendra (India)
MDG	Millennium Development Goal
MERET	Managing Environmental Resources to Enable Transitions to More Sustainable Livelihoods (Ethiopia)
MoARD	Ministry of Agriculture and Rural Development (Ethiopia)
MoFA	Ministry of Food and Agriculture (Ghana)
MYRADA	Mysore Resettlement Development Agency
NDC	National Democratic Congress (Ghana)
NGO	nongovernmental organization
NORSAAC	Northern Sector Awareness on Action Centre
NPP	New Patriotic Party (Ghana)
NPW	National Policy on Women (Ethiopia)
OBC	other backward castes
PBS	Protection of Basic Services (Ethiopia)
PDS	Public Distribution System
PSCAP	Public Sector Capacity Building Program (Ethiopia)
RELC	research and extension linkage committee (Ghana)
SC	scheduled caste
SIGI	Social Institutions and Gender Index
SGRY	Sampoorna Grameen Rozgar Yojana (India)
SNNP	Southern Nations, Nationalities, and Peoples (region) (Ethiopia)
ST	scheduled tribe/caste
TISS	Tata Institute of Social Sciences (India)
TPLF	Tigray People's Liberation Front
UNDP	United Nations Development Programme
UNICEF	United Nations Children's Fund
UNIFEM	United Nations Development Fund for Women
USAID	U.S. Agency for International Development
WATSAN	water and sanitation committee (Ghana)
WASH	Multi-stakeholder water, sanitation, and hygiene coalition (Ethiopia)
WIAD	Women in Agricultural Development (Ghana)
WoARD	Woreda (District) Office of Agriculture and Rural Development
WoWR	Woreda Office of Water Resources
WYTEP	Women Youth Training and Education Program (India)

All dollar figures are U.S. dollars.

EXECUTIVE SUMMARY

Three out of four poor people in the developing world live in rural areas, and most of them depend—directly or indirectly—on agriculture for their livelihoods. Providing economic services, such as agricultural extension, is essential to using agriculture for development. At the same time, the rural poor need a range of basic services, such as drinking water, education, and health services. Such services are difficult to provide in rural areas because they are subject to the "triple challenge" of market, state, and community failure.

As a result of market failure, the private sector does not provide these services to the rural poor to the extent that is desirable from society's point of view. The state is not very effective in providing these services either, because these services have to be provided every day throughout the country, even in remote areas, and because they require discretion and cannot easily be standardized, especially if they are demand driven. Nongovernmental organizations (NGOs) and communities themselves are interesting alternative providers of these services, but they too can fail, because of capacity constraints and local elite capture. This triple challenge of market, state, and community failure results in the poor provision of agricultural and rural services, a major obstacle to agricultural and rural development.

The perception bias that "women are not farmers" makes it even more challenging to provide agricultural services—to women. Providing better services to women is not only necessary for them to be able to realize their rights, it is also essential to promote development and to use agriculture for development. Yet the multifaceted role that women play in agriculture and livestock rearing is often overlooked, and the perception that "women are not farmers" remains widespread, despite ample evidence to the contrary. This perception bias against the role of women in agriculture adds a fourth challenge to the triple challenge of market, state, and community failure.

Various governance reform approaches have been adopted to improve agricultural and rural service provision, but major knowledge gaps remain regarding what works where and why. The past two decades have seen a range of governance reforms that can help improve agricultural and rural service provision, including democratization, decentralization, public sector management reforms, and community-driven development. These approaches have been linked with diverse efforts to make service provision more gender responsive, including the reservation of seats for women in local councils and national parliaments, the formation of women's self-help groups and quorums for women in community meetings, gender budgeting, and the creation of gender-specific units in the public administration ("gender machinery"). The empirical evidence on their effectiveness has been mixed. In particular, it is often unclear how to create effective mechanisms of accountability that result in a better provision of agricultural services for rural women and the rural poor.

OBJECTIVES OF THIS REPORT

As the first output from the Gender and Governance in Rural Services project, this report presents descriptive findings and qualitative analysis of accountability mechanisms in agricultural extension and rural water supply in India, Ghana, and Ethiopia, paying specific attention to gender responsiveness. The Gender and Governance in Rural Services project seeks to generate policy-relevant knowledge on strategies to improve agricultural and rural service delivery, with a focus on providing more equitable access to these services, especially for women. The project focuses on agricultural extension, as an example of an agricultural service, and drinking water, as an example of rural service that is not directly related to agriculture but is of high relevance for rural women. A main goal of this project was to generate empirical microlevel evidence about the ways various accountability mechanisms for agricultural and rural service provision work in practice and to identify factors that influence the suitability of different governance reform strategies that aim to make service provision more gender responsive.

This report presents the major descriptive findings from the quantitative and qualitative research conducted in the three countries. It identifies major patterns of accountability routes and assesses their gender dimension. Because the report is exploratory, the policy implications derived from it have been formulated in a cautious way. The results should nevertheless be of interest to a wide audience interested in agricultural and rural service provision, including researchers, members of the public administration, policy makers, and staff from NGOs and international development agencies involved in the design and management of reform efforts, projects, and programs dealing with rural service provision.

RESEARCH METHODS

The findings presented in this report are based on quantitative surveys of households, community members, community-based organizations, and service providers and on qualitative case studies. The quantitative analysis draws on household surveys (of about 1,000 households in each country), in which both male and female household members were interviewed; surveys of service providers for extension and water supply; surveys of user organizations involved in water supply and agricultural extension; and surveys of local political representatives. Case studies investigated similar agents and employed various interview techniques to explore the research questions in greater depth.

This study applies an extended version of the conceptual framework used in the 2004 *World Development Report* (figure 1). Within this framework,

Figure 1   The Long and Short Routes of Accountability

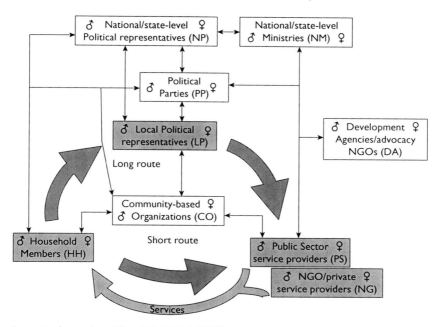

Source: Authors, adapted from World Bank (2003).

accountability is achieved through a short route, through which citizens hold service providers directly accountable, and a long route, through which citizens hold to account local political representatives, who seek to ensure that service providers deliver services effectively.

The framework adopted in this report disaggregates and expands the World Bank Accountability Framework in several ways:

- It includes male/female gender signs in all boxes to indicate the gender dimension of all actors involved in service delivery.
- It distinguishes between public sector service providers at the local level and the ministries at the national/federal or state level to which the local public sector service providers may belong.
- It disaggregates political representatives at different levels of local government and members of parliaments at state and federal levels.
- It includes NGOs and private sector organizations that provide services as a separate category.
- It includes development agencies and advocacy NGOs as a separate category because they often influence service provision.
- It explicitly introduces community-based associations, which may empower citizens to interact more effectively with their political representatives or act as service providers themselves.
- It includes political parties, which can play an important role in formulating policies and laws that influence the gender responsiveness of public service provision and in selecting political candidates and at times public officials.

EMPIRICAL FINDINGS

The accountability framework guided the collection of empirical data on agricultural extension and drinking water supply in the three study countries. The findings are summarized below.

Agricultural Extension

Access to extension is moderate in India and Ethiopia and low in Ghana. In Ghana, the gender gap in access to extension is pronounced. Access to extension by women was highest in Ethiopia, where 20 percent of the women covered in the sample were visited by an extension agent at home or on the farm (27 percent of the men in the sample had access to agricultural extension visits, the same percentage as in Karnataka, India). However, access to extension in Ethiopia varied widely across regions, ranging from 2 percent in Afar to 54 percent in Tigray. Moreover, a high level of access does not necessarily mean the service is being used or that it is of good quality. As a result of the top-down approach and the focus on getting model farmers to adopt fixed-technology packages, extension tends to neglect poor farmers, particularly women. The extension system is not client oriented, and users have limited demand capacity.

Access to extension was lowest in Ghana. About 12 percent of the male-headed households received individual visits of agricultural extension officers, and 10–15 percent attended group meetings organized by agricultural extension officers, with some variation across agroecological zones. Access to a livestock agent was best in the savannah zone, where livestock is most important. Despite the predominant role of women in Ghanaian agriculture, access of female-headed households to agricultural extension turned out to be very low: 2 percent of the female-household heads in the transition zone received agricultural extension visits, and none of the sampled female-headed households in the forest and savannah zones received such visits. Less than 2 percent of female spouses in male-headed households received agricultural extension visits. Access to livestock extension was somewhat better.

Access to agricultural extension was also limited in Karnataka, India. During the year before the survey (2006), 29 percent of male-headed households with land and 18 percent of female-headed households with land met with extension agents. Access to livestock services was better for male-headed households (72 percent) and for female-headed ones (79 percent).

Alternative providers of extension still play a rather limited role. NGOs were not active in providing extension in the surveyed districts in Karnataka, and they played only a limited role in Ghana and Ethiopia. In Ghana, only one of all sampled farmers had received a visit from an NGO extension provider in the year preceding the survey. Private sector enterprises did not feature as providers of extension services per se in any of the surveyed regions in any of the three countries. However, farmers who buy inputs from private input dealers receive advice related to these inputs.

The involvement of farmer-based organizations (FBOs) in extension services remains low, and these organizations are not typically inclusive. The case study evidence from Karnataka and Bihar indicates that the main farmers' organizations, the farmers' cooperatives, play roles chiefly in facilitating access to subsidized inputs. Dairy cooperatives play an important role in providing livestock services, such as veterinary services and artificial insemination, which may contribute to the fact that livestock services have higher coverage. The survey in Karnataka indicates that the leadership of the farmers' and dairy cooperatives is not inclusive with regard to gender.

In Ghana, it has been a policy of the Ministry of Agriculture to form village-based FBOs to improve access to extension. These organizations have limited coverage, and women are less likely to join them than men.

In Ethiopia, cooperatives are the main type of FBO. They are in charge of providing inputs and, therefore, are closely linked to the "package approach" used by the Ethiopian extension system (they do not provide extension services themselves). Government rules mandate that women be represented on the committees of cooperatives, but they generally do not serve as chairpersons.

Making agricultural extension demand driven remains a challenge, for a variety of reasons. These reasons differ across countries, as explained below.

Lack of Capacity in India

In India, the main problem seems to be the lack of overall capacity. As a result of a policy of not hiring agricultural extension workers for more than a decade, there is almost no public capacity left for providing extension, and the private and civil society sectors have not filled that gap. Also, the extension agents' main task was to implement a wide range of government programs, most of which focused on the provision of subsidized inputs. The survey also indicates that agricultural extension workers and veterinary assistants identify political interference in their work as another main constraint, along with staff shortages.

Lack of Focus on Outcomes in Ghana

The ratio of extension agents to farmers is higher in Ghana than in India, although vacancies in remote areas are high. There seems to be little direction as to what kinds of goals extension agents should actually achieve, however. Extension agents seem to be able to respond to farmers' individual demands, but they do not seem to be focused on reaching overall goals for the sector.

Overreliance on a Package Approach in Ethiopia

Staff capacity is generally not a problem in Ethiopia. It is the top-down nature of public service delivery in Ethiopia that makes it difficult to tailor agricultural extension to farmers' demands. Strategies to increase women's access to agricultural extension suffer from the general problems faced by the extension system and from the perception bias regarding the role of women in agriculture.

Strategies to Increase Women's Access to Extension Services Differ Across Countries

The three countries have adopted very different strategies for promoting women's access to agricultural extension. In India, these efforts were confined largely to the extension reform model called the Agricultural Technology Management Agency (ATMA). Case study evidence indicates that extension workers make dedicated efforts to increase the participation of women in extension activities under ATMA.

Ghana can be seen as the most advanced of the three countries in terms of institutionalizing attention to gender in the public agricultural extension system. Its Women in Agricultural Development (WIAD) directorate is one of seven directorates at the national level. There is also one designated senior officer in charge of WIAD in each district agricultural office. The perception bias regarding women's role in agriculture was less pronounced than in the other two study countries. Ghana also had the highest share of female extension agents of the three countries, and female extension agents proved more effective in reaching female farmers. Despite these efforts, women's access to extension in Ghana was lower than it was in the other countries.

Ethiopia mainstreams gender though the "gender machinery" in the public administration. Access of women to extension services is nevertheless weaker than it is for men, as proportionally many fewer women attend community meetings organized by extension agents and substantially fewer women visit demonstration homes and plots. The study finds strong evidence for a cultural perception that "women don't farm," a perception that persists even though women engage in a wide range of agricultural activities.

The Long Route of Accountability

The long route of accountability plays a limited role in agricultural extension. The reasons differ across the three countries.

Agricultural extension remains a deconcentrated rather than a devolved service in India and Ghana. In India, agricultural extension agents are located at the block level. Their line of accountability remains within the Department of Agriculture. Unlike *gram panchayat* (village council) members, block panchayat (council) members are involved in extension, but their role seems largely confined selecting beneficiaries of subsidized input programs, such as subsidized tractors.

In Ghana, the district assembly has little authority over the agricultural extension system—or any agricultural programs. Agriculture has been decentralized to the district level, but it remains a deconcentrated rather than a decentralized service. The district directors of the district agricultural offices have more authority and discretion than they did before decentralization, but the lines of accountability for both staff and funds remain within the Ministry of Food and Agriculture. The district assembly members are more accessible to rural people, but they lack the authority to influence agricultural extension.

In Ethiopia, the short route of accountability is more accessible for rural households, at least in terms of physical proximity. In view of the top-down approach to agricultural extension, the challenge remains of making agricultural extension more responsive to the needs of farmers, including female farmers.

Drinking Water

Access to drinking water is high in India, moderate in Ghana, and very low in Ethiopia. In Karnataka, 88 percent of households surveyed use safe drinking water sources, and 97 percent have a water source within 1 kilometer of their home. In Ghana, 60 percent of households have access to safe drinking water (access rates differ slightly across zones). The average time needed to get to the water source and fetch water is less than half an hour. In Ethiopia, just 32 percent of surveyed households use safe drinking water sources, and the average time to fetch water from the most frequently used sources is approximately two hours.

Households identified drinking water as their top concern in Ghana and Ethiopia, yet they reported high satisfaction rates and only rarely complained. In India, 90 percent of respondents report being satisfied with the drinking water provision. In Ghana, the reported satisfaction rates for drinking water were also high, even though access was much lower. Surprisingly, households also indicated high satisfaction rates with unsafe water sources, such as streams and rivers. Likewise, reported satisfaction rates were high in Ethiopia, despite low access to safe drinking water. The share of households that took any action, such as contacting political representatives or public officials to complain, was low in all three countries.

Several reasons may explain the inconsistency between the problem ratings on the one hand and the satisfaction ratings and low inclination to complain on the other. First, awareness about the health advantages of using safe drinking water sources seems to be limited. Second, respondents may feel uncomfortable giving answers that might be seen as critical to the government. Third, households may not take action because they may feel that it would have little effect and, therefore, it is not worth the (opportunity) costs involved.

Community-based organizations have been promoted as the main strategy for improving access to drinking water—a strategy that faces different challenges in the three countries. More than agricultural extension, drinking water lends itself to management by local government councils rather than specific community-based organizations, because every citizen needs access to safe drinking water. Yet it has been a major strategy in all three countries to promote community-based organizations. The surveys reveal that these groups are not inclusive and that households prefer to approach their elected representatives directly rather than through user group functionaries.

COUNTRY-SPECIFIC POLICY RECOMMENDATIONS

A set of policy recommendations was derived for each country. Each set addresses the country-specific challenges identified in this study.

India

This section first presents recommended strategies for India's general decentralization policy. It then offers recommendations for agricultural extension and drinking water provision.

General Decentralization Policy

The following strategies can be used to address the challenges of decentralization identified by the study:

1. *Pay attention to elite capture when designing programs to be implemented by gram panchayats.* A formula-bound allocation of fiscal grants to the gram panchayats was successfully implemented, but the allocation of funds to the villages within the gram panchayats turned out to be subject to severe targeting failures. Villages represented by female gram panchayat members from scheduled castes received significantly fewer resources than others. This problem could be addressed by applying a formula for distributing grants among villages. Possible mechanisms to implement such a formula include using the block officials and gram panchayat secretary to oversee implementation, creating awareness about the problem in the training of gram panchayat members, and increasing the transparency of the intervillage distribution of funds through more stringent reporting in *gram sabha* (village assembly) or *jamabandhi* (social audit) meetings.

2. *Increase administrative support at the gram panchayat level.* Evidence from the case studies indicates that the gram panchayat secretaries are overburdened with the increasing number of programs that have been decentralized to the gram panchayat level. Hiring additional staff (as already foreseen by the government of Karnataka) is essential to address this problem. Doing so provides a unique opportunity to improve the gender balance of this important type of front-line staff. Female gram panchayat members may be more comfortable interacting with female administrative staff.

3. *Create better conditions for women to attend gram sabha meetings.* To increase women's participation in gram sabha meetings, meetings need to be held at times that are more convenient for women to attend. Information about the meetings and their agenda should also be improved.

Agricultural Extension

The following approaches appear promising in addressing the problems identified by the study:

1. *Address the staff shortage problem.* The number of agricultural extension agents can be increased in various ways; hiring more staff under the civil service system may not always be the preferred option. Hiring staff on a contract basis for specific programs is a more flexible approach, one that is currently pursued by the government of Karnataka. Other options include contracting NGOs that work in the agricultural sector, contracting private sector companies that can provide extension services, and

establishing public-private partnerships. Before hiring more agricultural extension staff, states should conduct a thorough analysis of the human resources in terms of numbers, qualification, and skill mix required for improving agricultural extension.

2. *Provide better services to female farmers.* Addressing the staff shortage problem also provides opportunities to provide better services to female farmers. In view of the positive experience in other countries (Ghana in particular), the strategy to hire female extension agents to better serve female farmers deserves special attention. The standing committees on agriculture and industry in the district panchayats could also play a proactive role in mobilizing public awareness for the inclusion of gender issues in plans and policies of decentralized bodies and government departments.

3. *Address the management challenges within the public sector.* The management challenges identified by the study deserve attention, particularly political interference and the low prevalence of merit-based promotion. Because both problems are deeply entrenched in the general public administration, they cannot be resolved in isolation within the agricultural departments. The hiring of new staff outside the civil service system offers new opportunities for merit-based promotion and other incentive systems, such as merit-based wage compensation. The problem of political interference could be reduced by strengthening the role of agricultural extension staff in improving the knowledge and skill base of the farming population rather than by using extension agents mainly for implementing subsidized input programs. It is also worthwhile exploring the extent to which a right-to-information approach could be used to reduce political pressure and elite capture.

4. *Reestablish the function of agricultural extension as a bridge between agricultural research, farmers, and markets.* The linkages between agricultural research and extension can be strengthened in various ways. If participatory planning approaches for the introduction of new technologies, commodities, and farming practices are implemented (as piloted by ATMA), extension agents may have stronger incentives to contact agricultural researchers to meet farmers' needs. The establishment of governing structures that involve both agricultural researchers and extension agents, as foreseen under ATMA, can also improve the bridging function of agricultural extension.

5. *Form functioning FBOs.* Extension agents are not only limited in numbers, but they also lack the skills required to form and supervise groups. Furthermore, they tend to work with better-off farmers and male farmers. If the strategy of forming farmers' interest groups is to be pursued, appropriate investments have to be made in hiring qualified facilitators for group

formation and training group representatives. Special attention needs to be paid to making farmers' interest groups inclusive in terms of gender and caste, something that has proved to be a challenge in the past. Although the best strategy to improve rural service provision will always depend on the specific situation, it may be promising to link agricultural service provision to existing groups. Women's self-help groups may be an option, especially for livestock-related services. However, one needs to take care not to overload these groups with too many functions. Federations of community-based organizations and agricultural producer companies are other promising options. As group-based approaches place demands on farmers' time, however, alternatives should be considered. The provision of extension services through Internet kiosks and cell phones deserves attention; further analysis is needed to assess the gender responsiveness of these approaches.

Drinking Water Supply

Karnataka already has good access to safe drinking water. The following strategies can be used to address the remaining problems identified by the study:

1. *Strengthen the accountability and inclusiveness of Water and Sanitation Committees.* This project did not conduct an impact evaluation of the committees. The study findings indicate two potential challenges regarding them, however: accountability and inclusiveness in terms of gender.

    To ensure the accountability of the Water and Sanitation Committee within the gram panchayat system, the gram panchayat member who represents the village or ward in which the committee is located could be an ex officio member of the committee. The Water and Sanitation Committee could be formally constituted as a subcommittee of the gram panchayat, a strategy that is already being pursued in Karnataka. Committee members may also be required to report in gram sabha or ward sabha meetings to improve accountability.

    A quota system could be used to increase the representation of women in leadership positions of the Water and Sanitation Committees. The rule that one-third of members and chairpersons should be women has already been promoted under the Second Karnataka Rural Water and Sanitation project. Special attention should be paid to implementing the quota system because women's representation in leadership positions is currently low, despite affirmative action policies in more than half of the surveyed committees.

2. *Focus more attention on drainage.* The low satisfaction rates with drainage suggest that policy should shift in this direction, given the importance of drainage for sanitation. Strategies to achieve this goal may include increased allocation of funding for sanitation, including drainage and awareness creation among panchayat council members and front-line professionals.

3. *Pay attention to gender issues.* It appears useful to analyze the content of the training programs junior engineers receive, assess areas in which a focus on gender is appropriate, and adjust training programs and material accordingly. Moreover, in view of the small share of female junior engineers, efforts could be made to increase this share when hiring new staff.

Ghana

This section first presents recommended strategies for Ghana's general decentralization policy. It then offers recommendations for agricultural extension and drinking water provision.

General Decentralization Policy

Ghana's decentralization policy was successful in bringing government closer to the people; the district assembly member is a major link between rural citizens and the government. Yet district assembly members describe themselves as a "glorified beggars" because they have to beg the administration and donors to get projects done. The following strategies could be used to address these challenges:

1. *Empower district assembly members.* Increasing the share of discretionary district-level resources that are not earmarked or tied to specific programs would enhance the role district assembly members play with respect to the administration. To facilitate closer interaction with the district administration, it would be useful to provide assembly members with dedicated office space at the district assembly and to increase their travel allowances so that they can interact with the administration on a regular basis; better remuneration for the work they do could also be considered. Providing more training to the district assembly members with the aim of improving their capacity to deal effectively with the district administration could strengthen their role, too.

2. *Increase the share of female district assembly members.* Cross-country evidence suggests that a quota or reservation system would be the most effective way of increasing the share of female district assembly members. Adopting such a policy requires a sovereign political decision that only the Ghanaian people and their political representatives can make. Formally recognizing the partisan nature of the local government system might allow the political parties to take more deliberate steps in promoting female candidates. The main strategy that could be used within the current political system is encouraging and supporting female candidates and female district assembly members. Possible ways of doing so include establishing mentors and special funds for female district assembly candidates and members, training male and female district assembly members on gender mainstreaming, and

providing special training for female members. Such efforts are already being pursued by the Institute of Local Government Studies, but unlike in India, the institute has no budget for this purpose; funding for such activities has to be raised on a case-by-case basis. Increasing gender equity in political representation can be considered a goal in its own right. It is not necessarily a sufficient strategy to achieve better outcomes for women, however. As the case of India shows, female political representatives may even be disadvantaged in achieving better outcomes for women, depending on local power structures and program design. Hence additional efforts are necessary to reach better outcomes for women.

3. *Strengthen the district gender focal points.* Piloted by the District Capacity Building Project (DISCAP), gender focal points have been promoted at the district level. The focal points need to have a working environment that is suitable for their task, which includes relieving them of other obligations. Providing systematic training to the focal points and strengthening their relationships with the district assembly members may also help increase their effectiveness.

4. *Strengthen area councils and unit committees.* The study indicates that these bodies of representatives at the subdistrict level may already play a larger role than is commonly assumed. Allowing them to play a more important role in planning, monitoring, and evaluating development activities while collaborating with the district assembly members could strengthen the long route of accountability.

Agricultural Extension

The study indicates that access to agricultural extension is low, despite an extension agent–to–farmer ratio that is comparatively high. The following strategies may be considered to address these challenges:

1. *Improve the management of agricultural extension.* To improve the focus on agricultural productivity and other outcome-related targets, it will be useful to make such targets explicitly part of the extension agents' agenda. The Ministry of Food and Agriculture could introduce awards for communities and districts that are most successful in increasing agricultural productivity at the community or district level rather than just rewarding individual farmers. Research and extension linkage committees (RELCs) at the district level are supposed to create linkages between research and extension, yet this strategy does not seem to be sufficient. Increasing farmers' demand for new knowledge—by strengthening participatory extension planning and technology development approaches, for example— may be a useful strategy for creating more incentives for extension agents

to channel this demand to the research system. In view of the low percentage of farmers who try new technologies, it also seems useful to devise incentive systems that reward extension agents for the number of male and female farmers who adopt new technologies. It will be useful to critically review past efforts to reform the Ministry of Food and Agriculture and to try reform approaches such as Appreciative Inquiry, which use the best values of an organization as a starting point of reform and rely on internal change agents rather than considering the organization only as a problem that has be resolved (usually by restructuring using external consultants).

2. *Increase the access of female farmers to agricultural extension.* The following strategies could be explored:
   - Identify and address the factors that prevent female household members from attending extension-related community meetings, perhaps by organizing such meetings at times and locations that make them more accessible for female household heads. Explore the extent to which the WIAD units have already tried to address these problems, and identify the implementation problems WIAD officers may have faced in this respect.
   - Increase the share of female extension agents, who were found to be more effective than male extension agents in reaching female farmers.
   - Create incentives for reaching female farmers by, for example, rewarding such outreach in performance reviews.

3. *Prepare extension agents for Local Government Service.* One of the planned changes to strengthen the local government system is the introduction of a Local Government Service, a separate category of public officials besides the civil service that will probably include agricultural extension. It would be useful to proactively use this opportunity for increased accountability and to pilot test approaches by which extension agents, district assembly members, and district assembly staff can work together effectively under this new system.

4. *Reconsider the role of FBOs.* FBOs have been promoted as a major strategy to deliver agricultural extension services more effectively. Several strategies could be pursued to address the challenges with this strategy that the study identified:
   - Encourage FBOs to engage in activities that will make them sustainable, such as joint agricultural marketing, agroprocessing, joint purchasing of agricultural inputs, and joint use of agricultural machinery. The experience of projects that already tried this strategy needs to be reviewed.
   - Analyze the problems women face in joining FBOs. Promote the formation of FBOs made up only of women (an intervention that is already in operation).

- Consider alternative strategies to improve access to agricultural extension. Such approaches may involve the use of cell phones. Using the radio more extensively for agricultural extension also seems to be a promising approach, although this tool is not suited for providing farm-specific advice.

Drinking Water Supply

The formation of water and sanitation committees (WATSANs) has been a central element in the strategies used by the government and donors to improve access to drinking water in rural areas. The study indicates that this approach faces some challenges, in particular, low coverage. A variety of strategies could improve drinking water supply:

1. *Strengthen the role of the WATSANs in the local accountability system.* Although the WATSANs are in charge of water and sanitation, rural citizens are more likely to contact their district assembly member or their unit committee member rather than a WATSAN member if they experience problems with drinking water supply. This is not necessarily a problem, as it may indicate that the short route and the long route of accountability are used in a synergetic way. However, it may also indicate a lack of trust in the capacity of the WATSANs to resolve problems. Hence, it appears useful to consider how accountability can be created within these organizations and with respect to the population they serve. Making them subcommittees of the unit committees may be one approach, as the unit committees are elected.

2. *Strengthen unit committees as an alternative strategy.* As drinking water supply is a service needed by the entire population rather than specific groups, unit committees may be considered as an alternative organization that can perform the tasks of the WATSANs. Unit committees could also provide other rural services. As an alternative to specialized user organizations, unit committees could, for services that everyone needs, be turned into multipurpose committees that also play a formal role in the local government system.

Ethiopia

This section first presents recommended strategies for Ethiopia's general decentralization policy. It then offers recommendations for agricultural extension and drinking water provision.

General Decentralization Policy

The government is engaged in ongoing efforts to strengthen the local government bodies that are most important to the majority of decentralized public services. Assistance to the decentralization process and, in particular, to public service provision at the local level, could take into account the following strategies:

1. *Strengthen the organizations tasked with building the capacity of the relevant local agencies.* Regional governments operate various programs to strengthen the key public sector bodies at the local level. Among these are regional training institutes that take on the responsibility of providing training to district cabinet members. Creation of such organizations is an important step toward institutionalizing district government training and scaling back reliance on fragmented ad hoc training done through consultants and far away in the capital city. Such organizations can be valuable to provide support to such region-level training institutes that strengthen the capacity of key players and decision makers at the local level, such as the district cabinets.

2. *Pay more attention to gender dimensions in the delivery of public services.* This study highlights the development impact of implementing policies on public service provision in a way that enhances the productive contribution of women as well as men in rural areas. The study's findings may be useful in introducing gender dimensions into the training modules used by the regional training institutions targeting local governments.

3. *Better understand intraparty processes that affect service delivery.* Processes and mechanisms within the ruling party may be important drivers of policy design and policy implementation in agricultural extension and water supply. Very little is known about these processes. Further research efforts could go a long way in helping to understand the driving forces, incentives, and accountability systems that influence how public services for men and women are delivered. This understanding would clarify the opportunities and constraints that exist for interventions seeking to improve agricultural extension and drinking water supply.

4. *Take the political reality into consideration when deciding how to target support.* This study reveals that members of the local council play a limited role in influencing decisions regarding which and how services are delivered to residents. In contrast, executive bodies are a much more influential local player. Hence, resources committed to training and capacity building of local councils may not achieve the desired results. Understanding political realities such as this one can help donors target support.

Agricultural Extension

Agricultural extension is a high government priority, but coverage of extension services across regions varies widely, and extension agents have limited discretion to adapt technology packages to the context of individual communities. The gender gap in access to extension can also be improved. Some approaches to addressing these issues could include the following:

1. *Give more discretion to extension agents.* To increase technology adoption by more farmers, it seems useful to give extensions agents—together with farmers—more space to experiment with technology and input packages other than those they are currently required to promote. Microlevel adaptation of existing packages could make new inputs and practices more credible to farmers. This is particularly important with regard to extension agents' work with women.

2. *Expand extension coverage where it is low, including to pastoral areas.* Extension coverage varies widely across sites, with as few as 2 percent and as many as 54 percent of respondents having access to extension agents. Reducing these stark differences in access seems justified.

3. *Bridge the gender gap in access to extension services.* The study identifies some promising ways to reduce the gender gap. One is the engagement of women's associations to serve as a bridge between extension workers and women farmers. External assistance may include better and more detailed documentation on how and through which mechanisms women's associations are successful in bringing extension advice to their members. Lessons learned could be taken into account in expanding and scaling up this approach.

Drinking Water Supply

Several strategies could address the problems identified in the study:

1. *Increase access to safe drinking water.* Increasing the very low access to safe drinking water would address citizens' priorities and improve productivity— by reducing the amount of time women spend fetching water (time they could spend engaging in agricultural activities) and reducing health problems associated with unclean water. External support may help address the problem.

2. *Provide training to water committees on community relations.* Training to water committees concentrates on technical topics. It could be expanded to cover community relations. One of the important reasons for the nonfunctioning and nonuse of drinking water facilities in rural areas is the poor governance of facilities by water committees, particularly their lack of success in mobilizing community resources to maintain facilities. Training for managing community relations, raising awareness for the need of users to ensure that facilities get maintained after initial construction, and similar "soft" skills are much needed.

3. *Ensure that water maintenance systems are in place.* Service providers responsible for constructing water facilities should plan carefully for maintaining the facilities after construction.

4. *Consider local knowledge when selecting water sites.* Local governments and NGOs should draw on both geological expertise and the local knowledge of the community to minimize mistakes in site selection.

5. *Expand local government efforts to change cultural norms around water.* In some areas, the local government has brought attention to the usually female-borne burden of fetching water, displaying posters appealing to men to take on some of the burden. Efforts such as these to change cultural norms could be considered more widely and assessed for their ability to effect changes in behavior. Other local policies that take a more formal nature, such as mandating that water committee chairs be women, could also be considered, taking into consideration the strong variation in the cultural acceptability of such policies.

IMPLICATIONS FOR FUTURE RESEARCH

The accountability linkages for rural service provision vary widely across countries, depending on the political system and the approach to decentralization in service provision. Understanding these linkages is essential for identifying entry points to make rural service provision more responsive to gender needs.

Many important questions require further research, experimentation, and learning. Which mechanisms in the local governance system create political incentives in obtaining better outcomes for the rural population in general and rural women in particular? How do these mechanisms differ across political systems? Which mechanisms work within a (de facto) one-party system? Which mechanisms work in multiparty systems that are subject to political competition but plagued with clientelism and elite capture? Future research—including research using the data collected under this project—will have to address these questions.

The political reforms of the past decade have created new opportunities for improving the provision of agricultural and rural services to those who have benefited least from them in the past: the rural poor and rural women. The author team hopes that this report will help rural communities and their organizations, governments, NGOs, and development partners grasp these opportunities.

CHAPTER ONE

Introduction

PROVIDING AGRICULTURAL AND RURAL SERVICES: WHAT IS THE PROBLEM?

Three out of four poor people in the developing world live in rural areas, and most of them depend—directly or indirectly—on agriculture for their livelihoods. In the 21st century, agriculture remains a fundamental tool for lifting them out of poverty, as highlighted in the *World Development Report 2008* (World Bank 2007e). The 2008 food crisis underscored the urgency of supporting agricultural development.

Providing economic services, such as agricultural extension, is essential to using agriculture for development. The rural poor also need a range of basic services, such as drinking water, education, and health services.

Such services are difficult to provide in rural areas, because they are subject to the triple challenge of market failure, state failure, and community failure (box 1.1). Because of market failures, the private sector does not provide these services to the rural poor to the extent that is desirable from society's point of view. The state is not very effective in providing these services either. Non-governmental organizations (NGOs) and communities themselves are alternative providers of these services, but they often also fail.

The reasons for market failure, state failure, and community failure differ across services. For agricultural credit, market failures arise from the fact that the risks of crop failure affect large numbers of clients at the same time.

Box 1.1 Market Failure, State Failure, and Community Failure in Agricultural Extension

Agricultural and rural service provision is challenging because of market failure, state failure, and NGO and community failure. This box discusses the reasons behind these failures, using agricultural extension as an example.

Market Failure

In a market economy, one would expect the private sector to provide agricultural extension services. There are several reasons why it does not:

- Knowledge that is not farm specific, such as information about agricultural prices, is typically a public good, which limits the incentives for the private sector to provide it. Extension services can also have the characteristics of a "merit good"—that is, a good whose true value is not recognized or that consumers cannot afford, limiting demand.
- Extension has positive externalities, because some of its benefits, such as improved food security and environmental sustainability, benefit not only the farmers who use it but society as a whole.
- Provision of extension benefits from economies of scale, but reaching a large enough number of smallholders is difficult, because they are spatially dispersed and transportation costs in rural areas are high.

State Failure

The market failures of extension services have induced most countries to provide these services through public sector organizations. Extension has two characteristics that make provision by the public sector inherently difficult: transaction intensity and discretion (Pritchett and Woolcock 2004). Extension is transaction intensive, because it has to be provided frequently throughout the country, even in the most remote areas. It requires discretion on the part of extension agents, especially if solutions are tailored to farmers' needs. These characteristics create state failures for a variety of reasons:

- Information asymmetry exists between extension agents and their managers because of the spatially dispersed nature of agriculture and because agricultural outcomes, such as crop yields, are influenced by many factors other than extension. This asymmetry makes good extension services difficult to provide.
- Although public sector agencies can use various instruments, such as merit-based promotion, to create incentives, they cannot usually provide salary incentives, limiting their ability to reward excellent work. Together with the fact that extension agents often have lower social status than other public sector employees, this reduces their morale. The lack of operational funds that would allow them to get to the field and work effectively also affects morale.

(continued)

Box 1.1 (Continued)

- Public sector agencies often lack the incentives to invest in the capacity of their extension staff. As a result, staff knowledge is not always up to date.
- Because large-scale farmers have more political influence than smallholders, politicians often induce the public administration to serve larger farmers better. At the same time, extension service providers find it easier to work with them. Because extension agents are often the only government agents able to interact with a considerable part of the rural population, governments can also misuse their positions for political purposes, such as campaigning for the ruling parties in elections.
- Public sector extension agents are often burdened with activities that fall outside the mandate of agricultural extension. They are frequently involved in organizing subsidized input supply and implementing credit schemes. They may also be asked to help implement public health programs and other government schemes that are not related to agriculture.
- Bureaucratic procedures make it difficult for extension agents to respond flexibly to local demands, especially in highly centralized systems. Bureaucratic culture is also an obstacle to the reform of public sector agencies. Bureaucratic structures often discourage the coordination of agricultural extension with other departments. Farmers may also suffer from attitudinal problems, which are widespread in traditional public sector agencies.
- Public sector extension often lacks financial sustainability, especially if cost recovery is not pursued. After donor-funded programs end, extension agencies are frequently left with a large number of extension agents they can no longer fund.
- Corruption is not a common problem in extension (knowledge services offer little scope for corruption). However, the more extension agents are involved in the distribution of inputs and credit or in the enforcement of laws, the wider the scope for corruption.

NGO and Community Failure

In view of the problems of state and market failure, NGOs have been promoted as an alternative solution. In the absence of a market mechanism, however, they are subject to the same types of information problems the public sector faces.

NGOs are usually smaller than public sector agencies. This contributes to their flexibility, but it reduces their outreach. The percentage of farmers reached by NGO extension is often small. In India, for example, which has a vibrant NGO community, NGOs constitute an information source for less than 1 percent of farmers (NSSO 2005).

NGOs are also subject to accountability problems. In principle, public sector agencies can be made accountable to farmers through political channels; NGOs are accountable only to their funding agencies. They often face problems of financial sustainability and have to cope with wide fluctuations

(continued)

Box 1.1 (Continued)

in funding. At the same time, NGOs are not immune to problems of mismanagement, misuse of funding, and inappropriate attitudes. The NGO staff may treat farmers in a patronizing way. Moreover, they may have incentives to combine extension with other goals, including promoting the world view or religion of the NGO. Frequently, NGOs do not have their own extension staff; they use public sector extension agents.

Another option for providing agricultural extension is the use of community-based or farmer-based organizations (FBOs). These organizations face the classical problem of collective action. If the benefits of FBO action are "nonexcludable" (that is, FBOs cannot exclude nonmembers from enjoying the benefits of their action), farmers have limited incentives to incur the transaction costs of participating (this is the classic free-rider problem [Olson 1965]). The incentives to join local farmer groups for the purpose of group-based extension may be high, because participants expect to benefit directly from their participation. However, to participate in extension planning and management beyond the district level, farmers need to become organized at a more aggregate level, which poses its own challenges. For all of these reasons, organizations formed for donor-funded projects often collapse once project funding ends.

A major challenge of FBOs is preventing social exclusion and elite capture. FBOs are often dominated by middle-class and wealthy farmers. Poor farmers and socially marginalized groups typically play a limited role in the leadership of FBOs, even if they are represented among its members. The representation of women in FBOs is often low, a problem linked to the sociocultural role of women in most societies as well as to the time constraints faced by women.

Source: Birner and Anderson 2007.

State failures occur because politicians have a strong incentive to write off agricultural debt. Community-based solutions need to overcome the pervasive collective action problem.

BETTER SERVING THE RURAL POOR, INCLUDING RURAL WOMEN

The rural poor suffer disproportionately from poor service provision (World Bank 2003). Where elite capture prevails, they have less access to agricultural and rural services; where the public system fails in general, they cannot easily resort to private service providers. They have to spend more of their time accessing services, which affects their productivity; often they also have to pay bribes. Rural women, especially those from poor households, face a particularly heavy burden, because the gender division of labor requires them to spend more time fetching water, getting health care for their children, and reaching markets. In most of the developing world, girls have less access to education than boys. Maternal mortality is high if the specific health care needs of women are not met. Providing better services to women is therefore not only necessary to realize their rights, it is also essential to promote development. As research has shown, when women have more education and better access to assets, their children are better nourished, healthier, and more likely to go to school (Quisumbing and others 1995; IFPRI 2000, 2005). An impressive body of evidence documents the positive relationship between gender equality, economic growth, and poverty reduction (Mason and King 2001). The global community formally recognized gender inequality as one of the major hurdles to development when it set gender equality and the empowerment of women as the third Millennium Development Goal (MDG).

Providing better services to rural women is essential to using agriculture for development, as the *World Development Report 2008* (World Bank 2007e) and the *Gender in Agriculture Sourcebook* (World Bank, FAO, and IFAD 2008) show. Women play an important role in agriculture: in many parts of Africa, they are the main producers. In Uganda, for example, 75 percent of agricultural producers are women (World Bank, FAO, and IFAD 2008). In the Indo-Gangetic plains, the main rice and wheat production region of South Asia, women provide more than 60 percent of the labor for crop production and more than 70 percent of the labor for livestock production (Ladha and others 2000). Migration and the effects of HIV/AIDS have increased the share of women in charge of managing family farms in many parts of the world (World Bank, FAO, and IFAD 2008). Women also play a prominent role in the production of high-value commodities, such as fruits and vegetables, which are increasingly in demand, as incomes rise. Despite these contributions, the role of women in agriculture is often unrecognized, a perception bias with serious implications.

Lack of recognition of the role of women in agriculture constitutes a serious problem. The perception of the roles men and women play in agriculture is biased toward men.[1] As a consequence, the perception that agricultural services are needed is biased toward men, too. Because of this bias, fewer efforts are made to reach women with agricultural services. The perception bias adds a fourth challenge to the triple challenge of market, state, and community failure, because it weakens efforts to provide agricultural services to women.

Ample evidence indicates that access to agricultural services is particularly poor for rural women, as documented in the *Gender in Agriculture Sourcebook*. Women have less access to agricultural extension and training, less access to agricultural credit, and less access to irrigation and modern inputs. They are also less likely to be organized in farmers organizations or agricultural interest groups that make their voices heard. The result is a tremendous loss of opportunity. Achieving gender equity is not only a goal in its own right, it is essential if agriculture is to be used to spur development. Gender equity is an essential precondition to meeting the first MDG of halving hunger and poverty.

In view of the food crisis, governments and the international development community have pledged to invest more in agriculture; agricultural service provision is an essential part of this investment agenda. Even before the food crisis, which underscored the urgency of investing in agriculture, agriculture had reemerged as a priority on the international development agenda. In Africa, heads of states made a commitment in 2003 to spend at least 10 percent of their budgetary resources on agriculture. The New Partnership for African Development launched the Comprehensive Africa Agricultural Development Program, which aims to achieve 6 percent growth in the sector. Foundations such as the Bill & Melinda Gates Foundation have also turned their attention to agriculture.

Investing is important, but more funds alone will not improve agricultural and rural services. The triple challenge of market failure, government failure, and community failure must be overcome, and the perception bias must be changed if such services are to reach the people who need them.

GOVERNANCE REFORMS AND THEIR PROMISE FOR BETTER SERVICE PROVISION

The past decades have seen a range of governance reforms that can help improve agricultural and rural service provision (Birner 2007). Democratization is one of the most promising of these reforms. The number of countries that have become democracies increased rapidly in recent decades. Although many of them are not yet fully institutionalized democracies, democratization provides more voice to the rural poor and rural women, because their votes count.

Another important governance reform is decentralization, which entails a far-reaching change in the structure of the state. Eighty percent of all developing countries have engaged in some form of decentralization during the past several decades (Work 2002). Although local empowerment is not always the explicit or implicit goal of this reform, decentralization brings government closer to the people, thereby improving people's ability to make their demands heard and to hold public sector agencies accountable. Community-driven development and group-based approaches, which have gained increasing relevance in recent years, pursue similar goals.

Other types of reform approaches have targeted the providers of agricultural and rural services. Important examples include the introduction of new management approaches, civil service reforms, the contracting out of service provision, public-private partnerships, and the involvement of NGOs in service provision. These governance reform approaches have been linked with various efforts to improve gender sensitivity in service provision, as discussed in chapter 2 (see box 2.2). They include gender budgeting, the establishment of quotas for women in political leadership positions, the reservation of seats for women in national parliaments and local councils, and the formation of self-help groups and quorums for women in community meetings.

MAKING SERVICES WORK FOR THE POOR: THE WORLD BANK ACCOUNTABILITY FRAMEWORK

Understanding the accountability relations between clients, service providers, and politicians is essential to understanding how governance reforms can improve service provision (World Bank 2003). The conceptual framework developed in the *World Development Report 2004*: *Making Services Work for Poor People* (hereafter referred to as the World Bank Accountability Framework) distinguishes three main actors: citizens/clients, politicians/policy makers, and service providers (figure 1.1). Citizens/clients can use two "routes of

Figure 1.1   World Bank Accountability Framework

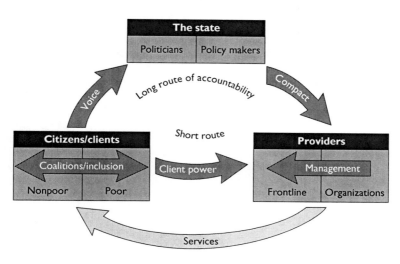

Source: World Bank 2003.

accountability" to get better services, the long route and the short route. Holding service providers directly accountable, referred to as *client power*, constitutes the short route of accountability. Exercising *voice* to induce politicians and policy makers to interact with service providers with the goal of improving service delivery, using a "compact," is the long route of accountability.

The 2004 *World Development Report* focused attention on a pervasive problem that has far-reaching implications for service provision: clientelism (box 1.2). Strategies to improve public service provision will not be successful without addressing this problem, which is particularly relevant in agriculture and in rural areas.

Box 1.2 The Pervasive Problem of Clientelism and Elite Capture

In the context of service provision, clientelism refers to the excessive tendency of political patrons to provide public services to specific clients in exchange for political advantage. Clientelism leads to inequality in service provision, typically to the disadvantage of women and the poor. It may involve the provision of private goods to political supporters. Agricultural services that have the nature of public goods, such as subsidized inputs or farm-specific advice, are particularly prone to this form of clientelism. In fact, elite capture in agriculture is often the consequence of clientelism. Clientelism can also involve the preferential provision of public infrastructure, such as drinking water facilities, to locations that are strategically important for politicians, such as their home constituencies. In socially fragmented societies, clientelism often functions along ethnic, religious, or caste lines.

Clientelism has an important psychological effect: it undermines the ability of citizens to demand better services, because they consider services as gifts provided by political patrons rather than something to which they are entitled. Clientelism can also undermine collective action, because community-based groups can be co-opted by clientelistic networks, thereby undermining the empowering role they could play.

Clientelism is frequently encountered in democracies with political party competition, where politicians use public services to gain votes. Lack of transparency and lack of trust foster clientelism in democratic regimes. Clientelism can play an equally important role in authoritarian states, with both left-wing and right-wing regimes relying on clientelism to stay in power. Clientelism is so pervasive that Nobel Prize winner Douglass North and his coauthors describe it as "the natural state." In fact, overcoming clientelism is one of the major challenges of development.

Sources: Oi 1991; World Bank 2003; Keefer 2005; North, Wallis, and Weingast 2009; authors' interviews.

WHERE ARE THE KNOWLEDGE GAPS?

The World Bank Accountability Framework has been widely used and greatly advanced our the understanding of different strategies that can be used to improve service provision. However, its application has focused on social services, especially health and education. It is less well understood which role short routes and long routes of accountability play in agricultural service provision and how clientelistic environments influence these relations, especially in decentralized settings. (For a glossary of terms, see box 1.3.)

Decentralization adds an additional layer of complexity to the framework. How do rural men and women interact with their elected representatives at the local and national level? How do they interact with local and national service providers, such as ministries of agriculture and agricultural extension agencies? Local governments often have different tiers; little is known about what happens between these tiers.

Knowledge gaps also exist regarding the role of political parties, which are not an explicit element of the World Bank Accountability Framework but play a major role. The literature suggests that the way in which political parties function, in both multiparty and one-party regimes, has important implications for the types of clientelism and elite capture that may affect agricultural and rural service provision (Keefer and Khemani 2005; Van de Walle 2001) Collective action approaches have been widely promoted to improve the provision of agricultural services by supporting farmer-based organizations (FBOs). How well have FBOs performed? Have they been inclusive or subject to elite capture? Have they been sustainable?

These knowledge gaps regarding the accountability routes in agricultural service provision are linked to the general dearth of studies in this sector. Very few studies thoroughly analyze the wide-ranging recent reforms in agricultural extension, one of the major agricultural service sectors (Anderson 2008).

Additional knowledge gaps exist with regard to the gender dimension of these routes of accountability. As an extensive literature review shows, there are considerable knowledge gaps regarding the reform strategies that are most suitable for different country-specific conditions (Horowitz 2009). Most of the literature focuses on the link between citizens and their elected representatives, such as the reservation of seats in local councils. Evidence on strategies that target service providers, such as gender desks (administrative units in charge of gender mainstreaming) and equal opportunity structures in the public administration, is much more limited. There is also a lack of knowledge about how to best combine strategies that aim to strengthen long and short routes of accountability. The evidence on how macrofactors, such as the political system and the role of women in society, influence the appropriateness of different reform strategies is also limited. In sum, there is limited knowledge regarding what works where and why in making rural services more responsive to gender-specific needs. These knowledge gaps are particularly pronounced in agricultural service provision.

Box 1.3   Glossary

Accountability: Obligation or willingness of a person, organizational unit, or organization to accept responsibility and to account for one's actions. In the context of service delivery, accountability entails the responsibility for performance in meeting expected objectives and standards; the obligation to answer for all actions involved in service delivery, including transparency regarding funding; and the availability of enforceable mechanisms of corrective action. One can distinguish upward accountability (such as of extension agents with respect to their supervisors) and downward accountability (such as of extension agents with respect to their clients).

Actors: Individuals; households; communities and community-based organizations; firms; government bodies at different levels; and other public, nongovernmental, and private organizations that are involved in the financing, provision, regulation, delivery, or consumption of services.

Clients/users/citizens: The term *clients*, which is used here interchangeably with the term *users*, refers to people who use services. The term *citizens* refers to people who participate individually or in groups or organizations in political processes to shape and attain collective goals. All clients are citizens (in most settings), but depending on the service, not all citizens are clients.

Community-based organizations: All types of membership organizations at the community level, including economic associations such as farmers' cooperatives, self-help groups, savings and credit groups, sociocultural and identity-based organizations such as religious groups, and caste associations, and customary organizations such as funeral societies. User groups (see below) are one type of community-based organization. One can distinguish formal and informal organizations, depending on whether or not they are registered or governed by formal law. Community-based organizations may be customary, in the sense that they have existed for centuries, or they may have been created by more recent social movements or development interventions.

Clientelism: Excessive tendency for political patrons to provide public services to specific clients in exchange for political advantage, which leads to inequality in service provision, typically to the disadvantage of the poor and women (box 1.2).

Discretionary services: Services, such as farm-specific agricultural advice, for which front-line professionals must exercise significant judgment over what to deliver and how to deliver it. In the case of discretionary services, there is often also a considerable gap in information between the front-line professional and the client/farmer (for example, on new technologies available) on the one hand and between the front-line professional and his or her supervisor (for example, regarding the needs of the clients/farmers) on the other. Creating accountability for discretionary services is inherently difficult, especially if the ultimate outcome for which the service is provided is also

(continued)

Box 1.3 (Continued)

influenced by factors outside the control of the front-line professional (for example, yield increases depend not only on technologies promoted by the extension agents but also on weather conditions).

Front-line professionals: Service providers who are in direct contact with the clients, such as agricultural extension agents, engineers in charge of village infrastructure, or community facilitators. The term *front-line staff*, or *field staff*, is used interchangeably here with the term *front-line professionals*.

Gender-responsive service provision: Service provision based on the goal of providing men and women with equal opportunities to flourish in their productive and private lives. The provision of services is considered to be gender responsive, or gender sensitive, if one or more of the following conditions are met:

- *Sensitive to gender differentials*: Service provision takes into account that men and women have different service needs. For example, female farmers may require different agricultural advice, because they grow different crops and have different obligations and demands on their time. For this reason, it may be necessary to provide advice at times and locations that allow women to access service.
- *Gender specific*: Men and women have service needs specific to their gender (for example, women have specific needs regarding their reproductive health). Gender-specific service provision addresses such gender-specific needs.
- *Empowering women*: Services, such as assistance to women's self-help groups, may empower women by, for example, strengthening their capacity to act collectively.
- *Transformative*: Services may aim at altering gender relations in society by, for example, changing prevalent attitudes that lead to gender-based discrimination.

Long and short routes of accountability: Clients can hold service providers accountable for performance in two ways. First, they may be able to interact directly with the management of organizations providing the services or interact with them through their community-based organizations. In this report, this route is referred to as the *short route of accountability*. Second, clients or community-based organizations may be able to hold accountable their political representatives, who then must be able to hold the service providers accountable. This chain of accountability is referred to as the *long route of accountability* (fig. 2.1).

Political representatives: People who hold political office, such as members of councils at different levels of local government and members of parliaments at the state and federal levels. Political representatives may be elected (in competitive or noncompetitive elections) or appointed.

(continued)

Box 1.3 (Continued)

Service providers/service provision organizations: Public, private non-profit, and private for-profit entities that provide services. These include government ministries, departments, and agencies. User groups can also be service providers (by providing maintenance services for drinking water facilities, for example).

Transaction-intense services: Services that require a high volume of transactions in terms of time and space. Agricultural extension services are transaction intensive because they have to be provided every day throughout the country, even in remote areas. Provision of infrastructure for drinking water is transaction intensive in terms of space but not time; the maintenance of drinking water facilities is transaction intensive in both regards. Discretionary services that are transaction intensive are particularly hard to monitor, both for the client and for the policy maker. They pose particular challenges for all the relationships of accountability.

User groups/user organizations: Community-based organizations formed with the specific objective of facilitating access to services or taking part in service provision. Examples are water and sanitation committees for drinking water supply, water user associations for irrigation, and parent-teacher associations for schools. User groups can be service providers (see above).

Voice: Mechanisms citizens can use to hold political representatives accountable, including voting in elections, campaign contributions, advocacy and lobbying, public meetings where politicians have to justify their actions, legal actions, media activities, and various forms of political protest, including demonstrations.

Source: Authors, based on World Bank (2003) and Horowitz (2009).

THE GENDER AND GOVERNANCE IN RURAL SERVICES PROJECT

This report is the first output of the Gender and Governance in Rural Services project, which aims to generate policy-relevant knowledge on strategies for improving agricultural and rural service delivery, with a focus on providing more equitable access to these services, especially for women. The project has been implemented in India, Ghana, and Ethiopia. These countries were chosen to capture variation in important macrofactors, especially the level of economic development; various aspects of governance, such as political system and party system; the role of women in society; and strategies adopted to promote gender equity.

The project focuses on agricultural extension as an example of an agricultural service and on drinking water as an example of rural service that is not directly related to agriculture but is of high relevance for rural women.[2] Including one agricultural and one nonagricultural service makes it possible to assess the interaction between different types of services and to learn from the comparison of service provision in different sectors.

The findings from these two services are expected to provide interesting lessons for other types of agricultural and rural services that are subject to some type of market failure. The findings will be less relevant for services that can be provided at a socially desirable level by the private sector without any type of state involvement.

The Gender and Governance in Rural Services project combines quantitative research—specifically, surveys of household members, community-based organizations, political representatives, and service providers—with qualitative case studies. Its goals include the following:

- Identify the extent to which strategies to improve rural service provision—such as involving community-based organizations, outsourcing service provision to NGOs, adopting participatory planning methods, and strengthening the role of locally elected government members—are associated with better service delivery outcomes, especially for the rural poor and rural women.
- Identify context-specific factors that influence the institutional and policy reforms that can effectively address the well-known constraints faced by rural women in channeling their preferences to policy makers and the well-known incentive problems faced by rural service providers to respond to clients' needs.
- Develop gender-specific governance indicators that measure the performance of providing these services and make it possible to track changes over time.
- Increase the capacity for inclusive local government by working with training institutes to develop gender-specific training material for actors involved in rural service provision.

The project is managed by the World Bank's Agricultural and Rural Development Department and implemented by the International Food Policy Research Institute (IFPRI) in collaboration with four partner research organizations: the Institute of Social and Economic Change (ISEC) and the Tata Institute of Social Sciences (TISS) in India; the Institute of Statistical Social and Economic Research (ISSER), University of Ghana, Legon; and the Ethiopian Economic Policy Research Institute (EEPRI) in Ethiopia. The project is funded by the Bank Netherlands Partnership Program (BNPP) Trust Fund and cofinanced by IFPRI's Ghana and Ethiopia Strategy Support Programs, which are financed by multiple donors.

OBJECTIVES AND STRUCTURE OF THIS REPORT

As a first output from the Gender and Governance in Rural Services project, this report is mainly explorative in nature. It presents major descriptive findings from the quantitative and qualitative research, which are analyzed to identify major patterns of accountability routes in agricultural and rural service provision and to assess their gender dimension. A limited number of regression analyses was conducted to identify factors associated with some key service provision outcomes of interest. Subsequent outputs of the research project will build on this report and on associated country-specific reports to conduct more extensive quantitative analyses of the gender-specific relations between accountability routes and service provision outcomes. The exploratory nature of this report limits the possibility of deriving strong implications about causality. Therefore, the policy implications derived from this report were carefully formulated, specifying the areas in which more evidence is needed.

The report provides empirical information on a range of questions. Although the results have limitations, they should nevertheless be of interest to a wide audience interested in agricultural and rural service provision, including researchers, members of the public administration, policy makers, and staff from NGOs and international development agencies involved in the design and management of reform efforts, projects, and programs dealing with rural service provision.

The report is structured as follows. Chapter 2 describes the conceptual framework of the study, which builds on the World Bank Accountability Framework. It uses that framework to classify various strategies for making agricultural and rural service provision more gender sensitive. It then summarizes major findings from the literature on the effectiveness of these strategies.

Chapter 3 provides contextual information about the three study countries. It presents major economic, political, and gender-related indicators and describes the system of decentralized governance and the institutional arrangements under which agricultural extension and rural water supply are provided in the three countries. The annex to this chapter reviews the country-specific literature on gender and rural service provision, overviews the strategies the three countries have used to promote gender equity, and describes the major initiatives by international agencies in this field.

Chapter 4 describes how the quantitative and qualitative data were collected in each of the three study countries.

Chapters 5 and 6 present the main empirical findings. Chapter 5 deals with the short route of accountability. It focuses on households, community-based organizations, and service providers. For each of the three study countries, it examines service provision outcomes as well as household members' interactions with service providers and community-based organizations. The chapter also opens the "black box" of service providers and presents the perspective of the front-line staff responsible for service provision.

Chapter 6 deals with the long route of accountability. It assesses the interaction of political representatives with households and other actors and discusses the factors that influence the effectiveness of local politicians in improving service provision.

Chapter 7 presents a comparative discussion and a qualitative analysis of the findings presented in chapters 5 and 6. It applies the conceptual framework introduced in chapter 2 to examine how the country-specific conditions and the strategies adopted to provide agricultural extension and drinking water on the one hand and the different strategies to promote gender equity on the other hand influence service provision outcomes.

Chapter 8 draws conclusions and policy implications and identifies areas for further analysis and research.

NOTES

1. In a seminal article, Nobel Prize winner Amartya Sen identifies the perception bias against women's economic role as an important reason for persistent gender inequality (Sen 1990a).
2. In India, veterinary services are also studied.

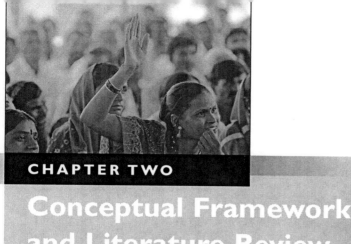

CHAPTER TWO

Conceptual Framework and Literature Review

This chapter presents the conceptual framework used for this study, which is based on the World Bank Accountability Framework (World Bank 2003) discussed in chapter 1 (see figure 1.1). The framework is used to classify strategies for making service provision more gender-sensitive and to guide a review of the literature in this field.

CONCEPTUAL FRAMEWORK

The conceptual framework used for this study is shown in figure 2.1. It disaggregates and expands the World Bank Accountability framework in order to increase its suitability for analyzing the provision of agricultural and rural services in a decentralized setting, taking the role of the political system into account.[1]

The box depicting household members in figure 2.1 corresponds to the citizens/clients box in the World Bank Accountability Framework. The household is added as an additional analytical category, as gender relations within the household, which are shaped by sociocultural norms, influence the service needs of men and women, their possibilities to access services, and the mechanisms they can use to hold service providers accountable. The gender division of labor within the household, for example, may restrict the ability of women to attend meetings organized by agricultural extension agents.

The framework distinguishes between public sector service providers at the local level (box PS) and ministries at the national/federal or state level

Figure 2.1   Conceptual Framework Applied in the Report

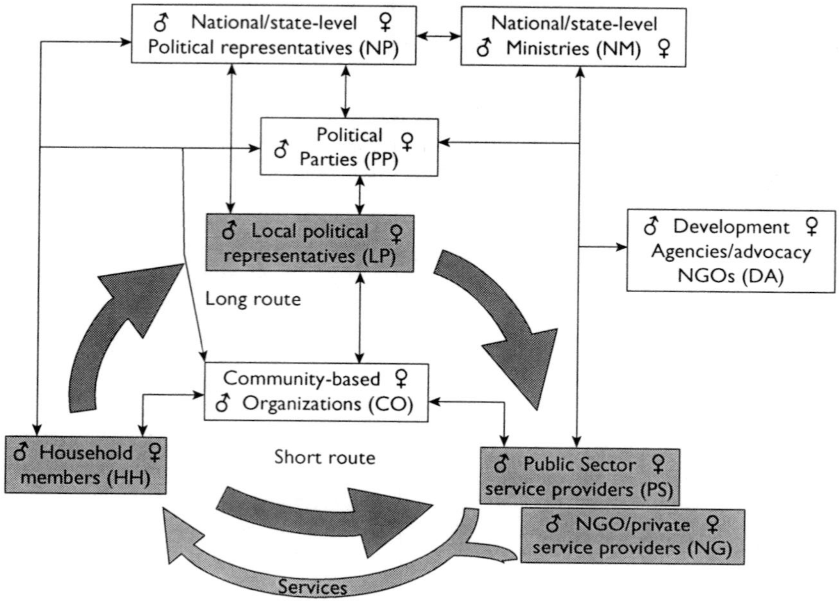

Source: Adapted from World Bank (2003).

(box NM) to which the local public sector service providers may belong. This disaggregation makes it possible to draw attention to the upward accountability linkage between local service providers and their respective ministries (the PS–NM link). This linkage can play an important role in service provision, especially if the reform model is "deconcentration" rather than "devolution."[2]

The framework presents nongovernmental organizations (NGOs) and private sector organizations that provide services (box NG) as a separate category.[3] Because this study is concerned with services that are subject to some kind of market failure, the private sector providers that are relevant are expected to have some link with public sector agencies (for example, they may be contracted by the public sector to provide services, as in the case of water supply in Ghana). Following the World Bank Accountability Framework, these service providers comprise "front-line professionals," who are in direct contact with the clients, such as agricultural extension agents, as well as staff involved in management and administration, such as supervisors of front-line professionals, clerical staff, and others. As discussed below, the gender composition of front-line professionals can play an important role in making service provision responsive to gender needs. Management practices also play an important role in this regard.

In this report, the term *political representatives* is used to refer to men and women who hold political office, such as members of councils at different levels of local government and members of parliaments at state and federal levels. The term also refers to politicians in executive political functions at different levels, such as district chief executives in Ghana, *kebele* (peasant association) cabinet members in Ethiopia, or government ministers. Political representatives may be elected (in competitive or noncompetitive elections) or appointed.

To capture the effect of decentralization, the framework distinguishes between political representatives at the local government level (box LP) and the national level (box NP). To keep the diagram in figure 2.1 manageable, not all tiers of local government are represented. Federally constituted countries may have elected representatives at the state level and the federal/national level; box NP refers to both. Gender equity among political representatives can be improved in a variety of ways, ranging from support to female candidates to mandatory quotas.

The links between households and service providers (links HH–PS and HH–NG) correspond to the short route of accountability in the World Bank Accountability Framework. The long route of accountability is indicated by the links between household members and elected representatives (links HH–LP and HH–NP), who in turn interact with different types of service providers (links LP–PS und NP–NM).

The framework used here extends the World Bank Accountability Framework in several other aspects. It explicitly includes community-based associations (box CO), defined here as membership organizations at the community level. These organizations include economic associations (such as farmers cooperatives, self-help groups, and savings and credit groups); sociocultural and identity-based organizations (such as religious groups and caste associations); and customary organizations (such as funeral societies). Community organizations may be formal or informal organizations (formal organization are those that are registered or governed by formal law). They may be customary (in the sense that they have existed for centuries) or created by more recent social movements or development interventions.

One type of community-based organizations is a user group or association formed with the objective of facilitating access to services or taking part in service provision. Examples are water and sanitation committees for drinking water supply, water user associations for irrigation, and parent-teacher associations. This report considers user associations that create links between service providers and households (links PS/NG–CO and CO–HH) to be part of the short route of accountability. Community-based organizations, such as self-help groups, may also empower citizens to interact more effectively with their political representatives, thus strengthening the long route of accountability. Male and female household members may join user groups as individuals; households may also be represented by a single member, typically the male household head. As discussed below, user groups may have affirmative action rules, such as requirements for women in the executive body of the organization.

The framework also includes development agencies and advocacy NGOs (box DA), which often affect service provision through projects, policy advice, or advocacy. International development agencies typically work with ministries at the national/state level (link DA–NM), but they may also directly interact with public or nongovernmental service providers at the local level by providing funding and technical advice (links DA–PS and DA–NG). They may promote gender-sensitive service provision through the design of their projects and programs and in policy dialogues with governments. Advocacy NGOs may lobby local and national political representatives (links DA–LP and DA–NP). NGOs that specialize in advocacy for women's rights may play an important role in improving the gender responsiveness of service provision, for example, by lobbying for changes in the legal framework and providing support to female politicians.

Another extension of the World Bank Accountability Framework is the inclusion of political parties (box PP). Political parties can play an important role in formulating policies and laws that affect the gender responsiveness of public service provision. They are also influential through their role in the selection of candidates for elected and appointed positions at local and national levels (links PP–LP and PP–NP). Even where formal rules require that local representatives be elected on a nonpartisan basis, as in Ghana, political parties often play an important informal role (by, for example, supporting certain candidates). They can also be involved in the recruitment and promotion of staff in public sector service providers (links PP–PS and PP–NM). As explained below, political parties can use various strategies to promote gender equity.

ACTIONS AND MECHANISMS THAT CREATE ACCOUNTABILITY

Along the chain of service delivery, various actions and mechanisms can create accountability between the actors involved (figure 2.2). These actions and mechanisms can also be related to the actors involved in service delivery specified in the framework (box 2.1). Each action or mechanism has its own gender dimension. An important accountability mechanism in the planning stage is the ability of clients to express their needs and demands and the obligation or willingness and capacity of service providers to consider their needs and demands in the planning process. The ability of male and female clients to express their needs and demands may differ; the willingness and capacity of providers to respond to gender-differentiated or gender-specific needs may differ as well. For example, district agricultural offices may involve fewer female than male farmers in planning meetings and pay less attention to their needs.

The allocation of funding is a crucial stage in the service delivery chain; access to budget information is an important mechanism for creating accountability at that stage. Gender budgeting has been introduced to improve gender

Figure 2.2 Creating Accountability along the Service Delivery Chain

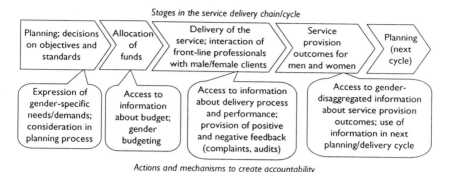

Stages in the service delivery chain/cycle

| Planning; decisions on objectives and standards | Allocation of funds | Delivery of the service; interaction of front-line professionals with male/female clients | Service provision outcomes for men and women | Planning (next cycle) |

| Expression of gender-specific needs/demands; consideration in planning process | Access to information about budget; gender budgeting | Access to information about delivery process and performance; provision of positive and negative feedback (complaints, audits) | Access to gender-disaggregated information about service provision outcomes; use of information in next planning/delivery cycle |

Actions and mechanisms to create accountability

Source: Authors.

responsiveness for this element of the service delivery chain. Accountability in the stage of actual service delivery is enhanced if users have access to information about the delivery process, its finances, and performance. Users can hold providers accountable by requesting information, providing positive and negative feedback, and launching complaints. Information about ultimate service delivery outcomes, such as adoption rates for technologies promoted by agricultural extension agents, can also be used to create accountability.

These mechanisms are effective only if providers have the obligation or willingness and capacity to respond and enforceable means of corrective action exist (UNIFEM 2009). As in the case of planning, male and female clients may differ in their capacity to use these mechanisms, and providers may respond differently to actions taken by male and female clients. The threat of sexual harassment or abuse from state officials may lead women to avoid state agents and contact or engagement with the state.

Clients and their organizations play an essential role in holding service providers accountable; important mechanisms also create accountability within organizations, including service provision organizations, political parties, and community-based organizations. To create accountability within their staff, public, nongovernmental, and private sector organizations that provide services can use human resource management approaches, such as merit-based promotion, reporting rules, performance reviews, monitoring and evaluation systems, and disciplinary action in the case of misconduct. They can promote financial accountability through financial management rules that increase transparency and through audits.

Political parties can create accountability through internal party democracy (voting for leadership positions, democratically selecting candidates); incentives (for example, campaign support); and disciplinary measures (such as, in the extreme case, exclusion of party members). Community-based

Box 2.1 Mechanisms and Actions That Create Accountability in Service Delivery

The actors involved in service delivery can use the following mechanisms and actions to create accountability:

■ Citizens (HH) or community-based organizations (CO) can hold service providers (PS, NM) accountable by obtaining information about the planning and execution of service delivery, the monitoring of service delivery results, and complaints about performance.

■ Mechanisms by which accountability is created within service provision organizations (PS, NM), such as government departments, include service standards or contracts, reporting rules, monitoring and evaluation systems, audits, disciplinary actions, and the use of incentives such as merit-based promotion for good performance.

■ Citizens (HH) can hold political representatives (LP, NP) and political parties (PP) accountable through voting; other forms of political support, such as campaign contributions; lobbying; meetings at which politicians provide information; and political protest, which may range from issuing complaints to demonstrating.

■ Political representatives (LP, NP) can hold service providers (PS, NM) accountable by setting policies, guidelines, and standards; allocating budgets; providing oversight (for example, through performance reviews and audits); and inducing disciplinary actions, such as transfer of staff. Politicians may misuse their influence over service provision organizations for personal political gain.

■ Political parties (PP) can hold their members accountable through incentives, such as facilitating access to political office (for example, choosing candidates for elections, providing campaign support), as well as through disciplinary measures (in the extreme case, exclusion from the party).

■ Members of community-based organizations (CO) and political parties (PP) can hold their leaders accountable through mechanisms such as selecting candidates and voting for executive positions, participating in membership meetings, and monitoring activities and finances.

■ The media can play an important role in strengthening various mechanisms of accountability by increasing access to information.

Source: Authors.

organizations can also create accountability through internal democratic mechanisms, such as voting for members in executive body positions and making decisions in membership meetings. Voting is only one way to create accountability; community-based organizations can also use important alternative or customary mechanisms, such as reputation and local recognition.

GENDER AND GOVERNANCE IN RURAL SERVICES

Women may be disadvantaged in using either of these mechanisms. For example, voting rights in community organizations may be restricted to one household member, and traditional accountability mechanisms do not necessarily recognize women.

The mechanisms citizens can use to hold their political representatives accountable are often referred to as "voice." These mechanisms include voting in elections, providing campaign contributions, lobbying, holding meetings at which politicians have to justify their actions, and engaging in various forms of political protest, including demonstrations. The opportunities for women's voice are often limited by male- and elite-dominated political processes (UNIFEM 2009).

Some recently developed frameworks that deal with governance highlight additional aspects of accountability. The World Bank's governance and anti-corruption strategy (World Bank 2007d) emphasizes the role civil society and the media can play in improving various accountability mechanisms, especially by increasing transparency. It also emphasizes the role of formal oversight institutions—including an independent judiciary and legislative and independent oversight bodies, such as supreme audit institutions—as well as transparency initiatives (such as income and asset declarations).

The Local Governance Framework of the World Bank (2007e) has three important elements that relate to the topic in this study. First, the framework emphasizes the relationship between discretion and accountability, showing how the lack of discretion can undermine accountability. Second, it notes that the effectiveness of decentralization for improved service delivery depends on the extent to which it is implemented in all three dimensions—fiscal, political, and administrative. Third, it distinguishes between upward and downward accountability, identifying the appropriate role of each. Other frameworks that deal with local governance, even those that are not centered on accountability dynamics, focus on institutional design features and processes, and institutional context. (see Agarwal and Perrin 2009 for an example).

STRATEGIES TO MAKE SERVICE PROVISION MORE GENDER SENSITIVE

The framework presented in figure 2.1 can be used to identify and classify strategies to make the provision of agricultural and rural services more gender sensitive (box 2.2). This section presents some major findings regarding these strategies derived from *Getting Good Government for Women: A Literature Review* (Horowitz 2009), hereafter referred to as "the review." The review, conducted by the late Leah Horowitz as part of the Gender and Governance in Rural Services project, covers 166 peer-reviewed studies written in English. Unless otherwise stated, all quotations and page numbers in this section refer to this review.

Box 2.2 Strategies to Make Service Provision More Gender Sensitive

The following types of strategies can make service provision more gender sensitive:

Strategies that target household members and community organizations (boxes HH and CO in figure 2.1):

- Organizing women and girls; promoting political awareness, leadership, and advocacy abilities
- Creating and strengthening women's self-help groups
- Conducting gender-sensitive citizen monitoring and auditing
- Establishing gender-sensitive complaint mechanisms
- Requiring gender quorums at community meetings
- Adopting affirmative action in user group membership
- Providing gender-sensitive training for members of user organizations
- Creating programs and projects that target women and girls

Strategies that target the public administration (boxes PS and NM):

- Establishing ministries/agencies of gender in national and local governments ("gender machinery")
- Creating gender focal points in sectoral ministries and decentralized departments
- Establishing equal opportunity structures in the civil service (antidiscrimination bureaus, merit protection agencies, equal opportunity commissions)
- Adopting affirmative action in the civil service

Strategies that target all types of service providers (boxes PS and NG):

- Establishing performance contracts with attention to gender
- Designing and implementing programs and projects in a gender-sensitive manner
- Monitoring indicators in a gender-disaggregated and gender-sensitive manner
- Employing female fieldworkers and giving them sufficient discretion to address the needs of female clients

Strategies that target local and national political representatives (boxes LP and NP):

- Adopting affirmative action in electoral politics (for example, reserving seats for women in local councils and national parliaments)
- Creating parliamentary committees on women's affairs; giving responsibility for gender to subject-specific parliamentary committees

(continued)

Box 2.2 (Continued)

- Establishing party-independent bodies that provide financial and moral support to female candidates
- Providing gender-focused training and support programs for local and national representatives (targeting male and female representatives)

Strategies that target political parties (box PP):

- Creating women's wings in political parties
- Adopting affirmative action in political parties
- Creating party manifestos for women
- Recruiting, mentoring, and developing women as leaders

Cross-cutting strategies:

- Establishing gender-responsive budgets
- Creating organizational gender structures, such as gender working groups and advisory councils
- Establishing institutions that respond to women's needs with respect to the timing of meetings, the type of pay, safety in travel, child support, and related issues.

Source: Adapted from Horowitz (2009).

Strategies That Target Household Members and Community Organizations

Cross-country evidence indicates that gender norms, domestic responsibilities, and opportunity costs inhibit women from participating in political activities. Women are less likely than men to attend community meetings in India; in contrast, other disadvantaged groups attend village meetings, thus improving the targeting of resources toward them. In South Africa's democratic transformation, the concept of "structured participation" was promoted at the local level. This concept entails the establishment of rules and procedures that specify who is to participate, on behalf of whom, through which organizational mechanism, and to what effect. Still, many black women found this process inaccessible. In Zimbabwe, female smallholders hardly took action to secure the services they needed from the government. In Indonesia, "most of the opportunities for women to participate in civil society are in their roles as mothers, wives, and household managers, but not as empowered citizens. Community meetings are still not a forum for women in their current form, at least not in the places in India, Indonesia, or southern Africa that have been studied" (p. 33).

The review indicates that community-based organizations can play an important role in overcoming these obstacles, with the effect depending on the type of organization. Women's participation in organizations such as women's associations, self-help or microlending groups, social networks, and civic and religious groups play an important role in strengthening their social networks. In fact, "such organizations may provide individual women with new platforms to exercise agency and may motivate women to access existing forums for political voice or create new ones" (p. 35). Women are often creative in carving out space for action at the local level. For example, if they are formally silenced and, thus, cannot show opposition or approval through public statements, they may resort to "unusual" modes of participation, such as evocation of the supernatural and song. Such strategies are often overlooked.

The literature highlights the role of women's movements in developing accountability to women, which helps women and their allies identify and mobilize around an issue of common concern. "Feminist political scientists have contributed to a growing literature on women's movements in comparative perspective, and a good deal is now known about how women in different places come to politicize their identity and to choose organizational and advocacy strategies" (p. 20). This literature focuses on Latin America and Eastern Europe; less is known about the role of women's movements in other parts of the world.

A body of literature deals with groups that formed to support the provision of a particular service, such as water and sanitation committees. The limited evidence about such organizations suggests that they are often required by donors rather than the outcome of an emancipatory social movement. The space they create for women to tailor service provision to their needs is limited by the fact that such organizations are often assigned fairly limited tasks, such as selecting beneficiaries or implementing already planned programs or projects. As the review points out, they rarely have the power to influence program implementation or policy design.

The literature also draws attention to the fact that selection criteria for user committees are often established by less than democratic means and can, therefore, exclude women, either by definition or by process. To avoid this problem, donor agencies have used guidelines for the inclusion of women, which they have enforced by excluding noncompliant groups from benefits. This strategy, used by the United Nations Development Programme (UNDP) and the United Nations Children's Fund (UNICEF) for water and sanitation committees in Ghana, did not bring women into positions of responsibility. The literature also criticizes participatory development initiatives that overemphasize consensus and mask or silence dissent, making it difficult for women to make their voices heard. The creation of user committees can also lead to the fragmentation of popular participation, limiting their effectiveness.

Strategies That Target the Public Administration and Other Service Providers

Strategies that target the public administration and other service providers include women's or gender machinery (public sector agencies in national and local governments that are set up to promote gender equity); affirmative action, such as quotas for women in the civil service; the employment of female staff with sufficient discretion to respond to gender needs; gender-sensitive design and implementation of programs and projects; and the use of gender-disaggregated monitoring and evaluation data. The sparse evidence on gender machinery indicates that "promoting a cross-cutting issue like gender in the average bureaucracy is a supremely difficult task for even the best situated agency" (p. 24). The review concludes that gender machinery has the potential to strengthen the capacity of bureaucracies to deliver gender-sensitive administration in terms of technical skills and managerial systems but often lacks the political buy-in required to demand real accountability to women from the greater bureaucracy. National gender machinery is often criticized as being imposed by external actors. It can be misused as political support units for the ruling party and can alienate women's activities in the NGO community. It is also often subject to restructuring, changes in leadership, and lack of sufficient resources to fulfill its mandates. A common strategy for dealing with the challenge to providing oversight in a wide range of sectoral ministries and agencies is to install gender focal points in them, but such focal points suffer from challenges similar to those facing dedicated agencies. The gender machinery has also been criticized for depoliticizing gender equality. However, there have also been positive examples, especially following democratic transitions, as in Chile, the Philippines, South Africa, and Uganda.

Some countries, such as Bangladesh, have implemented gender quotas or target systems for public employment. Such systems are often capriciously administered, especially where there is not genuine commitment to gender equity from the administration. There is almost no peer-reviewed literature on the gender-specific aspects of civil service and public administration reform, which may reflect the lack of attention to gender in such reform efforts. Indeed, UNIFEM (2009) finds that less than 5 percent of World Bank lending for public sector governance from 2002 to 2007 had a gender focus.

To be responsive to gender needs, public administrations require both adequate capacity and incentives. The limited evidence on this issue suggests that "performance reviews and indicators, bureaucratic communication flows, and informal professional cultures all implicitly undervalue the work necessary to tailor services specifically to the needs of women and to help women overcome barriers to accessing these" (p. 26). Little is known about how to overcome this challenge. In particular, "there is very little understanding of how to craft bureaucratic incentive systems that reward the extra effort needed to work for women's advancement" (p. 25). The review suggests that collecting more gender-disaggregated data at every point in the chain of service delivery—demand, expenditure, benefit incidence, impact—would help foster gender-sensitive policy analysis, monitoring, and evaluation.

The evidence on the responsiveness of female front-line staff in providing services to female clients is mixed. Several studies show that female staff in rural credit organizations and community health programs catered to the needs of female clients. In Tanzania, female farmers prefer female extension agents. Studies of nurses and midwives in maternity wards in Benin and South Africa, however, document critical, judgmental, or abusive behavior by women nurses toward female patients, including significant levels of physical abuse (p. 17). The literature suggests that the institutional and political context influences the ability and incentives of female staff to cater to specific needs of female clients. Moreover, to meet the specific needs of women and girls, female staff must also have the discretionary power to do so.

The sparse literature on the gender dimension of privatization—in rural water supply, for example—deals mainly with the potential negative implications of increased cost recovery for women. The review concludes that "privatization may increase the number of choices, but it does not change the conditions of inequality and dependency that constrain women's access to services in the first place" (p. 29).

Strategies That Target National and Political Representatives and Political Parties

Measures that target political representatives include affirmative action in electoral politics, especially the reservation of seats for women in local councils and national parliaments; the establishment of parliamentary committees on women's affairs and the granting of responsibility for gender to sector-specific parliamentary committees; and the creation of party-independent bodies that provide financial and moral support to female candidates. Strategies that can be pursued by political parties include the creation of women's wings in political parties; the adoption of affirmative action, such as party quotas female candidates; the inclusion of women-specific elements in party manifestos; and the recruitment, mentoring, and leadership development of women in political parties.

National Level

Much of the literature on gender and governance deals with women as politicians at the national level. It finds that labor market participation and better education are not necessarily associated with the number of women in national parliaments. Instead, it finds that the structure of the electoral system is one of if not the most important factor in accounting for variations in women's representation in national politics. In particular, many more female politicians are elected under proportional representation systems in which voters choose from closed party lists in multimember districts than in systems in which individual candidates are chosen in single-member districts.

The review emphasizes the role of political parties, often described as the "gatekeepers" of women's political inclusion. The political prospects of female party members are influenced by factors such as candidate selection mechanisms, recruitment, branch structure, systems of mentoring and leadership development, and the procedures by which party activists make it to the national executive committee. According to the review, women's wings or sections are conducive to promoting women's interests within parties, but they can also segregate women's influence and activities while remaining excluded from central decision-making bodies. The literature also indicates that women who reach elite positions in political parties are able to aid other female candidates. The way in which they do so is shaped by the opportunities provided by the electoral system. Although political parties allow women to enter politics, women's participation rarely translates into formal power within the party.

The review finds substantial evidence that left-leaning or progressive political parties are more receptive to gender-oriented public policy goals and to higher levels of female representation than centrist parties or parties on the right. Such parties may focus on short-term concessions in areas that are less costly and less contentious, however, rather than addressing more far-reaching concerns, such as women's access to the labor market.

Affirmative action mechanisms that help women enter politics, such as quotas and reservations, are effective in increasing the number of women in politics. But they can also reduce the effectiveness of female politicians by undermining their perceived legitimacy or by making them dependent on political patronage.

The question of whether female politicians pay special attention to the needs of their female electorate has also received substantial attention in the literature. The evidence is mixed. Some studies find that female parliamentarians do indeed focus on issues particularly relevant to women and children; other studies indicate that factors such as party affiliation, caste, and class are more important than gender in influencing the political activities of female legislators.

Local Level

Most of the empirical literature on the role of women as local politicians deals with India, where close to a million women came to power following the adopting of two constitutional amendments that mandated local elections to three tiers of local government and reserved one-third of the seats in local councils for women (for more detail on this issue, see the annex to chapter 3). Studies that analyze the role of women in local governments in several African countries (including Ghana, Nigeria, Senegal, South Africa,

Uganda, and Zimbabwe) find that social restrictions on women's mobility, low levels of literacy, and low socioeconomic status are important obstacles to the effectiveness of female politicians at the local level. The literature highlights the role that training programs by governments, NGOs, and development agencies can play in addressing these challenges. Some observers of this training landscape have made a distinction between programs offered by governments and those offered by NGOs. Government programs are typically organized around information dissemination. In contrast, NGO programs are often "transformative," focusing on skill and confidence building, role clarification, and gender awareness.

Political parties often exert significant discipline at the local level. According to one study, female members of local (panchayat) councils in India felt that "the local party machinery exercised considerable control over them and that they were not able to function independently or without partisan bias to implement a development agenda" (p. 33). In Zimbabwe, one party used its Women's League to intimidate families of opposition politicians.

The literature also points to structural tensions between the recognition of traditional authorities and the empowerment of women in rural areas. In South Africa, local authorities, who have considerable influence in local governments, may resist granting women access to land or allowing women to participate in decision-making bodies. More generally, tradition and patriarchy may be particularly strong in local politics. As a result, women who do break through the barriers into public life often face male ridicule, harassment, and even physical intimidation and violence for transcending conventional gender roles. In Uganda, women campaigning for local councils were required to perform "socially submissive acts," such as kneeling for the electorate at the campaign podium. Men also use procedural subversion to silence women members, scheduling meetings at times when women's domestic responsibilities inhibit participation, for example. Quorums in council meetings can help overcome this problem, but they are not widely implemented, and they can be undermined if male council members ensure that only their female supporters attend. Male officials of line departments do not give due recognition to female representatives even in a comparatively advanced Indian state like Kerala. The literature advocates associations of elected female local representatives, which can be supported by the women's machinery.

Corruption

The debate on the effect of female politicians on corruption was launched by two cross-country studies that found that greater representation of women in parliament is associated with lower levels of corruption (Dollar, Fisman, and Gatti 2001; Swamy and others 2001). Swamy and others (2001) also suggest that women have less tolerance for and involvement in bribery.

Subsequent literature does not support the claim that women are intrinsically more honest and thus a "tool" for combating corruption. Political scientists who have engaged in the debate hold the following view:

> It is opportunities for corruption that are gendered, not people's reactions to [them]. In particular, in socially conservative societies, it is difficult for women to become either clients or patrons in the male-dominated patronage networks through which corrupt exchanges occur. Where corrupt acts are condoned by social networks, or even required by social convention, women have been shown to be no less willing than men to engage in such behavior, especially if required to create a sustainable livelihood (p. 18).

Recent research has shifted interest from investigating whether women help combat corruption to investigating how governments can reduce the disproportionate effects of corruption on women.

Cross-Cutting Strategies

Among the strategies that can be considered cross-cutting in terms of the framework applied for the study, gender budgeting has received particular attention. Gender-responsive budget initiatives assess the adequacy of policy and budgetary allocations for addressing the nature of gender inequity; they can thus expose gender bias in macroeconomic policy.

Gender budgeting has been used in more than 60 countries since being pioneered in Australia in the 1980s. The results have been mixed. In some cases, it has been translated into administrative rules. The Philippines, for example, mandated that every national agency allocate 5 percent of its budget for "gender and development." Elsewhere the main advantage of gender budgeting has been the building of "coalitions between members of civil society, the parliament, and the bureaucracy, and even between different bureaucratic actors of the budget planning process who may not have previously worked together" (p. 27). Almost all initiatives have some sort of training and capacity-building component. In many cases, the effect has been limited because those involved in the initiatives did not have the power to change budgets. The review concludes that gender-responsive budget work is most effective when it supports the direction that particular policy makers already want to take by providing information that strengthens their position.

Questions for Further Research

Three types of gaps are relevant to the provision of agricultural and rural services. The first is the lack of information on "how governments actually work at the local level, and thus how specific men and women work within it to get things done. In particular, increased attention should be paid to how the informal rules that govern formal institutions exclude women—or create unconventional opportunities" (p. 42). The role of different tiers of governments for empowering women also deserves attention. The second gap in the literature is the "disconcerting silence in the public administration literature on gender" (p. 43). As a consequence, there is little empirical information on how to integrate gender sensitivity into the norms, incentives, and practices of mainstream agencies in the public administration. The third major gap is in the analysis of the links between women's participation in politics and actual outcomes for poor women in their lives and livelihoods. As indicated in chapter 1, the Gender and Governance in Rural Livelihoods project aims to contribute to filling these important knowledge gaps. As the first output from the project, this report responds to the first two knowledge gaps by providing descriptive information and focusing on a qualitative analysis (box 2.3).

Box 2.3   Research Questions for Descriptive and Qualitative Analysis

Based on the literature review, the following research questions were identified. They are presented here with reference to the conceptual framework shown in figure 2.1.

Households and Community-Based Organizations (Boxes HH and CO)

- To what extent do priorities regarding rural services differ between men and women and between female-headed and male-headed households?
- What role do community-based organizations (for example, farmer organizations, water and sanitation committees, and self-help groups) play in demanding better service provision?
- What mechanisms and channels do household members use to demand better service provision (for example, contacting political representatives or line department staff, or participating in community-based organizations)? What is their experience with different strategies? If women have demands for specific services or experience problems in this regard, whom do they approach and how, if at all, do their problems get solved? What motivates women to participate in community forums and community-based organizations? What gender-specific challenges do they face in participation?

(continued)

Box 2.3 (Continued)

Service Providers (Boxes PS, NG, and NM)

- What role do different types of organizations (public sector, NGOs, and private sector) play in the provision of agricultural extension and drinking water? How do service providers and the general public administration interact at different levels of government?
- How do households interact with different types of service providers? Are there gender-specific differences?
- How important are different aspects of service provider capacity (quality of human resources, availability of funds, incentives, mission orientation) for responding to citizens' demands and delivering services effectively? Do service providers have incentives and the capacity to respond specifically to the needs of female clients?
- How effective have different initiatives and reforms to improve local government capacity (for example, training, technical assistance regarding organization and management) been in increasing the ability to provide infrastructure and services? How effective have different approaches been in improving the gender responsiveness of local governments and decentralized line agencies (gender desks, gender-related training, efforts to collect gender-specific data, special programs)? Which approaches can bring about attitudinal changes? What role do development organizations and advocacy NGOs play in inducing service providers to address the needs of female clients?

Political Representatives (Boxes LP and NP)

- How do household members interact with their political representatives (voting, contacting in case of problems, and so forth)? Are there differences between male and female household members/heads? Does the gender of the political representative influence this interaction?
- What motivates women to seek political leadership? What role do political parties play? What role do development organizations and advocacy NGOs play? How do capacity-development activities influence the effectiveness of female representatives?
- What strategies do political representatives at different levels of government use to influence the provision of agricultural and rural services? What is their experience in using different strategies?
- How do members of the local public administration, line agencies (at different levels), and political representatives interact in the provision of agricultural extension and drinking water? Does the gender of the political representative affect this interaction?

Source: Authors.

NOTES

1. The diagram displays only one arrow between every two different actors. This arrow can indicate different types of relations, however, as discussed in this chapter. The male/female signs in every box indicate the gender dimension of all actors involved in service delivery.

2. In the public administration literature, the term *deconcentration* refers to the situation in which authority is transferred to lower levels of administration (for example, the district) but these offices remain accountable to the headquarters of their respective ministries. The term *devolution* refers to the situation in which these offices become accountable to locally elected governments (see Rondinelli 1981). In the literature on natural resource management, the term *devolution* is also used to refer to the transfer of authority from government agencies to user associations (Meinzen-Dick and Knox 2001).

3. Although the diagram in the 2004 *World Development Report* does not disaggregate different types of service providers, the text describing the framework acknowledges that service providers may include public sector organizations as well as different types of nonprofit and private for-profit organizations (World Bank 2003).

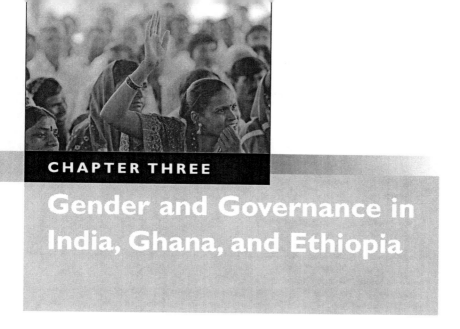

CHAPTER THREE

Gender and Governance in India, Ghana, and Ethiopia

his chapter provides background information about the study countries. It first presents basic comparative data and then provides more detailed information on the system of local government and on the two services the study concentrates on, agricultural extension and drinking water supply. For each country, the chapter's annex reviews the literature and information on decentralization, gender, and rural service provision; identifies strategies to promote gender equity; and describes initiatives by international development agencies.

THE THREE COUNTRIES IN COMPARATIVE PERSPECTIVE

This section provides basic information on the economy and agriculture of the three study countries, followed by information on governance and gender roles. The data presented come from international databases.

Economy and Agriculture

India has the highest per capita gross domestic product (GDP) of the three countries (table 3.1). All three countries experienced rather high growth rates in the years leading up to the recent global financial crisis. The reported female labor force participation is close to one-half in Ghana and Ethiopia but only slightly above one-quarter in India.

Table 3.1 Selected Economic Indicators in India, Ghana, and Ethiopia, 2006

Indicator	India	Ghana	Ethiopia
GDP per capita (constant 2000 $)	634	294	146
GDP growth (annual percent)	9.2	6.2	9.0
Female labor force (percent of total labor force)	28	48	45
Rural population (percent of total population)	71	52	84
Poverty headcount ratio at rural poverty line (percent of rural population)[a]	30	40	45[b]
Improved water source (percent of rural population with access)	83	64	11[c]

Source: World Development Indicators database (www.worldbank.org/data).
a. Data for Ethiopia and India are for 2000.
b. According to the 2004/05 Household Income, Consumption and Expenditure Survey (HICES) of the Central Bureau of Statistics of Ethiopia, the rural poverty rate in 2004/05 was 39.3 percent.
c. Data for Ethiopia are for 2004.

Ethiopia is the least urbanized of the three countries. In all three countries, rural poverty is endemic. Access to an improved drinking water source ranges from 11 percent in Ethiopia (2004) to 83 percent in India (2006).

India's economy is the least dependent on agriculture of the three countries: in 2006 agricultural value added accounted for 17.5 percent of GDP in India, 37.4 percent in Ghana, and 47.3 percent in Ethiopia (table 3.2). Agriculture still employs more than half of India's population. Despite their relatively poor irrigation infrastructure, Ghana and Ethiopia registered impressive gains in crop and food production between 1999–2001 and 2004. In contrast, India saw only modest improvement.

Governance

Governance indicators vary markedly across the three countries (table 3.3) (Kaufmann, Kraay, and Mastruzzi 2008).[1] Although these aggregate indicators have to be interpreted with care, as they are subject to measurement and aggregation errors, they help broadly identify the position of the three countries with respect to one another and to the rest of the world.

On the voice and accountability indicator, which captures citizen's political rights and the quality of democracy, Ethiopia ranks lowest, and its ranking decreased considerably between 1998 and 2007. Ghana's value increased, slightly topping that of India. India and Ghana registered a slight improvement in government effectiveness from already comparatively high levels; Ethiopia started from a low level and showed considerable improvement. With regard to

GENDER AND GOVERNANCE IN RURAL SERVICES

Table 3.2   Selected Agricultural Indicators in India, Ghana, and Ethiopia

Indicator	India	Ghana	Ethiopia
Agriculture, value added (percent of GDP), 2006	17.5	37.4	47.3
Agricultural raw materials exports (percent of merchandise exports), 2003	1.3	10.0	25.9
Agricultural land (percent of total land area), 2005	61	65	34
Irrigated land (percent of cropland), 2003	22.9	0.5	2.5
Crop production index (1999–2001 = 100), 2004	104	121	111
Food production index (1999–2001 = 100), 2006	109	132	134

Source: World Development Indicators database (http://www.worldbank.org/data).

Table 3.3   Governance Indicators (percentile rank)

Indicator/year	India	Ghana	Ethiopia
Voice and accountability			
2007	58.7	62.0	13.5
1998	58.2	37.0	24.0
Government effectiveness			
2007	57.3	55.0	37.4
1998	53.6	50.2	12.3
Regulatory quality			
2007	46.1	53.9	18.9
1998	33.7	47.3	12.7
Control of corruption			
2007	47.3	56.0	27.5
1998	48.1	44.7	34.5

Source: Kaufmann, Kraay, and Mastruzzi 2008.

control of corruption, India remained slightly below the 50th percentile, Ghana managed to move beyond this level, and Ethiopia experienced a deterioration.

Gender Roles

The indicators on mortality, schooling, and literacy can be viewed as outcome indicators of providing health and education services (table 3.4). India leads Ghana and Ethiopia in most cases, although in some instances the discrepancies between males and females are most pronounced there, indicating that women and girls remain disadvantaged despite the country's economic and

Table 3.4 Social Indicators in India, Ghana, and Ethiopia, by Gender

Indicator	India Female	Male	Ghana Female	Male	Ethiopia Female	Male
Adult mortality rate (per 1,000 adults of respective gender), 2006	168	260	283	289	329	367
Infant mortality rate (per 1,000 children under the age of 1 of respective gender), 2003[a]	37	25	52	44	56	56
Primary school enrollment rate (net percent of respective gender), 2005	87	90	64	64	56	63
Primary school completion rate (percent of relevant age group of respective gender), 2005	82	87	68	73	34	48
Adult literacy rate (percent of respective gender 15 and older)[b]	48	73	50	66	23	50
Child employment in agriculture (percent of children 7–14 of respective gender)[c]	77	70	68	89	91	97

Source: World Development Indicators database (www.worldbank.org/data).

a. 2005 in Ethiopia.

b. 2000 in Ghana, 2001 in India, and 2004 in Ethiopia.

c. 2000 in India, 2003 in Ghana, and 2005 in Ethiopia.

social progress. As in the case of economic indicators, Ghana represents a middle ground between India and Ethiopia.

India's female adult mortality rate is about half that of Ethiopia (168 per 1,000 versus 329 per 1,000). It is also much lower than the male adult mortality rate (260 per 1,000). In Ethiopia, infant mortality rates for boys and girls are identical; in India infant mortality is far higher for girls than for boys, for reasons that have been discussed in the literature (Sen 1990b). In Ghana, girls are also significantly more likely to die during their first year of life (52 deaths per 1,000 for girls, 44 for boys), although this gender differential is not as pronounced as in India.

India has achieved fairly high rates of primary school enrollment for both boys (90 percent) and girls (87 percent); the rates for Ghana and Ethiopia are still below 65 percent. A similar disparity exists in primary school completion rates. Only one-third of girls in Ethiopia complete primary school. Adult literacy rates are lowest in Ethiopia, where only 23 percent of women—less than half the percentage for men—are able to read. Although the rates are higher in the other two countries, the share of women that can read does not exceed 50 percent in either country. Child employment rates in agriculture are high in all three countries. India is the only one of the three countries in which employment in agriculture is higher for girls than for boys.

Gender-related indicators derived from the Social Institutions and Gender Index (SIGI) database of the Organisation for Economic Co-operation and Development (OECD) present a mixed picture (table 3.5). The violence against women indicator is based on the existence of legislation against domestic violence, sexual assault or rape, and sexual harassment. India has the best rating in this regard, followed by Ghana. The freedom of movement indicator measures the degree to which women have freedom of movement outside of the home. It reveals that women have full freedom in both Ghana and Ethiopia but that significant restrictions still exist in India. India scores best on the women's access to land indicator; the scores for both Ghana and Ethiopia indicate significant obstacles to women's ownership of land. (The findings reported in the annex indicate that access to land is far more limited than these indicators suggest. They also indicate that Ethiopia has made major steps to include women in land titling programs.) The three countries score equally on the women's access to bank loans indicator. With regard to national-level political participation, women make up 22 percent of the members of Ethiopia's parliament, a significantly larger percentage than in India (8 percent) or Ghana (10 percent).

Table 3.5 Social Institutions and Gender Index Indicators in India, Ghana, and Ethiopia

Indicator	India	Ghana	Ethiopia
Violence against women	0.3	0.6	0.8
Freedom of movement	0.6	0	0
Women's access to land	0.5	0.7	0.7
Women's access to bank loans	0.5	0.5	0.5
Percentage of women in parliament	8	11	22
Gender-Related Development Index (rank out of 136)	96	101	n.a.
Gender, Institutions, and Development Index (rank out of 117)	106	92	86

Source: OECD SIGI database (http://genderindex.org/).
Note: The first four indicators are measured on a 0–1 scale on which 0 represents full equality or gender sensitivity and 1 represents maximum discrimination or the absence of gender sensitivity. The indicators are based on statistical data and country-specific expert assessments published by the OECD in 2008. The percentage of women in parliament refers to 2006. n.a. = Not available.

The last two indicators are composite indices of other gender-related indicators. The Gender-related Development Index (GDI) measures achievement in three basic facets of development—health, education, and livelihood—accounting for intracountry differences between men and women. India (96th) ranks slightly higher than Ghana (101st) on this index (Ethiopia was not ranked). The Gender, Institutions, and Development Index (GIDI) measures gender inequality in four social institutions: family code, physical integrity, civil liberties, and ownership rights. Ethiopia ranks highest on this measure, followed by Ghana and India.

INDIA

This section provides background information about India. It first describes India's political system and the role of decentralization, focusing on Karnataka and Bihar, the two states in which the empirical research was carried out. This section also describes major government initiatives to promote gender equity and provides an overview of agricultural service provision and drinking water supply.

Political System and Decentralization

India is a federally constituted country with a multiparty system and an electoral system of proportional representation. The early years after independence were dominated by the Congress Party at both the federal and the state level.[2] Since the 1970s, an increasing number of regional parties has emerged that has led to the phenomenon of coalition politics and strong electoral competition.

The Congress Party can be described as center-left; its main opposition party, the Bharatiya Janata Party (BJP), has a right-wing Hindu nationalist orientation. Apart from the Communist parties, which play a role at both the federal and state levels, other parties are not characterized by a strong ideological orientation. In contrast, caste affiliation and identity-based voting play important roles in India's party politics (Ahuja 2005).

The three main levels of local government in India, each of which has an elected council, are the *gram panchayat* (cluster of villages), the *taluk panchayat* (block), and the *zilla panchayat* (district) (figure 3.1). Decentralization received a major impetus in 1992 with the 73rd and 74th constitutional amendments. The 73rd Amendment granted constitutional recognition to the local government institutions in rural areas, which are referred to as *panchayati raj* institutions; the 74th Amendment did so for municipalities in urban areas. Although this was not the first time decentralization had been promoted in India, the amendments laid down the general framework for decentralized governance.

The constitutional amendments granted considerable administrative and fiscal discretion to the states. In their state-specific decentralization laws, states

Figure 3.1   Levels of Government and Types of Elected Government Bodies
in India, Ghana, and Ethiopia

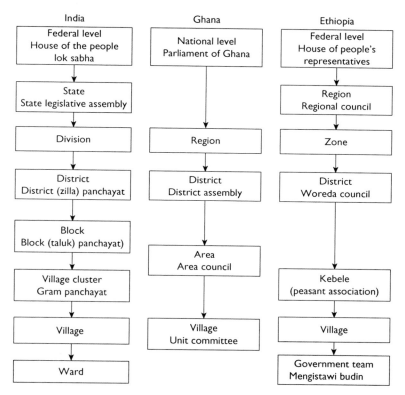

Source: Authors.
Note: Some zones have elected bodies (see text).

can determine which of 29 subject areas they want to transfer to the three
different levels of local government, where transfer refers to "functions,
functionaries, and funds." These subject areas include a wide range of services
and infrastructure, such as agriculture (including agricultural extension),
livestock and veterinary services, minor irrigation, drinking water, and health
and education. As a consequence, there is considerable variation across states
regarding the decentralization of these services. Karnataka and Bihar, the two
states in which this study was carried out, present two different points along
this spectrum.

Karnataka

The government of Karnataka is one of the earliest to have adopted legislation
incorporating the provisions of the constitutional amendments. Karnataka's

experience with decentralized governance dates back to the "local fund" and "local fund committees" constituted in every district in the 1860s and 1870s, which can be regarded as precursors of the current system (Aziz and others 2002).

Karnataka is regarded as one of the forerunners of decentralized governance reforms in India. It is the first state in the country to have devolved funds, functions, and functionaries for all 29 subjects, channeling about 30 percent of its revenues to rural local governments (Rao, Nath, and Vani 2004). The system of transferring authority to different levels of government is differentiated: for each type of service, different functions are allocated to different levels of government (table 3.6). (For a discussion of the rationale for this differentiation that draws on the fiscal federalism and New Institutional Economics literature, see Birner and von Braun 2007 and World Bank 2007b.)

Although many steps have been undertaken in Karnataka to strengthen and streamline rural decentralization in the state, some weaknesses remain. One relates to the predetermination of expenditure allocations, which, except in certain public works programs, offers too little scope for reflecting local priorities. Works frequently cannot be completed in the planned time, mainly because of delays in the release of grants (Sivanna 2002).

Bihar

The state of Bihar has lagged far behind in decentralizing power to elected local self-governments, including both the panchayati raj institutions and municipal bodies. Following the constitutional amendments, Bihar passed its

Table 3.6 Devolution of Agriculture and Drinking Water Functions to Different Tiers of Government in Karnataka

Sector	Gram panchayat (village cluster)	Taluk panchayat (block)	Zilla panchayat (district)
Agriculture	Promotion and development of agriculture and horticulture	Training of farmers and extension activities; opening and maintenance of agricultural seed farms and horticultural nurseries	Management of agricultural and horticultural extension and training centers; opening and maintenance of agricultural and horticultural farms and commercial farms
Drinking water	Construction, repair, and maintenance of drinking water wells, tanks, and ponds	Establishment, repair, and maintenance of rural water supply schemes	Promotion of drinking water and rural sanitation programs

Source: Karnataka Panchayati Raj Act, Government of Karnataka 1993.

first panchayat raj act in 1993, but its first elections to the panchayat institutions were held only in 2001. The 2001 elections implemented the reservation policy for women in a restrictive way, which some observers have attributed to a particularly high level of patriarchy in Bihar (Panth and Puri 2006). After a change in state government, a new panchayat act was passed in 2006, which in many aspects is more advanced than that of other Indian states:

- The 2006 act reserves half of all seats in panchayat councils at all levels of local government for women.
- It reserves 20 percent of all seats in panchayat councils at all levels for members of lower backward castes. These castes, which constitute one-third of Bihar's population, had previously not been recognized as a group that deserved special consideration; it was the upper backward castes in Bihar who benefited socially and economically (Gupta 2002).
- Under the act, the gram panchayat president must be an ex officio member of the block panchayat. This provision fosters better coordination between the two levels.
- The act introduced *gram kachahri* (village courts) to increase local people's access to justice. This local court system follows the same reservation policy as the panchayat councils.
- The act transferred more functions to the gram panchayat level than any other state. For example, the gram panchayats in Bihar are in charge of hiring primary school teachers.

Gender Strategies

A range of government initiatives has been implemented to address the disadvantaged position of women in Indian society. As the SIGI data in table 3.5 indicate, India ranks relatively high with regard to implementing legislation to protect women. With regard to local governance, the most far-reaching strategy to promote gender equity adopted by India is the reservation of seats in local councils. All states have reserved one-third of the seats in all panchayati raj institutions at all three levels for women; Bihar has gone beyond the constitutional mandate and reserved half of all seats—including the chair positions of the panchayati raj institutions at all levels—for women. Some states have also introduced quorums to increase the attendance of women in village (gram sabha) meetings, which play an important role, for example, in the selection of beneficiaries of government programs.

India has also promoted women's self-help groups, most of them centered on microfinance. These groups are seen as a major vehicle for empowering women in society. Self-help groups are promoted not only under government programs such as the Sampoorna Grameen Rozgar Yojana (SGRY) scheme (a public works program); they are also at the center of programs supported by international development agencies (see annex).

A third major initiative of more recent origin is the introduction of gender budgeting, which involves the reservation of funds for female-specific purposes. To date, gender budgeting has been applied mainly in government programs, although there are initiatives to promote it more generally to the state and federal budgets. Under Karnataka's Mahila Abhivrudhi Yojane scheme, for example, the government reserves one-third of the resources for women in individual beneficiary-oriented and labor-intensive schemes. At the federal level, gender budgeting is applied to more than 200 schemes of various departments. (Annex table 3.A.1 describes the strategies adopted by the federal and state governments to promote gender equity in service provision and in society in general.)

Agricultural Service Provision

This section provides an overview of agricultural service provision in India. It starts with a brief review of the role of women in Indian agriculture.

Role of Women in Agriculture

Women play a pivotal role in Indian agriculture, as farmers, agricultural laborers, and livestock rearers. Traditionally, they perform a number of agricultural tasks in both preharvest and postharvest operations, such as seed selection; seedling production; sowing; application of manure, fertilizer, and pesticides; weeding; transplanting; threshing; winnowing and harvesting; and seed preservation (NRCWA 2004). Women are also the main workers in animal husbandry, where they collect fodder, water livestock, and market livestock products locally.

Women's contribution at almost all stages of work in agriculture and allied activities is unrecognized. As Agarwal (1994) shows, women are treated as marginalized workers and deprived of rights over land and other rural economic assets because of the traditions of India's patriarchal society. They are also excluded from accessing direct benefits from their labor because of lack of ownership titles, which has caused extreme deprivation (NRCWA 2004). With more than 80 percent of female workers in rural areas engaged in agriculture and allied sectors, ignoring their roles will adversely impact development programs, resulting in misguided policies (World Bank 2007e). The fact that 15 percent of rural households are headed by women (IIPS and Macro-International 2007) makes the integration of women's needs in agriculture development plans all the more important.

In the absence of men, women are able to manage their agriculture land and livestock well, often better than male-headed households (Vecchio and Roy 1998). Despite this, women's access to assets and services remains limited in Indian agriculture.

To understand the role of women in India's agriculture, one has to take into account the fact that most landholdings in India are small and marginal (Deshpande and others 2008). Moreover, the growth of agriculture has been rather slow in recent years. Both factors have contributed to relatively high poverty levels in the agricultural sector, a situation that is widely discussed in India as "agricultural distress." Farmers' suicides, which are attributed to this situation, have serious consequence for their widows.

Provision of Agricultural Extension

India achieved remarkable agricultural productivity gains starting in the late 1960s as a result of the Green Revolution, which made this huge country self-sufficient in food within a few years. This success still constitutes a source of pride for India. The Green Revolution was concentrated mainly in irrigated areas; the productivity of agriculture in nonirrigated areas remains low.

Agricultural productivity growth has slowed in the past decade, partly because of a poorly performing extension system. To control public spending, most state governments adopted a policy of restricting the hiring of new extension staff (Government of India 2007a). Agricultural extension by the public sector played an important role in making India's Green Revolution possible. Beginning in 1977, agricultural extension was organized according to the training and visit system, which was phased out in the late 1990s. Subsequent reform efforts aimed to establish a more pluralistic and demand-driven model of agricultural extension.

The ATMA (Agricultural Technology Management Agency) model is currently being promoted as a major reform approach throughout India (box 3.1). It is a decentralized system, implemented at the district and block

---

Box 3.1   India's ATMA Model for Agricultural Reform

ATMA (*atma* means "soul" in Hindi) stands for Agricultural Technology Management Agency. The Indian government originally pilot-tested the ATMA approach in different phases in 28 districts in seven Indian states under the World Bank–funded National Agricultural Technology Project. With the implementation of the Support to State Extension Program for Extension Reforms, the ATMA model had been implemented in 268 districts in 28 states and two union territories by the end of January 2007. It now extends to all districts in India.

ATMA is a semiautonomous agency designed to enhance agricultural productivity, agricultural growth, and rural development by pursuing broad-based, bottom-up participatory developmental approaches that link research and extension activities at the district level, involve farmers and the private sector in planning and implementing extension programs, promote technology dissemination, and center on community mobilization and agricultural

(continued)

Box 3.1   (Continued)

diversification. ATMA has full discretion over its budget and can thus respond to changing technological and environmental requirements.

ATMA seeks to bring together district administration, line departments, NGOs, and local farmer representatives in order to facilitate decentralization in planning and implementation and promote interdepartmental coordination and demand-driven service provision at the district, block, and village level (box figure). Stakeholder representatives are directed by a governing board, which identifies the programs and procedures for district-level research and extension activities, reviews the progress and the functioning of ATMA, and approves the strategic research and extension plan. A management committee implements the district-level research and extension program and conducts participatory rural appraisals to identify problem areas in the implementation of the strategic research and extension plan. At the block level, programs are implemented through a farm information and advisory center. This institution, which constitutes the operational arm of ATMA, is operated by a block team of technical advisors and a farmer advisory committee. The farmer advisory committee serves as a platform for encouraging interaction among all key stakeholders (for example, farmers and line department staff), partly by stimulating the formation of commodity-oriented farmer's and women's interest groups at the block and village level.

Organizational Structure of ATMA

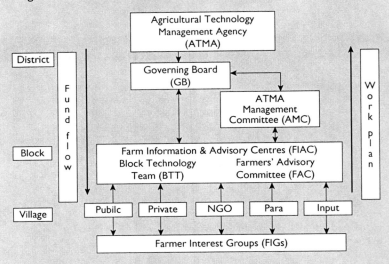

Source: Singh, Swanson, and Singh 2006.

(*continued*)

Box 3.1   (Continued)

To improve the access of women to agriculture and women's income, ATMA requires that 30 percent of the farmer representatives on its governing board and the block-level farmer advisory committees be women and that female farmers be included at every level of the ATMA model. It also asks two nonofficial members at the federal level to represent the interests of female farmers. In addition, the ATMA governing board is mandated to encourage agriculture lending institutions to increase the availability of capital to female farmers.

How successful was ATMA in meeting these provisions and in mainstreaming gender concerns in agriculture? The National Agricultural Technology Project completion report indicates that 30 percent of the members of the ATMA governing boards and block-level farmer advisory committees in the 28 pilot districts were women. It is not clear to what extent this provision has been met in nonpilot districts.

At least in the pilot phase of the program, women's self-help and farmer interest groups were slow to emerge, mainly because no budget allocations were made for promoting the role of women in agriculture. In response, the extension reform's agenda dedicates 30 percent of the resources for programs and activities to initiatives that promote the participation of women in agriculture. Similarly, 30 percent of resources for extension workers are supposed to be spent on female functionaries.

Assessments of the effectiveness of these provisions are unavailable. However, evidence from the 2008 ISEC-TISS-IFPRI study in Karnataka and Bihar casts doubt on the extent to which funds have been allocated to women-specific purposes in agriculture. Neither the agricultural field staff nor officials of the Department of Agriculture at the district and block level could confirm the existence of a budget component for women. In Karnataka, gender mainstreaming activities appear to be financed largely under the Women Youth Training and Education Program (WYTEP) of the Danish International Development Agency (DANIDA). The representation of women in the ATMA governing board differs across districts. Asked for the share of female representatives in the ATMA governing board, block and district officials of the Department of Agriculture in Karnataka report a number that ranges from 0 to 50 percent.

Sources: Sulaiman 2003; World Bank 2005; Reddy and Swanson 2006; Singh, Swanson, and Singh 2006; Birner and Anderson 2007; Government of India 2007b; Raabe 2008.

levels. However, although the states decentralized various agricultural functions under the Panchayti Raj Act, the panchayti raj institutions are not part of ATMA's formal design.

Despite efforts to make agricultural extension more pluralistic by encouraging private sector and NGO involvement, the public sector has remained the major provider of agricultural advisory services in India. A nationally representative survey published in 2005, the State of the Indian Farmer Survey, found that only input dealers, whose advisory services are presumably limited to the inputs they sell, have substantial coverage, reaching 13 percent of the households nationwide as a source of information about new technologies (NSSO 2005). The survey suggests that agricultural extension agents reach less than 6 percent of farmers and that less than 1 percent of farmers use private agencies or NGOs as a source of information about new technologies. These findings point to a major constraint that is not adequately addressed by the ATMA reform model: India's departments of agriculture no longer seems to have adequate staff numbers to reach farmers (male or female), and the private sector or NGOs had not filled this gap by 2005. It remains unclear to what extent private sector initiatives that use new information technologies, such as the *e-choupal* approach by Indian Tobacco Company, have increased access to agricultural knowledge and information since 2005. E-choupals are village Internet kiosks, from which farmers can access agricultural information. They also facilitate the sale of farm produce.

Drinking Water Supply

Drinking water supply is one of the few services that many states, including Karnataka, decentralized to the lowest tier of local government, the gram panchayats. In Karnataka, functional responsibility for drinking water supply depends on the source of rural drinking water supply. Maintenance of mini–water supply schemes and piped water supply schemes is the responsibility of block panchayats; responsibility for borewells with hand pumps rests with the gram panchayats. A variety of schemes for the provision of drinking water supply and sanitation facilities to rural residents are implemented by the central government (for example, the Accelerated Rural Water Supply program, the Total Sanitation Campaign, and sector reform projects) and the states (for example, the Karnataka Rural Water Supply and Sanitation project).

In 1999, the government of India introduced reforms in the rural water supply and sanitation and promoted programs for institutionalizing community-based drinking water supply management. The approach incorporates three basic principles: adoption of a demand-driven community-participation approach based on the empowerment of villagers to plan, design, implement, and manage water supply schemes; a shifting of the role of the government from direct service delivery to that of a facilitator; and partial capital cost sharing and shouldering of full responsibility of operation and maintenance by users (Government of India 2003).

Estimates of the effects and effectiveness of these principles in improving drinking water supply are not available. However, it appears that the government is still an important source of drinking water supply. Paul and others (2006) show that 80 percent of households in India received water from protected (government and private) sources; 62 percent of households use government drinking water supply, and 38 percent use private sources of drinking water supply. The majority of households using public water sources enjoy easy access to the source (within 100 meters), with greater access in Sikkim (90 percent), Tamil Nadu (83 percent), Arunachal Pradesh (81 percent), and Karnataka (79 percent) than in Nagaland (19 percent), Bihar (16 percent), and Assam (9 percent).

GHANA

This section provides background information about Ghana, the second case-study country. After describing Ghana's political system and the role of decentralization, it presents the government's gender strategies and describes agricultural service provision and drinking water supply.

Political System and Decentralization

Under its constitution, approved in 1992, Ghana is a representative democratic republic. The president of Ghana is both head of state and head of government. He or she is elected for a term of four years by popular vote and is eligible for reelection to a second term. The winning candidate must receive more than 50 percent of the valid votes cast.

Ghana's Political Parties Act prohibits the formation of ethnic or religious parties or parties that operate only in specific regions. The country has a multiparty system, but because parliamentary elections are held on the basis of the first-past-the-post rule (majoritarian system of representation), two parties dominate the political system, the New Patriotic Party (NPP) and the National Democratic Congress (NDC). The presidential and parliamentary elections in December 2008 brought the NDC to power. Before the election, the NPP had formed the government. This peaceful change of government has been widely acclaimed, as it demonstrated that Ghana is a well-functioning democracy.

The public administration system in Ghana consists of ministries, departments and agencies, state-owned enterprises, regional coordinating councils, district assemblies, area councils, and unit committees (see figure 3.1). The decentralized government system consists of regions, which are governed by the regional coordinating units, and districts, which are governed by district assemblies. The area councils are in charge of the subdistricts; the lowest government level, located at the village level, is the unit committee. The district assemblies were established by the Local Government Act of 1993 (Act 462), with the aim of empowering people to participate in the development process and to have access to decentralized services. The regional coordinating council has a coordinating and facilitating role but no planning authority of its own.

The term *district assemblies* is often used to refer to both the legislative and the administrative branches at the district level. The general assembly, consisting of elected and appointed members, is the legislative branch of local government at the district level. The district chief executive, who is appointed by the president, is the political head of the district. He or she also chairs the executive committee, which includes several assembly members but not the presiding member of the general assembly. The general assembly has a number of committees and subcommittees corresponding to major sectors, such as agriculture, health, and education, and to general affairs, such as administration, finance, and citizen petitions. The district coordinating director is the administrative head of the district.

Elections to district assemblies and corresponding subdistrict institutions are organized by the Electoral Commission. Officially, local government elections are nonpartisan. Thirty percent of the members of the district assembly are appointed by the president. Despite the previous government's stated policy of ensuring that 40 percent of appointed district assembly members were women, women have been generally underrepresented in the district assemblies. Although the percentage of female district assembly members doubled between the 1998 and the 2002 elections, the percentage of elected female district assembly members still reached only 8 percent.

The districts have the authority to raise their own revenues. Under a provision in the 1992 constitution, they are also entitled to transfers of not less than 5 percent of the total revenues of Ghana. These transfers are administered by the District Assembly Common Fund, which is allocated annually to the districts, based on a formula approved by the parliament, and has to be spent on investment projects according to guidelines issued by the parliament. Funds are also spent in the districts by programs and activities of the different sector ministries and by various donor programs and NGOs.

The role played by traditional authorities in local administrative matters varies widely across Ghana, where some areas have chieftaincy systems with clear hierarchies and others do not. Traditional authorities are frequently consulted on district assembly affairs, even though they have no formal role in the district assemblies. At the regional and national levels, chiefs form regional houses and the National House of Chiefs. The president of the National House of Chiefs is a member of the Council of State and hence wields considerable political power.[3]

Although Ghana was considered a leader in decentralization in Africa when it first started the process at the end of the 1980s, the impetus for decentralization slowed during the 1990s, and the decentralized system has been criticized in a number of areas (box 3.2).

Under the government that was in power until 2008, a number of reform initiatives were started that have far-reaching implications for rural service provision:

- To improve administrative decentralization, a Local Government Service was created (as of 2009, implementation had not begun). This service will have

Box 3.2 Challenges of Decentralization in Ghana

Decentralization has considerable potential to improve public service provision by "bringing government closer to the people." However, recent reviews of decentralization identify a number of challenges that have prevented Ghana from realizing this potential. They affect the political, the administrative, and the fiscal dimension of decentralization.

Political decentralization

Potential limitations on political accountability arise from the following factors:

- The district chief executive and one-third of the district assembly members are politically appointed rather than elected, limiting their direct accountability to the citizens.
- Although local elections are supposed to be nonpartisan, party politics play an important role in local governments.
- There are parallel systems of authority that stem from the fact that the role of traditional authorities such as village chiefs in the local government system is not clearly specified.
- Subdistrict structures (area councils and unit committees) are not fully implemented, which limits the possibilities of citizens to participate in development planning and implementation.

Marginalized social groups and women have limited representation in elected local bodies, which reinforces problems of inequity and social exclusion. Other challenges to social accountability emerge from the inadequate functioning of existing complaint mechanisms, such as the Public Relations and Complaints Committee.

Administrative decentralization

The functions of local governments and decentralized ministries, departments, and agencies overlap, resulting in problems regarding planning, funding, and human resources management. District assemblies lack effective control over decentralized line agencies, whose staff continues to report to line ministries rather than to the district assemblies. Moreover, important constraints to administrative and managerial capacity of local governments persist. Efforts to mainstream gender in the local government machinery have been met with limited success because gender desk officers have no legal status within the district assembly system.

Fiscal decentralization

Deficiencies in the design of fiscal decentralization include insufficient alignment of planning and budgeting procedures; fragmented fiscal transfers from

(continued)

multiple sources (various central government sources, donors, and others); and low capacities of local governments to raise their own revenues. Despite ongoing decentralization efforts, district assemblies still have extremely limited discretion over the allocation of financial resources. They also have to cope with unreliable timing in the release, and sometimes only partial release, of intergovernmental transfers such as the District Assembly Common Fund. Difficulties also persist in funding gender-specific activities at the district level. Under the District Capacity Building Project (DISCAP), District Gender Action Plans were introduced, but it proved difficult to raise funds to implement them.

Sources: Asante 2006; Cusack 2007; Malena, Daddieh, and Odei-Tettey 2007; NCG and Dege Consult 2007.

the authority to appoint, recruit, and fire staff operating at the local government level. In essence, it will bring all decentralized departments under its fold (NCG and Dege Consult 2007).

■ The government is in the process of scaling up the composite budget approach. Under this approach, the budget allocations of decentralized departments—such as health, education, and agriculture—are to be sent directly to the district assemblies.

■ To foster financial decentralization, the government decided to set up a performance-based grant system for local governments in the form of a district development facility accompanied by a functional and organizational assessment tool (MLGRDE 2007).

■ The ongoing review of the payment structure in the public administration may create better incentives for the local government system, especially for attracting qualified staff to remote and disadvantaged areas (NCG and Dege Consult 2007).

As a strategy to build the demand side of local governance, a World Bank study recommended public education campaigns and the strengthening of local governments to disclose and manage information (Malena, Daddieh, and Odei-Tettey 2007).

Gender Strategies

Ghana has adopted a range of strategies to promote gender equity in service provision (see annex table 3.A.3). Unlike India, however, Ghana does not reserve seats for women in the district assemblies, area councils, or unit committees, and the number of women who win seats in elections is low. The previous government had a goal of reaching a 30 percent share of women among the appointed district assembly members. This goal was not met in all districts. The current government increased this goal to 40 percent and expanded it to all positions appointed by the president, including the district chief executives. If implemented, this type of affirmative action is expected to increase the presence of women in local governments considerably.

Several strategies have been applied to strengthen the gender machinery in the public administration. At the district level, district focal points have been introduced. The Ministry of Food and Agriculture (MoFA) has a Women in Agricultural Development (WIAD) directorate, and every district is supposed to have at least one agricultural officer in charge of WIAD, who is typically female. There are also guidelines requiring extension agents to report separately how many male and female farmers they interact with. With regard to drinking water supply, it is an explicit policy of the Community Water and Sanitation Agency that women be represented in user organizations (water and sanitation committees), as described below. This policy is not a mandate, however, so it depends on communities to enforce this rule (except in cases where donors withhold funding in case of noncompliance).

Agricultural Service Provision

Agriculture in Ghana is practiced mainly on smallholder, family-operated farms, which produce about 80 percent of the country's agricultural output. According to the 2000 census, agriculture employs 50.6 percent of the labor force. About 90 percent of farm holdings are less than 2 hectares in size.

As is typical in West Africa, the agroecology varies considerably, from the humid forest zones in the south to the semiarid north. Data were collected in three agroecological zones: the humid forest zone, the semiarid savannah zone, and the transition zone.

As agricultural production is generally dependent on rainfall, production of the major food crops, roots, tubers, and vegetables fluctuates widely across years, depending on the weather. Despite efforts to promote agricultural diversification, cocoa has remained the most important agricultural export commodity. It is also the driving force behind agricultural growth in Ghana.

Role of Women in Agriculture

About half (48.7 percent) of Ghana's adult female population is self-employed in agriculture, with the majority engaged in food production (MoFA 2007). Cultural and institutional factors often limit women's access to land ownership, labor, and capital. Access to land is often restricted to usufruct rights (that is, use but not ownership rights); women cannot provide collateral for credit because they may not have legal ownership of tangible assets. A study of the evolution of land tenure institutions in western Ghana, however, shows that the gender implications of land ownership are complex and subject to change over time (Quisumbing and others 2001). Traders of agricultural produce are mostly women, yet official credit programs do not usually cover small-scale trading activities. Women also lack the financial capability to hire labor to supplement their own. In some cultural settings, they are also likely to be missed by public extension services because they are not as visible as male farmers. Morris and Doss (1999) find that gender-linked differences in the adoption of modern varieties of maize and chemical fertilizer are not attributable to inherent characteristics of the technologies themselves but instead reflect gender-linked differences in access to key inputs.

Agricultural Extension Services

MoFA is the main public sector organization providing agricultural extension services. One of its seven technical directorates is in charge of agricultural extension services. It also has a technical directorate in charge of WIAD. Under the decentralization policy, MoFA was restructured with the creation of regional agricultural development units and district agricultural development units (referred to here as *district agricultural offices*). They are in charge of managing agricultural projects and programs; provision of agricultural extension services is their single most important task. As a result of decentralization, the district directors of MoFA have considerable discretionary authority. The district agricultural offices prepare their own plans and budgets; the regional agricultural development units have only a coordinating and supervising role. Front-line extension workers are called *agricultural extension agents*; their supervisors are called *district agricultural officers*. The officers are responsible for different subject areas, one of which is WIAD.

In principle, the district agricultural offices are decentralized departments of the district assemblies. Their link to the district assemblies has been limited, however, because the assemblies control neither the budget nor the staff of the district agricultural offices. This is expected to change if two of the reform initiatives mentioned above—the composite budget, which would provide transparency to the district assemblies regarding the budget of the district agricultural offices, and the Local Government Service, which would shift responsibility for human resource management of the district agricultural office staff to the district assemblies—are implemented. Agricultural research organizations are under a different ministry, but Research and Extension Linkage Committees (RELCs) have been set up at the regional level to promote exchange between agricultural research and extension.

Farmer-based organizations (FBOs) have been promoted under various projects and programs, such as the World Bank–sponsored Agricultural Sector Investment Project. Apart from other functions, they are supposed to enable agricultural extension agents to use a group-based approach to extension. Some FBOs, especially those that focus on agroprocessing, include only women.

A community-based approach is also being promoted for irrigation, which entails the formation of water user associations.

Drinking Water Supply

The organization of the drinking water supply is different from that of agricultural advisory services because the authority for drinking water supply has been decentralized to the district assemblies. There is no dedicated line ministry in charge of drinking water. Rather, district water and sanitation teams (DWSTs) are formed in the district assembly to provide rural water. (Urban water supply continues to be provided by the Ghana Water Company Ltd.) DWST members are not specifically hired for this purpose; staff members of the district assembly who perform related functions, such as health, are designated to become members of the team. At the regional level, the Community Water and Sanitation Agency (CWSA) was formed as a coordinating and facilitating agency but not as an implementing agency.

The current approach to drinking water supply was introduced under the National Community Water and Sanitation Program, which was supported by the World Bank–funded Community Water and Sanitation Project I (1994–2000). The project aimed to establish a community-based or demand-driven approach, which (in principle) works as follows: Communities are expected to express a demand for drinking water facilities and form water and sanitation committees (WATSANs). Selected members of the beneficiary community serve on the WATSAN, which is in charge of one borehole. The WATSANs are expected to organize the community in the process of acquiring a borehole, which includes the collection of 5 percent of the capital cost of a borehole as a community contribution. The WATSANs are also responsible for maintaining the infrastructure. They are expected to collect regular fees from water users (on a volume or time basis) to cover maintenance costs. They are also supposed to organize collective cleaning of the surroundings of the borehole, and they are equipped to do minor repairs of the infrastructure. Maintenance requirements that are beyond the capacities of the WATSAN committee members are reported to the water and sanitation teams of the district assemblies. Under their procurement system, the district assemblies contract private sector organizations for the drilling of boreholes. District assemblies do not have dedicated field staff to work on water and sanitation issues; they are expected to hire NGOs or "partner organizations" to help communities form WATSANs.

ETHIOPIA

This section provides background information about the third case-study country, Ethiopia. As in the previous cases, this section first provides an overview of the political system and the role of decentralization and then presents the government's gender strategies, followed by an overview of agricultural service provision and drinking water supply.

Political System and Decentralization

Ethiopia is a federal republic with five administrative tiers: the federal level, regions, zones, *woredas* (districts), and *kebeles* (peasant associations) (see figure 3.1). At the federal, regional, district, and kebele levels, and in some cases at the zonal level, governance institutions take a parliamentary form, with citizens electing councils that formally appoint the executive bodies and judges in the judicial branch of government. In principle, there is multiparty competition to fill the legislative seats at all levels. In practice, the Ethiopian People's Revolutionary Democratic Front (EPRDF) has been the prime political force in the country since taking power in 1991 following a civil war. EPRDF affiliates, including the leading affiliate, the Tigray People's Liberation Front (TPLF), which is chaired by the country's current prime minister, are organized along Leninist lines,[4] although EPRDF policy advocates a mixed economy with a substantial role for both the state and market forces (Vaughan and Tronvoll 2003).

The EPRDF government has organized political and administrative life according to a system of "ethnic federalism," with the regions constituting "national homelands" for particular ethnic groups. The current political system emerged with the constitution adopted in 1995. The administrative structure consists of nine regions and two city administrations.[5] A region may have more than one ethnic group, and it may create "special zones" for minority groups, which constitute an additional administrative and political tier between the regional and district levels.

The EPRDF is composed of affiliated parties in the four largest regions. In addition, in the five smaller regions, there are allied parties that are not considered full-fledged Front members. Following disputed elections at the federal and regional levels in 2005 and a period of suppression of dissent, the EPRDF won nearly all of the 3.6 million council seats in countrywide district and kebele council elections in 2008 after electoral officials disqualified many opposition party and independent candidates (Aalen and Tronvoll 2008).

In principle, then, Ethiopia has a multiparty system, elections are held periodically, and some opposition parties are permitted to exist. In practice, the EPRDF has had uninterrupted control over the federal government since the overthrow of the previous military dictatorship in 1991; through its affiliated and associated parties it controls all regional governments and has dominated nearly all local government councils at all times throughout this period (Pausewang, Tronvoll, and Aalen 2002).

The strict curtailment of political freedoms in Ethiopia affects the political space not only of opposition parties but also of civil society, the media, and ordinary citizens (Pausewang, Tronvoll, and Aalen 2002; World Bank 2004; Aalen and Tronvoll 2008; U.S. Department of State 2009). Ethiopia's relative status in terms of voice/accountability and political stability—two of six governance indicators analyzed in Kaufmann, Kraay, and Mastruzzi (2008)—is weak, as indicated in table 3.3.

Structure of Local Government

At the federal level, the executive branch consists of the president, who is the head of state; the prime minister, who is the head of government; and the cabinet of ministers (see figure 3.1). Ministers may or may not be members of parliament. The parliament organizes standing committees on various subject areas (for example, agriculture and water).

This basic structure is more or less replicated at the lower tiers of government. Below the federal and regional levels, tiers that are explicitly provided for in the constitution, is the zone as a unit of administration. With the exception of the zones in the multiethnic Southern Nations, Nationalities, and Peoples (SNNP) region and a few "special zones" for ethnic minority groups in other regions, this tier generally does not have an elected council. Rather, zonal administrators are assigned by the regional government. They provide administrative links between the region and the lower levels of government structure or act as oversight bodies.

Districts are contained in zones, and kebeles are contained in districts. Both levels of government have elected councils that appoint executive cabinets. Below kebeles are villages. Villages are not administratively created units, but they are often a relevant unit for government initiatives and programs—notably agricultural extension and drinking water—at the local level. A yet smaller unit is the *Mengistawi budin* (government team).[6] Mengistawi budin are collections of about 30 households that implement a range of government activities, including mobilizing household labor for community projects.

Waves of Decentralization

Since the EPRDF took power, governance and rural service provision have undergone two significant waves of decentralization. In 1992, the EPRDF–dominated transitional government issued a decree devolving significant administrative responsibilities to the regions. The federal and parallel regional constitutions firmly establish popular sovereignty, under which governmental bodies at all administrative levels are subject to periodic elections. These constitutions provide citizens with access to services, the right to censure elected officials, and the right to participate in planning and budgeting decisions. First-round decentralization kept development of broad policy frameworks in the hands of the federal government but made the regions responsible for implementing policy, with broad discretionary authority. Nevertheless, the first wave of decentralization was characterized by ongoing fiscal dependence on the federal government (Gebre-Egziabher and Berhanu 2007). In practice, this limited the discretion regional governments could exercise (World Bank 2001) (box 3.3).

Box 3.3 Results from a World Bank Field Study of Decentralization in Ethiopia

In the 1970s, the Derg bypassed Ethiopia's traditional community organizations in creating modern participatory structures. These highly centralized structures extended to the grassroots level and provided a mechanism for both service delivery and the exercise of political control. This is the system the EPRDF inherited and has put to use. The formal authority entrusted to these representative structures under the federal and regional constitutions of 1995 is considerable; the constitutional and legal basis for devolution of power is thus in place. In reality, however, Ethiopia's system of governance is still highly centralized.

Planning at the local level is largely subordinated to national and regional priorities. Most plan resources available for districts and kebeles are spoken for by the recurrent budget needs of the civil service, over which local governments have no say. Where off-plan resources (emergency food or cash funds, donor and international NGO contributions) are available, they are generally programmed by external development agencies. Local governments are generally left to focus on the planning of capital projects, but capital budgets are very limited. Capital project selection, moreover, is ultimately determined by civil servants at the zonal level, where priority is given to sector ministry objectives and to the national five-year plan. A 2001 World Bank study found no evidence that traditional community structures were tapped in planning; labor power, not ideas, appears to be the main contribution sought from communities. Groups with little voice, in particular pastoralists and women, are not specifically catered to in the planning cycle.

Citizens are passive beneficiaries of public service delivery rather than active participants in its management. The Ethiopian service delivery model is based on area coverage and direct service provision by cadres of professional staff, whose salaries account for the bulk of public development resources (more than 60 percent in most study districts). Capital resources and funds for operating costs are scarce. This imbalance reflects the clearly stated federal focus on increasing primary school enrollments and the numbers of farmers reached by the extension service; it has undermined service quality quite seriously.

The traditional community structures prevalent in Ethiopian life play little part in formal service delivery; the capacity, leadership, and resources embodied in them lie untapped by the official development effort. Apart from site selection and the contracting of individual artisans, communities and user groups exercise little discretion over government staff, procurement processes, or service evaluation. Channels for complaint are little used. Hierarchical control is strong, the formal development process is directed in detail by the technical bureaucracy, and local or alternative energies are underused.

(continued)

Box 3.3 (Continued)

Why does a system that so strongly empowers elected structures operate in this hierarchical manner? That it does so reflects Ethiopia's historical legacy, weak institutional structures, and lack of capacity. The situation also attests to the role of the ruling EPRDF in development. The party exercises considerable leadership and control throughout local government, as respondents at all levels acknowledge. Government strategy under these circumstances mixes commitment to eventual decentralization and economic democracy with a reliance on authoritarian practice. This hierarchical approach has permitted a strong budgetary emphasis on key priorities of agricultural development–led industrialization, in particular universal primary education and increased agricultural production, with impressive results through the mid-1990s. The civil service remains well disciplined, and absenteeism and fraud are rare by any standards. Funds appear to flow on time and to the purposes intended. Considerable stores of community labor power are tapped for their own benefit.

But these achievements come with a price. Foremost among them is the stifling of the development of the district as a democratic, accountable unit of government and the failure to capture the resourcefulness, resilience, and adaptability of Ethiopian communities. Second is the related self-reinforcement of the bureaucracy. Evidence of this is found in the high proportion of development resources devoted to maintaining regional and zonal bureaucratic superstructures and in the strong budgetary preference for salary expenditures over either capital projects or operating costs, despite what community preferences appear to indicate. There is also a relationship between the centralized control of service delivery and inflexibility. Service products are uniform in nature and not well tailored to different target groups (the poor, pastoralists, women). Valuable lessons that could be learned from bilateral and NGO activities are virtually ignored by the technical bureaus. The private sector, far from being seen as a legitimate complementary channel for service provision, tends to be regarded by officials as undesirable and exploitative. Indications from other sources suggest that the spread of rural entrepreneurship envisaged under agricultural development–led industrialization has faltered.

Source: Excerpted from World Bank (2001).

During 2001 and 2002, Ethiopia began an ambitious second wave of decentralization, further devolving responsibility for many public goods and services to district governments in the four most populous regions (Amhara, Oromia, Tigray, and SNNP, in which 86 percent of Ethiopians live). The process has entailed redeployment of civil servants from the regions to the districts, the formal empowerment of district governments to hire and fire staff, and a substantial measure of autonomy in planning and budgeting. However, the district governments remain heavily dependent on the regional and federal governments for revenues, and total district government budget allocations are fixed according to formulas established at the higher levels. Moreover, allocations are reduced by the amount of additional revenues that districts may secure (directly from donors, for example) (Dom and Mussa 2006a, 2006b).

In theory, district governments have discretion over the sectoral allocation of expenditures and the allocation of resources among their kebeles. In practice, they receive planning targets from the regional governments that are much more than indicative (Dom and Mussa 2006a, 2006b; Gebre-Egziabher and Berhanu 2007).

One important aspect of the second wave of decentralization has been to bring governance closer to citizens and to expand voice and participation in decision making. The process has sought to turn the district governments into nodes in which bottom-up and top-down modes of planning and accountability meet and are harmonized. However, the combination of budget ceilings and strong planning guidance from above tends to trump these downward accountability processes. Gebre-Egziabher and Berhanu (2007, p. 48) observe that "the Ethiopian decentralization drive is centrally controlled in spite of the fact that it appears to be a form of political devolution." As a result, they add, power is deconcentrated but not truly devolved, a point that is "corroborated by the fact that the ruling party that is prone to upward accountability dominates the entire realm of political governance at all levels" (p. 49).

An important aspect of service provision throughout the country is mobilization of community labor (and sometimes financial) contributions. In most of the country, these contributions are treated as voluntary, although in practice they are mandatory. In the Tigray region, labor contributions are explicitly treated as a compulsory tax. Labor contributions play an essential role in the construction and maintenance of conservation works, roads, and drinking water systems, as well as in reforestation efforts. Too often, ostensibly participatory rural development programs in Ethiopia have the character of "stone-carrying participation."

Gender Strategies

To address the problem of gender inequality, the government of Ethiopia has implemented a range of strategies (see annex table 3.A.4). In 1993, the government introduced the National Policy on Women (NPW). The 1995 constitution enshrines equality between men and women. Among the major objectives of the NPW are creating conditions that ensure equality between men and women so that women can participate in the political, social, and economic decisions of their country and facilitating the necessary conditions for rural women to have access to basic social services. The policy is also intended to create the appropriate structures within government offices to establish and monitor the implementation of different gender-sensitive and equitable public policies. National action plans on gender issues were devised in 2000 and 2006 to achieve the objectives of the NPW (Government of Ethiopia 2000; MoWA 2006). The plans included steps to enhance rural women's access to and control over productive resources such as land, extension, and credit.

At the various tiers of government, there are now ministries, bureaus, and offices of women's affairs. At the federal level, the Ministry for Women's Affairs is responsible for conducting and monitoring women's affairs activities and creating the environment for the implementation of the NPW in different sectors. At the regional, zonal, district, and kebele levels, there are offices (in the case of the kebele, a single individual in lieu of an office). As with the case of other line bureaus and offices, the women's affairs bureaus and offices are formally accountable to their respective councils, many of which have a women's affairs or social affairs committee that engages in oversight.

In addition to these agencies, several line ministries have departments, desks, and individual "focal points" focusing on gender issues affecting their sector. These entities exist from the federal to the district level. They are mandated to identify gender gaps and develop strategies to address inequalities in the line ministries and their subsectors (AfDB 2004).

The Women's Affairs Department of the Ministry of Agriculture and Rural Development (MoARD) acts as a gender focal point in the ministry. At the Bureau of Agriculture and Rural Development (BoARD) at the regional level, gender focal points are assigned in the respective women's affairs bureaus. At the district level, gender desks have been set up in the Woreda (District) Office of Agriculture and Rural Development (WoARD). In such a system, which is organized to penetrate the grassroots level, agricultural services, such as extension and credit, are supposed to reach men and women in an equitable way.

The Ethiopian Water Resources Management Policy recognizes the importance of incorporating gender issues in the development of the water sector. The policy has a section on gender issues with the aim of "promoting the full involvement of women in planning, implementation, decision making and training as well as empowering them to play a leading role in self-reliance initiatives"(MoWR 2004).

Spring and Groelsema (2004) suggest that the government introduced gender budgeting at the district level as a way to hold public spending activities accountable to principles of gender equality. There is no information on the ground on the extent to which gender budgeting has been implemented. The ruling party has also incorporated within its statutes the participation of women through the formation of an EPRDF women's league to work for the implementation of its strategies of development and to serve as "an agent of struggle to free Ethiopian women from all kinds of oppressions" (EPRDF 2006). This may be a relatively new focus, as EPRDF's five-year development plan for 1995–2000 did not mention women (Vaughan and Tronvoll 2003, citing Fekade 2000).

Agricultural Service Provision

Agriculture dominates economic life in Ethiopia, accounting for 85 percent of employment, 80 percent of exports, and 46 percent of GDP. Coffee is the principal export crop, with hides, pulses, oilseeds, khat, and sugar also important export commodities. Mixed crop and livestock production are found in both the northern highlands and the central Rift Valley. Commercial crop production, intercropped with *enset* (false banana) as a staple, characterizes the south-central region; pastoralism is the main livelihood in the arid eastern and far southern parts of the country.

The state owns all rural land, with usufruct rights allocated in 1991. These rights can be passed on to heirs and divided among them, but land cannot be sold or mortgaged. Land rental markets exist but remain underdeveloped.

The average farm plot is 0.5 hectares, with many farmers engaging in subsistence or semisubsistence production. Government policy emphasizes agricultural development–led industrialization, but Ethiopian agriculture faces severe constraints, including underdeveloped transportation networks that inhibit market development; serious land degradation, caused by overgrazing, deforestation, population pressure, and poor soil and water conservation practices; and periodic droughts, which appear to be occurring more frequently as a result of climate change.

Role of Women in Agriculture

Anyone who has spent time in rural Ethiopia can readily observe that in most parts of the country women are intimately involved in all aspects of agricultural production, marketing, food procurement, and household nutrition. Despite this reality, the view is widely held that "women do not farm." This cultural perception remains strong even though numerous agricultural tasks are deemed "women's work," including weeding, harvesting, preparing storage containers, managing all aspects of home gardens and poultry raising, transporting farm inputs to the field, and procuring water for household use and some on-farm uses (EEA/EEPRI 2006).

There is some variety across crop commodity type, region, and farming system in the traditional allocation of agricultural activities between men and women. For example, in a medium- to high-altitude area in the central Oromia region dominated by teff production, men undertake nearly all tasks in cereal production, including land preparation, planting, fertilizing, and harvesting, with the exception of weeding, which is the women's task (Bishop-Sambrook 2004). Participation of women in agricultural activity is constrained by cultural norms, such as the norm that women should not engage in plowing. In some areas, such as Sidama in the SNNP region, restrictions go even farther, prohibiting women from plowing, sowing, hoeing, and even weeding. Women often predominate in the cultivation of horticultural, especially vegetable crops. Such crops are commonly grown on small land plots in the vicinity of the house or in the compound.

Crop marketing and the control over revenues from these sales are often gender differentiated and in some cases vary by crop type. Many female farmers bring vegetables and fruits that they produce to the market and may retain the income they earn to pay for household needs. In contrast, the marketing and income from cash crops grown by the household at a larger scale, such as coffee, teff, and khat, are controlled by the household head, who is nearly always male in households in which the head has a spouse in the household, although small quantities of these important crops may be sold by the head's wife.

Tending to livestock is usually performed by boys and young men. Women are frequently responsible for providing feed and water for livestock kept near their home and for dairy production. In some areas, they are also involved in collecting animal dung from grazing lands.

Sole cattle ownership by women is not common in Ethiopia, although joint ownership by spouses is found in many regions. Control over the sale of and proceeds from livestock and livestock products is generally gender differentiated, with women tending to market small livestock and poultry, dairy products, and eggs. The sale of cattle and other large livestock is for the most part in the male domain.

This gender division of agricultural activities has constrained women's access to extension services. Until recently, horticultural production and the raising of poultry and small ruminants were considered "home economics," excluding women from other agricultural extension advice, training, and credit. Recent extension packages tailored for women have emphasized sheep and goat husbandry.

Both the federal constitution and all regional land proclamations stipulate that land rights are to be granted equally to men and women. Empirical evidence, however, reveals important gender asymmetries in access to and control over land. Upon forming a new household through marriage, women bring only a negligible amount of land into the household; nearly all land is brought in by the male spouse (Fafchamps and Quisumbing 2005), suggesting high intrahousehold land inequality upon the formation of a household. Traditionally, this inequality in land was perpetuated later in the household's life cycle upon the death of the spouses' parents, because men nearly always inherit land and women very rarely do so. Recently, however, in the northern regions of the country, women have regularly inherited their parents' land.

Even in regions where women formally receive individual rights to use land, land tenure security continues to be precarious for women (Crewett, Bogale, and Korf 2008). In the Oromia region, for example, tenure insecurity prevails for divorced women, arising from several exceptions to such land rights in the legal framework. Some articles in Oromia's land proclamation link land rights to social status, which in effect constrains the rights of divorced women and widows. Fafchamps and Quisumbing (2005) find husbands generally keep the land upon the dissolution of a marriage. Although female household heads may have access to land, they frequently lack other productive resources, such as labor, oxen, and credit, making it difficult for them to obtain inputs. As a result, they frequently must sharecrop out their land and usually do so from a weak bargaining position that results in unfavorable arrangements.

Agricultural Extension

During the early 1990s, the government initiated a big push to disseminate agricultural packages to farmers, which included fertilizer, improved seeds, credit, and the provision of extension services. Within the decentralized federal administrative structure, the main government institutions responsible for planning and implementing agricultural policies and projects are MoARD at the federal level and the corresponding regional bureaus and zonal and district offices.

The government is the major provider of extension through the WoARDs, which are generally divided into such subsectors as agricultural development, natural resources, environmental protection and land administration, water supply and rural roads, input supply and cooperative promotion, marketing, and disaster management and food security (Berhanu, Hoekstra, and Azage 2006). Agricultural extension service provision falls under the agricultural development sector; it is subdivided into extension on crop production, livestock production, and natural resources management.

The second wave of decentralization in Ethiopia gave district governments in the four largest regions responsibility for providing rural services, including extension and drinking water, to the kebeles. Until 2006 each kebele had access to the services of a single extension agent based in the WoARD. Selected kebeles were able to draw on a larger extension team under specialized projects such as the Managing Environmental Resources to Enable Transitions (MERET) soil and water conservation project supported by the World Food Programme (Cohen, Rocchigiani, and Garrett 2008). WoARDs also have more highly trained specialists who can provide services as needed to address specific problems.

As part of its extensive "good governance" reform in the wake of the disputed 2005 elections, the federal government directed all districts in the four largest regions to dramatically expand extension services so that every kebele would have a team of at least three extension agents, with training in crops, livestock, and natural resource management, respectively. According to this plan, agents are based in the kebeles, rotate to new communities every few years, and remain accountable to the WoARD. The extension team leader in the kebele serves as the agriculture portfolio holder in the kebele cabinet. In some cases, there are additional extension agents, such as those who specialize in beekeeping, veterinary health, cooperatives, or other topics; where they are present, they usually serve multiple kebeles.

The team deploys in the kebele on a watershed basis, with each member taking responsibility for all agricultural advice within his or her territory, drawing on the technical expertise of colleagues as needed. The team meets frequently and reports to supervisors who are deployed to a kebele and take responsibility for teams in a cluster of three to four surrounding kebeles. The team members work closely with contact and model farmers in their respective territories and facilitate the development of kebele-level agricultural planning.

The rapid expansion of the extension service increased the number of agents who hold postsecondary diplomas and opened up opportunities for women to fill extension slots. Farmer training centers have been established in many kebeles, through which extension agents will train farmers in both classrooms and field demonstrations. Short-term training, as well as more modular training for farmers with a fourth-grade education or higher, is envisaged. The government's goal is to eventually establish one farmer training center in each kebele. Extension agents and other agriculture staff receive training through the 25 agricultural, technical, and vocational education and training colleges in Ethiopia.

Drinking Water Supply

Lack of access to clean drinking water is a serious problem in Ethiopia. In 2004, only 11 percent of the rural population had access to improved drinking water sources. In the absence of such access, women must walk to the nearest river, lake, or stream to fetch water.

In line with decentralization, different responsibilities for supplying drinking water are assigned to the different levels of government bodies to implement the Ethiopian water resource management policy. The federal Ministry of Water Resources takes on national-level water management. It is responsible for formulating policies for the water sector and for developing long-term policy strategies. At the regional and zonal level are the bureaus and zonal offices of water resources.

Water service provision was long the responsibility of a "desk" within the WoARDs—a subcabinet agency that had to compete with other such agencies for resources, personnel, and policy attention. Since the district-level decentralization in 2001/02, districts have established woreda (district) offices of water resources (WoWR) to provide drinking water and hygiene education services, among others.[7] These offices have the status of technical agencies within the district government; in contrast to the head of the agriculture office, the office head is not considered a full member of the district cabinet. In some districts, the district cabinet members are elected members of the district council, even if they also have professional training in their areas of competence and rose through the civil service ranks. The limited capital budgets of district governments constrains their ability to fund construction of new drinking water systems. This often leads to a breakdown in communities' trust in the district government as promised systems do not get built.

Unlike extension agents, drinking water technicians are posted to district capitals and focus on training kebele residents who serve on local water committees. The committees are expected to organize users of improved and protected drinking water systems, carry out programs of health and hygiene education, establish fee schedules and collection, hire guards for the security of the water facility and other necessary personnel, and mobilize users for operation and maintenance of the system. WoWR staff are available for more difficult repairs and can help gain access to spare parts, but the local committees are supposed to achieve a degree of self-reliance. WoWRs often have limited access to vehicles, do not maintain regular contact with the committees, and do not evaluate their performance.

As with extension, the training of water committees is technically focused, with members expected to figure out how to mobilize the community, encourage payment of fees, and promote maintenance of systems more or less on their own. This tends to work better in Tigray than in many other regions, as Tigray has a strong tradition of political mobilization and self-reliance dating back to the anti-Derg struggle.

ANNEX: BACKGROUND INFORMATION ON DECENTRALIZATION, GENDER STRATEGIES, AND INTERNATIONAL DEVELOPMENT INITIATIVES

This annex reviews the literature and information on decentralization, gender, and rural service provision; identifies strategies to promote gender equity; and describes initiatives by international development agencies in India, Ghana, and Ethiopia.

India

Research Findings on Decentralization, Gender, and Rural Service Provision

This section provides a brief review of the literature on gender and governance in rural services, particularly agriculture extension and rural drinking water services, in India. It also looks at the effects of "women reservation" policies, as affirmative action strategies are an important feature of decentralized local governance in India. The review emphasizes the determinants of the reservation policy and discusses the effects of reservation on local governance and rural service provision.

Reservation policy. Most studies on the effects of reservation policies begin by identifying the variables that affect the selection of politicians. In a widely cited study of West Bengal and Rajasthan, Chattopadhyay and Duflo (2004) observe that female presidents in gram panchayats with reservation policies are less educated, less likely to be literate, less politically knowledgeable, younger, and poorer than presidents in gram panchayats without reservation policies. Chattopadhyay and Duflo hypothesize that female presidents in such gram panchayats are likely to be weak and subservient to local elites.

Other researchers argue that reservation policies result in the selection of strong women. Besley, Pande, and Rao (2005b) suggest that the level of education, landholdings, and political past of the politician explain his or her selection: local politicians tend to be better educated than their constituencies, have larger landholdings, and belong to families with a political history. Using the same data set as Besley, Pande, and Rao (2005b), Ban and Rao (2008b) show that women reservation policies do not lead to an unbiased election of female gram panchayat presidents. "Reserved" female presidents are significantly less educated, less knowledgeable, less politically experienced, and younger than unreserved presidents. However, they tend to be more politically knowledgeable, wealthier, and older than the average woman in the population and to have the same level of education. Ban and Rao (2008b) conclude that female presidents are not mere tokens.

The empirical literature approximates the effect of reservation on local governance by determining the effect of women reservation policies on the attendance and participation rate of local (female) citizens in local government (village) councils. In a study of West Bengal, Ghatak and Ghatak (2002) observe that the village constituency meetings are dominated by men and non–SC/ST groups and thus fail to be an effective mechanism for inclusive local governance. The caste and gender bias in the attendance rates of village constituency meetings is attributed to the ineffectiveness of voice and the corresponding feeling of not being heard.

Chattopadhyay and Duflo (2004) explain the gram sabha attendance rate using information from West Bengal and Rajasthan. They show that the reservation of presidential seats for women has a positive effect on the attendance rate of female citizens in gram sabha meetings in West Bengal but not in Rajasthan. Jayal (2006) provides counterevidence in a theoretical and empirical study for India that argues that women face institutional and social constraints that preclude their effective participation in panchayati raj institutions. Women who attend meetings might be unable to articulate their interests or to translate them into locally relevant policy outcomes.

Besley, Pande, and Rao (2005a) suggest that female, illiterate, and wealthy constituents are less likely to attend gram sabha meetings and that marginalized groups, such as SCs, STs, and the landless, are more likely to attend these meetings. They claim that the reservation of seats for women does not influence the frequency of gram sabha meetings. Village differences are attributable to differences in population size and literacy, with larger villages and villages with a higher literacy rate being more likely to hold gram sabha meetings.

Ban and Rao (2008a) find that gram sabhas in reserved gram panchayats headed by women are significantly more likely to be dominated by landowners. Landowners are more likely to have their priorities discussed during meetings, and deliberations over their issue tend to last longer. Ban and Rao (2008a) argue that this finding may point to the relative ineffectiveness of female leadership (similar results prevail for SC, ST, and OBC reservation). Other researchers show that women reservation policies improved the access of women to political office in West Bengal (Beaman and others 2008) and urban areas of Mumbai (Bhavani

2009). In both studies, more than 10 years of experience with women reservation policies appear to raise the probability that women directly compete with men for and win seats in villages.

Duflo, Fischer, and Chattopadhyay (2005) and Besley and others (2004) provide evidence of the service delivery effects from gram panchayats with a reserved SC or ST president. Munshi and Rosenzweig (2008) present evidence from wards with a reserved SC, ST, or OBC leader (wards are subunits of gram panchayats; 1 gram panchayat consists of 10–15 wards). The evidence suggests that caste reservation policies may result in the inefficient allocation of public goods to individuals. Munshi and Rosenzweig (2008) attribute this finding to the absence of a numerically dominant caste in reserved wards and the associated selection of relatively inexperienced and less competent leaders.

In a study of West Bengal, Bardhan, Mookherjee, and Torrado (2005) show that women reservation policies improve the targeting of subsidized loans to poor and SC/ST households but worsen the targeting of employment grants. The net effect is that the reservation of seats for women makes it less likely that SC/ST and landless households are welfare beneficiaries.

Besley, Pande, and Rao (2005b) determine the effect of women reservation for the targeting of Below Poverty Line (BPL) cards in Andhra Pradesh, Karnataka, Kerala, and Tamil Nadu. Reserved and unreserved gram panchayats do not differ in the targeting of BPL cards to SC and ST households. Gram panchayats with reserved female presidents are more likely to target BPL cards to ineligible members of the gram panchayat, however. This selection bias suggests that the reservation of seats for female presidents reduces access to antipoverty programs.

The literature also examines the effect of reservation policies on service quantity and quality. Chattopadhyay and Duflo (2004) show that female presidents in reserved gram panchayats in Rajasthan and West Bengal invest more in drinking water infrastructure than presidents in unreserved gram panchayats. The reservation effect on other public goods, including education and roads, is either insignificant or signficant in the other direction. Foster and Rosenzweig (2004) note that the interpretation of gender differences in rural service provision is complicated by the absence of information on the nature of the preferences of female and male gram panchayat presidents. Ban and Rao (2008a) suggest that female- and male-headed gram panchayats provide similar drinking water, health, sanitation, roads, transport, and electricity services. Significant differences are evident only in education: gram panchayats reserved for female presidents pursue significantly more education activities than unreserved constituencies. Munshi and Rosenzweig (2008) find that the reservation of seats for women increases the efficiency of service delivery in wards with a dominant caste and leadership commitment.

Agriculture and water service provision. Sweetman (1999), Kumar (2000), and Jain (2007) find that the productive contribution of women in rural regions in India has been constantly increasing and expanding. The increase has been particularly large in agriculture and associated fields, such as animal husbandry, dairy, fishery, and forestry, and even in nonfarm areas, such as construction and mining.

Shoba (1999) shows that a gender policy in the framework of institutional support for providing agricultural inputs, technology, extension service, and rights of land ownership enabled women to increase agricultural output, leading to gender equality and empowerment. Such an approach also succeeded in setting new social norms and power structures between men and women.

Grover and Grover (2004) note that provisions for institutional support and services, however inadequate, encouraged the process of women's participation in agricultural activities, reducing their drudgery. The provision of technological and extension services and training for skill development to improve their working conditions and supply of infrastructural inputs further enabled women to develop their capabilities. They show that the pattern of energy use in rural areas and the management of natural resources by rural women, including training to empower women in agriculture, have influenced policy approaches.

Sharma (2004) shows that the policy framework for mainstreaming women in agriculture needs to be adopted by the states to create suitable motivation, employment, leadership, and participation. Her study also provides evidence that self-help groups are more effective than individual approaches. Gain (2004) argues that the supply of credit and the provision of extension services enhances women's access to opportunities and ensures the sustainability of their agricultural activities. Rao (1996) observes that women in India did not benefit from participation in water development projects because of lack of equal opportunities. Swarnalatha (2007) argues that participation of women in development should not be measured by participation in the labor force or presence at meetings. Their effective participation is ensured only by integrating them in the decision-making process and developing in them a sense of belonging. In a randomized field experiment in Kenya, Leino (forthcoming) shows that the participation of women in the maintenance of water infrastructure does not affect the quality of maintenance of the spring. A livelihood approach should be adopted to address the nonagricultural needs of women, including food security, drinking water, savings, credit, transport, and communication, and non-land-based income-generation activities.

Strategies to Promote Gender Equity

Table 3.A.1 summarizes the main strategies to promote gender equity in India. The table is based on the classification scheme presented in box 2.2.

Initiatives by International Development Agencies

The government of India limits international involvement in local governance and agricultural and rural service provision to four agencies: the World Bank, the International Fund for Agricultural Development (IFAD), the British Department for International Development (DFID), and the German Development

Table 3.A.1 Strategies to Promote Gender Equity in India

I. Strategies that target household members and user organizations (boxes HH and CO in figure 2.2)

Strategy	Provisions	Status
Organizing women and girls; promoting political awareness, leadership, and advocacy abilities	■ Self-help groups perceived to be necessary precondition for promoting political participation of women. ■ Election of women self-help group members as representatives in local government institutions. ■ All India Women's Association; All India Women's Democratic Forum at the national level. ■ Women Power Connect coalition promotes the political participation for women at all levels of the government, including 33 percent reservation for women in parliament and gender-just budgeting (received USAID support).	■ Self-help groups as incubators for creating political leaders still in rudimentary form. ■ Formal links between self-help groups members and elections to local government institutions are lacking. ■ At national level, advocacy NGOs play important role in promoting gender equity in India, pressuring political parties and administration with variable success; using media to influence public opinion.
Creating and strengthening women's self-help groups	■ Since India's Eighth Five-Year Plan, major thrust has been on forming self-help groups and gender budgeting as main channels of female empowerment. ■ Formation of women's self-help/user groups under various development programs, including watershed development, women entrepreneurship, and microcredit programs for farm women. ■ Strengthening links between civil society organizations (MYRADA, Gram Vikas); women's self-help groups; and elected bodies to facilitate networking.	■ Women's participation in self-help groups centers mainly on microfinance. ■ Women user groups—particularly groups formed under programs that require rights/ownership over resources (for example, land or livestock), as in watershed development or agriculture-related programs—often constrained in accessing the benefits of programs. ■ Links between elected representatives and civil society are primarily for advocacy and not directly for policy formulation.
Conducting gender-sensitive citizen monitoring and auditing	■ Statewide campaigns initiated by various civic rights groups, such as Citizens' Forum.	■ Focus has been on monitoring that benefits of programs and policies reach women across all sections and ensuring that women gain access and control over resources, inputs, and decision-making processes.

Establishing gender-sensitive complaint mechanisms	■ Standing Committee on Social Justice at all tiers of local government for addressing gender-related issues and complaints. ■ National Commission on Women for promoting women's welfare and safeguarding women against atrocities. ■ Constitution of gender-redressal cells in all public offices. ■ Independent media and Right to Information Act important tools for addressing gender-related complaints.	■ Standing Committee on Social Justice involved largely in ensuring that there is no social exclusion in selecting beneficiaries for development programs. Committee plays almost no role as a gender-sensitive mechanism for addressing complaints. ■ Citizens lack easy access to this largely political body, which responds mainly to pressure groups, such as the media and civil society groups.
Requiring gender quorums at community meetings	■ Quorum for a gram sabha meeting remains one-tenth of adult population of gram panchayat area; one-third of quorum must be women.	■ Minimum participation rates differ across states (0 in Bihar and Tamil Nadu; 10 percent in Rajasthan; 30 percent in Himachal Pradesh, Karnataka, and Orissa). In Maharashtra, political participation of women is encouraged by requirement that women members of gram sabha meet before regular meeting of the gram sabha.
Adopting affirmative action in user group membership (for example, quota for women in user groups)	■ Mandatory representation of women (one-third of total) in user groups such as village drinking water management committees, watershed committees, joint forest management committees, and school development monitoring committees.	■ Provision for mandatory representation for women in local government bodies supply driven and often fails.
Providing gender-sensitive training for members of user organizations	■ Many gender-sensitive training programs for user organizations with NGO partnerships.	■ Training programs target women's groups. Little focus on mixed groups. ■ Mismatch between people trained and their access to resources often results in poor outcomes.
Creating programs and projects that specifically target female household members (women and girls)	■ 11th Five-Year Plan (2007–12) confirms government's commitment to ensuring equal access to basic infrastructure and health and educational services and to supporting agricultural growth. ■ Mainstreaming gender concerns in development programs by providing women with access to land rights and access to asset ownership.	■ There is often limited gender focus in agricultural programs. ■ Promotion of income-generating activities is main thrust in agriculture and animal husbandry sectors.

(continued)

Table 3.A.1 (Continued)

Strategy	Provisions	Status
	■ Programs and projects focusing on women and girl children. Examples include wage employment programs Swarnajayanti Gram Swarozgar Yojana/National Rural Employment Guarantee Act, livelihood girl fund for girl children [Bhagyalakshmi]; social security programs for women (pensions for widows and old women). ■ Strengthening of entrepreneurial skills of women through self-help groups in income-generating activities.	
2. Strategies that target the public administration (boxes PS and NM)		
Establishing ministries/agencies of gender in national and local governments ("gender machinery")	■ Ministry of Women and Child Development at center, Department of Women and Child Development at state level. ■ National Commission on Women. ■ Linking women's empowerment and gender equality issues to various national policies, such as the National Agricultural Policy (2000), the National Policy for the Empowerment of Women (2001), and the National Water Policy (2002), which view women's self-help groups as important instrument for alleviating gender inequality. ■ National Project for Repair, Renovation, and Restoration of Water Bodies Directly Linked to Agriculture advocates formation of district implementation committees on which representation of women is mandatory.	■ Implementation of specific programs for women and children through ministries and departments of women and child development, but limited influence on other ministries/departments (see below). ■ National Commission on Women plays important role in advocacy.
Creating gender focal points in sectoral ministries and decentralized departments	■ Interface meetings (open forums) between elected women, women's groups/collectives, and policy makers/ministers to articulate their concerns and influence policies. ■ The five-year plans of the Planning Commission define actions of positive discrimination in favor of women's empowerment (from Eight Five-Year Plan onward).	■ Mainstreaming of gender in sector ministries and departments (such as agricultural or public works departments) limited by lack of gender focal points in such departments. ■ Departments in charge of decentralization and panchayati raj typically very active in promoting gender mainstreaming.

- Adopting affirmative action in the civil service (for example, quota for female staff)

  - Preferential policies in government employment in the All-India services.
  - A few initiatives impose lower bounds on participation of women in public service agencies.
  - Bihar has reserved half of the 200,000 posts of government school teachers and the *nyaya mitras* (law aides) in all 8,500 panchayats for women.
  - Under the Karnataka Mahila Abhivrudhi Yojane scheme, 30 percent of all positions in departments, boards, and corporations in direct recruitment are reserved for women.

  - Limited representation of women in administrative positions such as secretaries of departments in state and national governments. Women in administrative services form only 5.7 percent of civil service personnel. Even within the premier civil services in India, women are underrepresented (Government of India 1997).

3. Strategies that target all types of service providers (boxes PS and NG)

- Designing and implementing programs and projects in a gender-sensitive manner

  - Shifts in rural service provision to public goods that reflect gender sensitivity in program design.
  - Panchayats as institutions of engendered decentralized rural service provision.
  - Agricultural Technology Management Agency (ATMA) approach mandates that 30 percent of farmer representatives on the ATMA Governing Board and the block-level Farmer Advisory Committees be women.

  - Provisions for gender in government programs important strategy to promote gender-equity; implementation varies across states.

- Monitoring indicators in a gender-disaggregated and gender-sensitive manner

  - Acknowledged need at policy level for gender-disaggregated data to plan for mainstreaming women in sectors of economic activities where their contribution is invisible, such as agriculture and food security/livelihood activities.

  - Few gender-disaggregated data are available. Those that are collected are done so largely to meet donor guidelines.

- Employing female fieldworkers and giving them sufficient discretion to address the needs of female clients

  - Appointment of female facilitators under Department of Women and Child Development for providing integrated child development services (under Integrated Child Development Services program).
  - Appointment of women as auxiliary nurses and midwives at primary rural health centers.
  - In most states, no specific policies to hire female field staff in sector ministries and departments such as those in charge of agriculture, irrigation, or public works.

  - Strategy to hire female field staff for child development programs and as auxiliary nurses and midwives universally followed in India.
  - Percentages of female field staff in sector ministries and departments such as those in charge of agriculture, irrigation, or public works are very low.

(continued)

Table 3.A.1 (Continued)

Strategy	Provisions	Status
4. Strategies that target local and national elected representatives (boxes LP and NP)		
Adopting affirmative action in electoral politics (for example, reserving seats for women in local councils and national parliaments)	■ At least one-third of all seats and offices of chairs in local councils (panchayats) at all three levels of local government reserved for women.	■ State electoral commissions enforce implementation of this reservation policy; implementation problems can also be resolved in court. ■ States can increase level of reservation. Bihar provides for 50 percent reservation for women in the local bodies; legislative initiative to prescribe this rule for all states ongoing.
Providing gender-focused training and support programs for local and national representatives (targeting male and female representatives)	■ Planning and strategizing for women's participation in decision-making processes, particularly through training and capacity-building programs. ■ Strategic capacity building for women of panchayati raj institutions. ■ Documentation and dissemination of capacity-building efforts for women for learning lessons and replication of strategies. ■ Gender-sensitization training for men and women representatives.	■ Gender-sensitization training of men and women in power is institutionalized in India. ■ Gender-focused training as a strategy has been accepted within organizations, action groups, and political parties. ■ Government departments, NGOs, and other institutions, including administrative training institutes and state institutes of rural development, have taken initiatives to sensitize local government bodies about women's issues and needs. ■ A National Centre for Gender Training and Research has been set up in the National Academy of Administration in Mussourie to train young administrators and policy makers on gender issues.

5. Strategies that target political parties (box PP)

Creating women's wings in political parties	■ Most major political parties in India have women's wings. ■ The Communist Party of India (Marxist) established the All India Democratic Women's Association in 1981, with regional affiliations. ■ Members of women's wings of political parties contribute to making the manifestos of their parties gender sensitive; they function as "vote gatherers" and as critical arm of their party's electoral machinery. ■ Women's wings are also used to launch collective struggles against social evils such as dowry and child marriage. They also promote education, equality, and empowerment of women (special focus on violence against women) and fight for greater representation of women in state legislature and parliament. ■ Women made up just 9.2 percent of the parliament following the 2005 Lok Sabha elections.
Adopting affirmative action in political parties (for example, quotas and reservations for female party members)	■ Many political parties in India have shown great reluctance to field women candidates. ■ Reservation of seats in local bodies, particularly for district panchayats, in which elections are conducted on a party basis, and municipal and local urban bodies has put pressure on political parties to identify and field more female candidates.
Creating party manifestos for women	■ Representation of women in public bodies outlined in manifestos of political parties. ■ Targets in party manifestos not implemented in view of political opposition (for example, the Indian National Congress did not yet implement provision in its party manifesto to reserve seats for women in state legislatures and national parliament).
Recruiting, mentoring, and developing women as leaders	■ Membership drive in political parties for women. ■ Mentoring of female candidates within parties occurs, but mostly on an individual (rather than an institutionalized) basis.

(continued)

Table 3.A.1 (Continued)

Strategy	Provisions	Status
6. Cross-cutting strategies		
Establishing gender-responsive budgets	■ Scheme of intersectoral budget allocations for women in local government institutions (for example, under the Karnataka Mahila Abhivrudhi Yojane scheme, the government reserves one-third of the resources for women in individual beneficiary-oriented schemes and in labor-intensive schemes). ■ Gender budgeting in 208 schemes of various government departments, such as departments of social welfare, agriculture, and backward classes. ■ Provision in ATMA to allocate one-third of funding to women-specific activities.	■ Gender budgeting is a promising approach to increase gender equity; however, implementation and monitoring constitute a challenge because ministries and departments often do not collect sufficient gender-disaggregated information on their programs and schemes.

Source: Authors' compilation.

Agency (GTZ). These agencies play a much more limited role in India than they do in Ghana and Ethiopia; total funding of international development agencies accounts for a miniscule share of India's overall budget (although the share is substantial in some states, such as Bihar).

These agencies fund a variety of development projects that are relevant for local governance, gender, and agricultural/rural service provision (table 3.A.2). Community- or group-based approaches play a central role in these projects, and the formation of women's self-help groups is a prominent approach within these projects. The projects focus either on livelihoods generally or on watershed development, taking into account that the majority of the poor live in nonirrigated watershed areas.

Ghana

Research Findings on Decentralization, Gender, and Rural Service Provision

Although there is a substantial body of literature on Ghana's decentralization and governance system, very few studies examine the role of gender in this respect. According to Issaka (1994) and Ofei-Aboagye (2000, 2004), two main driving forces have spurred the concern with promoting women's interests and gender equity in local governance in Ghana. First, the design of the assembly system has considerable potential for enhancing the effective involvement of women in local development, as it includes features such as appointed memberships, the use of English and local languages, the use of subcommittees, and the nonpartisan status of the assemblies. Second, Ghana has committed itself to such international requirements as the 1995 Beijing Platform for Action and the 1998 International Union of Local Authorities Declaration on Women.

Allah-Mensah (2003) notes that diverse interventions by various agencies have addressed the invisibility of women in local governance in Ghana. Civil society organizations have invested in awareness creation and gender mainstreaming, and grassroots participation has yielded dividends. The district assemblies proved to be a good starting point for women, as reflected in the increasing number of elected female assembly members. Using district assemblies as channels for addressing development paradigms and acceptable policies makes gender considerations even more critical.

According to Ofei-Aboagye (2004), efforts to increase women's presence, visibility, and influence over the business of local authorities have met with some success, but much remains to be done. Obstacles that need to be overcome include low levels of literacy, time constraints, and problems related to socialization.

A study by ActionAid Ghana (2002) finds that decision making at the district assembly level appears to be centralized in the executive committee. The lack of regular district assembly meetings implies that only those assembly members with clout are able to lobby the district chief executive and the district coordinating director for development projects. The study notes that the traditional

Table 3.A.2 Projects by International Development Agencies That Support Local Governance and Agricultural/Rural Service Provision in India

Agency	Project	State	Period	Description	Funding (Million)
DFID	Karnataka Watershed Development Project	Karnataka	1998–2005	Developed the watershed.	£4
DFID	Eastern India and Western India Rainfed Farming	Eastern and western India	Completed 2005, 2007	Used paraprofessionals to promote innovation at the village level, participatory varietal selection, and plant breeding for sustainable improvements of crop yield.	£6.7 (Eastern India), £15.5 (Western India)
DFID	Knowledge to Action: Enhancing Traditional Dairy Value Chains	Assam	2008–11	Promotes awareness and enhances demand for good-quality locally produced fresh milk and the capacity to provide it through the informal sector.	n.a.
DFID	Poverty Alleviation through Rice Innovation Systems	Eastern Uttar Pradesh, Bihar, West Bengal	2008–11	Collaboratively develops new methods of knowledge transfer for the introduction of direct-seeded rice to improve productivity of rice-based cropping systems used by poor farmers.	n.a.
DFID	Promoting Sustainable Livelihood Development	Bihar, Uttar Pradesh, Madhya Pradesh	2008–11	Develops innovative agricultural services that will meet needs of women and extremely poor alongside credit intervention.	n.a.
GTZ	Strengthening Capacity Building for Decentralised Watershed Management	National	2006–09	Strengthens implementing capacity of service delivery agencies. Focus is on systemic capacity development for large public investment program of Ministry of Food and Agriculture for watershed management.	n.a.
GTZ	Rural Financial System Development Program	National	2005–12	Works on technical issues such as management information systems, credit risk management, design of demand-oriented financial products, and viability analysis and promotes strengthening of the cooperative credit structure in rural areas.	n.a.

IFAD	National Microfinance Support Program	National	2002–09	Improved and expanded access to microfinance services for poor people in both rural and urban areas.	$134.0
IFAD	Tejaswini Rural Women's Empowerment Program	Several	2007–15	Improves livelihood opportunities by developing participants' skills, fostering market linkages, and providing market and policy support.	$208.7
IFAD	Women's Empowerment and Livelihoods Programmed in the Mid-Gangetic Plains	Uttar Pradesh, Bihar	Not in effect	Will introduce market-linked enterprises, form producers' groups, and enhance capacity of financial institutions and private sector to operate in targeted areas.	$52.5
World Bank	Karnataka Watershed Development Project	Karnataka	2003–09	Improved rural livelihoods and reduced poverty by developing and strengthening community-based approaches to improving and managing selected tank systems. Project aimed to demonstrate viability of community-based approach to tank improvement and management by returning main responsibility of tank development to village-level user groups.	$98.9
World Bank	Karnataka Panchayats Strengthening Project	Karnataka	2006–12	Improves effectiveness of service delivery by gram panchayats, particularly with respect to management of public resources and delivery of relevant services that rural people prioritize. The project has four components: Component A: Block grants to gram panchayats would finance services listed in panchayat participatory plans and budgets. Component B: Information systems for constituents would increase ability of rural people—in particular the poorest and most excluded people—to voice their demands on local governments and elicit responses from them. Component C: Building the capacity of all three levels of panchayats in managing resources, collecting revenues, and delivering services. Component D: Building the capacity of the state to enable it to oversee, facilitate, and manage the panchayat system.	$82.2

(continued)

Table 3.A.2 (Continued)

Agency	Project	State	Period	Description	Funding (Million)
World Bank	Bihar Rural Livelihoods Project (Jeevika)	Bihar	2007–12	Project has four components: Component I: Community Institution Development. This component builds and strengthens primary and federated social and economic community institutions. Component II: Community Investment Fund. This component transfers financial and technical resources to community-based organizations Component III: Technical Assistance Fund. This component improves the quantity and quality of service provision by public, cooperative, community, and private service providers. It also promotes use of public-private partnerships in improving supply of key support services for community organizations and federations in institution building, finance, and livelihoods enhancement. Component IV: Project Management.	$63.0

Sources: Web sites of the DFID, GTZ, IFAD, and World Bank.

Note: n.a. = not available.

authorities play important roles in both local governance and development. Although they are nondemocratic institutions, they could become agents of development if they became open to discussions. The study indicates that the inability to operationalize the area councils and motivate unit committees greatly reduces the ability of the district assemblies to ensure broader participation and to monitor development project implementation. Most decentralized departments do not have the technical staff to support the district assemblies; most districts did not have communication facilities or computers.

A quantitative study by Engel, Iskandarani, and Useche (2005) assesses community-based water management. The authors find that among households with access to improved water, 43 percent continued to use unsafe sources as their main domestic water source. Using a discrete choice model (in which the dependent variable is a household's decision to choose an improved water source versus an unimproved source), the authors find that the price of water per bucket has a highly significant negative effect on both the decision to use the improved source and the quantity of improved-source water consumed. The perceived good quality of alternative water sources (a river in this case) tends to discourage farmers from buying improved water. The study also finds that about 40 percent of households participated in decisions on location or technology of the drinking water facility. Regression analysis shows that the poorest and the least-educated segment of the community and the richest and most-educated segment were more likely to participate in decision making for improved domestic water supply than the "middle class." Better-off and highly educated members have a strong bargaining power; participation by the poor may reflect the Community Water and Sanitation Agency policy of including the poor.

Strategies to Promote Gender Equity

Table 3.A.3 summarizes the main strategies to promote gender equity in Ghana. The table is based on the classification scheme provided in box 2.2.

Initiatives by International Development Agencies

Donor-funded projects and programs have played an important role in supporting the decentralization process in Ghana. Examples include the following:

- The World Bank's Community-based Rural Development Program provided a significant amount of training to the personnel of district assemblies, area councils, and regional bodies (about 40,000 trainee days between November 2004 and June 2007). Training areas included leadership, participatory planning, resource mobilization, procurement, financial management, transparency, and accountability. About 70 percent of the funding was spent on education, health, and potable water; demand for agricultural infrastructure was surprisingly low. The project also supported rural

Table 3.A.3 Strategies to Promote Gender Equity in Ghana

Strategies that target household members and user organizations	Strategies that target the public administration	Strategies that target all types of service providers	Strategies that target local and national elected representatives	Strategies that target political parties	Cross-cutting strategies
Local NGOs (such as Abantu for Development) promote activities and issues concerning women and girls.	Domestic violence unit created within the Ghana Police Service to address abuses of women.	Principle of Community Water and Sanitation Agency to promote the role of women in planning and management of services, especially in rural water supply.	Government uses its 30 percent appointment to the district assembly to increase the number of women as assembly members.	All political parties have women's wings and national women's organizers. There are also women's organizers in the regional executives of the various parties.	All public universities encourage admission of women, usually by increasing the cutoff point for admission.
WIAD has special programs for women, such as demonstration homes.	Ministry for Women and Children created.	Some agricultural extension agents are women.	Parliament has a women's caucus, made up mainly of female members.	The manifestos of almost all political parties include commitments to reserving a certain percentage of government appointments for women.	
WATSANs usually have a woman on their executive committee, although a woman is usually not the chairperson or secretary.	Women in Agriculture Department (WIAD) in the Ministry of Food and Agriculture.	Most socioeconomic indicators are disaggregated by gender.	Local and international NGOs support female candidates by providing campaign funds, sponsoring radio announcements, printing posters, and so forth.		

At the district level, there is an agricultural extension officer responsible for women in development issues.

Most ministries have gender desks.

Districts have a gender focal person.

Conscious effort by government to have women represent 40 percent of appointees.

Education Service has girls' division.

Manifestos of political parties have sections on how they intend to promote women in public office.

NGOs, donors, and the Institute of Local Government Studies Ghana train electoral representatives.

Source: Authors' compilation.

enterprise development/learning centers and natural resource management activities. The project experimented with innovative methods, such as the Rapid Response Initiative approach, to improve local governance (World Bank 2007a).

- The 2000–07 District Capacity Building Project (DISCAP), supported by the Canadian International Development Agency, focused on streamlining the institutional relationships among water supply–related institutions at the local and regional levels and on developing a system for operation and maintenance, revenue collection, and governance related to water and sanitation. DISCAP pioneered gender mainstreaming strategies in the local government system, including the establishment of gender desk officers and gender support networks in the three northern regions.

- Other development partners have also been active in supporting local governance. GTZ developed methods for poverty profiling, mapping, and pro-poor planning that were incorporated into the planning guidelines of the National Planning Commission for the 2006–10 medium-term development plans of the districts (GTZ 2007). DANIDA supports four pillars under its Support to Decentralisation Reform project: policy and institutional arrangements, a district development facility, capacity building and human resources development, and partnerships and participation for accountability.

Ethiopia

Research Findings on Decentralization, Gender, and Rural Service Provision

In their comprehensive review of the literature on decentralization in Ethiopia, Gebre-Egziabher and Berhanu (2007) find that culture and religion contribute to women's social marginalization and limited access to resources, services, and political power. Historically, Ethiopian culture has put a strong emphasis on hierarchy and upward accountability. This was reflected in the unitary state and tightly centralized governance of both the imperial and the Derg eras. Some 85 percent of Ethiopians practice culturally conservative interpretations of Orthodox Christianity and Sunni Islam that reinforce these mores. Social norms discourage women from participating in public forums; according to Gebre-Egziabher and Berhanu (2007), decentralized governance since 1994 has not appreciably improved this situation. The establishment of women's affairs agencies in all levels of government and the election of women to office within the structures of governance has not challenged systemic gender bias. No systematic study has been conducted of how decentralization affects women's access to services or their involvement in decision-making or governance structures.

Studies of agricultural extension in Ethiopia note the country's top-down approach to service provision. Agents are required to meet quotas for enrolling farmers in technology packages and are evaluated on the extent to which they meet those quotas. Extension also works through "model" or "progressive" farmers, who tend to be better off and male. Communication is mostly one way, with extension agents transferring knowledge to farmers. There is little effort to marry new agricultural research and development with farmers' knowledge or to learn what kind of services farmers would like to receive (Buchy and Basaznew 2005; EAA/EEPRI 2006; Lemma 2007). Except in home economics, most agents are men, who provide services mainly to heads of household, regardless of gender (Buchy and Basaznew 2005; EAA/EEPRI 2006).

Historically, extension policy was made in Addis Ababa and merely implemented in the field. Changing the delivery mode can have benefits: deployment of extension teams to kebeles can facilitate communities' ability to plan and manage development activities for themselves on a sustainable basis (Cohen, Rocchigiani, and Garrett 2008). In addition, extension services generally have positive impacts on nutrition and poverty reduction (Dercon and others 2007). Few agents have university degrees, although an increasing number have postsecondary technical training. Extension personnel with more advanced training tend to work in administrative positions (Lemma 2007).

The EPRDF is pervasive in all policy matters and at all levels of governance in Ethiopia, including agricultural and rural development policy (Aalen 2002; Pausewang, Tronvoll, and Aalen 2003; Gebre-Egziabher and Berhanu 2007). Civil society organizations for women, youth, elders, and veterans are basically mass organizations of the party, in keeping with the EPRDF's Leninist character (Vaughan and Tronvoll 2003). This is true even of farmer cooperatives, which are supposedly organized to advance farmers' interests and secure them tangible benefits. Members of EPRDF parties routinely fill cooperative leadership positions. Moreover, the cooperatives are often more responsive to the desires of the government and donors than to those of their members (Bernard, Taffesse, and Gabre-Madhin 2008; Francesconi 2009).

In their analysis of the agriculture bureaucracy in southern Ethiopia, Buchy and Basaznew (2005) find critical shortcomings in both the gender sensitivity of extension provision and in the way gender and women's affairs are situated within the agriculture bureaucracy. For example, in the Awasa Bureau of Agriculture in the Sidama Zone of SNNP region, where farmers in general are underserved by extension agents, women farmers make up only a small fraction of farmers receiving extension services. Women farmers almost never attend field visits unless the visit is related to home economics. Even where training by agricultural staff is in principle open to farmers of both sexes, the training times are selected without consideration to women farmers' schedules and the timing of their traditional agricultural commitments. The Ethiopia National Action Plan for Gender points to the challenge inherent in the way in which traditional social norms filter into bureaucracies, leading to a resistance within these bureaucracies to consider gender experts in agencies as on par with other officials (Government of Ethiopia 2000).

Buchy and Basaznew (2005) identify the major push toward gender awareness as coming from donors. Despite donor efforts, the Awasa Bureau of Agriculture in the Sidama Zone of SNNP region had no gender policy and therefore no gender-specific guidelines or procedures. The unit responsible for gender outreach had the characteristics of many similar gender desks in line ministries: it had an all-female staff and a precarious position within the bureau; it was heavily specialized in home economics and nutrition and short on other core skills, such as project planning and preparation; it operated mostly in isolation from the rest of the bureaucracy; and it had no mandate to monitor gender-related performance of the bureau.

In contrast to many other countries, gender representation in government in Ethiopia does not consistently decrease with the level or tier of government. For example, as of 2004, women made up 8 percent of federal, 13 percent of regional, 7 percent of district, and 14 percent of kebele parliament/council seats (Government of Ethiopia 2004). These figures mask substantial regional variation in women's presence in subnational government structures, reflecting the highly disparate role of women in different regions: women's representation in regional councils ranged from 1 percent in the Somale region to 28 percent in the Tigray region (IFAD 2005).

A detailed analysis of the 1993 National Policy on Women warned that decentralization could weaken the government's ability to effectively implement the policy in light of more limited capacity at the district and kebele levels to translate the policy into investments and programs (Government of Ethiopia and World Bank 1998). There are no formal quotas to ensure a degree of representation of women in the government's electoral bodies, and the constitution does not mandate representation of women in political office (in contrast, there are mandates for certain ethnic minorities). Adoption of the constitution was not followed by electoral legislation reserving seats or establishing quotas for women (Demessie, Kebede, and Shimeles 2005). At the same time, the constitution does not bar the use of affirmative action measures to reduce gender inequality. It has been proposed that such measures be employed to strengthen women's presence in local councils to overcome the absence of women's voice in government representative bodies (Government of Ethiopia and World Bank 1998).

At the local level, gender representation among elected representatives reflects the ghettoization of women in women's affairs units. Very few women sat on the standing committees of the district council in the Amhara region (formed around topics such as economic affairs, budget and finance, and legal and administrative affairs); in contrast, the standing committee for women's affairs was made up entirely of women (Dom and Mussa 2006b). The same pattern is common in the executive arm of the district government: the district cabinet typically contains only one woman, the official assigned the women's affairs portfolio.

Women's associations exist at every level of government, from the kebele on up. Their role and effectiveness vary by region. In the Tigray region, women's associations tend to be important and well organized. In contrast, in the Amhara region, their strength, effectiveness, and thus credibility are constrained, especially at the lower levels, by limited resources (Dom and Mussa 2006b). The size and vigor of membership in women's associations is also likely to be compromised by residents' perception that, despite their formally non-governmental status, they are an appendage of the government and, in particular, the ruling party. This perception discourages women farmers from greater participation (Muir 2004).

There is a stark discrepancy between formal procedures for local-level development planning under decentralization on the one hand and the reality and practice of the planning process on the other (Dom and Mussa 2006b; Yilmaz and Venugopal 2009): in practice, the participation of women in community planning and decision making is nearly nonexistent. A study of decentralization and service delivery in four regions finds several cultural, social, and economic barriers to women's ability to attend community meetings and to express their priorities and concerns when they did attend (World Bank 2001). Fear of violent reprisal from husbands, insecurity about speaking in public, a sense that their opinions would not be listened to, and pressure on women's time all combined to keep both attendance and expression of voice low. Despite these factors, in some places women were "ordered" to attend (World Bank 2001), perhaps in response to donor or higher-tier governmental pressure to create more gender balance at local meetings.

Strategies to Promote Gender Equity

Table 3.A.4 summarizes the main strategies to promote gender equity in Ethiopia. The table is based on the classification scheme provided in box 2.2.

Initiatives by International Development Agencies

In 2002, when Ethiopia embarked on district-level decentralization, the World Bank initiated a project to build capacity for improving public service delivery at the federal, regional, and local levels. The Capacity Building for Decentralized Service Delivery project sought to support the restructuring of the government's Civil Service Reform Program (initiated in 1996); the strengthening of local governments; and the Ministry of Capacity Building (World Bank 2002). The main objective of the local government component, the project's largest component, was to initiate and facilitate the process of building local governments that are financially sound and have the ability and incentives to improve service delivery, especially to the poor. This component sought to address three key constraints to the provision of services at the local level: finance, capacity, and an unclear mandate for local authorities. The project consisted primarily of technical assistance and training.

This project was followed by two other projects, the Public Sector Capacity Building Program Support Project (PSCAP) and the Protection of Basic Services Project (PBS). Both are described in box 3.A.1.

Table 3.A.4 Strategies to Promote Gender Equity in Ethiopia

Strategy	Provision	Status
I. Strategies that target household members and community-based organizations		
Organizing women and girls; creating and strengthening women's self-help groups	■ Policy to establish women's associations throughout the country	Women's associations help mitigate social constraints on women; help extension agents to get in touch with women farmers. Effectiveness varies by region.
Promoting political awareness, leadership, and advocacy abilities	■ Umbrella of all women/gender-focused NGOs exists (Network of Ethiopian Women's Associations) ■ Ethiopian Women's Lawyer Association (EWLA) ■ Women's Association of Tigray	Several NGOs have been very effective.
Creating programs and projects that target women and girls	■ Extension packages for women	Packages are targeted to women who are spouses of household heads; no evidence of packages tailored to female household heads, whose agricultural activities often differ from those of female spouses.
Adopting affirmative action in user group membership	■ Encouragement to increase women's membership in water committees ■ In one region: rule made by regional government that chairs have to be women	Women sit on water committees but tend not to chair them, even though users of water facilities are nearly exclusively women. Evidence that rule is implemented; rule reflects more egalitarian culture in this study area.
Providing gender-sensitive training for members of user organizations	■ Training for water committees	Training of water committees technically focused; lack of guidance on how to address gender issues in water facility use, mobilize the community, and handle other nontechnical issues.

2. Strategies that target the public administration

Establishing ministries/agencies of gender in national and local governments ("gender machinery")

- Ministry/Bureau/Office of Women's Affairs at the federal, regional, zonal, district, and kebele levels (kebele level has one official, not an office/unit)

  Functions as mechanism for reviewing gender aspects in sectoral ministries.

Creating gender focal points in sectoral ministries and decentralized departments

- Gender desks (departments, focal points, and so forth) within line ministries (at federal through district levels)

  Effectiveness varies, as gender desks are sometimes isolated from line ministries.

- Training of government officials in gender-sensitive programming (by an NGO)

  Case study evidence suggests that training is effective in sensitizing officials.

- Ethiopian National Action Plan (established to implement Ethiopia's women's policy)

Establishing equal opportunity structures in civil service (antidiscrimination bureaus, merit protection agencies, equal opportunity commissions)

- Federal Civil Servants Proclamation (Proclamation No. 262/2002) states that "there shall be no discrimination among job seekers or civil servants in filling vacancies because of their ethnic origin sex, religion, political outlook, or any other ground."

Adopting affirmative action in the civil service

- Civil Servants Proclamation (see above) incorporates affirmative action by stating that preference shall be given to female candidates who have equal or close scores to that of male candidates.

3. Strategies that target all types of service providers

Employing female fieldworkers and giving them sufficient discretion to address the needs of female clients

- Increase in number of female extension workers (largely a consequence of rapid expansion of total number of extension agents in the country)

  Case study evidence indicates that effectiveness of female extension agents varies; female extension agents no longer limited to women-oriented extension topics, such as home economics.

(continued)

Table 3.A.4 (Continued)

Strategy	Provision	Status
Designing and implementing programs and projects in a gender-sensitive manner	■ Encouragement (informal quotas) to get women to adopt "women's packages"	Strong pressure on extension agents to meet quotas (resulting in highly supply-driven instead of demand-oriented mode of service provision).
4. Strategies that target elected representatives		
Creating parliamentary committees on women's affairs; giving responsibility for gender to subject-specific parliamentary committees	■ Standing committees on women's affairs at all levels down to kebele	Assessment of effectiveness is difficult because phenomenon is new (first implemented following the 2008 district and kebele elections).
5. Strategies that target political parties		
Creating party manifestos for women	■ Rebel movement that turned into leading party had slogan "Women behind the plow."	Slogan no longer in use.
Adopting affirmative action in political parties	■ EDP (a now-defunct opposition party) had goal of affirmative action for women in its platform.	Not implemented (party was never elected).
Creating women's wings in political parties	■ Women's leagues of EPRDF (ruling party)	Creates political space for women to discuss issues that are relevant to them.
6. Cross-cutting strategies		
Establishing gender-responsive budgets	■ Gender-responsive budgeting at the district level; supposed to be checked by focal points/gender machinery	No evaluation conducted of whether gender budgeting was undertaken and if so whether it was useful.

Source: Authors' compilation.

Box 3.A.1 World Bank Support for Local Governance in Ethiopia

A central element of the World Bank's support for capacity building in Ethiopia is the Public Sector Capacity Building Program (PSCAP) support project. PSCAP operates through the federal and regional governments, not directly through the district governments. The federal component supports federal-level activities across each of the six subprograms, including capacity-building activities for which there are scale and network economies. The regional component constitutes the bulk of the program and is designed to enable regions to adapt and implement national reform and capacity-building priorities envisaged under PSCAP's six subprograms.

The District Level Decentralisation Programme (DLDP)—one of the six subprograms of PSCAP support—builds on the country's radical fiscal and administrative district-level decentralization agenda, pursued since 2002 based on far-reaching constitutional reforms in four regions. Decentraliza-tion has involved the transferring of a significant portion of the federal-to-regional transfers to districts, in the form of formula-driven block grants. By implication, the devolution of fiscal management responsibilities requires a massive redeployment of skilled staff, typically from regional bureaus and zonal sections to districts. The DLDP has sought to scale up these efforts through the systematic assignment of revenue and expenditure responsibili-ties within regions; the restructuring of regional bureaus; the transfer of sector-specific functions to districts; the development of fiscal transfer mechanisms and monitoring systems within regions; and the bulk training of local offi-cials, electorates, public servants, and other stakeholders.

After the national and regional May 2005 elections, which revealed serious governance problems, several donors felt that in the governance climate at the time it would be imprudent to continue to provide aid through direct budget support. To ensure service delivery, the donor community designed the Pro-tection of Basic Services (PBS) project (2006–08) (World Bank 2006).

The project's first component constituted the vast bulk of the project, making up 97 percent of total project costs and 85 percent of donor funds. This component primarily provided resources to regions and local authorities based on agreed plans for delivery of basic services (education, health, water and sanitation, and agriculture extension). The project used as the financing channel the government's own system of the federal block grant. The second component primarily financed procurement of health-sector-related com-modities. The third and fourth components were very small in size (together comprising 0.5 percent of the project and 2.5 percent of donor contributions to the project) but were important elements in the project because they were largely the product of the governance challenges identified in the post-election period.

Source: World Bank project documents.

NOTES

1. The authors provide the following disclaimer on their Web site: "The governance indicators presented here aggregate the views on the quality of governance provided by a large number of enterprise, citizen, and expert survey respondents in industrial and developing countries. These data are gathered from a number of survey institutes, thinktanks, nongovernmental organizations, and international organizations. The aggregate indicators do not reflect the official views of the World Bank, its executive directors, or the countries they represent. The Worldwide Governance Indicators are not used by the World Bank Group to allocate resources."

2. The Indian National Congress Party is the party of Mahatma Gandhi and Jawaharlal Nehru, which led India's struggle for independence.

3. The Council of State is mandated by the Constitution of the Republic of Ghana. It functions in an advisory role to the presidency.

4. According to their statute (Section II.7 and Article 7e), the EPRDF and its affiliated parties follow the principle of democratic centralism. See http://www.eprdf.org.et/ Eprdffiles/Basicdoc/Basicdocuments_files/statute.htm. The principle of democratic centralism was outlined by V. I. Lenin in *What Is to Be Done? Burning Questions of Our Movement* (1902). Party members and structures must adhere strictly to decisions the party has taken. Members are subject to sanctions (including expulsion) if they break discipline.

5. The nine regions and two city administrations are often referred to together as Ethiopia's 11 regions.

6. Recently, the Mengistawi budin have been renamed *lemat budin* ("development teams"). Both terms are now used interchangeably.

7. In some districts, these are called *woreda offices of water, mines, and energy*.

CHAPTER FOUR

Methodology

This chapter describes the methodology used to collect empirical data in the three study countries. It describes both the quantitative and qualitative data collection methods in each setting.

INDIA

Quantitative Data Collection

Two data sources were combined for the quantitative analysis of India. The first is the 2006 survey of Karnataka, conducted jointly by the Institute for Social and Economic Change (ISEC) and the International Food Policy Research Institute (IFPRI), which covered households, villages, gram panchayats, and elected gram panchayat members. The second is the 2008 follow-up survey, which covered public administration officials and community-based organizations in the same districts and blocks in which the 2006 survey was conducted.

The samples were selected from 12 districts of Karnataka's four administrative divisions (table 4.1). Three districts were randomly drawn from each division. The 12 districts consist of 85 blocks.

Using the Comprehensive Composite Development Index (CCDI) as defined in 2000 by the Government of Karnataka's High Power Committee for the Redressal of Regional Imbalances, the team stratified the blocks into five socioeconomic development categories. From each development category, a random sample of gram panchayats was drawn on the basis of the population

Table 4.1	Number of Units Surveyed in Karnataka in 2006
Respondent type	Sample size
Districts	12
Blocks	85
Gram panchayats	80
Villages	225
Households	966
Gram panchayat members	272

Source: Authors.

in the respective development category. The final gram panchayat sample consists of 80 units. From every gram panchayat, up to three villages were randomly chosen, resulting in a total sample of 225 villages. Within every sampled gram panchayat and from the sample of the 225 villages, one village was randomly selected. Interviews were conducted with households selected in a random draw of about 5 percent of all households in that village, yielding a final sample of 966 households.

A sample of gram panchayat members was drawn, as well. This sample includes members from the selected villages in every selected gram panchayat. For every village, one gram panchayat president/vice-president, one scheduled caste or scheduled tribe (SC/ST) member, and one female member was surveyed, for a total of 272 interviews with gram panchayat members. At the village level, a survey module was administered to collect information about the village's socioeconomic characteristics, facilities, and availability and accessibility of rural services. The household interviews collect information on the socioeconomic status and structure of households, political and institutional memberships, use of and satisfaction with public services, access to public benefit schemes, and attendance of and satisfaction with gram sabha meetings. The household questionnaire also provides insights into gender differences in satisfaction with rural services. The survey module administered to the 272 gram panchayat members collects information on their socioeconomic characteristics, their political and institutional history, and their views on the availability and quality of public services. Finally, gram panchayat presidents or vice presidents answered questions on gram panchayat activities, finances, budget allocation decisions, and on institutions and processes. The gram panchayat survey data are supplemented with 2001 census data on population, caste dominance, and literacy at the gram panchayat level, among others.

The gram panchayat module also includes detailed income and expenditure accounts of the gram panchayats for 2005–06. The data record the income and expenditures associated with all grants from the central and state governments and link these expenditures to the activities undertaken. For the Sampoorna Grameen Rozgar Yojana (SGRY), the largest and only universal program of public goods provision implemented through gram panchayats in Karnataka, information was collected on income or funds received by the gram panchayats and on expenditures taken out of these funds. Detailed data on the kinds of goods provided from these expenditures were also collected. Because each gram panchayat has more than one village, the survey also collected village-level expenditure data. These data include information on the expenditures for various activities implemented in the village and on the source of funds—that is, whether it was from the SGRY program or from other programs or funds devolved from the gram panchayat to its constituent villages.

In 2008/09 IFPRI, ISEC, and the Tata Institute of Social Sciences (TISS) extended the 2006 survey to cover public service providers and user groups at the district, block, and village levels. The survey was implemented in five departments (table 4.2). The first three departments—responsible for agricultural extension, livestock services, and drinking water supply—are directly relevant for this study. Findings from the other two services are presented for comparison purposes. The Food and Civil Supplies Department is in charge of the public distribution system (a food security program under which households below the poverty line receive food items at subsidized rates in so-called ration shops). *The anganwadi* centers are child care facilities staffed mostly by female volunteers who receive a modest remuneration. This department offers an interesting comparison because its staff is mostly female and hired in a manner that is different from that of other departments. The survey covered field-level staff (also referred to as *front-line staff or frontline service providers*) and senior officials, typically the direct supervisors of the front-line staff. One type of user organization associated with each department is involved in service provision and supervision. Representatives of these organizations were interviewed as well.

The study was carried out in the 12 districts from the 2006 survey round. In each district, two blocks were selected, one of which was more developed than the other. The selection was made on the basis of the CCDI indicator variable. Two gram panchayats for each block were selected from the set of gram panchayats included in the 2006 survey; user associations were then selected from these gram panchayats. In a number of blocks, the household survey covered only one gram panchayat. In those instances, the selection of the second gram panchayat was guided by the existence of user organizations for the largest number of service sectors. The interviews with field-level staff and user organization representatives were conducted using handheld computers. Paper questionnaires were used in all other interviews.

Qualitative Case Studies

This report draws on case studies conducted in Karnataka and Bihar. The Karnataka case study locations constitute a subsample of the quantitative survey described above. In Bihar, two districts were selected by using 2001 census

Table 4.2 Number of Service Providers and User Organizations Interviewed in Karnataka

Department	Service	Senior officials		Field-level staff		Users organizations	
		Type	Number	Type	Number	Type	Number
Agriculture	Agricultural extension	Assistant directors of agriculture	34	Agricultural extension workers	41	Farmers organizations	20
Animal husbandry	Livestock services	Assistant directors of animal husbandry	30	Veterinary assistants	40	Dairy cooperative societies	29
Rural Development and Panchayati Raj (RDPR)	Drinking water and sanitation	Assistant executive engineers	29	Junior engineers	41	Water users organizations	40
Food and civil supplies	Public distribution system	Block food and civil supplies officers	26	Food inspectors	34	Vigilance committees	37
Women and child development	Anganwadi (child care) centers	Child development project officers	36	Anganwadi workers	50	Women's self-help groups	50
Total			155		206		176

Source: Authors.

information and the insights from a poverty and social assessment study of districts in Bihar prepared by the Asian Development Research Institute, which ranked districts according to poverty, social vulnerability, livelihood potential, and social capital criteria, using a 1–5 scale. One district that performed better than and one district that performed worse than the average district in Bihar were selected. In each district, two blocks were selected, one better developed than the other. The selection of blocks was guided by the 2001 census infrastructure data on the number of villages with drinking water, schooling, health, post office, public transportation facilities, and other infrastructure. The selection of villages in the better-developed district was supported by insights from district officials. In the less-developed district, 10 villages were randomly selected in each block. With the assistance of block-level officials, one well- and one less-well-developed village from the list of 10 villages were identified. The choice of districts was also guided by the availability of user groups. In general, the letter A is used to refer to more developed districts, blocks, and villages, and the letter B is used to refer to less developed locations. (For a description of the ways in which the case study locations are identified, see appendix table 4.A.1 for Karnataka and table 4.A.2 for Bihar.)

The methods used for the field studies included semistructured interviews, focus group interviews, and field observations. Process-influence-mapping was also applied. In this participatory mapping method, respondents first identify relevant actors and processes and then rank the influence of the actors on the outcome of interest. This method was derived from Net-Map, the method used in Ethiopia.[1]

GHANA

Quantitative Data Collection

In Ghana, data were collected jointly with the Institute of Statistical Social and Economic Research (ISSER) of the University of Ghana, Legon. Six districts were purposively sampled to cover the country's three agroecological zones: the forest zone, the transition zone, and the savannah zone. For each zone, a pair of districts (referred to as F-1, F-2, T-1, T-2, S-1, and S-2) was selected in such a way that one district chief executive in each pair was female.[2] The strategy for sampling was based on the goal of keeping as many factors as possible constant within the agroecological zones (hence the district pairs) but to create variation on one variable of particular interest for the study: the gender of the political head of the district.

A sample of 90 electoral areas was selected in each district. Electoral areas rather than other sampling units commonly used in Ghana (such as enumeration areas) were used in order to be able to link the household and service provider data directly to the district assembly member responsible for this area. In each electoral area, the district assembly member representing the area was interviewed, which resulted in a target of 90 elected district assembly members. In addition, eight appointed district assembly members in each district were to be interviewed (table 4.3).

In each electoral area, three communities were randomly selected and surveyed. In one of the three communities, a random sample of about 12–13 households was selected for a head of household and spouse survey. A subsection of the household questionnaire (containing the key variables on service use, participation, exercise of voice, and related issues) was administered separately to both the household head and his or her spouse.

In each of the electoral areas in which the household survey was conducted, one farmer-based organization (FBO) member and one water and sanitation committee (WATSAN) member were interviewed if these organizations were present in that electoral area. If community training for water and sanitation was contracted out to NGOs, one NGO carrying out such activities on a contract basis was interviewed (table 4.3).

In the selected districts, the following staff members from the district assembly were interviewed: the political head of the district (the district chief executive), the administrative head of the district, the planning officer, and one member in charge of the water and sanitation team. In addition, five staff members from the district agricultural offices in the selected districts were interviewed. To shed light on factors influencing responsiveness to citizens' demands within the public administration, the sampling strategy ensured that lines of reporting (for example, extension agent, supervisor, district director) could be assessed. All extension agents who served in the 90 electoral areas in which the household surveys were conducted were interviewed. The sampling also ensured that staff members with special responsibilities for gender, such as gender desk officers and staff of Women in Agriculture Development (WIAD), were interviewed.

Table 4.3 Number and Type of Interview Respondents in Ghana

Type of respondent	Sample size
Household heads	1,168
Spouses	613
Communities	231
Elected District Assembly members	73
Appointed District Assembly members	41
Agricultural extension agents	70
NGOs	19
Members of farmer-based organizations	46
Members of water and sanitation committees	49

Source: Authors.

Qualitative Case Studies

A qualitative case study was conducted in the savannah region (Districts S-1 and S-2). A multiple-case embedded research design was used, meaning that data were not pooled across the sample but were instead clustered into cases. The primary unit of analysis was the individual service delivery case, such as a school, borehole, or electricity line. However, because each case of resource allocation is embedded in and predicted by political institutions that operate at the community, electoral area, and district assembly levels, data used in the analysis of each case were collected at these levels as well. The major data collection techniques were key informant interviews, including home stays, focus group discussions with community opinion leaders, and community meetings. Secondary data were also collected from the Electoral Commission and district assembly.

The study covered 10 communities in 6 electoral areas in the 2 districts. The district pair was chosen to illuminate the effect of different district assembly administrations within similar physical, social, and financial environments and to include one district headed by a female district chief executive (see above). Three electoral areas and assembly members were profiled in each district. They were selected to include a heterogeneous sample in terms of gender, tenure, age, strategy, and religion. (They are a subset of those covered by the survey described above.) Where the sampled assemblyperson represented more than one community, two communities were studied: the assemblyperson's hometown and either the larger or the farther community. The largest communities yielded insights into the assemblypersons' accountability to locations with high service pressures; the farthest communities revealed dynamics created by spatial dispersion in rural areas.

ETHIOPIA

Quantitative Data Collection

Quantitative surveys in Ethiopia were undertaken jointly by the Ethiopian Economic Policy Research Institute (EEPRI) and IFPRI. The surveys were conducted at two levels: the kebele level and the household/individual level. The sampling procedures are described below for each level.

Selection of Districts

Four pairs of districts (eight districts) were selected, located in 7 of Ethiopia's 11 regions. The pairs were chosen so that each would consist of nearby districts that belong to different regions. Of the two regions associated with a district pair, one is a "leading" region—that is, one of Ethiopia's four more institutionally advanced regions—in which local-level decentralization has taken place. The other district belongs to a "lagging" or "emerging" region.[3] In Ethiopia's four emerging regions, decentralization has been implemented only to the regional, not to the local (district), level.

This method of district pair selection applies to three district pairs (or six districts) from the sample. The fourth pair consists of one district in the Amhara region and one in the Tigray region. Both are considered leading regions, but local empowerment and community mobilization has a longer and distinct history in Tigray, making the Amhara-Tigray comparison an interesting one with which to contrast legacies of de facto local-level decision making.

The districts are referred to by the region in which they are located, followed by the letter D. They are Afar-D, Amhara-D1, Amhara-D2, Amhara-D3, Beneshangul Gumuz-D (BG-D), Gambella-D, Oromia-D, SNNP-D, and Tigray-D. In Amhara-D1, only qualitative research was conducted. (See the annex for more detail on the qualitative case studies.)

Sampling and Surveys at the Kebele (Peasant Association) Level

All 156 kebele in the eight districts were selected. Eight different questionnaire types were administered to the following groups or individuals:

- Focus groups consisting of about five individuals, including at least two women
- One of the three district council members representing each kebele
- One female kebele council member and one male kebele council member
- The kebele council speaker
- The kebele chairperson
- One agricultural extension agent specializing in crops and one agricultural extension agent specializing in livestock
- The head of an agricultural cooperative
- The head of a water committee.

Ten interviews were to be conducted in each kebele, for a total of 1,560 planned kebele-level interviews (table 4.4).

Sampling and Surveys at the Household or Individual Level

From each of the eight districts, four kebeles were randomly sampled. From each of the 32 kebeles, 35 households were randomly drawn. This resulted in a planned household sample size of 1,120 (the actual sample included 1,062 households). In each household, both the household head and the spouse were interviewed separately. If there was no spouse, as is often the case in female-headed households and sometimes the case for male-headed households, only the head was interviewed. Where there were multiple wives, the head and the first wife were interviewed.

The household questionnaire has two components. The first component, administered only to the household head, includes questions about the household

Table 4.4   Number and Type of Interview Respondents in Ethiopia

Type of respondent	Sample size	Survey type
Community members		
Male household heads	834	Household/individual level
Female household heads	238	survey (used in this
Male spouses	9	report)
Female spouses	680	
Total number of actual interviews	1,761	
Focus groups	156	
Political representative		
District council members	156	Kebele-level surveys
Kebele chairpersons	156	(fieldwork ongoing)
Kebele council members	312	
Kebele council speakers	156	
Extension agents	312	Kebele-level surveys
Cooperative heads	156	(fieldwork ongoing)
Heads of water committees	156	
Total number of planned interviews	1,560	
Total number of actual interviews	1,072	

Source: Authors.

roster, assets, and other household-level variables. The second, longer component, administered separately to both head and spouse, contains all the modules of direct research interest, relating to agricultural and water-related activities, access to and satisfaction with services, participation, social capital, and other issues.

Some 1,761 household/individual-level surveys (including interviews with household heads and their spouses) were administered in Ethiopia (table 4.4). (This actual sample is smaller than the planned sample by 48 households.) The kebele-level survey was ongoing when this report was written. For this reason, this report relies on data from the household-level survey only.

Qualitative Case Studies

Qualitative case studies were conducted in five districts (for descriptions of the districts, see annex table 4.A.3). In each district, the team conducted key informant interviews and focus group discussions in the district capital town and one kebele, meeting with 105 respondents (table 4.5). In the district capitals, the team interviewed district government officials responsible for finance and budget, agricultural extension, drinking water, and women's affairs; the speaker of the district council; and leaders of the district women's association, the cooperative union, and the governing party of the district. At the kebele level, the team interviewed agricultural extension agents; the kebele manager; the speaker of the kebele council; the kebele chairperson; members of the kebele

Table 4.5 Number and Sites of Qualitative Interviews in Ethiopia

District site	District capitals	Kebeles	Total
Amhara-D1	2	12	14
Amhara-D3	16	11	27
Beneshangul-Gumuz-D	4	6	10
Oromia-D	8	7	15
Tigray-D	15	24	39
Total	45	60	105

Source: Authors.

cabinet responsible for agriculture, drinking water, and women's affairs; leaders of the agricultural cooperative, the women's association, and the governing party; members of a water and sanitation committee; and male and female farmers. The team prepared interview guides for discussions with key informants and focus groups. For discussions with groups of farmers, the team relied on the Net-Map tool. Before starting the research, the team carried out a preliminary scoping exercise in Amhara-D1; findings from this district are also discussed in this report.

ANNEX

Case Study Sites

The tables in this annex indicate the labels used in the text to refer to the case study locations in India and Ethiopia. The names of the case study locations are not displayed in order to ensure the anonymity of the respondents. The two case study districts in Ghana are referred to as S-1 and S-2.

Table 4.A.1 Case Study Sites in Karnataka

	Districts	
	Better developed	Less developed
	Districts A, A1, A2	District B
Blocks		
Better developed	Block A-A	Block B-A
	Block A1-A	
	Block A2-A	
Less developed	Block A1-B	Block B-B
Gram Panchayats		
Closer to block capital	GP A2-A1	GP B-B1
Further from block capital	GP A2-A2	GP B-B2

Source: Authors.

GENDER AND GOVERNANCE IN RURAL SERVICES

Table 4.A.2   Case Study Sites in Bihar

	Districts	
	Better developed	Less developed
	District A	District B
Blocks		
Better developed	Block A-A	Block B-A
Less developed	Block A-B	Block B-B
		Block B-C
Gram panchayats		
Closer to block capital	GP A-A1	GP B-B1
	GP A-B1	GP B-C1
Further from block capital	GP A-B2	GP B-B2.1
		GP B-B2.2

Source: Authors.

Table 4.A.3   Case Study Sites in Ethiopia

Kebele	District	Region	Main Livelihood Pattern
Amhara-K1	Amhara-D1	Amhara (Western part)	Mixed crop and livestock
Amhara-K3	Amhara-D3	Amhara (Northern part)	Mixed crop and livestock
BG-K	BG-D	Beneshangul-Gumuz	Forest, cash crop, livestock
Oromia-K	Oromia-D	Oromia	Cash crop
Tigray-K	Tigray-D	Tigray	Mixed crop and livestock, horticultural products

Source: Authors.

NOTES

1. Net-Map is an interview-based mapping tool that helps people understand, visualize, discuss, and improve situations in which many different actors influence outcomes. By creating influence network maps, individuals and groups can clarify their views of a situation, foster discussion, and develop a strategic approach to their networking activities. Net-Map helps players determine which actors are involved in a given network, how they are linked, how influential they are, and what their goals are. For more detail, see http://netmap.wordpress.com/.

2. To ensure the anonymity of respondents, the district names are not disclosed here.

3. The leading regions are Amhara, Oromia, SNNP, and Tigray. The lagging regions included in the survey are Afar, Beneshangul-Gumuz, and Gambella.

CHAPTER FIVE

The Short Route of Accountability: Households, Community Organizations, and Service Providers

This chapter uses the survey and case study data for India, Ghana, and Ethiopia to analyze the short routes of accountability (figure 5.1). Expressed in terms of the framework displayed in figure 2.1, this chapter examines the links between households and service providers (HH–PS and HH–NG) and community-based organizations (HH–CO and HH–CO–PS) with regard to service provision.

Each country section starts by presenting data on access to and satisfaction with services (arrow PS/NG–HH). Each then deals with the extent to which households can hold service providers accountable (arrow HH–PS/NG) before discussing the role of community-based organizations. To keep the chapter focused, only the most relevant tables and figures are included here. Additional tables and figures are presented in the chapter annex.

INDIA

Households' Access to and Satisfaction with Services

This section describes access by male- and female-headed households to agricultural and veterinary services and to water and sanitation and reports on their satisfaction with the services they receive. It is based on the results of surveys of households in Karnataka.

Figure 5.1   Short Route of Accountability

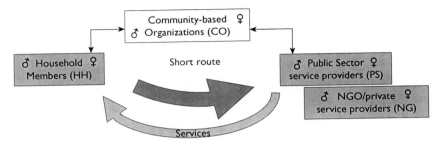

Source: Authors, based on World Bank (2003).

Female-headed households appeared to be disadvantaged on several counts: they were more likely to be casual laborers than farmers, were less literate, and had fewer assets than male-headed households (see annex table 5.A.1). Nine percent of sampled households were headed by women, 19 percent of whom were literate. In contrast, 64 percent of male heads of households are literate. Whereas the dominant source of livelihood for the majority of male-headed households was agriculture, a majority of female-headed households reported casual agricultural labor as their dominant occupation. Female-headed households were significantly less likely to possess a bicycle, a motorbike, or a TV set than male-headed households. They also owned fewer livestock than male-headed households.

Agricultural Extension and Veterinary Services

Among surveyed farm households, 29 percent of male-headed households and 18 percent of female-headed households reported having had at least one contact with an agricultural extension agent during the previous year (table 5.1). The visit was part of a group visit in 15 percent of the cases and an individual visit in 85 percent of the cases.

About 60 percent of both male and female respondents reported being very satisfied or somewhat satisfied with the agricultural extension service (figure 5.2). There were no substantial differences between male and female respondents.

Respondents from scheduled castes (SC) were more likely to be very satisfied with agricultural extension services than members of scheduled tribes (ST) or other backward classes (OBCs).[1] Household respondents who were dissatisfied with agricultural extension complained mainly about infrequent visits or the absence of visits. A sizable share of households were not able to

GENDER AND GOVERNANCE IN RURAL SERVICES

Table 5.1 Access to Agricultural Extension in Karnataka, by Gender of Household Head

Type of household	Sample size	Households visited at least once in year preceding the survey (percent)
Male-headed household with land	638	28.8
Female-headed household with land	38	18.4
Total	676	28.3

Source: ISEC-IFPRI Survey 2006.

assess the quality of the service, most likely because they did not receive extension visits.

Access to livestock services was better: 72 percent of male-headed and 79 percent of female-headed households had at least one contact with a veterinary assistant or officer during the 12 months preceding the survey (table 5.2). To receive livestock services, clients typically visit the office of the veterinary service provider. The better access to livestock services may be related to the fact that these services are provided not only by the animal husbandry department but also by dairy cooperatives (under the Milk Federation of Karnataka). (The survey question does not capture the source of service provision.)

Male-headed households had on average 3.5 contacts with a livestock officer during the 12 months preceding the survey; female-headed households had on average 3.7 contacts. Members of female-headed households traveled an average of 3.1 kilometers to the livestock office; male-headed households traveled 4.1 kilometers.

Women tended to be more satisfied with the veterinary extension services than men, but the differences were not large (figure 5.3). Members of STs were more likely to be very satisfied with the service than members of SCs and OBCs.[2] The main reason for dissatisfaction with veterinary services was insufficient veterinary hospitals within reach.

Drinking Water and Drainage Facilities

Eighty percent of respondents have access to safe drinking water sources (table 5.3). Only 9.5 percent obtain their water from open wells.

All respondents except those from general castes tend to be very or somewhat satisfied with rural drinking water supply (figure 5.4). Dissatisfied respondents complained mainly about the quantity of drinking water, especially during

Figure 5.2 Household Satisfaction with Agricultural Extension in Karnataka, by Gender and Caste

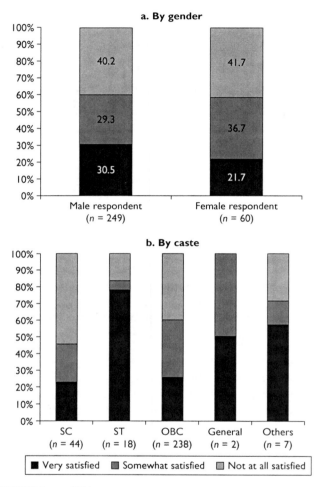

Source: ISEC-IFPRI Survey 2006.
Note: SC = scheduled caste; ST = scheduled tribe; OBC = other backward class. Sample surveyed households that own land. The answer category "cannot say/don't know" is not displayed.

summer; the high flouride content of the water; and the lack of electricity, which is required to operate pumps (see annex figure 5.A.1).

Satisfaction rates for drainage vary by caste, with general caste households the most likely to be dissatisfied (figure 5.5). Gender differences do not exist. Respondents perceive major problems with the availability and quality of

Table 5.2	Access to Livestock Services in Karnataka, by Gender of Household Head	
Type of household	Sample size	Percentage of households visited at least once in year preceding the survey
Male-headed household with livestock	564	71.8
Female-headed household with livestock	33	78.8
Total	597	72.2

Source: ISEC-IFPRI Survey 2006.

drainage facilities, and they complain about irregular cleaning. Of reporting households, 92 percent state that maintenance of the drainage facility is undertaken only when a complaint is made to the gram panchayat. More than one-third of reporting households indicate that they are involved in the maintenance of drainage facilities.

Factors Associated with Access and Satisfaction

Several regression models were estimated to determine the factors associated with visits by agricultural extension workers and the degree of household satisfaction with agricultural extension and households' asset ownership. These models take into account the gender and literacy of the household respondent; the size, gender, and age distribution of households; and the percentage of dependent household members (defined as those too young [under 15 years] or too old [over 59 years] to work).

Households with a larger percentage of dependent household members are less likely to have met with an extension worker during the year preceding the survey or to be satisfied with extension service delivery (table 5.4). This finding cannot be explained by the conventional notion that per capita landholdings decrease with the size of the household, because the Spearman rank correlation and cross-correlation coefficients point to insignificant or positive and significant relationships between the size of households' landholdings (various types) and the number of household members.

Households with more assets and households with a female head are more likely than other households to have reported being satisfied with extension service delivery. Controlling for assets, the gender of the household head does not affect satisfaction with extension services. Although such simple regressions have to be interpreted with care, the findings suggest that agricultural

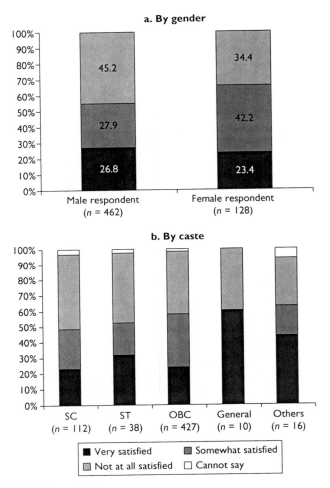

Figure 5.3 Household Satisfaction with Veterinary Services in Karnataka, by Gender and Caste

Source: ISEC-IFPRI Survey 2006.
Note: SC = scheduled caste; ST = scheduled tribe; OBC = other backward class. Respondents included households that own livestock.

extension is subject to elite capture by better-off households. This disadvantages female-headed households, which have fewer assets.

The degree of satisfaction with drinking water supply and quality does not depend on any of the household characteristics included in the analysis (table 5.5). The statistical insignificance of asset holdings is in line with the observation that access to drinking water facilities in rural areas is more

GENDER AND GOVERNANCE IN RURAL SERVICES

Table 5.3	Sources of Drinking Water in Karnataka
Source	Percentage of respondents (n = 966)
Piped water	23.1
Mini water supply scheme	43.7
Hand pump/borewell	19.9
Open well	9.5
Multiple sources	2.3
Others	1.6

Source: ISEC-IFPRI Survey 2006.

likely to depend on the location of households in a village than on household characteristics (see Raabe, Sekher, and Birner 2009).

Large households and households with access to water from protected public sources that are subject to regular or complaint-based maintenance works are significantly more likely to be satisfied with drinking water supply than other households (table 5.6). Maintenance thus appears to be critical for ensuring the long-term functionality and reliability of drinking water sources.

Service Providers: Capacity, Constraints, Incentives, and Accountability

This section deals with the providers of agricultural and livestock services, drinking water, and drainage, all of which were provided by public sector agencies. Applying the framework outlined in chapter 2, it presents evidence on the capacity, constraints, and incentives of service providers and examines the extent to which accountability for gender-responsive service delivery is created within the service provision organizations.

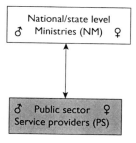

Demographic Characteristics

This section presents a profile of the front-line professionals responsible for service provision in Karnataka, including extension workers for agricultural

Figure 5.4   Household Satisfaction with Drinking Water Service in Karnataka, by Gender and Caste

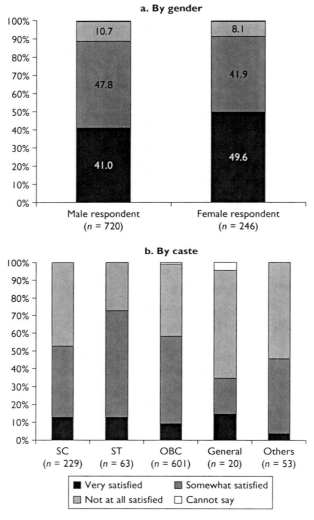

a. By gender

Male respondent (n = 720): 41.0, 47.8, 10.7
Female respondent (n = 246): 49.6, 41.9, 8.1

b. By caste

SC (n = 229)   ST (n = 63)   OBC (n = 601)   General (n = 20)   Others (n = 53)

■ Very satisfied   ■ Somewhat satisfied
■ Not at all satisfied   □ Cannot say

Source: ISEC-IFPRI Survey 2006.
Note: SC = scheduled caste; ST = scheduled tribe; OBC = other backward class.

extension, veterinary assistants for livestock services, and junior engineers for drinking water facilities and drainage. These officers are located at the block level.

Staff members from two other departments were also interviewed; findings on them are presented for purposes of comparison. The front-line professionals

Figure 5.5   Satisfaction with Drainage in Karnataka, by Gender and Caste

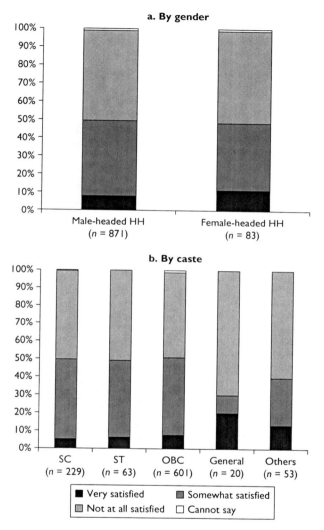

Source: ISEC-IFPRI Survey 2006.

for the Public Distribution System (PDS) are food inspectors, who are located at the block level. The staff of child care centers are called *anganwadi* workers. They are volunteers at the gram panchayat level and receive a small remuneration from the government. They are included because they present an interesting alternative mode of service provision and because they belong to a department that has

Variable	Household met extension worker during previous year[a]		Household satisfaction with extension[b]	
	(1)	(2)	(3)	(4)
Female household head	1.099	1.143*	1.422***	1.353**
	(0.716)	(0.623)	(0.467)	(0.531)
Literate household head	−0.037	−0.314	0.241	0.112
	(0.425)	(0.497)	(0.306)	(0.312)
Number of household members	−0.015	−0.078	−0.147***	−0.170***
	(0.082)	(0.084)	(0.049)	(0.051)
Percent of dependent household members	−0.031***	−0.026**	−0.018***	−0.015**
	(0.011)	(0.011)	(0.006)	(0.007)
Percent of female household members	0.006	0.009	−0.006	−0.006
	(0.015)	(0.015)	(0.011)	(0.011)
Household asset ownership[c]	0.687		0.904	
	(0.704)		(0.642)	
Sum household assets[d]		0.290***		0.154**
		(0.115)		(0.061)
Constant	−0.626	−0.694		
	(0.935)	(0.754)		
Number of observations	177	177	305	305
Hosmer-Lemeshow chi-square	7.08	5.890		
Log-likelihood ratio	31.723***	36.116***	118.722***	121.457***
McFadden's R^2	0.170	0.193	0.179	0.183

Source: Authors, based on data from ISEC-IFPRI Survey 2006.
Note: The standard errors are clustered at the village level and reported in parentheses.
District effects are fixed in all regressions. The marginal effects of the model are available
on request.
a. Logistic regression.
b. Ordered logistic regression. The dependent variable is an ordered response variable coded
as follows: 1 = not at all satisfied, 2 = somewhat satisfied, 3 = satisfied with service delivery.
c. The household owns any of the following assets: bicycle, scooter/motorbike, radio, TV
set, fan, fridge, tractor, bullock cart, plowing implements, thresher, or pump for irrigation.
d. The number of consumer assets owned by a household refers to the existence of an asset.
A household can have up to 11 assets.
***Significant at the 1% level; **significant at the 5% level; *significant at the 10% level.

primarily female staff. A government staff member, the gram panchayat secretary, is also assigned to each gram panchayat (box 5.1).

No female agricultural extension worker was employed in the blocks included
in the survey (table 5.7). Among the 41 junior engineers was 1 woman; among

Table 5.5 Variables Associated with Satisfaction with Drinking Water Quantity and Quality in Karnataka

Variable	Household satisfaction with drinking water quantity		Household satisfaction with drinking water quality	
	(1)	(2)	(3)	(4)
Female household head	-0.082 (0.336)	-0.084 (0.338)	-0.115 (0.302)	-0.108 (0.308)
Literate household head	0.224 (0.173)	0.177 (0.171)	-0.029 (0.188)	-0.029 (0.189)
Number of household members	0.011 (0.035)	-0.004 (0.037)	0.068 (0.050)	0.067 (0.050)
Percent of dependent household members	-0.001 (0.003)	0.000 (0.003)	-0.002 (0.003)	-0.002 (0.003)
Percent of female household members	-0.001 (0.005)	-0.001 (0.004)	-0.002 (0.005)	-0.002 (0.005)
Household asset ownership	-0.030 (0.213)		-0.067 (0.256)	
Sum household assets		0.051 (0.042)		-0.008 (0.040)
Number of observations	949	949	949	949
Log-likelihood ratio	90.071***	91.904***	64.964***	64.867***
McFadden's R^2	0.050	0.051	0.047	0.047

Source: Authors, based on data from ISEC-IFPRI Survey 2006.

Note: See notes to table 5.4.

***Significant at the 1% level.

Table 5.6 Variables Associated with Satisfaction with Drinking Water Quantity from a Public Source in Karnataka

Variable	(1)	(2)	(3)	(4)
Female household head	-0.177	-0.158	-0.166	-0.155
	(0.305)	(0.302)	(0.294)	(0.293)
Literate household head	0.216	0.170	0.239	0.222
	(0.166)	(0.169)	(0.184)	(0.187)
Number of household members	0.084**	0.071*	0.107***	0.102**
	(0.039)	(0.039)	(0.039)	(0.040)
Percent of dependent household members	-0.003	-0.002	-0.003	-0.002
	(0.003)	(0.003)	(0.003)	(0.003)
Percent of female household members	-0.003	-0.003	-0.003	-0.003
	(0.004)	(0.004)	(0.004)	(0.004)
Household asset ownership	-0.139		-0.116	
	(0.216)		(0.229)	
Sum household assets		0.033		0.004
		(0.048)		(0.054)
Maintenance[a]			1.02***	1.027***
			(0.363)	(0.369)
Number of observations	945	945	880	880
Log-likelihood ratio	136.056***	136.091***	153.345***	152.870***
McFadden's R^2	0.073	0.073	0.088	0.088

Source: Authors, based on data from ISEC-IFPRI Survey 2006.

Note: See notes to table 5.4.

a. Maintenance is a binary dummy that equals 1 if the water source is regularly cleaned or immediately cleaned after a complaint is made, or 0 otherwise.

***Significant at the 1% level; **significant at the 5% level; *significant at the 10% level.

40 veterinary assistants, 4 were women. All of the food inspectors were male, and all of the anganwadi workers were female.

The percentage of SC/ST members ranged from 13 percent to 22 percent, suggesting that the government's reservation policy for these groups is being implemented. About a quarter of the junior engineers, agricultural extension workers, and food inspectors have urban backgrounds. The percentage is lower for veterinary assistants and negligible for anganwadi workers. One-third of the junior engineers do not reside in the block in which they perform their duty. This percentage is lower for the staff of the other departments and is negligible for the anganwadi workers.

Box 5.1   Challenges of Staff at the Gram Panchayat Level in Karnataka

In Karnataka, the gram panchayat secretary is the main government official responsible for the gram panchayat. He is assisted by several staff members who can be hired by the gram panchayat directly. These staff include the bill collector, the electrician/lineman, the office attendant, and the waterman (the water tax-collector), who work in the villages under the gram panchayat's jurisdiction.

The gram panchayat secretary has many responsibilities that sometimes affect his or her performance as the administrator in the lowest tier of the local government structure. When asked about the work pressure, the gram panchayat secretary of A2-A1-GP in Karnataka said the following:

We have been assigned with 28 new activities, but without the requisite staff. At least in the block panchayat office there is one person assigned for each scheme. Here, what happens is that my staff goes to collect tax in the village and I am left with having to open and close the daybook and the cashbook. In fact, I take homework every night like a child going to school, and that is how I complete my work every day. The work is tight and it is like that every day. There are complaints in other gram panchayats about improper or incomplete records. I can understand this problem because it involves a lot of work. Should I leave the cashbook and the daybook and attend the *Vikas* and *Abhivruddhi Karyakrama* (development programs) in the village? When a higher official comes to evaluate, the first thing he asks for is the previous day's closing balance for all the accounts. I have to come from 40 kilometers and go 40 kilometers to my house. Look at these villagers who are waiting for me to issue checks for the *Indira Awas Yojana Kaccha* House scheme. They have been waiting for two days to get it, although I assist you to finding the relevant records for your research. I feel that we are understaffed to carry out both the administrative and the developmental works.

Table 5.7 Demographic Characteristics of Front-Line Staff Providing Rural Services in Karnataka

Characteristic	Junior engineer (n = 41)	Agricultural extension worker (n = 41)	Veterinary assistant (n = 40)	Food inspector (n = 34)	Anganwadi worker (n = 50)	Total (n = 206)
Gender						
Male	98	100	90	100	0	74
Female	2	0	10	0	100	26
Caste						
SC/ST	22	17	13	21	16	17
OBC	66	71	75	65	78	71
General	12	12	8	12	6	10
No response	0	0	5	3	0	1
Birthplace						
Rural	76	76	85	74	96	82
Urban	24	24	15	26	4	18
Residence in block in which duty is performed						
Resident	66	88	78	59	96	79
Nonresident	34	12	23	41	4	21

Source: ISEC-TISS-IFPRI Survey 2008.

More than 70 percent of the agricultural extension workers serving the surveyed blocks are over 50; just 2 percent are under 40 (figure 5.6). The food inspectors have a similar age distribution. This distribution is probably the result of a policy of not hiring this type of field staff for many years, adopted to control public spending (Government of India 2007a). The age distribution of the veterinary assistants and the anganwadi workers is spread more equally across age groups.

Education and Training

Education and training are major determinants of the capacity of front-line professionals to deliver quality services. A large share of the interviewed agricultural extension workers and food inspectors have high school or bachelor's degrees. The specialization of those with bachelor's degrees did not always match the requirements of the profession, however. For example, only 17 percent of agricultural extension workers with bachelor's degrees had degrees in agriculture or biology; the remainder held degrees in areas such as the arts. The majority of veterinary assistants held bachelor's or master's degree in veterinary science or animal nutrition. Most junior engineers had diplomas or completed vocational training. Those with bachelor's degrees tended to have specialized in civil engineering. Most anganwadi workers held high school degrees.

Figure 5.6   Age Distribution of Staff in Karnataka (percent)

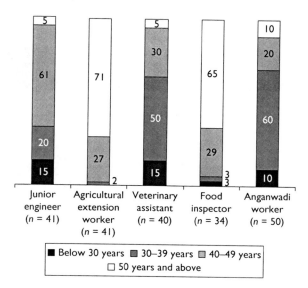

Below 30 years ■   30–39 years ▨   40–49 years ▨
□ 50 years and above

Source: ISEC-TISS-IFPRI Survey 2008.

Preservice training rarely took place. All agricultural extension workers and 95 percent of the veterinary assistants and anganwadi workers received training after joining the respective departments. About one-quarter of junior engineers and food inspectors never received any training on the job. No clear pattern distinguishes those with and without training. Front-line staff with a degree in a subject relevant to the departments were no more or less likely to receive training than staff without relevant education. Frequently, months or even years passed between the time a person joined a department and received training.

Agricultural extension workers were trained predominantly in technology transfer and dissemination, the use of agricultural input material, and crop disease monitoring and prevention. At the time of the survey, none of the extension workers in the sample had received training regarding the Agricultural Technology Management Agency (ATMA) or the formation of farmer-based organizations (FBOs). Veterinary assistants were trained mainly in cross-breeding and animal disease prevention. About one-third of the interviewed veterinary assistants were also trained in technology transfer and dissemination and animal disease monitoring. The junior engineers reported 68 training events on various topics (see annex table 5.A.3). Only one of these training events included a focus on women's issues, although the topics of some of the trainings (water harvesting and conservation, for example) indicate that a focus on women's issues might have been appropriate.

Constraints

Field staff of the five departments faced a variety of constraints in fulfilling their duties and responsibilities (table 5.8). For agricultural extension workers and

		Agricultural			
Constraint	Junior engineer (n = 41)	extension worker (n = 41)	Veterinary assistant (n = 40)	Food inspector (n = 34)	Anganwadi worker (n = 50)
Lack of staff	39	88	75	65	4
Political interference	51	51	40	71	8
Lack of funds	27	7	18	12	12
Inadequate work environment	10	5	6	10	10
Complex admin. procedures	7	7	8	3	2

Table 5.8 Constraints Identified by Front-Line Staff in Karnataka (percentage of respondents)

Source: ISEC-TISS-IFPRI Survey 2008.
Note: Multiple answers possible.

veterinary assistants, lack of staff was the most frequently cited constraint. Among junior engineers and food inspectors, political interference was reported most frequently. Neither the work environment nor complex administrative procedures were perceived as major constraints in any of the five departments.

Most agricultural extension workers and veterinary assistants ranked the human resource constraint to be strong. The political interference constraint was ranked strong by about half of the junior engineers and food inspectors and by about one-third of agricultural extension workers and the veterinary assistants (see annex table 5.A.4).

Perceptions of Work Environment

The work environment is important because it can create incentives for front-line staff to deliver quality services. One aspect of the work environment is satisfaction with the training opportunities that front-line professionals receive. The percentage of respondents who agree with the proposition that they have received adequate training to meet their current duties and responsibilities ranges from 56 percent among junior engineers to 90 percent among agricultural extension workers (table 5.9).

For female staff, attention to gender-specific needs is an important aspect of the work environment. Most anganwadi workers believe that their department pays special attention to the needs of female staff. In contrast, only 15 percent of veterinary assistants and 20 percent of agricultural extension workers believe this is the case in their department.

Merit-based recruitment and promotion are particularly important mechanisms for creating accountability within service organizations. Staff in all departments observe that hiring but not promotion is done largely on the basis of merit.

In line with the general pattern, most agricultural extension workers felt that hiring in the Department of Agriculture was done fairly, with only 9 percent believing that staff were not hired purely on the basis of merit. However, only 28 percent of workers felt that promotions were granted on the basis of merit. This indicates that one of the most important mechanisms that public sector organizations can use to create accountability is not working. Sixty-four percent of anganwadi workers believe that promotion in their department is done purely on the basis of merit. All categories of workers overwhelmingly indicated that men and women had equal opportunities of promotion within the department. Given that four out of five departments had staff almost exclusively of one gender, gender differences in promotional opportunities were difficult to observe. However, all four female veterinary assistants and the lone female junior engineer in the sample agreed with the statement that promotional opportunities are equal.

Payment plays an important role as a motivating factor. Only 31 percent of all workers felt that salaries in their department were commensurate with

Table 5.9 Perceptions of Staff in Different Departments Regarding Work Environment in Karnataka (percentage of respondents agreeing with statement)

	Junior engineer (n = 41)	Agricultural extension worker (n = 41)	Veterinary assistant (n = 40)	Food inspector (n = 34)	Anganwadi worker (n = 50)	Total (n = 206)
I have received adequate training to meet my current duties/responsibilities.	56	90	68	74	84	75
There are good opportunities for promotion in my department.	34	29	25	29	22	28
Male and female staff of my department have equal opportunities for getting promoted.	85	90	88	91	86	88
My department pays special attention to the transportation and accommodation needs of the female workers in my department.	20	41	15	18	82	38
The staff of my department is paid equally to staff in other departments that does comparable work.	49	34	13	50	14	31
The pay scales in my department reflect differences in workload and responsibility of different grades.	41	49	68	41	58	52
My workload is adequate.	78	73	83	65	36	66
The staff of my department is hired purely on the basis of merit.	78	93	85	85	96	88
The staff of my department are promoted purely on the basis of merit.	20	10	20	15	64	28

Source: ISEC-TISS-IFPRI Survey 2008.

the pay of staff in other departments who performed comparable work. Among veterinary assistants, this rate was particularly low (13 percent). Less than half of junior engineers, agricultural extension workers, and food inspectors reported that pay scales adequately reflect differences in the workload and responsibilities of different grades. Despite identifying staff shortages as a major constraint on their ability to perform their jobs, more than 70 percent of junior engineers, agricultural extension workers, and veterinary assistants agreed with the statement that their workloads are adequate.

Most staff feel that their work is recognized by their supervisors (table 5.10). Awards do not seem to play a major role. All employees except anganwadi workers report being paid in a timely manner. Almost all staff members report

Table 5.10 Incentives and Transportation among Service Providers in Karnataka
(percentage of respondents answering "yes")

Question	Junior engineer (n = 41)	Agricultural extension worker (n = 41)	Veterinary assistant (n = 40)	Food inspector (n = 34)	Anganwadi worker (n = 50)
Have you ever received an award for good performance?	0	15	3	6	14
Is your work recognized by your supervisor?	98	85	93	88	100
Do you receive your monthly salary regularly?	90	93	80	94	62
Do you have to incur own out-of-pocket expenses to provide services?	73	85	78	91	—
Do you have access to a motorbike or vehicle for work?	54	32	50	35	—

Source: ISEC-TISS-IFPRI Survey 2008.
Note: — = Not available.

incurring out-of-pocket expenses. One-third of agricultural extension workers and food inspectors and half of junior engineers and veterinary assistants have a motorbike or other vehicle for work. Among the four female veterinary assistants, only one had access to a vehicle.

Food inspectors are required to cover the largest area in their work by a substantial margin (annex table 5.A.5). The number of gram panchayats, villages, and population served are similar for all other groups, with veterinary assistants covering the largest number of gram panchayats and villages but a slightly smaller estimated population than the junior engineers and agricultural extension workers. Junior engineers served the largest proportion of female-headed households (more than 20 percent). Comparing the population numbers with the number of villages covered suggests that front-line staff may overestimate the number of households they are responsible for.

Interactions with Other Actors

This section deals with the interactions front-line professionals have with other actors, including local political representatives (panchayat members at different levels) and NGOs. As all five departments covered in the survey come under the purview of the panchayti raj system, in principle all the functionaries should be accountable to local governments at the appropriate level.

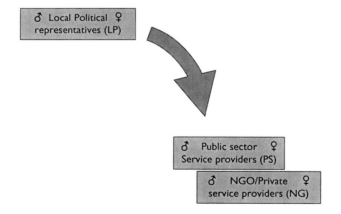

Only 32 percent of the sampled agricultural extension agents visited one of the *Krishi Vigyan Kendras* (KVKs), which are meant to impart training and knowledge to extension personnel (table 5.11). This indicates a serious problem regarding the knowledge flow between agricultural research and extension.

More than three-quarters of the extension workers interacted with the gram panchayat for the delivery of subsidized inputs, crop disease prevention, or crop insurance. Seven percent of respondents mentioned communicating

Table 5.11 Professional Contacts of Agricultural Extension Workers in Karnataka

Institution	Percentage of respondents reporting contacts with institution (n = 37)
Gram panchayat	81
KVK/training center	32
Block panchayat	22
Rural bank	5
Local NGO	5
District panchayat	3

Source: ISEC-TISS-IFPRI Survey 2008.
Note: Results indicate responses to unprompted question, "During the past year, which institutions did you talk to or visit?" Multiple answers are possible.

women-specific needs as a reason to contact the gram panchayat. There was less interaction with panchayats at higher levels.

Senior agricultural officers interacted with a wider group of actors and had more intensive interactions with the block and district panchayats than did agricultural extension workers (annex table 5A.6). One-quarter reported frequently interacting with members of the legislative assembly. The case study evidence suggests that the influence of members of the legislative assembly on public officials is enormous, mainly because of their power to transfer administrative staff. As one official in Block A1-A in Karnataka put it, "Anyway, we have to perform under instructions from the local member of the legislative assembly, who has powers to transfer us."

For veterinary assistants, there is evidence of some interactions with NGOs about addressing women-specific needs. Veterinary assistants also reported contacting NGOs for the transfer and dissemination of technology and the promotion of public-private partnerships. Similar to agricultural extension workers, veterinary assistants contacted the KVKs for technology transfer and dissemination and for training and capacity building. Farmers' complaints about issues related to the work of veterinary assistants were communicated mainly during visits of the gram panchayat.

Junior engineers reported interacting with gram, block, and district panchayats for a number of reasons, mainly related to the construction, rehabilitation, inspection, and maintenance of water and sanitation facilities; the management of water sources; the introduction and coordination of water and sanitation projects; and the preparation and submission of cost estimates. Except for the preparation and submission of cost estimates, most issues were more likely to be discussed with the gram panchayats. For cost estimates, the importance of the block and district panchayats likely reflect the budgetary authority of these institutions.

Agricultural Extension Activities

The qualitative case studies in Karnataka and Bihar shed additional light on the activities of the agricultural extension workers. In all case study blocks, most of these positions were vacant. Very few agricultural extension workers were responsible for an entire block. Most worked largely on implementing various government schemes, typically involving the distribution of subsidized inputs. In some cases, the outreach of these schemes was marginal. For example, only one livestock training program was implemented in District B in Bihar. It trained about 20 people, half of whom did not return to livestock activities following the training. In Block B-B, a seed distribution program entailed distributing 6 kilograms of improved seed to one better-off farmer—by design of the program, the only beneficiary in the entire gram panchayat. According to case study respondents, block panchayats in Block A-A in Bihar were involved to some extent in the selection of beneficiaries. Some of the schemes had a targeting component for households below the poverty line or for SC/ST members. Yet the team could not identify a single case in which the gram panchayat was involved in selecting beneficiaries or implementing an agricultural or livestock program.

The implementation of ATMA was underway in some of the case study locations in Bihar. The staff shortage prevented agricultural extension workers from promoting the formation of farmer interest groups foreseen under ATMA. Consequently, in Blocks B-A and B-B, farmers who had connections with agricultural extension workers represented the farmer interest group, which did not exist. Case study interviews in the B-B Block indicated that both farmers and agricultural extension workers perceived ATMA as another subsidized input scheme, in which the representative of the farmer interest group has to sign for the release of funds.

The case study evidence suggests that the ATMA guidelines stipulating the participation of women did induce agricultural extension workers to seek women's participation in ATMA–sponsored programs. Such efforts were not always geared toward improving agricultural production or the marketing practices of women, however. This problem was encountered in the A-A1-GP in Bihar, where a group of landless female members of a self-help group were selected for an exposure visit to West Bengal to learn about new agricultural technologies that, it turned out, required access to land. Moreover, instead of sending five women for the exposure visit, as specified, only three were sent; the remaining two positions were filled by men from a dominant caste group.

Despite such challenges, linking agricultural programs with self-help groups seems to be a promising approach to reaching women. Survey evidence in Karnataka shows that they are the only community-based group with wide coverage. Case study evidence from Bihar suggests that self-help groups have become increasingly widespread as a result of various programs by the government, development agencies, and NGOs.

Drinking Water Supply Activities

Drinking water supply is the service that has been most effectively decentralized to the gram panchayats. It is therefore interesting to note that junior engineers did not consider the gram panchayats to be responsible for the construction of drinking water facilities. Among junior engineers, 65 percent reported that projects constructing drinking water facilities had been conducted the previous year in the area they were responsible for. Of the 68 projects carried out, almost half were seen as the responsibility of the district panchayat; only 7 were seen as the responsibility of the gram panchayat (see annex table 5.A.7). With regard to the rehabilitation of drinking water facilities, a similar picture emerges. Forty-nine projects for rehabilitating drinking water facilities were conducted in the blocks of the surveyed junior engineers. In just one case was the gram panchayat reported to be the organization mainly in charge of the rehabilitation. Although drainage was considered to be the more severe problem by the households, drainage facilities were constructed in only 34 percent of the blocks included in the survey.

Most district-level engineers (who have a supervisory function over junior engineers) considered the decentralization of drinking water supply beneficial (see annex table 5.A.8). For the three respondents who felt that decentralization had not helped target project funds and cited other reasons than those indicated in the table, one cited political interference, one political pressure, and one the fact that local officials divided funds among themselves instead of distributing them as intended.

Role of Community-Based Organizations

This section deals with the role of community-based organizations, part of the short route of accountability. Membership in such organizations is low, and few household members belong to more than two such organizations. (The data should be intepreted with care, as a large number of missing responses may cause membership levels to be overestimated.)

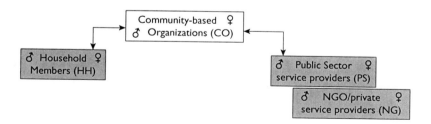

Women participate mainly in self-help groups and women's groups, the only group with substantial coverage (figure 5.7). Men belong to forest groups, cooperative societies, and caste associations.[3]

Figure 5.7   Membership in Community-Based Organizations by
Men and Women in Karnataka

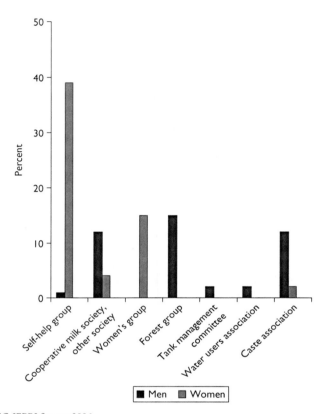

Source: ISEC-IFPRI Survey 2006.
Note: Percentage refers to percent of all valid answers.

Literate household members and members of large households are significantly more likely to belong to a larger number of institutions (table 5.12). The positive relationship between household size and the number of household organizational memberships is not surprising, as the opportunity cost of spending time in an organization may be lower for larger households, which have greater availability of family labor.

User groups and community-based organizations—farmers cooperatives, dairy cooperatives, water and sanitation committees for drinking water supply (not water users associations for irrigation), vigilance committees, and women's self-help groups—were surveyed for each of the services covered in the survey. Most of the respondents from farmers cooperatives mentioned the distribution of input and access to loans among their most important activities.

GENDER AND GOVERNANCE IN RURAL SERVICES

Table 5.12 Factors Associated with Membership in Community-Based Organizations in Karnataka

Variable	(1)	(2)
Female household head	0.033	0.028
	(0.086)	(0.085)
Literate household head	0.126***	0.116***
	(0.039)	(0.042)
Number of household members	0.032***	0.030**
	(0.011)	(0.012)
Percent of dependent household members	−0.001	−0.001
	(0.001)	(0.001)
Percent of female household members	0.001	0.001
	(0.001)	(0.001)
Household asset ownership	0.051	
	(0.053)	
Sum household assets		0.019
		(0.015)
Constant	0.661***	0.672***
	(0.148)	(0.160)
Fixed district effects	yes	yes
Number of observations	954	954
Log-likelihood ratio	79.835***	81.299***
Adjusted R^2	0.064	0.065

Source: Authors, based on data from ISEC-IFPRI Survey 2006.
Note: See notes to table 5.4. Figures show ordinary least squares regression. The dependent variable is the number of institutions to which a household belongs. The variable captures membership in the following institutions: village development committees, self-help groups, finance and credit groups, cooperative milk or other societies, women's groups, forest user groups, tank management groups, biogas user groups, water users associations, religious groups, caste associations, and other groups. The maximum number of memberships per household is 12.
***Significant at the 1% level; **significant at the 5% level.

Facilitation of access to agricultural extension was not listed. Milk marketing was cited as the main activity of dairy cooperatives, but they also provide livestock services, such as artificial insemination and veterinary services. The water and sanitation committees had been set up under various programs, including the World Bank–supported rural water and sanitation projects. Members of these committees mentioned the construction and maintenance of drinking water facilities as their main responsibilities; awareness creation regarding sanitation issues did not feature prominently in their description of activities. These committees do not seem to play a major role in collecting fees for the maintenance of drinking water facilities. As indicated above, households that did pay a water tax paid it exclusively to gram panchayat officials. Vigilance committees are somewhat different from the other groups, as they are not membership organizations. They were set up to supervise the ration shops of the Public Distribution System (PDS). Women's self-help groups have been promoted under a variety of schemes, programs, and projects, including those supported by international development agencies. Under some of the initiatives, they were formed with the help of anganwadi workers.

The size of groups ranges from less than 15 (in the case of women's self-help groups) to several hundred members (in the case of farmers cooperatives) (table 5.13). Excluding the women's self-help groups, which by definition include only women, the male-female ratio ranges from 1.8 in the water and sanitation committees to 4.2 in the farmers cooperatives. Participation in the last meeting of the groups varies considerably, from 11 percent in the water and sanitation committees to 100 percent in the self-help groups.

The groups also differed regarding the frequency of their meetings. All self-help groups had met within the last month. In contrast, about 40 percent of the farmers cooperatives and dairy cooperatives had not met for a year or more (see annex table 5.A.9).

Women appeared to be underrepresented in the leadership of most organizations: none of the farmers cooperatives and only about 10 percent of the water and sanitation committees and the dairy cooperatives had female chairpersons, and very few had female secretaries (table 5.14). Forty percent of the vigilance committees had female chairpersons. The low prevalence of female chairpersons in most organizations occurs despite the fact that a quarter of the farmers cooperatives, more than half of the dairy cooperatives, and 45 percent of the water and sanitation committees reserved seats for women in executive positions. None of these groups had reserved seats for the chairperson, the

Table 5.13 Group Membership and Attendance at Meetings by Men and Women in Karnataka

Group	Average number of members		Male/female ratio	Percent of members attending last meetings	
	Male	Female		Male	Female
Farmers cooperative	706 (n = 18)	169 (n = 18)	4.2	42 (n = 17)	31 (n = 13)
Dairy cooperative society	209 (n = 27)	81 (n = 27)	2.6	43 (n = 26)	25 (n = 26)
Water and sanitation committee	186 (n = 31)	103 (n = 31)	1.8	11 (n = 29)	8 (n = 24)
Women's self-help group	0	14 (n = 41)	n.a.	0	100 (n = 46)

Source: ISEC-TISS-IFPRI Survey 2008.
Note: n.a. = Not applicable.

Table 5.14 Characteristics of Leaders of User Organizations
in Karnataka
(percentage of members of each group)

Item	Farmers cooperative (n = 20)	Dairy cooperative society (n = 29)	Water and sanitation committee (n = 40)	Vigilance committee (n = 27)	Women's self-help group (n = 50)
Chairperson holds other community or political position	5	14	55	43	12
Chairperson is member of gram panchayat	0	0	68	69	17
Chairperson is male	100	89	90	60	0
Secretary is male	100	97	94	100	0
Organization reserves seats in executive committee for women	25	55	45	68	n.a.
Caste of chair					
SC/ST	5	4	30	31	16
OBC	85	96	60	60	74
General	10	0	10	6	8
Other	0	0	0	3	2

Source: ISEC-TISS-IFPRI Survey 2008.
n.a. = Not applicable.

vice-chair, or the secretary, however. The share of SC/ST chairpersons was particularly low in farmers cooperatives; in contrast, in water and sanitation committees and vigilance committees, almost a third of the chairpersons came from these groups.

Dairy cooperative societies appear to be the most democratic type of user organization: in about a third of these societies, members elect their chairperson (table 5.15). In almost half of farmers cooperatives, the chairperson is elected by the executive committee or board. In more than a quarter of the water and sanitation committees, the chairperson is appointed by the gram panchayat and gram panchayat members; members elect their chairperson in just 5 percent of these committees. These figures indicate that competitive elections by members are not a major mechanism for creating accountability. How well the other mechanisms worked could not be explored. However, it is likely

	Table 5.15	Method of Choosing the Chairperson of User Organizations in Karnataka (percentage of members of each group)			
Method	Farmers cooperative (n = 20)	Dairy cooperative society (n = 29)	Water and sanitation committee (n = 40)	Vigilance committee (n = 27)	Women's self-help group (n = 50)
Elected by members	16	32	5	17	10
Elected by executive committee/ board	47	25	0	0	0
Appointed by members in a meeting	16	32	33	37	52
Appointed by gram panchayat	0	0	28	43	0
Informal agreement among users	0	0	10	0	0
Other	21	11	25	3	38

Source: ISEC-TISS-IFPRI Survey 2008.

that appointment by members at a meeting creates more accountability to users than appointment by a government official.

GHANA

Households' Access to and Satisfaction with Services

This section presents the findings of the household survey regarding access to and satisfaction with services in Ghana. Because opportunities for and constraints on the provision of agricultural services and drinking water there vary widely across agroecological zones, the data are disaggregated by zone.

The percentage of households headed by women ranges across the zones, with women heading 9 percent of household in the savannah zone, 18 percent in the transition zone, and more than 30 percent in the forest zone (see annex table 5.A.10). Other variables—including occupation, household assets, availability of services, and village infrastructure and projects—also differ across zones (see annex tables 5.A.11 and 5.A.12).

Agricultural Extension

Extension coverage in Ghana was low among both men and women. Only about 12 percent of male-headed households received a visit from an agricultural extension agent (table 5.16). The percentage of male household heads who met with a livestock officer ranged from 5 percent in the forest zone to 34 percent in the savannah zone, reflecting the differences in livestock-keeping across these regions. Women had extremely limited access to agricultural extension in Ghana: only 2 percent of the female-headed households in the transition zone received a visit from an agricultural extension agent; none of the female-headed households in the other two zones received such a visit. Access of female spouses to agricultural extension was also very limited. In the transition and savannah zones, female household heads and spouses had better access to livestock services.

The number of respondents who did not receive a visit despite a request for one was very small. This may indicate either low demand for extension or a reluctance to answer this question. The only two respondents who did answer this question regarding agricultural extension agents said the reason was that they were not able to pay the money the agent requested for a visit. In the case of livestock officers, two out of five persons who answered the question offered the same reason.

Access to community meetings or group meetings held by extension agents or livestock officers was higher (table 5.17). Female spouses were more likely to participate in both community and group meetings than were female household heads. This may imply that they participate with their husband or that they have more time to participate in such meetings. As indicated above, the share of female-headed households was lower in the savannah zone, yet no female household head in this zone attended either a community or a group meeting about agricultural or livestock issues. The difference in attendance by

Table 5.16 Visits by Agricultural Extension Agents and Livestock Officers to Households in Ghana, by Zone and Type of Respondent (percentage of members of each group)

Service provider/zone	Male-headed households	Female-headed households	Female spouses
Agricultural extension agent	(n = 767)	(n = 125)	(n = 607)
Forest	11.7	0	1.8
Transition	12.3	2.1	1.4
Savannah	10.9	0	0.5
Livestock officer	(n = 677)	(n = 108)	(n = 92)
Forest	5.0	0	0
Transition	18.0	24.2	5.3
Savannah	33.9	15.0	15.0

Source: ISSER-IFPRI Survey 2008.
Note: Figures refer only to households in the sample that cultivated land (for extension agent visits) or kept livestock (for livestock officer visits).

Table 5.17 Attendance at Meetings on Agricultural or Livestock in Ghana, by Zone and Type of Respondent (percentage of members of each group)

Zone	Attended community meeting about agricultural issues			Attended group meeting with extension agent or livestock officer		
	Male household heads (n = 767)	Female household heads (n = 125)	Female spouses (n = 607)	Male household heads (n = 677)	Female household heads (n = 108)	Female spouses (n = 92)
Forest	17.5	1.9	5.4	10.8	1.9	5.3
Transition	17.1	6.3	7.7	15.2	4.2	6.4
Savannah	23.6	0	8.7	13.2	0	6.5

Source: ISSER-IFPRI Survey 2008.

male and female household heads was statistically significant. The vast majority of both men and women who did not attend meetings failed to do so because such meetings were not held in their villages (see annex table 5.A.13).

Only one respondent who received an extension visit at home indicated that the visit was from an NGO agricultural extension provider. This suggests that the public sector (the Ministry of Food and Agriculture [MoFA]) is almost the sole provider of home visits. Although the share of households that received home visits was low, those who received extension seemed to be satisfied with the quality of the service: 85 of 96 respondents (89 percent) who received a visit of an extension agent at their home were "highly satisfied" with the quality of information provided, and the remaining 11 were "somewhat satisfied." The percentages for spouses were similar.

MoFA organized two-thirds of the community meetings that dealt with agricultural or livestock issues; 14 percent were organized by NGOs and 30 percent by others (unit committees were mentioned most frequently among the others) (table 5.18). Chiefs and cooperatives also organized meetings. Private sector entities were not mentioned among the organizers of such meetings. In general, satisfaction rates with meetings were very high: 90 percent of respondents were very satisfied with the information provided at the MoFA meetings. For NGO meetings, the percentage was 72 percent. The NGO meetings tended to be slightly more demand driven: 28 percent of respondents said the NGO meeting was held on request; the figure for MoFA meetings was 19 percent.

NGOs and other organizations organized more than one-third of the community meetings that dealt with agriculture or livestock issues. In contrast, 90 percent of the meetings with farmers' groups were held by MoFA extension agents. Only 4 percent of such group meetings were held by NGOs. Satisfaction rates for the group meetings were similar to those for community-based meetings.

Item	MoFA (n = 193)	NGO (n = 39)	Other (n = 59)
Share of all meetings	66	14	20
Level of satisfaction			
Very satisfied	90	72	80
Somewhat satisfied	6	23	15
Somewhat dissatisfied	1	0	2
Very dissatisfied	3	5	3

Table 5.18 Satisfaction with Community Meetings in Ghana, by Type of Provider (percentage of respondents)

Source: ISSER-IFPRI Survey 2008.

Very few farmers received services beyond those they received from their local agricultural extension agents and livestock officers. Among the 4 percent of households that sought services, most sought extension at MoFA district offices. Only 2 percent of farmers visited agricultural research stations, and only 3 percent visited demonstration plots outside their village.

In view of the limited role of NGOs and others as service providers of agricultural extension services, the analysis concentrated on MoFA as service provider. MoFA extension agents transfer various types of technologies to farmers (see annex table 5.A.14). Extension agents often promoted technologies and practices that are not directly related to agriculture, such as HIV/AIDS sensitization,[4] which reached women to a considerable extent. Sanitation and hygiene reached almost twice as many women as men. This high percentage may reflect the fact that such activities may be promoted under the Women in Agriculture program, which targets women.

The share of women who had access to extension regarding marketing is also relatively high. This finding may reflect the prominence of women in agricultural marketing in Ghana. Additional information collected during the survey suggests that the main planting technique promoted is the planting of maize in rows, which seems popular among extension agents because it can be adopted without requiring purchased inputs.

The number of technologies promoted is impressive—but the share of households that actually tried a new practice was low. Only 15 percent of male household heads and 7 percent of the female household heads and 5 percent of the spouses had tried a new technology or farming practice in the past two years (table 5.19).

For more than half of both household heads and spouses, the MoFA extension agent was the main source of information (table 5.20). Radio was more frequently the information source about new technologies for spouses than for household heads.

Table 5.19 Use of New Technologies and Farming Practices in Ghana, by Type of Respondent

Respondents	Percentage using new technology and farming practices
Male household heads (n = 751)	14.8
Female household heads (n = 127)	7.1
Female spouses (n = 612)	4.6

Source: ISSER/IFPRI Survey 2008.
Note: The interview question was, "During the past two years, did you start some new farming practice, such as a new variety, new crop, new input, new cultivation technique, etc.?"

Table 5.20 Sources of Agricultural Information in Ghana, by Type of Respondent (percentage of members of each group)

Main source of information	Male household heads (n = 122)	Female household heads (n = 9)	Female spouses (n = 33)
Extension agent	61.5	66.7	60.6
Other farmer	15.6	22.2	6.1
Input dealer	2.5	0	9.1
Radio	7.4	0	9.1
NGO	4.9	11.1	3.0
Other	8.2	0	12.1

Source: ISSER/IFPRI Survey 2008.

Although the sample covered almost 1,200 household heads and more than 600 spouses, the figures on information sources are sparse because of low adoption rates. Still, they seem to indicate that public sector extension agents remain the main source of new technology and farming practices. In about 60 percent of the cases, the new farming technology or practice involved additional costs. In one-third of the cases, the new technology adopted required more family labor input. There were no major differences between household heads and spouses in this respect. All spouses and 94 percent of household heads indicated that they wanted to continue the new practice because it was beneficial to them.

Drinking Water

The main sources of drinking water vary across ecological zones (table 5.21). In the forest zone, about one-third of households obtained their water primarily from rivers or lakes, wells without pumps, and other potentially unsafe water sources. Obtaining water from open natural water bodies was less common in the savannah region, which has dry agroecological conditions. In both

Table 5.21 Primary Water Sources of Households in Ghana, by Zone
(percentage of households)

Source of water	Forest (n = 386)	Transition (n = 330)	Savannah (n = 377)	Total (n = 1,093)
Potentially unsafe sources				
River/lake/spring	22.3	31.2	18.8	23.8
Well without pump[a]	8.6	12.4	12.7	11.2
Water vendor	0.3	0.3	0.0	0.2
Other	0.3	4.4	8.8	4.4
Subtotal	31.4	48.4	40.3	39.5
Safe sources				
Borehole/well with pump	40.7	29.4	27.9	32.9
Public standpipe	22.3	17.3	28.9	23.1
Private standpipe	2.1	2.1	0.8	1.7
Rainwater	3.6	1.5	1.3	2.2
Indoor plumbing	0.0	0.6	0.0	0.2
Inside standpipe	0.0	0.9	0.5	0.5
Subtotal	68.7	51.8	59.4	60.4

Source: ISSER-IFPRI Survey 2008.
a. Wells without pumps are considered safe if covered.

the transition and the savannah zones, about 60 percent of households reported getting their water from safe water sources, mostly boreholes and public standpipes; the proportion of households that obtained water from private standpipes, indoor plumbing, and indoor standpipes was negligible. Few households reported using rainwater, and only one household reported using a water vendor as primary water source.

In all zones, the person in charge of fetching water was most likely to be a child. However, a significant proportion of household heads (12 percent of male household heads and 18 percent of female household heads) reported being responsible for fetching water for the house. The percentage for male household heads was lower in the savannah zone.

The average time to travel to and fetch water varies by zone and gender (table 5.22). Members of households with political connections tended to have access to safer drinking water (see annex table 5.A.15).

In each ecological zone, the proportion of people satisfied with the quality of water was lowest among those whose primary water source was an open lake or spring (table 5.23). Less than 60 percent of households who obtained their water from this source were satisfied with the quality in the transition and savannah zone; in the forest zone, 82 percent were satisfied. There is no statistically significant difference between the responses of female and male respondents.

More than 90 percent of all surveyed household members did not contact anyone when they were dissatisfied with their drinking water. Male household heads (11 percent) were most likely to contact someone, followed by female

Table 5.22 Average Time Required to Access Water in Ghana (minutes)

Group of respondents	Forest	Transition	Savannah
Female household heads	25	25	31
	(n = 63)	(n = 103)	(n = 26)
Male household heads	19	20	26
	(n = 308)	(n = 225)	(n = 329)
Female spouses	23	22	23
	(n = 205)	(n = 147)	(n = 163)

Source: ISSER-IFPRI Survey 2008.

Table 5.23 Satisfaction with Drinking Water in Ghana (percentage of households satisfied with quantity or quality of water from primary source)

Zone/source of water	Satisfied with water quantity	Satisfied with water quality
Forest zone		
River/lake/spring	90	82
	n = 99	n = 78
Borehole/well with pump	88	84
	n = 89	n = 73
Well without pump	86	86
	n = 37	n = 28
Public standpipe	92	87
	n = 48	n = 37
Transition zone		
River/lake/spring	95	56
	n = 86	n = 85
Borehole/well with pump	96	97
	n = 157	n = 157
Well without pump	100	84
	n = 33	n = 32
Public standpipe	100	100
	n = 86	n = 81
Savannah zone		
River/lake/spring	87	57
	n = 71	n = 68
Borehole/well with pump	93	99
	n = 105	n = 98
Well without pump	90	78
	n = 48	n = 45
Public standpipe	99	97
	n = 109	n = 108

Source: ISSER-IFPRI Survey 2008.

household heads (8 percent) and female spouses in male-headed households (6 percent). Considering that drinking water was reported to be the main concern of the households (see next section), it is surprising more households did not take action to address the problem. Even in the forest zone, where 44 percent of the 30 percent of households whose primary water source was a lake or spring were unsatisfied with the quality of their water, only 6 percent of household heads ever complained to an authority.

Priorities for Service Provision

In each zone, district assembly members, male household heads, female household heads, female spouses, and community leaders were asked to list the three most important areas of concern and then to rank the three. The results show little disagreement between the priority concerns of men and women.

In the savannah zone, the majority of respondents in all categories ranked drinking water as the main area of concern (table 5.24). Drinking water is the main concern for the majority of female spouses and community leaders in the forest and transition zones as well. In the transition zone, the majority of female household heads also rank water first. In contrast, male household heads and district assembly members more often identify roads as their top concern. Among all household heads and community leaders in the transition zone, roads were the second most important concern. In the forest zone, district assembly members and all household heads ranked water, sanitation, and roads in almost equal shares as their top concern.

Lack of livelihood opportunities was the second most popular concern for female spouses in all ecological zones. District assembly members in the savannah zone also ranked this concern high. In the transition zone, the proportion of both community leaders and district assembly members that cited lack of livelihood opportunities or lack of electricity as the primary concern was considerably lower than the proportion of households that did so. In the savannah zone, the proportion of district assembly members and community leaders that cited sanitation as the priority concern was significantly higher than it was among households.

The next most important problem is road infrastructure. Problems related to sanitation are more often reported as a priority in the forest and transition zones than in the savannah zone. Female spouses appeared to be more concerned with livelihood opportunities than were household heads (male or female) in all ecological zones.

Factors Associated with Access and Satisfaction

Being a male-headed household seems to be the most important factor associated with being visited by an agricultural extension agent (table 5.25). Some measures of wealth (measured by ownership of a TV, sheep, and chickens) also had a positive and significant impact on receiving an extension visit. Such an

Table 5.24 Top-Ranked Service Area of Concern in Ghana, by Zone (percentage of respondents citing concern as most important)

Zone/Service area	District assembly members (n = 36)	Male household head (n = 264)	Female household head (n = 120)	Female spouses (n = 167)	Community leaders (n = 83)
Forest					
Water	22	17	17	21	25
Sanitation	19	17	24	13	17
Roads	22	17	17	15	13
Livelihoods	3	12	12	15	2
Electricity	6	11	13	14	7
Education	8	9	4	6	8
Irrigation	0	0	0	1	0
Health facilities	0	4	3	4	11
Street lights	0	0	0	1	0

	District assembly members (n = 37)	Male household head (n = 316)	Female household head (n = 69)	Female spouses (n = 221)	Community leaders (n = 64)
Transition					
Water	19	15	32	27	20
Sanitation	3	12	9	13	11
Roads	24	16	26	16	16
Livelihoods	5	14	10	18	11
Electricity	11	12	10	12	14
Education	16	9	7	6	14
Irrigation	0	0	0	0	0
Health facilities	3	12	3	7	9
Street lights	0	2	0	0	0

	District assembly members (n = 40)	Male household head (n = 346)	Female household head (n = 30)	Female spouses (n = 185)	Community leaders (n = 84)
Savannah					
Water	33	45	45	40	43
Sanitation	15	4	0	4	7
Roads	10	18	18	15	14
Livelihoods	13	12	6	23	8
Electricity	5	7	6	8	5
Education	3	4	6	4	12
Irrigation	0	0	0	1	1
Health facilities	0	5	9	6	1
Street lights	0	1	3	0	0

Source: ISSER-IFPRI Survey 2008.
Note: Respondents were asked to list the three most important service areas of concern and then rank the three in terms of their importance. The table refers to percentage of respondents in the respective category that ranked the respective service number 1.

Table 5.25 Factors Associated with Visit of Agricultural Extension Agent in Ghana

Variable	(1)	(2)	(3)	(4)	(5)	(6)
Literate	-0.00872	-0.00665	-0.00670	-0.0271	-0.00809	-0.0191
	(0.0493)	(0.0490)	(0.0491)	(0.0496)	(0.0496)	(0.0497)
Male head	0.0441	0.0403	0.0433	0.0384	0.0450	0.0403
	(0.0297)	(0.0295)	(0.0296)	(0.0304)	(0.0309)	(0.0305)
Male head*literate	0.0346	0.0303	0.0339	0.0453	0.0362	0.0390
	(0.0528)	(0.0524)	(0.0526)	(0.0530)	(0.0532)	(0.0531)
Forest zone	-0.0243	-0.0250	-0.0241	-0.0195	-0.0223	-0.0196
	(0.0238)	(0.0237)	(0.0238)	(0.0239)	(0.0240)	(0.0240)
Transition zone	-0.0151	-0.0133	-0.0158	-0.0121	-0.0137	-0.0117
	(0.0217)	(0.0216)	(0.0217)	(0.0218)	(0.0219)	(0.0219)
Goat index	0.00604					
	(0.00783)					
Sheep index		0.0248***				
		(0.00737)				
Chicken index			0.0159**			
			(0.00741)			
TV				0.0290***		
				(0.00956)		
Radio					-0.00272	
					(0.00880)	
Mobile phone						0.0172*
						(0.00895)
Constant	0.0283	0.0302	0.0279	0.0381	0.0257	0.0335
	(0.0304)	(0.0302)	(0.0303)	(0.0315)	(0.0318)	(0.0316)
Number of observations	861	861	861	849	849	849
R^2	0.012	0.024	0.016	0.022	0.011	0.015

Source: Authors, based on ISSER-IFPRI Survey 2008.

Note: Standard errors in parentheses. All livestock indices (wealth indicators) refer to Z scores within agroecological zones.

***Significant at the 1% level; **significant at the 5% level; *significant at the 10% level.

agent visit was positively and significantly associated with adoption of a new agricultural technique. The literacy of the household head mattered for male-headed household. Richer households (using ownership of a TV and sheep as a measure of wealth) were more likely to adopt new practices (table 5.26).

Male-headed households were more likely to access a primary improved water source and to live near a water source (tables 5.27–5.31). Wealth (using TV and mobile phone ownership as a proxy) increased access to improved water sources, and households with literate heads spent less time accessing water. People who got their water from an improved water source were more likely to be satisfied with the quantity and quality of water. Literate households tended to be less satisfied with quality than illiterate ones. Regarding satisfaction with water quantity, there was no difference between literate and illiterate household heads or between male and female household heads. Wealthier households (proxied by mobile phone, chicken, and goat ownership) were less likely to complain about water; households with access to improved water sources were more likely to do so.

Service Providers: Capacity, Constraints, Incentives, and Accountability

This section presents findings on the capacity, constraints, and incentives faced by front-line staff in Ghana. It also examines mechanisms for creating accountability within service provision organizations.

Agricultural Extension

This section deals with agricultural extension. It is based mainly on the survey of extension agents.

Profile and capacity of extension agents. The extension agent survey covered 70 agricultural extension agents who served in the areas in which the household survey was conducted. Ten were female (2 out of 24 in the forest zone, 3 out of 28 in the transition zone, and 5 out of 16 in the savannah zone). About 40 percent of the male extension agents were 29–40; about the same share were 50 or older (table 5.32). The age distribution was younger among women.

Under the training and visit system, the predominant mode of operation was individual visits to leading farmers or model farmers, who were then expected to pass on information to other farmers in their location. Since the abolishment of the training and visit system in the late 1990s, more emphasis has been placed on the group approach. Despite this official policy shift, the main mode of interaction with households remains farm visits, which about half of all agents cited as the main mode of extension. Meeting with FBOs was identified as the main mode by 34 percent of extension agents. There was no statistically significant difference between the types of technologies promoted by female and male extension agents in the last year. Among both male and

Table 5.26 Factors Associated with Adoption of New Agricultural Practices in Ghana

Variable	(1)	(2)	(3)	(4)	(5)	(6)
Visit by agricultural extension agent	0.189***	0.181***	0.187***	0.169***	0.177***	0.177***
	(0.0448)	(0.0450)	(0.0449)	(0.0453)	(0.0452)	(0.0453)
Literate	-0.0441	-0.0418	-0.0351	-0.0588	-0.0441	-0.0445
	(0.0645)	(0.0644)	(0.0644)	(0.0653)	(0.0651)	(0.0653)
Male head*literate	0.115*	0.112	0.121*	0.123*	0.115*	0.116*
	(0.0691)	(0.0690)	(0.0687)	(0.0697)	(0.0698)	(0.0697)
Male head	0.0314	0.0302	0.0153	0.0265	0.0316	0.0302
	(0.0390)	(0.0389)	(0.0373)	(0.0400)	(0.0406)	(0.0401)
Forest zone	0.0611*	0.0606*		0.0611*	0.0593*	0.0589*
	(0.0312)	(0.0311)		(0.0315)	(0.0315)	(0.0316)
Transition zone	0.0107	0.0116		0.0134	0.0123	0.0121
	(0.0284)	(0.0284)		(0.0287)	(0.0287)	(0.0288)
Goat index	0.00873					
	(0.0102)					
Sheep index		0.0174*				
		(0.00976)				
Chicken index			0.000964			
			(0.00976)			
TV				0.0218*		
				(0.0126)		
Radio					-0.00290	
					(0.0115)	
Mobile phone						-0.00122
						(0.0118)
Constant	0.0365	0.0372	0.0646*	0.0464	0.0364	0.0374
	(0.0398)	(0.0397)	(0.0337)	(0.0415)	(0.0417)	(0.0415)
Number of observations	861	861	861	849	849	849
R^2	0.048	0.051	0.042	0.047	0.044	0.044

Source: Authors, based on data from ISSER-IFPRI Survey 2008.

Note: Standard errors in parentheses. All livestock indices (wealth indicators) refer to Z scores within agroecological zones.

***Significant at the 1% level; *significant at the 10% level.

Table 5.27 Factors Associated with Access to Clean Water in Ghana

Variable	(1)	(2)	(3)	(4)	(5)	(6)
Literate	0.0323	0.0332	0.0334	0.00679	0.0283	0.0107
	(0.0651)	(0.0651)	(0.0650)	(0.0655)	(0.0658)	(0.0660)
Male head	0.0829*	0.0790*	0.0772*	0.0806*	0.0768	0.0774*
	(0.0451)	(0.0451)	(0.0451)	(0.0458)	(0.0470)	(0.0461)
Male head*literate	0.00740	0.00843	0.00965	0.00504	0.00988	0.00919
	(0.0717)	(0.0716)	(0.0716)	(0.0718)	(0.0724)	(0.0721)
Forest zone	−0.207***	−0.211***	−0.211***	−0.193***	−0.204***	−0.196***
	(0.0370)	(0.0369)	(0.0369)	(0.0372)	(0.0374)	(0.0374)
Transition zone	0.141***	0.138***	0.137***	0.155***	0.145***	0.152***
	(0.0356)	(0.0355)	(0.0355)	(0.0358)	(0.0359)	(0.0359)
Goat index	−0.00836					
	(0.0135)					
Sheep index		0.00550				
		(0.0134)				
Chicken index			0.0157			
			(0.0135)			
TV				0.0518***		
				(0.0139)		
Radio					0.00810	
					(0.0140)	
Mobile phone						0.0329**
						(0.0141)
Constant	0.295***	0.299***	0.301***	0.300***	0.298***	0.301***
	(0.0455)	(0.0455)	(0.0455)	(0.0466)	(0.0476)	(0.0468)
Number of observations	1,143	1,145	1,145	1,129	1,129	1,129
R^2	0.102	0.102	0.103	0.113	0.102	0.106

Source: Authors, based on data from ISSER-IFPRI Survey 2008.

Note: Standard errors in parentheses. All livestock indices (wealth indicators) refer to Z scores within agroecological zones.

***Significant at the 1% level; **significant at the 5% level; *significant at the 10% level.

Table 5.28 Factors Associated with Average Time Taken to Access Water in Ghana

Variable	(1)	(2)	(3)	(4)	(5)	(6)
Clean water	0.891	0.904	0.829	0.713	0.669	0.692
	(1.034)	(1.032)	(1.033)	(1.046)	(1.040)	(1.042)
Literate	−5.417**	−5.439**	−5.411**	−5.234**	−5.231**	−5.204**
	(2.329)	(2.327)	(2.327)	(2.354)	(2.352)	(2.363)
Male head	−7.327***	−7.179***	−7.370***	−7.133***	−6.967***	−7.113***
	(1.624)	(1.624)	(1.623)	(1.658)	(1.688)	(1.659)
Male head*literate	7.911***	7.932***	7.924***	7.810***	7.715***	7.799***
	(2.562)	(2.559)	(2.559)	(2.581)	(2.586)	(2.581)
Forest zone	−1.628	−1.540	−1.651	−1.587	−1.534	−1.603
	(1.351)	(1.350)	(1.350)	(1.360)	(1.360)	(1.362)
Transition zone	−3.993***	−3.938***	−3.989***	−3.962***	−3.905***	−3.968***
	(1.254)	(1.251)	(1.251)	(1.268)	(1.263)	(1.270)
Goat index	0.153					
	(0.468)					
Sheep index		−0.532				
		(0.500)				
Chicken index			0.450			
			(0.472)			
TV				−0.242		
				(0.497)		
Radio					−0.275	
					(0.497)	
Mobile phone						−0.229
						(0.500)
Constant	18.53***	18.35***	18.58***	18.37***	18.25***	18.36***
	(1.670)	(1.673)	(1.670)	(1.715)	(1.739)	(1.717)
Number of observations	1,061	1,062	1,062	1,049	1,049	1,049
R^2	0.026	0.027	0.027	0.024	0.024	0.024

Source: Authors, based on data from ISSER-IFPRI Survey 2008.

Note: Standard errors in parentheses. All livestock indices (wealth indicators) refer to Z scores within agroecological zones.

***Significant at the 1% level; **significant at the 5% level; *significant at the 10% level.

Table 5.29 Factors Associated with Satisfaction with Quantity of Water in Ghana

Variable	(1)	(2)	(3)	(4)	(5)	(6)
Clean water	0.0320*	0.0320*	0.0315*	0.0364**	0.0373**	0.0368**
	(0.0173)	(0.0173)	(0.0173)	(0.0174)	(0.0173)	(0.0173)
Literate	-0.00150	-0.00143	-0.00129	-0.00482	-3.78e-05	-0.00457
	(0.0393)	(0.0393)	(0.0393)	(0.0395)	(0.0396)	(0.0397)
Male head	0.0158	0.0161	0.0152	0.0116	0.0165	0.0115
	(0.0270)	(0.0270)	(0.0269)	(0.0274)	(0.0280)	(0.0275)
Male head*literate	-0.0160	-0.0156	-0.0152	-0.00984	-0.0128	-0.00965
	(0.0432)	(0.0432)	(0.0432)	(0.0433)	(0.0434)	(0.0433)
Forest zone	-0.00912	-0.00942	-0.01000	-0.0105	-0.0103	-0.0106
	(0.0226)	(0.0226)	(0.0226)	(0.0226)	(0.0226)	(0.0227)
Transition zone	0.0637***	0.0634***	0.0631***	0.0638***	0.0634***	0.0636***
	(0.0208)	(0.0208)	(0.0208)	(0.0209)	(0.0208)	(0.0210)
Goat index	0.00382					
	(0.00791)					
Sheep		0.000914				
		(0.00828)				
Chicken			0.00600			
			(0.00780)			
TV				0.00236		
				(0.00833)		
Radio					-0.00735	
					(0.00825)	
Mobile phone						0.00119
						(0.00838)
Constant	0.887***	0.887***	0.888***	0.889***	0.884***	0.889***
	(0.0276)	(0.0277)	(0.0276)	(0.0283)	(0.0288)	(0.0284)
Number of observations	1,064	1,065	1,065	1,051	1,051	1,051
R²	0.023	0.022	0.023	0.025	0.026	0.025

Source: Authors, based on data from ISSER-IFPRI Survey 2008.

Note: Standard errors in parentheses. All livestock indices (wealth indicators) refer to Z scores within agroecological zones.

***Significant at the 1% level; **significant at the 5% level; *significant at the 10% level.

Table 5.30 Factors Associated with Satisfaction with Quality of Water in Ghana

Variable	(1)	(2)	(3)	(4)	(5)	(6)
Clean water	0.142***	0.142***	0.142***	0.146***	0.146***	0.147***
	(0.0231)	(0.0231)	(0.0231)	(0.0235)	(0.0233)	(0.0233)
Literate	-0.109**	-0.110**	-0.109**	-0.108*	-0.103*	-0.0995*
	(0.0557)	(0.0557)	(0.0557)	(0.0564)	(0.0564)	(0.0566)
Male head	0.00654	0.00390	0.00410	0.00471	0.0123	0.00607
	(0.0378)	(0.0378)	(0.0378)	(0.0389)	(0.0396)	(0.0389)
Male head*literate	0.0575	0.0578	0.0581	0.0574	0.0527	0.0560
	(0.0608)	(0.0608)	(0.0608)	(0.0614)	(0.0615)	(0.0613)
Forest zone	0.0474	0.0457	0.0458	0.0437	0.0454	0.0416
	(0.0320)	(0.0320)	(0.0320)	(0.0322)	(0.0322)	(0.0322)
Transition zone	0.0384	0.0374	0.0375	0.0337	0.0343	0.0307
	(0.0278)	(0.0277)	(0.0277)	(0.0281)	(0.0280)	(0.0281)
Goat index	-0.00632					
	(0.0104)					
Sheep index		0.00471				
		(0.0111)				
Chicken index			0.00476			
			(0.0103)			
TV				-0.00135		
				(0.0115)		
Radio					-0.0114	
					(0.0114)	
Mobile phone						-0.0146
						(0.0114)
Constant	0.795***	0.798***	0.798***	0.798***	0.791***	0.795***
	(0.0386)	(0.0387)	(0.0386)	(0.0401)	(0.0406)	(0.0400)
Number of observations	976	977	977	963	963	963
R^2	0.047	0.047	0.047	0.048	0.049	0.049

Source: Authors, based on data from ISSER-IFPRI Survey 2008.

Note: Standard errors in parentheses. All livestock indices (wealth indicators) refer to Z scores within agroecological zones.

***Significant at the 1% level; **significant at the 5% level; *significant at the 10% level.

Table 5.31 Factors Associated with Complaints about Water in Ghana

Variable	(1)	(2)	(3)	(4)	(5)	(6)
Clean water	0.0511**	0.0529***	0.0545***	0.0537**	0.0528**	0.0560***
	(0.0204)	(0.0204)	(0.0205)	(0.0208)	(0.0207)	(0.0207)
Literate	-0.0358	-0.0379	-0.0355	-0.0311	-0.0312	-0.0213
	(0.0457)	(0.0459)	(0.0460)	(0.0468)	(0.0469)	(0.0470)
Male head	0.0150	0.0103	0.0117	0.0114	0.0137	0.0141
	(0.0320)	(0.0322)	(0.0323)	(0.0332)	(0.0340)	(0.0332)
Male head*literate	-0.0590	-0.0565	-0.0605	-0.0609	-0.0626	-0.0615
	(0.0503)	(0.0505)	(0.0506)	(0.0514)	(0.0515)	(0.0513)
Forest zone	0.00701	0.00583	0.00589	0.00739	0.00791	0.00497
	(0.0262)	(0.0263)	(0.0263)	(0.0267)	(0.0267)	(0.0267)
Transition zone	0.0734***	0.0733***	0.0732***	0.0742***	0.0751***	0.0708***
	(0.0248)	(0.0248)	(0.0249)	(0.0254)	(0.0253)	(0.0254)
Goat index	-0.0323***					
	(0.00944)					
Sheep index		-0.0183*				
		(0.0101)				
Chicken index			-0.0165			
			(0.0115)			
TV				-0.00427		
				(0.00991)		
Radio					-0.00326	
					(0.0100)	
Mobile phone						-0.0197**
						(0.00996)
Constant	1.881***	1.884***	1.883***	1.880***	1.879***	1.875***
	(0.0327)	(0.0328)	(0.0329)	(0.0342)	(0.0347)	(0.0342)
Number of observations	1,000	1,001	1,001	988	988	988
R^2	0.048	0.040	0.039	0.037	0.037	0.040

Source: Authors, based on data from ISSER-IFPRI Survey 2008.

Note: Standard errors in parentheses. All livestock indices (wealth indicators) refer to Z scores within agroecological zones.

***Significant at the 1% level; **significant at the 5% level; *significant at the 10% level.

Table 5.32 Age Profile of Extension Agents in Ghana		
Age	Male (n = 59)	Female (n = 9)
Below 30	1.7	11.1
30–39	15.3	22.2
40–49	44.1	22.2
50 and above	39.0	44.4

Source: ISSER/IFPRI Survey 2008.

female extension agents, 40 percent reported learning of some of the technologies they transfer after they joined the service. Two-thirds of all extension agents stated that they received training that had a gender component; 7 percent reported receiving training that was totally targeted to gender issues.

Both male and female extension agents believed that a bad extension agent is one who makes limited farm visits. Based on self-reported activities by extension agents, female agents were just as likely to establish and run demonstration plots as their male counterparts. However, there seems to be a difference in terms of outreach. Female extension agents reported that they serve on average 430 farmers; the average for male extension agents is 2,220. Although the literature suggests that limited transportation is an important obstacle for female extension agents, this does not seem to be the reason for the lower reported outreach figures (see below). There may be differences in reporting between male and female extension agents.

According to self-reported figures, female extension workers serve a higher proportion of female farmers than male extension workers (the average ratio of women to men is 1.3 for female agents and 0.53 for male agents). This difference may partly reflect the fact that men and women promote different technologies. However, even for the major agricultural technologies—planting techniques, improved planting materials, and postharvesting techniques—female extension agents serve a higher proportion of women. The ratio of females to males in technologies disseminated by female extension agents is 0.75; the corresponding ratio for male extension agents is 0.45–0.52. This suggests that extension services from female extension agents are better targeted to female farmers. This conclusion is supported by the fact that when asked what their major responsibilities as extension agents were, 20 percent of the female extension agents mentioned improving income opportunities for women. In contrast, just 11 percent of male extension agents considered this a primary responsibility. The proportion of extension agents that viewed it their duty to address the specific concerns of female farmers was low among both male and female extension agents.

Mission orientation and constraints. No major gender differences could be observed regarding extension agents' perceptions of the central mission or job of their office: about 80 percent of both male and female extension agents considered increasing farmer's income as the main mission of their MoFA district office, followed by the distribution of technology. More than half considered monitoring crop and livestock diseases among their central tasks, and one-fifth cited distribution of agricultural input. Sixty percent of both male and female extension agents cited improving nutrition among the central tasks of their office.

Responses to the question, "What do you consider to be the biggest success in your professional career so far?" vary (table 5.33). Of the extension agents who gave answers related to farmers' adoption of the technology they promoted, 37 percent were male and 13 percent female. One-quarter of male extension agents and half of female extension agents considered the biggest success of their career to be that farmers they had supported had won a best-farmer award. Other top achievements included career-related objectives (such as promotions), the formation of farmers groups, and increases in farmers' income and well-being. Only one of the 70 agents interviewed considered an increase in productivity to be the biggest success of his career.

The answers to this question have to be interpreted with care, as perceptions of success do not necessarily imply that extension agents align their efforts accordingly. Still, one may ask whether the attention given to winning awards induces extension agents to spend more time working with farmers who have the prospects of doing so (and may already be advanced) than working with a broader group of disadvantaged clients.

Male extension agents considered transportation the biggest constraint to achieving their mission, whereas half of the female extension agents considered farmer-related problems, such as lack of access to credit, to be the most important constraint (table 5.34). (These figures have to be interpreted with care, as the

Table 5.33   Achievements Male and Female Extension Agents View as "Biggest Success" in Ghana

Achievement	Male (n = 59)	Female (n = 8)
Farmers adopted new technologies	37.3	12.5
Helped farmers to win award	23.7	50.0
Personal career advancement	13.6	12.5
Disease control in livestock	6.8	0.0
Group formation by farmers	5.1	0.0
Farmers' income or well-being increased	3.4	12.5
Collaboration/appreciation by farmers	3.4	0.0
Increased production/productivity	1.7	0.0
Other	5.1	12.5

Source: ISSER/IFPRI Survey 2008.
Note: Question was asked as an open question and postcoded.

Table 5.34 Self-Reported Constraints Facing Male and Female Extension Agents in Ghana (percent)

Constraint	Male (n = 59)	Female (n = 10)
Lack of transportation	33.9	10.0
Lack of funds or inputs	23.7	10.0
Farmer-related problems	20.3	50.0
Lack of staff	6.8	10.0
Inputs not timely	3.4	10.0
Low income	5.1	0.0
Other	6.8	10.0
Total	100.0	100.0

Source: ISSER/IFPRI Survey 2008.
Note: Question was asked as an open question and postcoded.

number of female respondents is small.) This difference may partly reflect the fact that female extension agents are more likely to work with female farmers, who may face more obstacles to adopting new practices.

None of the extension agents cited political interference as a constraint in response to an open question. However, when asked whether they agreed or disagreed with the statement "There is hardly any political interference in your work," about 40 percent of both female and male extension agents disagreed.

Setting performance targets can play an important role in helping organizations achieve their mission. Forty-seven percent of the extension agents reported setting their own targets. Most agents cite the number of farmers to meet as targets, and these numbers vary considerably. Very few extension agents indicate production-related goals as targets.

Interactions between extension agents and political officeholders. Across ecological zones, a large proportion of extension agents had frequent (one to several times a month) interactions with individuals who hold political office in their area. The most common interaction (other than with farmers or supervisors) was with district assembly members, whom 75 percent of extension agents in the savannah zone, 52 percent in the transition zone, and 43 percent in the forest zone met (table 5.35). The large number of agents who meet with district assembly members may explain in part why political interference seems to be a problem in the savannah zone, where only 30 percent of male extension agents and 40 percent of female extension agents agreed with the statement that there is "hardly any political interference" (table 5.35).

The percentage of agricultural extension agents that met an agricultural researcher at least once during the previous year ranged from 7 percent in the transition zone to 38 percent in the savannah zone, suggesting weak linkages between agricultural research and extension. (To put these figures in perspective,

Table 5.35	Extension Agents' Interactions in Ghana, by Zone (percent)		
Person with whom extension agent met at least once during past year	Forest	Transition	Savannah
Assembly person	43	52	75
Unit committee member	13	59	44
District assembly member	17	22	44
Chief	35	30	38
NGO	35	26	56
Private input supplier	30	44	19
Farm gate buyer	9	33	13
Rural bank employee	13	11	19
Agricultural researcher	22	7	38
Regional MoFA staff	17	19	31
National ministry staff	0	7	6

Source: ISSER-IFPRI Survey 2008.

under the training and visit system, all extension agents were supposed to meet with researchers every two weeks.)

Extension agents' perceptions of work environment. Ninety percent of both male and female extension agents state that male and female extension staff have equal opportunities in getting promoted (table 5.36). Thirty-five percent of male extension agents and 56 percent of female agents disagree with the statement that corruption and misuse of funds is not a problem in the district office in which they are working; more than 60 percent of male extension agents and almost 45 percent of the female extension agents disagree with the statement that this is not a problem at other district offices and the head office. About half of both male and female extension agents disagree with the policies that they have to implement; 12 percent of the male extension agents strongly disagree. This can be interpreted as an indication that field staff have little influence on the policies developed by MoFA.

Extension agents' perceptions of farmers' constraints. In all ecological zones, respondents of all types identify financial constraints and poor access to credit as the main impediments preventing farmers from increasing crop production (table 5.37). Households rank issues related to pests and diseases as the next most important constraint. In the savannah zone, assembly members, community leaders, and extension agents do not recognize this as an important constraint to farmers. Although 2–5 percent of households state that their greatest constraint is lack of extension service, extension agents do not perceive a shortage of their services as a priority constraint. Although financial

GENDER AND GOVERNANCE IN RURAL SERVICES

Table 5.36

Table 5.36 Perceptions of Male and Female Extension Agents in Ghana (percent)

Statement	Male	Female
Male and female MoFA staff have equal opportunities in getting promoted	(n = 60)	(n = 10)
Strongly agree	20.0	30.0
Agree	71.7	60.0
Disagree	6.7	10.0
Strongly disagree	1.7	0.0
Corruption or misuse of funds is not a problem in this district office	(n = 60)	(n = 9)
Strongly agree	11.7	0.0
Agree	53.3	44.4
Disagree	26.7	55.6
Strongly disagree	8.3	0.0
Corruption or misuse of funds is not a problem in other districts and the head office	(n = 57)	(n = 10)
Strongly agree	5.3	0.0
Agree	31.6	44.4
Disagree	49.1	55.6
Strongly disagree	14.0	0.0
I often disagree with the policies or programs we are asked to implement	(n = 59)	(n = 10)
Strongly agree	8.5	0.0
Agree	35.6	50.0
Disagree	44.1	50.0
Strongly disagree	11.9	0.0
There is hardly any political interference in our work	(n = 60)	(n = 10)
Strongly agree	6.7	0.0
Agree	50.0	60.0
Disagree	28.3	40.0
Strongly disagree	15.0	0.0

Source: ISSER/IFPRI Survey 2008.

constraints are overwhelmingly the biggest constraint for the majority of farmers, a significant proportion indicate other constraints, such as lack of access to markets, the low price of outputs, or problems with diseases and pests. There may be an overemphasis on financial constraints as the main problem that farmers face.

Drinking Water Supply

Under Ghana's policy for drinking water supply, the Community Water and Sanitation Agency is in charge of rural drinking water. Unlike in the case of extension, this agency does not have district offices or field staff. The district

Table 5.37 Main Constraints to Increasing Income from Farming in Ghana, by Zone (percentage of group citing problem as main constraint)

Agroecological zone/constraint	Assembly members	Community leaders	Extension agents (of male farmers)	Extension agents (of female farmers)	Households
Forest zone	(n = 36)	(n = 220)	(n = 30)	(n = 30)	(n = 331)
Financial constraints	71	81	75	88	67
Pests and diseases	9	1	0	0	13
Lack of access to market or low prices	6	5	4	0	3
Lack of land or infertile land	0	4	0	0	1
Lack of extension or veterinary services	6	0	0	0	4
Postharvest losses	0	0	8	0	0
Lack of labor or tractor services	3	4	0	0	4
Poor weather	0	4	13	4	1
Other		1	0	8	6
Transition zone	(n = 36)	(n = 278)	(n = 24)	(n = 24)	(n = 251)
Financial constraints	65	92	60	53	64
Pests and diseases	16	0	10	3	12
Lack of access to market or low prices	3	3	0	3	5
Lack of land or infertile land	5	0	0	0	2
Lack of extension or veterinary services	0	0	0	0	2

	(n = 41)	(n = 296)	(n = 16)	(n = 16)	(n = 325)
Post harvest losses	0	0	10	13	1
Lack of labor or tractor services	0	0	0	0	4
Poor weather	8	3	17	16	3
Other	3	2	3	11	8
Savannah zone	(n = 41)	(n = 296)	(n = 16)	(n = 16)	(n = 325)
Financial constraints	66	66	88	81	56
Pests and diseases	0	0	0	0	16
Lack of access to market or low prices	2	2	0	0	17
Lack of land or infertile land	2	10	0	0	1
Lack of extension or veterinary services	5	0	0	0	5
Postharvest losses	0	0	13	6	0
Lack of labor or tractor services	0	0	0	0	4
Poor weather	22	17	0	0	9
Other	2	5	0	7	7

Source: ISSER-IFPRI Survey 2008.

administration is supposed to form district water and sanitation committees consisting of three people for each district. The team members are not hired specifically for the task and thus also serve other functions. Water and sanitation committees (WATSANs) at the village level are in charge of maintaining and operating drinking water facilities. NGOs are contracted to work with the communities and to assist the WATSANs. Private sector companies and NGOs are contracted by the district administration to establish drinking water facilities.

This section briefly describes the role of NGOs as service providers. WATSANs are discussed in the next section, on community-based organizations.

One field staff member from each of the 19 NGOs active in the area covered by the survey was interviewed. Just 3 of the 19 were female, suggesting that NGOs may not necessarily employ more female staff than public sector agencies. The average age was 41. One respondent mentioned empowerment of communities as the main mission of the NGOs; the others mentioned community access to safe drinking water. During the previous year, 33 percent of respondents interacted with district assembly members, unit committee members, and district assembly staff. NGOs interacted most frequently with chiefs (39 percent); 28 percent interacted with the Community Water and Sanitation Agency (CWSA). The least frequent interaction of the NGOs in the water sector was with other NGOs (6 percent). About 47 percent of the respondents interviewed said they had had some training with a gender component.

Twenty-eight percent of NGOs cited drilling boreholes as their main activity. The other activities cited related to domestic water supply, including facilitation of community organization, construction of water systems in small towns, and promotion of rainwater harvesting systems. Other activities not directly related to water included community-based rural development programs, construction of institutional toilets, and road construction.

The average size of the groups NGOs worked with varied: about 35 percent reported working with an average of seven people, 29 percent reported an average of four to five people, and 36 percent reported an average of eight or more. About a third of the NGOs (35 percent) report that their groups were more than 40 percent female. Forty-one percent of NGOs met a group once a month, and 35 percent met a group twice a month.

Role of Community-Based Organizations

This section deal with two important types of community-based organizations in Ghana: FBOs and water and sanitation committees.

Farmer-Based Organizations

The FBOs in the survey districts can be divided into two main groups: those formed with the help of the agriculture extension agents and those formed based on a common interest in the agricultural value chain, such as agroprocessors. FBOs formed with the help of agricultural extension agents were formed mainly to benefit from government programs, such as fertilizer or hybrid seed programs. The World Bank–funded Agricultural Sector Investment Project promoted innovation funds, which farmers could access only after forming a group. One condition for the formation of the FBO by the agricultural extension agents is that members be prepared to serve as guarantors for and to work with one another. Typically, agricultural programs allow farmers to access credit using group liability. The extension agents train the groups in skills such as basic bookkeeping and issues of group formation. Usually, the FBO elects a leader internally, with the help of agricultural extension agents.

The other group of FBOs, those formed based on a common interest, such as agroprocessing, usually have a constitution and bylaws governing their activities. They also elect executives to run the FBO for a specified period. The executives are usually the chairperson, the secretary, and the treasurer. The main purpose of this type of FBO is to market outputs. They are also formed to access funds from formal financial institutions.

Although FBOs have been widely promoted as a vehicle for agricultural development, the proportion of households in all the three zones that belong to an FBO was low (12 percent of households in the forest, 13 percent in the transition, and 20 percent in the savannah zone). In these households, it was typically the male head that was a member. Among female respondents who were not household heads, only 2 percent in the forest, 5 percent in the transition, and 5 percent in the savannah zones said they belonged to an FBO. Among female household heads, the percentage was only slightly higher (3 percent in the forest, 7 percent in the transition, and 6 percent in the savannah zones).

Male household heads were significantly more likely to belong to an FBO than female household heads, controlling for ecological zone, literacy of household head, and a proxy for household wealth (table 5.38). The regression analysis also indicates that wealthier households and households located in the savannah zone were more likely to belong to an FBO. The literacy of the household head was not significantly related to FBO membership.

Although FBO settings are an important mode of access to extension advice, all respondents viewed the main benefit of membership in an FBO as access to credit. Access to extension advice was rated as the main benefit of FBO membership by just 20 percent of FBO members (table 5.39).

Church groups were the most important form of social organization in all zones (see annex table 5.A.16). Parent-teacher associations also have fairly high membership rates. Forty-five percent of female household members in male-headed households are members of women's groups. The proportion of female-headed households in these groups is slightly higher. These figures suggest that such groups might be a better vehicle than FBOs for reaching women in rural areas.

Table 5.38

Table 5.38 Factors Associated with Membership in Farmer-Based Organization in Ghana (Probit Regression)

Variable	(1)	(2)	(3)	(4)
Male head	0.0796***	0.0713**	0.0714**	0.0682**
	(0.0296)	(0.0299)	(0.0298)	(0.0303)
TV	−0.00640			
	(0.0139)			
Literate	0.00399	0.00266	0.00417	0.00248
	(0.0282)	(0.0277)	(0.0276)	(0.0276)
Forest zone	−0.0630**	−0.0641**	−0.0638**	−0.0651**
	(0.0294)	(0.0289)	(0.0289)	(0.0288)
Transition zone	−0.0509*	−0.0517*	−0.0519*	−0.0514*
	(0.0287)	(0.0283)	(0.0282)	(0.0282)
Goat index		0.00926		
		(0.0102)		
Chicken index			0.0123	
			(0.00983)	
Sheep index				0.0184**
				(0.00931)
Number of observations	878	890	891	891
Pseudo R^2	0.0193	0.0191	0.0200	0.0229

Source: Authors, based on data from ISSER-IFPRI Survey 2008.
Note: Standard errors in parentheses. The relevant livestock index (a measure of wealth) is calculated at the agroecological zone level. The omitted ecological zone category is the savannah zone.
***Significant at the 1% level; **significant at the 5% level; *significant at the 10% level.

Table 5.39 Households' Perception of Benefit of Membership in Farmer-Based Organization in Ghana

Main benefit	Percent of households reporting ($n = 102$)
Access to credit	36
Communal farming help	21
Technical advice	21
Access to fertilizer/inputs	17
No benefit	6

Source: ISSER-IFPRI Survey 2008.

Water and Sanitation Committees (WATSANs)

Membership in WATSANs varies across zones: 14 percent of the communities in the forest zone, 27 percent in the transition zone, and 20 percent in the savannah zone have a WATSAN (see annex table 5.A.16). Forty-nine WATSANs were identified in the area the survey covered. Most WATSANs have three key members: chairperson, secretary, and treasurer. Some have other committee members, such as an organizer, caretaker, mechanic, and water vendor. A typical WATSAN has about seven to eight members. It is likely that district assembly members and unit committees manage the water facility in the many communities that do not have a WATSAN.

Although there is a policy to promote women in WATSANs, less than 20 percent of members surveyed were female. Three-quarters of the WATSANs were formed during the 2000s, mostly to manage boreholes with pumps (table 5.40).

Caretakers (both female and male) and groups of women are usually responsible for cleaning and maintaining boreholes and water sources. About half of the WATSANs in the forest and savannah zones and just 8 percent in the transition zone had access to a mechanic. About two-thirds of the mechanics lived in the community, among whom about 70 percent had received training, either from the district assembly or from an NGO. When repairs required external assistance, respondents indicated that they usually contacted the area mechanic, the assembly person, the district assembly administration, or the CWSA directly. Three-quarters of the WATSANs did not have the opportunity to express their opinion on the contractor selected to construct or rehabilitate the facility. According to the CWSA officials, involving the WATSANs in this step is desirable but difficult because (to enjoy economies of scale) one contractor is hired to drill boreholes in a large number of communities.

Information about the method of choosing executive members was collected to assess the types of accountability mechanisms used within the user organizations. According to the guidelines of the CWSA, members of the WATSANs are elected to promote accountability. However, the survey found that only one-fifth of WATSANs elected their chairperson (table 5.41). In more than half of the WATSANs surveyed, the chairperson was determined by consensus; in 20 percent of cases, the chairperson was appointed by the chief or another authority.

Table 5.40 Major Source of Water Supply in Ghana before and after WATSAN Formed
(percentage of respondents)

Major source of water supply	Before WATSAN formed (n = 47)	After WATSAN formed (n = 47)
Shallow well	7	4
Hand-dug well, no pump	23	12
Hand-dug well with pump	0	6
Borehole with pump	4	54
Small-town water system	2	9
Other	64	15

Source: ISSER-IFPRI Survey 2008.

Table 5.41	Method of Selecting WATSAN Chairperson and Executive Members in Ghana	
Procedure		**Percent of respondents** (*n* = 47)
Consensus reached by users at a meeting		55
Elected by members		21
Appointed by chief		11
Appointed by other authority		9
Informal agreement among users		2
Other		2

Source: ISSER-IFPRI Survey 2008.

About half of WATSANs met only when the need arose, 17 percent met every two weeks, and only 7 percent met every week. About one-third of WATSAN members had received recent training regarding management of the drinking water facility. In 40 percent of the cases, the WATSAN had organized a training for the community members in the previous year.

Complaints by households and response. According to the framework used for the study, complaints by households are an important mechanism for creating accountability. This section deals with the role the WATSANs play in this regard.

More than half of male household heads and their spouses approach the district assembly member in cases of problems with drinking water (table 5.42). Although the WATSANs are supposed to be in charge of drinking water, only about 10 percent of household heads (male or female) contact a WATSAN member with concerns; the share is even lower among female household heads, who are more likely to contact a unit committee member. These figures suggest that households mostly use the long route of accountability to deal with water problems.

Satisfaction rates with the action taken to correct drinking water issues were close to uniform (from 70–72 percent) across all groups of respondents (table 5.43). Female household heads were more likely to say they were "somewhat satisfied" as opposed to "very satisfied," however. Among those who were dissatisfied with the action taken, a significant majority said that they were "very dissatisfied" rather than merely "somewhat dissatisfied."

Contribution to the construction or rehabilitation of the water facility. WATSANs are supposed to leverage community involvement in the construction and maintenance of drinking water supply. About two-thirds of construction did go through a formal application procedure. More than half of the facilities were financed by the district assembly or CWSA; the rest were funded by other sources, such as international donor agencies. About 90 percent of the communities contributed to the construction, contributing labor, in-kind services, and cash (see annex table 5.A.17).

Table 5.42 Person Approached in Case of Dissatisfaction with Drinking Water in Ghana, by Type of Respondent (percentage of respondents)

Person approached	Male household heads (n = 84)	Female household heads (n = 16)	Female spouses (n = 31)
WATSAN member	12	6	10
Unit committee member	7	20	3
District assembly member	55	37	51
Others	26	37	36

Source: ISSER-IFPRI Survey 2008.

Note: Figures refer only to people who complained about drinking water problems.

Table 5.43 Satisfaction with Action Taken on Drinking Water Problems in Ghana, by Type of Respondent (percentage of respondents)

Satisfaction with action	Male household heads (n = 114)	Female household heads (n = 32)	Female spouses (n = 60)
Very satisfied	30	13	27
Somewhat satisfied	41	59	43
Somewhat dissatisfied	7	6	13
Very dissatisfied	22	22	17

Source: ISSER-IFPRI Survey 2008.

Among WATSAN respondents, 27 percent indicated that water facilities had been rehabilitated or undergone major repairs. All of the rehabilitation took place between 2004 and 2008. Most was undertaken to replace major parts or pipes or to change pumps. Usually, the assembly member or WATSAN committee took the first step in applying for such action. Most communities contributed 10 percent or less of the total cost; some contributed more (see annex table 5.A.19). In some cases, individuals within the community paid a large or substantial share of the community contribution. Such contributions may address the concern that poor communities face difficulties in meeting a share of the cost if this contribution has to be made in cash rather than labor.

Payments for water. The proportion of households that paid to access drinking water varied across zones. In the savannah and transition zones, about 80 percent of households reported paying for some aspect of their drinking water supply (table 5.44). In the forest zone, only 53 percent of households that used water from a borehole paid for it, compared with about 85 percent in the transition and savannah zones. For households whose primary source of water

Table 5.44 Payment for Water Services in Ghana, by Zone
(percentage of households that pay for water)

Source of water	Forest	Transition	Savannah
All water sources	46	77	80
	(n = 341)	(n = 331)	(n = 283)
River/lake/spring	31	20	50
	(n = 100)	(n = 49)	(n = 34)
Borehole/well with pump	53	86	83
	(n = 94)	(n = 154)	(n = 96)
Well without pump	55	41	60
	(n = 40)	(n = 22)	(n = 15)
Public standpipe	46	99	98
	(n = 56)	(n = 85)	(n = 105)

Source: ISSER-IFPRI Survey 2008.

was a public standpipe, a much lower proportion in the forest zone (46 percent) paid for water than in the transition and savannah zones, where almost all households did so.

All payment for water use was done by the household head. Of those who reported paying for water, 73 percent paid for the volume of water used, 49 percent paid by contributing toward the construction or setting up of the water source, and 31 percent paid for the maintenance and repair of the water source (annex table 5.A.19). In the savannah zone, more than half of households that paid for water paid to construct the source, paid for maintenance, paid a fixed cost to access the water, or paid for the water by volume. Paying for water was more pervasive in the savannah zone, and more types of payment were required. Payment frequency in the savannah zone was split between daily and monthly. In the forest and transition zones, most households that paid to use water paid for it daily. Where WATSANs were in charge, two-thirds of decisions about water fees were made during general community meeting by consensus and one-third by popular vote.

WATSAN committees or their members collected the fees. The survey did not establish who collected the fees where there is no WATSAN. Given that household members complained to unit committee members when dissatisfied with service, these committees may collect the fees. Informal organizations, which might be formed by district assembly members, may also play a role in this regard.

ETHIOPIA

Households' Access to and Satisfaction with Services

This section presents the findings of the household survey regarding access to and satisfaction with services in Ethiopia. Annex table 5.A.21 provides an overview of the major household characteristics.

Agricultural Extension

Access to and satisfaction with agricultural extension services varies in Ethiopia. The first subsection below examines agricultural extension provided by the public sector. The second subsection examines the extent to which NGOs and other nonpublic bodies engage in this service.

Extension service provision by the public sector. The public sector is the primary source of extension services in Ethiopia. In general, public service provision is neither client oriented nor demand driven. Historically, services have been provided via a top-down, command-and-control mode, in which extension agents are given quotas for signing up farmers for fixed technology "packages" and farmers are expected to serve as passive vessels for the knowledge transferred to them (Lemma 2007).

The most common form of formal extension provision in the study area was visits by the extension agent to the farmers' home or farm, with 23 percent of respondents reporting this form of extension contact. Twenty-seven percent of men and 20 percent of women stated that they were visited by an extension agent at their home or farm during the last year (figure 5.8). The gender gap in this access to extension is relatively small. It is possible that women may have responded in the affirmative as long as an extension agent was at their home or farm, whether or not they were being directly addressed by the extension agent during such a visit.

Figure 5.8   Use of Extension and Other Agricultural Services by Men and Women in Ethiopia
(percentage of respondents receiving service)

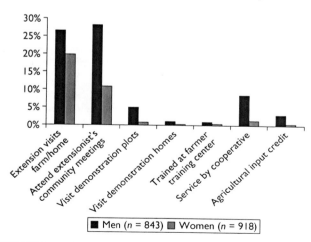

Source: EEPRI-IFPRI Survey 2009.

There is a significant gender gap when it comes to accessing technical advice through community meetings organized by extension officers: 11 percent of women and 28 percent of men participated in such meetings over a one-year period. Visits to demonstration plots and model farms and training received through the farmer training centers, a relatively new institution in Ethiopia, were rare among both men and women.

As many as 54 percent of respondents in Tigray-D had extension visits to their home or farm, in contrast to only 2 percent in Afar-D (annex table 5.A.21). Access to the other most common contact with extension agents, through community meetings they organize, varied similarly across sites, with Tigray-D and Afar-D again representing the extremes in access to such services.

Socioeconomic status also clearly plays a role in households' access to agricultural extension services (see annex figure 5.A.2). Better-educated farmers were somewhat more likely to receive farm or home visits by extension officers, and a much greater proportion of literate than illiterate farmers attend extension community meetings and visited demonstration plots. Better-endowed farmers accessed extension services more than asset-poorer farmers. These findings may result from the hard quotas for promoting technology packages that agents are expected to fill, which induce them to favor better-off and educated farmers, who are more inclined to adopt their advice.

Like in India and Ghana, individuals in Ethiopia reported being satisfied with extension advice at staggering rates: 92 percent of men and 94 percent of women who received extension or expert advice stated that they were very satisfied with these services, and another 7 percent of men and 5 percent of women reported being somewhat satisfied. Surprisingly, given these satisfaction rates, only 8 percent of respondents stated that they had tried something new in the past two years, making it unclear what farmers' near-100 percent satisfaction with extension agents means. Further research should address methodological issues and probe more deeply into farmers' perception of the quality of their interactions with extension agents.

The probability of being visited by an extension agent was strongly related to the district location of the respondents (table 5.45). Farmers in the Afar site, in which pastoralism is an important livelihood, were the least likely to receive an extension visit, followed by those at the Beneshangul-Gumuz site. (These are two of Ethiopia's four so-called emerging, or lagging, regions, which have fewer public services and less-developed local public institutions.) In contrast, farmers in Tigray were most likely to receive extension advice through farm or home visits.

Individuals in larger households were significantly more likely to receive extension services. This may be driven by the fact that larger households also have more land. The share of female dependents (children and the elderly) was negatively correlated with the probability of receiving extension visits. The gender of the respondent emerged as significantly correlated with extension services only when location was not accounted for.

Table 5.45

Variable	Visited by agricultural extension agent		Started agricultural practice for the first time	
Table 5.45 Relationship between Household and Geographic Characteristics and Extension Access and Innovation in Ethiopia				
Gender (1 = male)	0.158	0.206*	0.510***	0.553***
	(0.121)	(0.113)	(0.188)	(0.169)
Education (1 = literate)	0.101	0.022	0.183	0.110
	(0.087)	(0.081)	(0.113)	(0.103)
Respondent status (1 = head, 0 = spouse)	0.133	0.092	0.215	0.139
	(0.122)	(0.113)	(0.198)	(0.178)
Wealth (number of consumer asset types owned)	0.021	−0.025	0.057**	0.009
	(0.018)	(0.016)	(0.024)	(0.021)
Household size (number of household members)	0.038***	−0.013	0.063***	0.005
	(0.013)	(0.012)	(0.017)	(0.015)
Working-age women (percentage of household members)	−0.007	0.001	−0.006	−0.004
	(0.007)	(0.007)	(0.01)	(0.009)
Working-age men (percentage of household members)	−0.010	−0.003	−0.009	−0.006
	(0.007)	(0.007)	(0.01)	(0.009)
Female dependents (percentage of household members)	−0.012*	−0.004	−0.009	−0.006
	(0.007)	(0.006)	(0.01)	(0.009)
Male dependents (percentage of household members)	−0.009	−0.003	−0.012	−0.008
	(0.007)	(0.006)	(0.01)	(0.009)
Afar-D	−1.698***		−1.302***	
	(0.259)		(0.404)	
Amhara-D2	−0.405***		−0.410**	
	(0.134)		(0.187)	
Benesh G-D	−1.241***		−0.922***	
	(0.149)		(0.199)	
Gambella-D	−0.392***		−1.086***	
	(0.128)		(0.249)	
Oromia-D	−1.069***		−1.184***	
	(0.146)		(0.222)	
SNNP-D	−0.453***		−0.153	
	(0.124)		(0.16)	
Tigray-D	0.407***		0.386**	
	(0.126)		(0.156)	
Constant	0.159	−0.477	−1.306	−1.357
	(0.675)	(0.643)	(0.961)	(0.865)
Number of observations	1,753		1,740	
Likelihood ratio chi-square test	250.69***	29.65***	167.08***	59.31***

Source: Authors, based on EEPRI-IFPRI Survey 2009.

Note: Standard errors in parentheses. The excluded district is Amhara-D3.

***Significant at the 1% level; **significant at the 5% level; *significant at the 10% level.

Location also appears to play a major role in the adoption of new practices, with respondents in Afar-D least likely to have undertaken a new agricultural practice and those in Tigray-D most likely to have done so. The use of a new practice was more common among individuals in better-off and larger households, and men were significantly more likely than women to adopt a new practice. The gender effect was the only one among the demographic and socioeconomic variables that remained statistically significant whether or not location was controlled for.

National policy has promoted the rapid expansion of the extension service to enable the posting of at least three extension agents in each kebele. In Tigray-K and Amhara-K3, there were more than three extension agents, some of whom covered more than one kebele. In BG-D, where decentralization of service provision to the district level had not occurred, the extension agents were based in the district capital. Only two kebeles had extension centers, which were poorly developed and visited only irregularly by agents. More remote kebeles did not receive extension services. The case study fieldwork revealed that in these locations, agents often did not make visits and had essentially abandoned their positions, although they continued to collect their salaries through friends.

The deployment of extension agents to the kebele did seem to make services less top-down than they otherwise would have been (EEA/EEPRI 2006). Kebele-based extension agents had a good understanding of local conditions and often seemed to develop good rapport with the farmers they serve. In Tigray-K, the team observed that female extension workers had adopted the traditional dress and Muslim head covering of local women, although one of the extension agents informed the team that her background was urban and modern.

The Agricultural Technical Vocational Education Training (ATVET) curriculum continues to focus heavily on technical agricultural topics, without paying much attention to gender analysis, community organizing, or integration of modern agricultural science and traditional knowledge. The team observed that agents seem to learn these topics mainly on the job rather than through preservice training. In Amhara-K1 and Tigray-K, agents reported receiving formal in-service training on gender issues, sometimes from the district or regional government and sometimes from NGOs.

Extension agents work with model and contact farmers, who are supposed to pass extension messages on to follower farmers. The selection of these farmers is often not based solely on farming skills and social capital but may include political considerations or outright cronyism (Lemma 2007). Nevertheless, this system can be an effective way to disseminate extension advice, particularly if communication is two-way. At the study sites, the team did not find much evidence of this system providing for such links.

Extension service provision by user organizations, NGOs, and the private sector.
Where they existed, farmer cooperatives were a major source of agricultural inputs and credit. They were thus closely tied into the pervasive "package"

approach to extension that prevails in Ethiopia. These supposedly farmer-driven organizations were not free to set their own agendas based on leader or member needs and desires, according to local farmers. Instead, the government sets the parameters within which cooperatives operate.

In the districts of the qualitative research sites, cooperatives were more developed in Tigray-D than elsewhere. The cooperative union was engaged in projects such as dairy farms and beehive production in order to encourage its member cooperatives and individual farmers to engage in such activities. A cooperative union leader reported that these projects were successful in having such demonstration effects.

NGOs offer training to extension agents and other district-level civil servants on, for example, gender issues in development and community development (in both Tigray-D and Amhara-D3). Such training was not systematic, however, and varied considerably from district to district. Where NGOs were involved in rural development, there was weak collaboration and coordination between their interventions and those of the district government. Although community members, particularly women, appreciated the contribution of NGOs in Amahara-D3, government officials were blasé about it.

Drinking Water Supply

The vast majority of households in the study areas derived their water for drinking primarily from natural open sources: rivers, springs, ponds, or lakes. For 64 percent of households, this was the main drinking water source (figure 5.9). For improved drinking water sources, the public sector was the main provider,

Figure 5.9 Access to Drinking Water Sources in Ethiopia

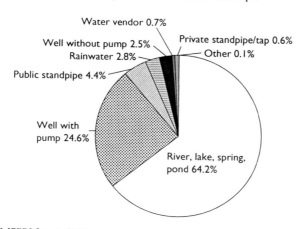

Source: EEPRI-IFPRI Survey 2009.
Note: Sample size: n = 959.

although NGOs, the private sector, and donor agencies were very active in constructing water systems. In the study sites, these actors were generally not involved in supporting operations and maintenance or the creation of user organizations, as they have elsewhere in the country, and they did not attempt to engage community involvement.

Regarding the type of improved water sources, for their primary source a quarter of households use wells without pumps and some 4 percent use public standpipes. A third of households use water sources that are considered to be safe (wells with pumps, public or private standpipes, taps, and rainwater). Although this information was obtained during the wet season, the use of primary water sources appears to be remarkably stable across the seasons, although diversification across water source types may change between wet and dry seasons.

For most water sources, the time it takes to fetch water does not change much across seasons either (table 5.46). For the most frequently used sources—unprotected sources such as rivers and ponds—it takes approximately two hours to fetch water.

When asked about their satisfaction levels, the majority of respondents expressed satisfaction with the water they obtain from their primary drinking water source (figure 5.10). The satisfaction rate was somewhat higher during the wet season, and it was slightly higher with regard to the quantity of water than the quality of the water.

Men were more likely than women to express their dissatisfaction with the water supply (see annex figure 5.A.3). This is the case even though in Ethiopia, as in nearly all countries, it is primarily women who are responsible for obtaining and handling the household's drinking water.

In the small number of households in which men were responsible or shared responsibility for fetching water, they were less likely than women to

Table 5.46 Average Time to Get Water from Different Water Sources in Wet and Dry Seasons in Ethiopia (minutes)

Water source	Wet season (n = 593)	Dry Season (n = 593)
River, lake, spring, pond	111	127
Rainwater	80	n.a.
Well without pump	80	102
Well with pump	107	119
Public standpipe	58	61
Household's private standpipe/tap	4	2
Water vendor	75	120
Other	28	75

Source: EEPRI-IFPRI Survey 2009.
Note: n.a. = not applicable.

Figure 5.10 Satisfaction with Quantity and Quality of Drinking Water Supply in Ethiopia in Wet and Dry Seasons

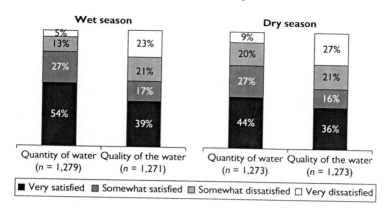

Source: EEPRI-IFPRI Survey 2009.

identify an improved water source as the household's primary source (table 5.47). This may suggest that men who share in the task of collecting water do so mostly in cases where the household's primary water use is from unimproved sources. In the model that accounts for the study sites, the wealth status of the respondent's household is positively and significantly correlated with the use of improved water.

Individuals in larger households stated longer water-fetching times, possibly because larger households have greater water needs. Individuals residing in Afar-D, an arid lowland region, spent substantially more time getting water than individuals elsewhere in the study area. Residents of this site were also more likely to be dissatisfied with water services and infrastructure than those in most other locations. After controlling for household size and household composition (which appear to be significantly correlated with satisfaction), the other factors that could have been hypothesized to correlate with expressions of dissatisfaction—gender, education, wealth— did not emerge as significant.

Priorities Regarding Service Provision

Men and women reported similar priority problems. Drinking water supply emerged as the most important problem, although women were somewhat more likely to state drinking water as the most significant problem (table 5.48). For both men and women, health facilities and services ranked as the second most frequently mentioned area of concern. Issues with electricity access and road infrastructure were, broadly, the third most often cited sectors of priority concern for men and women. Only a small percentage of respondents identified education facilities and services as their top concern.

Table 5.47 Factors Associated with Access to and Satisfaction with Drinking Water Sources in Ethiopia

Variable	Primary water source is improved source		Time taken to fetch water (minutes)		Dissatisfied with drinking water	
	(1)	(2)	(3)	(4)	(5)	(6)
Gender (1 = male)	−0.287*	−0.186	41.890	55.288	0.376	0.379
	(0.169)	(0.159)	(30.842)	(34.302)	(0.606)	(0.582)
Education (1 = literate)	0.017	−0.038	−4.581	−13.062**	0.104	0.197*
	(0.133)	(0.119)	(5.93)	(6.458)	(0.117)	(0.107)
Respondent status (1 = head, 0 = spouse)	0.119	0.259**	43.503	32.111	−0.524	−0.547
	(0.127)	(0.115)	(39.095)	(43.903)	(0.786)	(0.751)
Wealth (number of consumer asset types owned)	0.046*	0.014	−1.518	−5.637***	−0.020	0.015
	(0.024)	(0.02)	(1.402)	(1.444)	(0.027)	(0.024)
Household size (number of household members)	−0.019	−0.037**	1.850*	1.960*	−0.049***	−0.027*
	(0.018)	(0.016)	(0.954)	(1.003)	(0.018)	(0.016)
Working-age women (percentage of household members)	−0.010	0.002	−0.165	0.070	0.038**	0.027**
	(0.009)	(0.009)	(0.637)	(0.714)	(0.015)	(0.013)
Working-age men (percentage of household members)	−0.010	0.000	0.178	0.718	0.038**	0.025*
	(0.009)	(0.009)	(0.642)	(0.719)	(0.015)	(0.013)
Female dependents (percentage of household members)	−0.011	−0.001	0.059	0.330	0.040***	0.027**
	(0.009)	(0.009)	(0.619)	(0.694)	(0.015)	(0.013)
Male dependents (percentage of household members)	−0.009	0.000	0.252	0.746	0.038***	0.026**
	(0.009)	(0.009)	(0.613)	(0.687)	(0.015)	(0.013)

Afar-D	−0.334	176.958***	1.032***
	(0.217)	(15.466)	(0.3)
Amhara-D2	0.239	22.864*	0.426*
	(0.182)	(12.075)	(0.224)
Benesh G.-D	−0.088	−5.244	0.988***
	(0.173)	(9.942)	(0.197)
Gambella-D	0.437***	38.115***	0.602***
	(0.164)	(10.69)	(0.206)
Oromia-D	−1.579***	−4.090	0.837***
	(0.241)	(10.506)	(0.205)
SNNP-D	−1.193***	−8.599	1.506***
	(0.205)	(9.771)	(0.205)
Tigray-D	0.165	20.416	−0.669**
	(0.185)	(12.877)	(0.295)
Constant	0.595	−5.753	−4.411***
	(0.932)	(68.615)	(1.585)
	−0.374	−22.125	−2.879
	(0.871)	(76.598)	(1.414)
Number of observations	960	624	633
	LR χ^2: 196.53***	F-stat: 4.13***	LR χ^2: 114.46***
	18.86**	Adjusted R^2: 0.245	12.44
		13.6	
		0.043	

Source: Authors, based on data from EEPRI-IFPRI Survey 2009.

Note: Standard errors in parentheses. The excluded district is Amhara-D3. LR χ^2 = likelihood ratio chi-square test.

***Significant at the 1% level; **significant at the 5% level; *significant at the 10% level.

Table 5.48	Top Public Service and Infrastructure Concerns in Ethiopia, by Gender (percentage of respondents identifying concern as most important)		
Public service/infrastructure	Men (n = 843)	Women (n = 918)	Significance of difference
Drinking water	31	34	
Health	17	19	
Electricity	16	11	**
Roads	14	12	**
Education	5	3	
Livelihood opportunities	2	3	**
Small-scale irrigation	1	0	*
Sanitation/drainage	0	0	

Source: Authors, based on data from EEPRI-IFPRI Survey 2009.
**significant at the 5% level; *significant at the 10% level.

With regard to drinking water, the type and severity of specific problems faced seemed to have changed over time. Respondents who ranked water supply as the main concern were asked what type of water problems they encountered today and seven years ago. For both women and men, concern appeared to have shifted away from water quality to water quantity (figure 5.11). Almost no respondents identified inadequate collection of user fees as a problem with water services. This may reflect the efficiency and organization of fee collection or, perhaps more likely, the fact that respondents did not consider how this fee collection may link to the quality and quantity of the water they receive.

The illiterate and the poor identified drinking water as the community's greatest challenge by a wider margin than did literate and wealthier households (see annex table 5.A.23). The share of better-off households pointing to poor road infrastructure and insufficient access to electricity services as the greatest concern was substantially larger than the share of less advantaged. Although few respondents pointed to education as their primary problem, better-off respondents did so at twice the rate of the less-well-off.

Despite the geographic dispersion of the study sites, priority concerns across sites were similar. Across most areas, access to drinking water stood out as the most often stated top problem (table 5.49). Clear were the Tigray and Southern Region sites, where "hard" infrastructure, such as electricity and roads, was prioritized over water. This was particularly acute in the study site in Afar, an arid lowland. Health services rank second in most locations.

Service Providers: Capacity, Constraints, Incentives, and Accountability

Service providers' lines of accountability, their capacity, and the incentives and constraints they face determine the way in which they deliver services to

Figure 5.11   Changes in Concerns with Drinking Water Supply in Ethiopia, by Gender

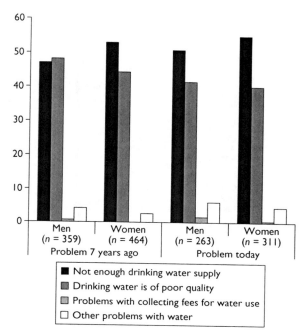

Source: EEPRI-IFPRI Survey 2009.

rural residents. This section discusses different facets of their interface with households, the local government bureaucracy, local political authorities, and one another.

Interaction with Households

This section elaborates on the findings on service providers' engagement with their clients. It examines their attitudes toward the rural residents they are there to serve, the extent to which they involve residents in planning exercises, and the manner in which they respond to complaints.

Service provider attitudes toward women and gender orientation of services.
Extension in Ethiopia has long focused on male farmers, in keeping with the cultural perception that "women do not farm," a perception that ignores the wide range of agricultural activities in which women engage. Extension traditionally concentrated services on "model" or "progressive" farmers, those who are open to new ideas and innovations. These farmers tended to be male. Because extension agents were evaluated on how many farmers they could get to adopt "packages,"

Table 5.49 Top Public Service and Infrastructure Concerns in Ethiopia, by Region (percentage of respondents identifying concern as most important)

Top-ranked concern	Afar-D (n = 127)	Amhara-D2 (n = 176)	Amhara-D3 (n = 226)	Benesh G-D (n = 262)	Gambella-D (n = 116)	Oromia-D (n = 193)	SNNP-D (n = 232)	Tigray-D (n = 184)
Drinking water	65	29	25	35	28	36	19	34
Health	21	31	22	31	8	9	11	14
Livelihood opportunities	2	4	4	1	2	1	6	3
Sanitation/drainage	1	0	1	0	0	0	0	0
Small irrigation	1	3	0	0	2	0	0	1
Education	1	8	3	3	1	9	2	5
Electricity	0	10	21	7	6	6	16	40
Roads	0	10	22	9	6	8	33	1

Source: EEPRI-IFPRI Survey 2009.

they preferred to work with the household decision maker, who in a husband-wife household was always the male (EAA/EEPRI 2006). In addition, extension agents were overwhelmingly male, and cultural taboos restricted their interaction with women. Home economics and nutrition agents were women and generally provided advice to women on household management and reproductive health (EAA/EEPRI 2006; Buchy and Basaznew 2005) (box 5.2).

The team found considerable evidence of gender bias in the provision of extension services in the study districts, even though national policy and EPRDF ideology strongly promote gender equality in all aspects of life. The findings from qualitative discussions contrast with the survey results discussed earlier. In Oromia-K, women complained that they had no access to extension services, although they hear on the radio about extension programs for women in other parts of the country. In Amhara-K1, an extension agent told the team that he works only with heads of household, providing even advice oriented toward women (on poultry and home gardens, for example) through their husbands. Female household heads in this kebele said that their contact with extension agents mainly involved mobilizing labor contributions.

Farmers, particularly in Tigray-K, pointed out that the gender of extension agents does not matter as long as they serve the needs of farmers. Extension

---

Box 5.2   Gender Blind Spot of an Agricultural Agency in Ethiopia

During the study period, the Awasa Bureau of Agriculture in the Awasa zone of the SNNP region was divided geographically into district bureaus and thematically into three departments, which were further divided into management, regulatory, and extension departments. The teams within the extension department were evaluated on the basis of output indicators: the number of livestock vaccinated, the quantity of illegal forest product seized, and so forth. Their targets were households; their clients were heads of households and therefore, de facto, men in the vast majority of cases.

The staff usually approaches individual male farmers on their farms or contact groups when there are field visits. These approaches excluded women, who did not go on field visits except for those organized by the home economics team. Staff members conducted training during their office hours, which may not have suited farmers' schedules, particularly those of female farmers. In the year examined, most training was conducted between March and May, when women in the region are busiest with the processing of enset, commonly known as "false banana." These oversights reflected both gender blindness and methodological inadequacy, in the form of a very top-down attitude. People-centered approaches should take account of seasonal and daily calendars; they should ensure that the method of delivery is both gender and culture sensitive.

(continued)

Box 5.2   (Continued)

The rural women's affairs team, which was housed in the extension department, was moved many times without a clear justification. Until 1990, there was no team; two experts were attached to the extension department. All members of the rural women's affairs team were women. In contrast, there were no women members of the microfinance, documentation, or farmers training teams; women made up 12–37 percent of other teams. Structurally, the part of the organization concerned with women (rather than gender) was working in isolation rather than as a fully integrated part of the organization.

There was no gender policy within the Awasa Bureau of Agriculture, despite the efforts of donors to introduce one. Ten of 39 respondents had participated in a gender workshop, 7 of them women. Gender was very much considered a women's issue; men attended this training only if they were specifically asked to do so. The rural women's affairs, tacitly expected to deal with gender issues, had no mandate to control or measure gender-related performances on other teams within the Awasa Bureau of Agriculture.

Source: Buchy and Basaznew 2005.

agents also shared this view. However, there are cultural barriers to male extension agents reaching women alone. In the study districts, male extension agents employed different approaches to reaching women farmers, such as contacting their husbands first and explaining the purpose of the visit; meeting women in groups (organized, for example, by the local women's association); addressing women in public meetings; and seeking the support of kebele cabinet women's affairs portfolio holders.

Extension agents in the study districts had a great deal of awareness of this gender bias and had employed strategies to get around it. In Amhara-K3, extension agents worked with the kebele women's association to organize women into extension programs, circumventing cultural taboos on women meeting one-on-one with men other than their husbands. Leaders of the women's association in Amhara-K3 reported that they work with husbands as well as wives. The team noted that many women leaders in the study kebeles were single (divorced, widowed, or never married) and that there was a great deal of resistance to women's empowerment among male farmers. For example, female leaders in Amhara-K3 told the team that when married women return home from meetings of the local women's association or the party women's league, their husbands urge them not to pay attention to the "nonsense" they heard about gender equality. In Amhara-K1 and K3, local women's association leaders reported that men frequently jeer at them when they speak up at public meetings.

In Amhara-D3, the district government carried out gender analysis as part of a comprehensive needs assessments (in Amhara-D1 and Tigray-D, all district government staff received in-service training on gender issues). The team observed that a female extension agent in Tigray-K was very popular with local farmers (both men and women), and the extension agent reported that she had won recognition for the high quality of her work. In some study sites, there was a great deal of social distance between educated extension agents and illiterate farmers, regardless of gender. In BG-K, extension agents felt that farmers should do what the agents said and were not willing to follow up with farmers who did not follow extension advice.

The gendered provision of extension services is evolving. Throughout the country, the effort to expand the extension service means that many more women have the opportunity to work as agents, in all subject matter areas. Nutrition and household management advice is now the purview of health extension agents rather than an agricultural responsibility. The Ministry of Agriculture and Rural Development (MoARD) has developed a broader variety of extension packages, recognizing that one size does not fit all farmers. This includes a "women's package," which emphasizes support for women's agricultural activities (poultry, small ruminants, and home gardens). Extension agents and district agricultural officials told the team that extension agents are expected to move toward advising at least as many women farmers as men. However, in Amhara-K3, the women's affairs portfolio holder in the kebele cabinet told the team that although extension agents will advise women if asked to do so, they do not tend to approach women on their own.

Moreover, the "women's development package" remains relatively standard and undiversified based on women engaging in different primary tasks. In particular, the package does not distinguish between the needs of female household heads and female spouses. According to an official in Amhara-K3, it is difficult for female household heads to raise chickens, for example, because they spend a great deal of time providing weeding services to male farmers to earn income. Informants in Amhara-K1, Tigray-K, and Amhara-K3 indicated that female household heads who have the right to use land typically sharecrop it out or exchange "women's" weeding services for "men's" plowing and planting, but they may engage in this work themselves on a portion of their land. To the extent that the women's package emphasizes poultry, it is really a "married women's development package."

With regard to water services, in most of the study districts, the local water committees were dominated by men (although all such water committees had female members), despite women's key role in fetching water for household use. This may impede the effectiveness of the water committees in mobilizing users around construction, operations, maintenance, and improved hygiene. The exception was BG-D, where women chair local water committees as a matter of policy. The team observed that the local Gumuz culture in this district is much more gender equitable than the culture elsewhere in Ethiopia.

Involvement of households in planning. Involvement in planning is an important mechanism for creating accountability (see chapter 2). Community engagement in planning varied considerably by region. In Tigray-K, extension agents and the kebele manager informed the team that there was a great deal of participation in sectoral planning and developing the overall kebele plan, with many active committees and citizen engagement. Extension agents work with *mengistawi budin* (government teams) to develop annual agricultural plans, and these bodies actively consult village residents about priorities. The team observed a large turnout of kebele residents for several full days of meetings with district government officials. In contrast, the team was also present for a kebele general assembly meeting to discuss the annual plan in Amhara-K3. No more than 15 people attended this desultory exercise. In general, district and kebele officials felt that planning at the community level was mostly symbolic in Amhara-K3, BG-K, and Oromia-K. The deeper citizen engagement in Tigray-K may reflect the institutionalization of self-reliance from the civil war era in the Tigray region. Whether community involvement in planning was symbolic or substantial, at all study sites, budgeting was carried out at higher levels of government.

Complaints by households and response. Citizens have a variety of channels for airing grievances, another mechanism through which accountability occurs. Farmers in Amhara-K1 usually take complaints to the kebele chairperson, who heads the executive branch of government. Certain disputes, such as those over land use, may go to the local court (composed of citizen judges), which in turn may refer issues to the traditional elders' council for advice or resolution. In addition, one farmer emphasized, "I have the right to go to the district government." In Tigray-K, the speaker of the kebele council said that citizens sometimes seek redress from the council. In Tigray-D and Amhara-D3, and the corresponding kebeles, a number of respondents pointed to grievance committees attached to the government's Productive Safety Net Program, noting that citizens who believe they are eligible but are not enrolled have successfully appealed to get into the program. In all, there appear to be effective recourse mechanisms for certain types of complaints in Amhara and Tigray.

In BG-D and Oromia-D, grievance systems did not work well. In Oromia-D, there were many land disputes, which governance structures do not resolve. In BG-D, people took dispute resolution into their own hands rather than relying on the legal system, as this was a "faster" way to get satisfaction.

At all of the study sites, the interaction of water committees (as service providers) with the communities was problematic. In Amhara-K3, BG-K, and Oromia-K, the water committees tended to be dysfunctional, unable to persuade residents to properly maintain systems or pay fees. The water systems eventually collapsed, as did the water committees. In Amhara-K3, BG-K, and Oromia-K, water users often simply voted with their feet when they had grievances over drinking water governance: they continued to fetch water from traditional sources. This put a heavy physical and time burden on women and often had negative health consequences. In these sites, the water committees received little support from the district water resources offices.

The situation was somewhat better in Tigray-K, where the research team observed a number of mechanisms through which users could hold water committees accountable. The head of the local women's association, who was also a member of the regional council, was very active in raising questions about water service provision. As is customary in Tigray, water committees and users frequently engaged in the process of criticism and self-criticism (*gimgema*).

But even in Tigray-K, there were many conflicts about water fees and labor and financial contributions for developing new water systems. The team observed that water users were dissatisfied with water service provision on grounds of fairness (some communities obtained free systems from the district, although others did not, and fees were regarded as unreasonable). However, the leader of the local women's association, who complained about some of these fairness issues, pointed out that the government had done a good job of improving things for women with respect to water, noting that most women had received free jerry cans, which are easier to fill and carry than traditional water vessels.

Collection of user fees and labor contributions. Farmers in Ethiopia receive advice from public sector extension agents without having to pay a fee. However, extension is not costless. Agents played a major role in mobilizing community labor contributions in all the study sites. In Amhara-K1, a female household head said that her main contact with the extension agents was when they wanted her to work on maintaining soil and water conservation structures. Farmers said that extension agents in this kebele spent a good deal of their time encouraging the repayment of fertilizer loans provided by the local cooperative, but a local agent said that even farmers who failed to do so would continue to receive basic extension advice, although they would not be eligible for packages until they covered their debts. (The collection of fees for drinking water supply is discussed below in connection with the water committees.)

Accountability of Public Sector Service Providers

This section deals with accountability mechanisms within the public sector organizations that provide services. It discusses funding mechanisms for public spending on services and planning and features of human resource management.

District and kebele administrations remain heavily dependent for revenues on the regional and federal governments, which exert tremendous influence over service provision. Although district governments are able to exercise some discretion over the sectoral and territorial allocation of funds, they cannot affect the total budget.

In all study districts, district finance, planning, and budget offices played a major role in aggregating sectoral plans and budgets and taking kebele priorities into account in devising overall district plans and budgets. In Amhara-D3 and Oromia-D, local priorities too often fell through the cracks in this process. In Oromia-D, the scarcity of capital project funds put severe constraints on service provision, which resulted in great dissatisfaction with the district government. In all study districts, recurrent expenses, mainly in the form of staff salaries and benefits, accounted for the vast bulk of expenditures.

BG-D is in a region in which decentralization to the district level has not yet occurred. The district government is explicitly an implementing agency for the regional government, without even nominal discretion over policy and expenditures.

Planning, service standards, and human resource management. MoARD and the Ministry of Water Resources provide the overall policy framework governing service provision. This may include technical standards—such as MoARD's Community-Based Participatory Watershed Development Guidelines, which provide extensive technical guidance on soil and water conservation—as well as guidelines on engaging communities in planning and management (Cohen, Rocchigiani, and Garrett 2008). Within federal policy parameters, the relevant regional bureaus offer planning guidance to the districts. In all study districts, officials told the team that this guidance is strictly indicative but that senior district government officials are evaluated by the regions on whether or not they meet these targets. In Oromia-D, officials complained to the team that regional targets make no reference to kebele needs and priorities and that budgetary resources received from the regional are inadequate to meet regional targets.

To ensure that gender is taken into account in the planning process, many districts have established a system of gender desks or focal points within sectoral offices. This provides the district office of women's affairs with a point of contact in each sectoral office and is supposed to guarantee that the office reviews budgets, plans, and operations through a gender lens.

The team found considerable variation in the effectiveness of this policy. There seems to be an assumption that gender is a women's concern. All of the gender focal points in the study districts were women, and in some instances they were rather junior staff members (there were male professional staff in some district offices of women's affairs, however). In Amhara-D1, the gender focal point at the Woreda Office of Agriculture and Rural Development (WoARD) informed the team that she had conducted training in gender analysis for all the extension agents in the district. In Tigray-D, the deputy head of the office of women's affairs said that gender is mainstreamed in all planning activities, so the focal point system is somewhat redundant. Her office organizes gender training for senior staff in all sectoral offices, carries out gender audits, and regularly reviews planning activities from a gender perspective. In Amhara-D3, the team met with the gender focal points of the agriculture and finance offices. Neither could explain the precise duties involved or how the focal point system is supposed to function. One characterized it as mainly symbolic and pointed out that her regular assignment is to conduct gender analysis for the needs assessment unit of the agriculture office; she did not see the focal point responsibilities as adding any additional duties. BG-D had only recently reestablished a women's affairs office and did not have a focal point system. In Oromia-D, there were focal points only in the office of education.

The study also identified challenges related to human resource management. Staff costs absorb most budget resources; in Amhara-D3, BG-D, and Oromia-D, senior officials complained that resources were inadequate to hire sufficient numbers of staff and people with adequate professional qualifications. In Amhara-D3 and BG-D, a high rate of staff turnover exacerbated these problems.

Overall, the legacy of six decades of top-down service provision weighs heavily on any efforts service providers undertake to induce higher levels of government to become more client oriented. The incentives to the providers strongly reinforce upward lines of accountability and render risky any efforts to support downward lines. In Amhara-K3, for example, the team noticed that an extension agent was much franker when the senior district official who accompanied the team was out of earshot. This extension agent complained directly about the lack of incentives for providing demand-driven services.

Service Providers' Relationship with the Local Bureaucracy

Extension agents remain primarily accountable to the WoARD. In Tigray-D and Amhara-D3, supervisors are based in kebeles and take responsibility for extension agents in three to four nearby kebeles. Supervisors then report to the WoARD on extension agents' activities in their territory. In Amhara-K3, an extension agent said that the supervisors and district-level experts had no greater technical knowledge than he did. He felt that he received inadequate support from supervisors, whose role is mainly one of control.

In Tigray-K, extension agents also met regularly with and worked closely with mengistawi budin. Mengistawi budin essentially constitute the political leadership at the subkebele level and are subject to some level of evaluation by these bodies and their contact farmers. The mengistawi budin meet regularly with the kebele cabinet to discuss extension agents' performance. However, lines of authority and accountability become somewhat muddled because recent practice is for the extension team leader to serve on the kebele cabinet as the member responsible for agriculture.

The new position of kebele manager, created as part of the good governance initiative in the wake of the 2005 elections, adds another accountability mechanism. This official is the chief civil servant of the kebele; all other staff report to him or her. The manager is available to residents 24 hours a day, seven days a week. The manager in Tigray-K instituted a suggestion box and meets frequently with residents on all issues. Managers are accountable to the district Office of Capacity Building.

Government bodies in the kebeles thus add another layer of oversight to extension service provision. The main lines of accountability remain upward, despite the elements in place to ensure some measure of downward accountability, because training and promotion opportunities depend on pleasing supervisors and the WoARD. Extension agents' incentives do not encourage efforts to draw on farmers' own knowledge or to tailor programs to farmers' demands; promoting package participation is the way to get a good evaluation.

In some study sites, extension agents complained about a lack of training opportunities and materials, as well as a top-down approach to supervision, whereby supervisors and technical experts enforce the promotion of packages rather than providing technical backup and coaching to front-line agents who respond to farmers' demands and work to combine modern and traditional knowledge. In Amhara-K3, an extension agent said that he sought to tailor services to local conditions and demand but added that he did not receive support from above for doing so.

The research team observed a well-functioning farmer training center in Tigray-K. In contrast, in Amhara-K3, an extension agent said that the center is nonfunctional, and agricultural officials in Oromia-D reported that the centers are often used as goat sheds. Links between research and extension were generally poor at all sites, as is common throughout Ethiopia (Lemma 2007).

Overall, the vertical and horizontal relationships of service providers are not well institutionalized and remain very weak. There is no systematic mechanism or coordinating body to align the activities of public sector, NGO, and user organization activities or provide a common framework in which all actors can operate. District governments are supposed to exercise this function, but in practice coordination is nonexistent, limiting the effectiveness and efficiency of services.

Interactions of Service Providers with Other Providers,
Community-Based Organizations, and Donors

At all sites, agricultural extension was provided exclusively by the public sector. In Amhara-D3, the private sector and NGOs were active in constructing but not operating water systems. In BG-D, NGOs provided water services. In Amhara-K3, members of a water committee complained about lack of consultation on the siting and construction of water points and about the failure of those involved in construction to draw on local knowledge about water sources (as a result of which, systems often did not function properly). Accountability is to the district government in Amhara-D3 and to the regional government in BG-D, not to local water users.

In Amhara-D1, extension agents based at the district headquarters promote the formation of farmers' cooperatives and membership in cooperatives (see next section) throughout the district. All districts have a cooperative promotion desk as a unit of the WoARD. In Amhara-K1, extension agents encourage cooperative membership and prompt repayment of loans obtained through the cooperative. In Amhara-K3, extension agents work closely with the local women's association on promotion of the "women's package" and other liveli-hood activities for women.

Donor agencies have played a major role in attempting to make extension services more client oriented. The World Food Programme and MoARD have collaborated on engaging communities in planning and management of soil and water conservation since the 1980s, culminating in national participatory watershed development guidelines in 2005. This effort has also included a major focus on gender equality in these activities. The effort was not donor driven; the World Food Programme took great pains to work in a collaborative mode with the ministry (Cohen, Rocchigiani, and Garrett 2008).

The Water, Sanitation, and Hygiene (WASH) Coalition—a multistakeholder initiative that includes several NGOs and is supported by a variety of donors, including the United Nations Children's Fund and the U.S. Agency for Interna-tional Development—has played an important role in the construction of water systems. NGOs have established water systems that include more active user groups (for example, a congress of users that meets annually or semiannually). No such bodies were present in the study communities.

Role of Community-Based Organizations

This section discusses the role of community-based user organizations, which are considered to be part of the short route of accountability. It examines agri-cultural and local water committees.

Agricultural Cooperatives

Cooperatives are becoming an increasingly important agricultural institution in Ethiopia. The government has been giving considerable attention to coop-eratives as a key vehicle for advancing the government's agricultural and rural development agenda.

Cooperatives have the function of both rural user organizations and service providers. They have the common characteristics of user organizations in that their members, and often their leadership, are local residents who directly use the services and resources that cooperatives facilitate. They are not strictly pub-lic agencies but rather voluntary local organizations of individuals interested in cooperating to achieve individual and mutual goals of increasing productivity and accessing markets. At the same time, agricultural cooperatives in Ethiopia can be characterized as service providers, because it is predominantly through them that farmers obtain agricultural inputs and in some cases agricultural equipment (Spielman, Cohen, and Mogues, forthcoming).

As a result of recent efforts by the government to expand and accelerate the formation of cooperatives and the membership of farmers in them, such mem-bership has increased significantly, albeit from a low base. In the study area, 24 percent of men and 4 percent of women belonged to some kind of cooperative (table 5.50); 13 percent of men and 2 percent of women belonged to agricultural (also called multipurpose) cooperatives. (Nationally, 9 percent of households belong to an agricultural cooperative [Bernard and Spielman 2009].) The small percentage of women who belong to cooperatives reflects the fact that almost all members are household heads. Men are five times more likely than women to hold a leadership position within a cooperative (3 percent of female and 15 percent of male cooperative members hold such roles).

The cooperatives in the study area appeared to have been relatively new (table 5.50). Three-quarters of male respondents and a majority of women who were in a cooperative had to pay an "establishment fee" upon joining. This fee helped defray the costs incurred in setting up the cooperative. A nontrivial proportion of men and even women were directly or indirectly involved in the development of the cooperative's rules and policies. Few members were obliged to pay regular membership fees. One of the reasons for this may be the diverse ways in which cooperatives obtain revenues, with many cooperatives marking up the price of agricultural inputs purchased from cooperative unions or the district government office of agriculture before selling them to members. Cooperatives engaged in output marketing may withhold a small amount of the revenues from commodity sales before paying farmers.

Cooperatives in the study area tend to be large. The prevalence of women is very low (figure 5.12).

Table 5.50	Involvement in and Contribution to Cooperatives in Ethiopia, by Gender (percentage of respondents, except where indicated otherwise)		
Residents' involvement in cooperative	Men (n = 843)	Women (n = 918)	Significance of difference
Member of any cooperative	24	4	***
Of those who are members of a cooperative	(n = 205)	(n = 39)	
Member of any agricultural (multipurpose) cooperative	13	2	
Hold a leadership position in the cooperative	15	3	**
Involved in development of cooperative's constitution/bylaws	34	15	**
Had to pay establishment fee upon joining the coop	74	62	
Had to contribute additional resources upon joining cooperative	25	26	
Have to pay periodic membership fee	17	26	*
Average number of meetings attended (per year)	12	13	*
Duration of membership (years)	6	4	

Source: Authors, based on data from EEPRI-IFPRI Survey 2009.
***Significant at the 1% level; **significant at the 5% level; *significant at the 10% level.

Figure 5.12   Size of Cooperatives in Ethiopia

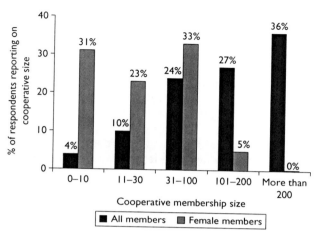

Source: EEPRI-IFPRI Survey 2009.
Note: Sample size: n = 225.

Water Committees

Local water committees, which function as both providers and user organizations, were the main source of water services in the study kebeles, although many households continued to rely on unimproved river, spring, or lake water. Local water committees registered users based on their willingness to pay fees and participated in construction, operations, and maintenance activities. In Tigray-D, some cooperatives provided spare parts for water systems, but this was not the norm among the study sites.

Water committees are made up of users of a water facility from the community. They are meant to have direct contact with facility users and to ensure that users follow the rules set out for the facility regarding water user fees, labor contributions for maintenance and small repairs, and so on. Committee members receive no training in community organizing or public speaking and persuasion; they often have difficulty persuading households of the advantages of protected water systems and paying fees to support them. In Amhara-D3, BG-D, and Oromia-D, the water committees receive little support from district water offices.

Local water committees are chosen by the district government, sometimes upon the recommendation of the local community. In Amhara-K3, a district government health extension worker deployed to the kebele sat in on one such committee, which its members and many other informants reported was the best-functioning water committee in the kebele. The team could not ascertain whether the presence of a civil servant on the body was decisive in this regard. Aside from its involvement in the formation of water committees, district governments tried to change cultural norms about the gender distribution of the burden of collecting water from unimproved sources or facilities. For example, in Amhara-D3 posters in district government offices exhorted men to share in the burden of procuring water for their families.

Water committee members varied in their willingness and capacity to persuade users of the value of using improved water sources instead of river, lake, and unprotected spring sources. In all study sites, the water committees had female members, but all sites except BG-D had male leaders. Water committees did not generally receive training in community mobilization in addition to technical issues.

In principle, local water committees are expected to collect fees from registered users to support operations, maintenance, and staffing (mainly guards to prevent damage and use by unregistered users). Water committee members at all study sites informed the team that community members object to paying even very minimal fees. In Tigray-K, residents expressed concern that the fees were actually taxes that would merely go into the district government's coffers without benefiting the community. In Amhara-K3, many residents were unwilling to pay fees when they could obtain water for free from unprotected sources. In BG-D and Oromia-D, fees generally go uncollected.

As with soil and water conservation activities, communities are expected to contribute labor toward the construction of water systems. In Tigray-K, the district government also asked for financial contributions, as a result of the lack of adequate capital budget resources. Farmers objected to this demand as unfair (district officials had not asked other villages within the kebele to contribute money and labor toward the construction of water systems).

At most sites there were many complaints about water services, including lack of availability and strong perceptions of unfairness. Perceptions of unfairness concerned the level of fees (Amhara-K3), whether villages should contribute financially to construction when their neighbors did not have to do so for previously constructed systems (Tigray-K), and whether the fees would go to the district government rather than supporting operations and maintenance (Tigray-K). Where the water committees were able to persuade users of the value of fees and protected water sources, as in Tigray-K, there was usually substantial community buy-in; where water committees did not engage in effective mobilization of users around "owning" the systems, the systems often fell into disrepair (for example, in Amhara-K3). In Amhara-K3, some users withdrew their registrations over issues of unfairness, even where water committees attempted to carry out hygiene education.

Residents in Amhara-K3 also complained that organizations that constructed water systems did not draw on local knowledge in site selection or design. This contributed to the breakdown of several local systems. Construction contractors also ignored property issues, such as the loss of land by some residents when a water system had to be located on their plot.

ANNEX

The Short Route of Accountability

This annex provides supplementary information on the short route of accountability in India, Ghana, and Ethiopia.

Table 5.A.1	Basic Indicators for Households Surveyed in Karnataka, by Gender of Household Head (percent, except where otherwise indicated)	
Indicator	Male-headed households (n = 871)	Female-headed households (n = 83)
Literacy rate of household head	63.6	19.3
Occupation of household head		
Agriculture	52.1	11.0
Agricultural casual labor	22.4	43.9
Own business	4.7	1.2
Self-employed in services	2.2	2.4
Nonagricultural casual labor	3.1	0.0
Salaried work	4.1	2.4
Self-employed in household industry	4.4	6.1
Household work	0.7	29.3
Livestock management	0.9	0.0
Other	5.4	3.7
Ownership of nonlivestock assets: Percentage of households that own		
Bicycle	12.5	4.8
TV	33.9	19.3
Motorbike/scooter	39.8	25.3
Livestock ownership (average number owned)		
Cows	1.15	0.73
Buffalo	0.47	0.29
Goats	1.16	0.37

Source: ISEC-IFPRI Survey 2006.

Table 5.A.2	Occupation of Household Head in Surveyed Households in Karnataka, by Caste (percent)					
Occupation	SC (n = 226)	ST (n = 62)	OBC (n = 592)	General (n = 20)	Others (n = 53)	Total (n = 953)
Agriculture	27.2	46.5	62.1	38.5	15.8	49.6
Agricultural casual labor	53.1	30.2	16.4	0.0	26.3	26.2
Own business	2.0	4.7	5.1	15.4	13.2	5.1
Salaried work	4.8	7.0	1.5	15.4	10.5	3.5
Nonagricultural casual labor	2.7	7.0	2.1	0.0	13.2	3.2
Self-employed in service industry	2.7	0.0	3.3	7.7	2.6	3.0
Self-employed in household industry	0.0	2.3	1.8	7.7	15.8	2.4
Household work	2.0	0.0	2.6	7.7	0.0	2.2
Livestock management	0.0	0.0	0.3	0.0	0.0	0.2
Others	5.4	2.3	4.9	7.7	2.6	4.8

Source: ISEC-IFPRI Survey 2006.
Note: SC = scheduled caste, ST = scheduled tribe, OBC = other backward caste.

Figure 5.A.1 Reasons for Dissatisfaction with Drinking Water Services among Surveyed Men and Women in Karnataka

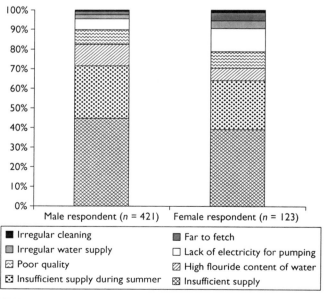

Source: ISEC-IFPRI Survey 2006.

Table 5.A.3 Training of Junior Engineers in Karnataka

Training subject	Number of trainings reported	Focus on women's issues
Construction of water supply facilities	10	0
Construction of sanitation facilities	8	0
Maintenance of water supply facilities	5	0
Rehabilitation of water supply facilities	4	0
Rehabilitation of sanitation facilities	4	0
Water source management arrangements	3	0
Training of rural population in water conservation	2	0
Training of rural population in water harvesting	2	0
Maintenance of sanitation facilities	2	0
Community organization	1	0
Other subjects	27	1
Total	68	1

Source: ISEC-TISS-IFPRI Survey 2008.

Table 5.A.4 Perceived Severity of Constraints on Service Providers in Karnataka
(percentage of respondents who identified constraint)

Constraint/severity	Junior engineer	Agricultural extension worker	Veterinary assistant	Food inspector
Staff shortage	(n = 16)	(n = 36)	(n = 30)	(n = 22)
Moderate	38	11	23	45
Strong	63	89	77	55
Political interference	(n = 21)	(n = 21)	(n = 16)	(n = 24)
Weak	5	0	0	4
Moderate	38	67	63	46
Strong	57	33	38	50

Source: ISEC-TISS-IFPRI Survey 2008.

Table 5.A.5 Self-Reported Outreach of Field Staff in Karnataka

Question	Junior engineer (*n* = 41)	Agricultural extension worker (*n* = 41)	Veterinary assistant (*n* = 40)	Food inspector (*n* = 34)	Anganwadi worker (*n* = 50)
For how many gram panchayats are you responsible in your work?	4.5	4.0	7.2	16.4	n.a.
For how many villages (including hamlets) are you responsible in your work?	35	26	41	106	n.a.
What is the total population in these villages?	23,800	26,290	22,040	120,460	1,775
What is the total number of households in these villages?	4,930	7,320	10,100	25,640	375
What is the total number of female-headed farm households in these villages?	1,050	1,030	570	2,480	n.a.

Source: ISEC-TISS-IFPRI Survey 2008.
Note: n.a.= Not applicable.

Table 5.A.6 **Frequency of Contacts by Senior Agricultural Staff in Karnataka (percentage of respondents)**

Institution	Frequent	Sometimes	Occasional	When need arises	Never
Gram panchayat	35	15	35	6	3
Taluk panchayat	41	15	18	15	6
Zilla panchayat	35	9	18	24	0
State agricultural universities/ agricultural research institutes	38	18	18	18	0
Training centers	35	15	15	3	6
Members of state legislative assemblies	24	3	24	32	3
Members of parliament	0	3	15	35	21
Private input supplier	26	9	12	65	6
Self-help group	29	0	12	35	15
Local NGO	15	6	6	0	24
Rural bank	9	6	18	21	9

Source: ISEC-TISS-IFPRI Survey 2008.
Note: Sample size is 34.

Table 5.A.7 Person or Institution Perceived to Be Mainly Responsible for Construction of Drinking Water Facilities in Surveyed Blocks in Karnataka

Type of facility	RDPR (Rural Development and Panchayati Raj) junior engineer	RDPR assistant director	RDPR executive engineer	Zilla panchayat	Gram panchayat	Water user organization	India rural water supply and sanitation agency	Other
Open Well	0	0	2	3	0	0	1	0
Bore Well with Hand Pump	0	0	2	7	1	0	0	0
Bore Well with Pump Set	1	1	6	6	3	0	0	2
Mini Water Supply Scheme	1	0	2	6	1	0	0	4
Piped Water Supply Scheme	1	0	2	6	0	1	0	0
Water Tank	0	0	2	3	1	0	0	1
Other	0	0	1	0	1	0	0	0
Total	3	1	17	31	7	1	1	7

Source: ISEC-TISS-IFPRI Survey 2008.

Table 5.A.8   Perceptions of District-Level Engineers in India Regarding Decentralization

Perception	Percent of respondents (n = 29)
Has decentralization helped better target project funds toward those most in need of drinking water and sanitation?	
Yes	79
How has decentralization helped?	
Better identification of the problems of beneficiaries	78
Better identification of beneficiaries	65
Transparency of funds availability	70
If not, why has it not helped?	
Improper identification of the problems of beneficiaries	20
Improper identification of beneficiaries	80
Lack of transparency of funds availability	40
Has decentralization increased the speed at which drinking water and sanitation facilities are installed?	
Yes	86
How has it increased the speed?	
Improved the accountability of service providers	28
Other	20

Source: ISEC-TISS-IFPRI Survey 2008.
Note: Multiple answers were possible.

Table 5.A.9   Time of Last Meeting of User Organization in Karnataka (percentage of members of each group)

Date of previous meeting	Farmers cooperative (n = 20)	Dairy cooperative society (n = 29)	Water and sanitation committee (n = 40)	Vigilance committee (n = 27)	Women's self-help group (n = 50)
Last week	0	0	12	3	60
Last month	6	14	30	44	25
Three months ago	0	7	18	35	0
Six months ago	17	14	9	3	0
One year ago	39	43	15	0	0
Other	39	22	15	15	15

Source: ISEC-TISS-IFPRI Survey 2008.

Table 5.A.10 Household Demographic Indicators in Ghana, by Zone (percentage of respondents)

Item	Forest (*n* = 385)	Transition (*n* = 384)	Savannah (*n* = 379)
Household head and literacy rate			
Household headed by female	32	18	9
Literacy rate among male household heads	71	64	22
Literacy rate among female household heads	41	36	8
Occupation of household head			
Farming	56[a]	78[b]	79[c]
Trading	12	5	4
Artisan	10	6	2
Nonagricultural laborer	9	4	4
Teaching	4	3	2
Percentage of households that own			
Mobile phone	41	49	28
TV	35	24	13
Percentage of communities with			
Assembly person resident	18	53	13
Water and sanitation committee	14	27	20
Agricultural extension agent resident	3	35	0

Source: ISSER-IFPRI Survey 2008.
a. Main crops grown are cocoa, cassava, oil palm, plantain, and rubber.
b. Main crops grown are yam and maize.
c. Main crops grown are maize, rice, yam, and shea nut.

Table 5.A.11 Average Number of Livestock Owned per Household in Ghana, by Zone

Type of livestock	Forest (*n* = 385)	Transition (*n* = 384)	Savannah (*n* = 379)
Chicken	8.0	8.3	8.6
Guinea fowl	3.6	0.5	6.0
Goats	1.0	1.7	4.1
Sheep	1.0	1.1	3.4
Pigs	0.3	0.2	0.4
Rabbits	0.1	0.0	0.1
Other poultry	0.1	0.3	0.1
Fish	0.0	0.0	0.5
Draught animals	0.0	0.0	0.1
Cattle	0.0	0.1	2.7
Grass cutter	0.0	0.1	0.0
Other	3.1	0.3	0.2

Source: ISSER-IFPRI Survey 2008.

Table 5.A.12 Infrastructure Stock and Development Projects in Ghana, by Zone (percentage of communities)

Item	Forest (n = 64)	Transition (n = 83)	Savannah (n = 84)
Infrastructure			
Primary school	73	75	75
Junior-secondary school	47	45	25
Health facility	22	23	13
Borehole	67	55	43
Other water facility	57	33	51
Public toilet	47	38	27
Road	0	0	0
Development project			
Microcredit	1	17	29
Water and sanitation	16	57	63
Child nutrition and health	2	40	26
Informal education	17	40	58

Source: ISSER-IFPRI Survey 2008.

Table 5.A.13 Reasons for Not Attending Community or Group Meetings about Agriculture in Ghana, by Zone (percentage of respondents)

Reason	Reason for not attending community meeting about agricultural Issues			Reason for not attending group meeting with agricultural extension agent or livestock officer		
	Forest (n = 163)	Transition (n = 266)	Savannah (n = 227)	Forest (n = 178)	Transition (n = 273)	Savannah (n = 259)
No such meeting held in village	88	89	81	89	85	81
Had other work to do	4	8	13	6	10	14
Meetings aren't very useful	2	2	2	2	1	2
Other	6	1	4	3	4	4

Source: ISSER-IFPRI Survey 2008.

Table 5.A.14 Types of Technologies Promoted in Ghana

Technology transmitted	Estimated number of farmers reached	Ratio of women to men
Planting techniques	14,400	0.39
Improved seed variety/plant material	14,000	0.38
Postharvest storage and handling	10,300	0.33
Group formation	10,000	0.39
Use of chemical fertilizer	9,500	0.44
Animal housing construction	9,500	0.34
Disease identification or control	8,600	0.38
Food processing	7,400	0.43
Animal parasite control	7,100	0.30
HIV/AIDS	6,900	0.89
Castration	6,700	0.31
Financial literacy	6,500	0.11
Use of agrochemicals for pests	5,100	0.42
Other interaction	4,000	0.50
Harvesting techniques	3,000	0.49
Use of herbicides	3,000	0.33
Other pest control techniques	2,500	0.45
Marketing of farm produce	2,200	0.60
Animal vaccination/deworming	1,700	0.33
Fire belts and safety	1,500	0.32
Disease in livestock	1,300	1.07
Sanitation and hygiene	600	1.94
Livelihood programs	600	0.66
Irrigation techniques	400	0.40

Source: ISSER-IFPRI Survey 2008.

Note: Figures are derived from estimations by the surveyed agricultural extension agents. Although the numbers may be subject to estimation errors, they indicate the relative outreach for different technologies and their gender dimension.

Table 5.A.15 Primary Source of Water for Households in Ghana (percentage of respondents)

Zone/primary source of water	Female-headed households	Male-headed households	p-value for test whether differences between the two groups are statistically significant	Politically connected[a]	Not politically connected	p-value for test of whether differences between the two groups are statistically significant
Forest	(n = 103)	(n = 223)		(n = 53)	(n = 211)	
River/lake/spring	24	35	0.06	21	31	0.13
Borehole	32	28	0.44	30	35	0.55
Well without pump	11	13	0.55	17	10	0.19
Public standpipe	20	16	0.35	17	16	0.81
Transition	(n = 680)	(n = 313)		(n = 61)	(n = 324)	
River/lake/spring	22	22	1.00	23	22	0.90
Borehole	28	43	0.02	41	41	0.97
Well without pump	19	6	00	5	9	0.27
Public standpipe	16	24	0.18	21	22	0.88
Savannah	(n = 31)	(n = 335)		(n = 85)	(n = 259)	
River/lake/spring	10	20	0.16	11	21	0.03
Borehole	39	27	0.15	29	25	0.48
Well without pump	3	13	0.10	12	12	0.89
Public standpipe	35	29	0.45	39	29	0.09

Source: ISSER-IFPRI Survey 2008.
a. A household is described as politically connected if it has or has had a member with political office.

Table 5.A.16 Awareness of and Membership in Community-Based Groups in Ghana, by Zone and Type of Respondent (percentage of respondents)

Type of group	Male household head			Female household head			Female respondents (female household heads and spouses)		
	Forest (n = 306)	Transition (n = 260)	Savannah (n = 339)	Forest (n = 68)	Transition (n = 119)	Savannah (n = 30)	Forest (n = 277)	Transition (n = 277)	Savannah (n = 199)
Awareness of group in community									
Self-help group	20	19	53	13	19	47	16	17	48
Finance credit union	08	15	26	13	22	40	10	13	28
Cooperative society	10	12	24	05	24	17	10	09	13
Women's group	23	41	71	21	35	67	24	37	68
Church group	73	86	53	70	91	60	78	90	44
School management committee	53	76	63	38	65	50	43	59	52
Parent-teacher association	74	90	77	54	82	67	71	84	66
Other religious group	21	45	63	21	37	70	27	38	59
Other	5	1	2	5	0	0	2	1	2
Membership in community group									
Self-help group	7	7	35	4	6	30	8	6	29

Finance credit union	2	3	12	2	04	20	2	2	11
Cooperative society	3	5	12	1	06	10	3	0	5
Women's group	2	2	8	11	18	47	14	20	45
Church group	35	36	11	53	59	13	56	56	15
School management committee	14	18	18	5	12	10	6	6	7
Parent-teacher association	38	44	52	32	29	47	36	39	35
Other religious group	5	6	46	5	4	60	08	06	42
Other	2	1	1	2	0	0	1	1	2

Source: ISSER-IFPRI Survey 2008.

Table 5.A.17   Financing of Construction of Water Facility in Ghana

Item	Percentage of respondents
Agency financing construction (n = 42)	
District assembly/Community Water and Sanitation Agency	55
District assembly through international donor	7
Local NGO	5
Other	33
Community contribution (number of communities) (n = 87)	
Labor	64
In-kind	57
Monetary contribution	66

Source: ISSER-IFPRI Survey 2008.

Table 5.A.18   Monetary Contribution of Community for Rehabilitation of Water Facilities in Ghana

Percent of monetary cost borne by the community	Percentage of respondents (n = 33)
0–10	76
11–30	15
31–100	9
Total	100

Source: ISSER-IFPRI Survey 2008.

Table 5.A.19   Payment for Water in Ghana, by Zone (percentage of respondents that pay for water)

Item	Forest (n = 387)	Transition (n = 351)	Savannah (n = 380)
Means of payment			
Contribute toward construction or setting up of a water source	24	60	62
Pay for maintenance and repair of water source	25	17	52
Pay fixed cost to use water	14	10	58
Pay for volume of water used	68	87	53
Frequency of payment			
Daily	86	87	50
Weekly	3	2	0
Monthly	11	3	47

Source: ISSER-IFPRI Survey 2008.

GENDER AND GOVERNANCE IN RURAL SERVICES

Table 5.A.20 Characteristics of Surveyed Households in Ethiopia (percentage of respondents, except where otherwise indicated)

Characteristic	Male household head (n = 833)	Female household head (n = 238)
Literacy	47.0	11.0
Main occupation		
Own farm cultivation/sharecropper	85.8	35.3
Livestock rearing	7.4	14.3
Student	3.1	2.5
Other government employee	0.6	0.0
Not in labor force due to age	0.6	5.0
Domestic work	0.5	34.5
Petty trade owner	0.5	1.3
Teacher	0.5	0.0
Casual labor	0.2	0.0
Disabled and unable to work	0.2	1.3
Herding	0.1	0.4
Prepared food or beverage seller	0.1	2.9
Religious worker	0.1	0.0
Other	0.1	0.4
Dung and firewood collection for sale	0.0	0.4
Forestry activities	0.0	0.4
Hired farm worker	0.0	0.8
Agricultural and consumer assets (ownership of at least one of each type of asset)		
Ox or bull	60.5	26.1
Goat or sheep	58.3	48.7
Radio/tape recorder	36.0	15.1
Donkey or mule	25.8	12.2
Camel or horse	10.9	13.0
Mobile/wireless phone	1.1	0.4
Number of agricultural assets	10.0	5.6
Material of roof		
Thatch	69.0	68.2
Iron	20.3	12.7
Wood	1.6	0.8
Bamboo	0.8	0.0
Mud	0.5	0.0
Cement/concrete	0.1	0.0
Other	7.7	18.2

Source: EEPRI-IFPRI Survey 2009.

Table 5.A.21 Use of Extension and Other Agricultural Services in Ethiopia, by Kebele (percentage of respondents)

Item	Afar-D (n = 139)	Amhara-D2 (n = 188)	Amhara-D3 (n = 230)	Benesh G-D (n = 295)	Gambella-D (n = 217)	Oromia-D (n = 284)	SNNP-D (n = 163)	Tigray-D (n = 187)
Visited by extension agent at farm or home	2	24	37	8	25	11	39	54
Attended extension agent's community meetings	1	24	27	13	18	15	27	39
Visited demonstration plots	0	5	3	3	3	1	1	4
Visited demonstration homes	0	3	1	0	0	0	0	1
Trained at farmer training center	0	3	1	0	0	1	0	1
Received service from cooperative	0	12	7	6	1	7	0	2
Received agricultural input credit	0	5	1	0	0	1	1	5

Source: EEPRI-IFPRI Survey 2009.

Figure 5.A.2   Use of Extension and Other Agricultural Services in Ethiopia, by Socioeconomic Status

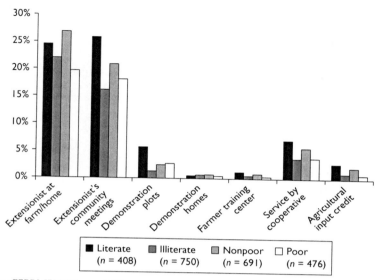

Source: EEPRI-IFPRI Survey 2009.

Figure 5.A.3   Tendency of Men and Women in Ethiopia to Complain When Dissatisfied with Drinking Water Facility

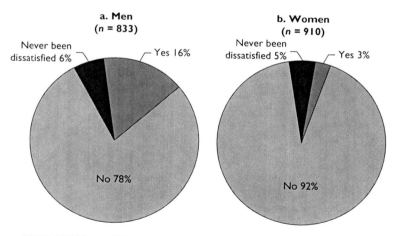

Source: EEPRI-IFPRI Survey 2009.
Note: Figure shows responses to following question: During the past 1 year, did you approach anyone when you were dissatisfied with the water quantity or quality?

	Education		Wealth	
	Literate ($n = 447$)	**Illiterate** ($n = 922$)	**Nonpoor**[a] ($n = 530$)	**Poor** ($n = 551$)
Public service				
Drinking water	28	34	28	36
Health	17	19	18	15
Roads	16	6	15	11
Electricity	14	8	17	13
Education	6	3	7	3
Livelihood opportunities	2	1	3	3
Small-scale irrigation	1	1	1	1
Sanitation/drainage	0	0	0	0

Table 5.A.22 Perceptions of Public Service Problems in Ethiopia, by Socioeconomic Status (percentage of respondents stating particular public service is most problematic)

Source: EEPRI-IFPRI Survey 2009.

a. Nonpoor are defined as households owning at least one ox.

NOTES

1. The category "other backward classes" comprises castes that traditionally have been disadvantaged but do not belong to the scheduled castes. The term *general castes* is used for castes that do not belong to the SC or OBC categories.

2. The number of observations is low for general castes and OBCs; the results are reported for completeness only.

3. Figure 5.7 must be interpreted with care, as missing answers may result in an overestimation of membership levels.

4. It is likely that such programs use agricultural field staff to reach the rural population because the health department or other departments lack sufficient field staff to reach rural households.

CHAPTER SIX

The Long Route of Accountability: Political Representatives and Their Linkages

This chapter examines the long route of accountability. In terms of the framework in figure 2.1, it focuses on the relationship between local political representatives with households (link HH–LP), service providers (link LP–PS), and political parties (link LP–PP) (figure 6.1). The most relevant tables and figures are included in the chapter. Additional tables and figures can be found in the annex.

INDIA

This section presents the results regarding the long route of accountability in India. It is based on the household survey and the survey among elected representatives (gram panchayat council members).

Characteristics of Political Representatives

Gram panchayat members surveyed in Karnataka overwhelmingly come from agricultural households in which cultivation is the main occupation (see annex figure 6.A.1). Almost one-fifth of the sample of elected leaders come from households in which the main occupation is agricultural wage labor. As expected, women and members from scheduled castes (SC) and scheduled tribes (ST) are overrepresented among leaders from agricultural wage households.

205

Figure 6.1   Long Route of Accountability

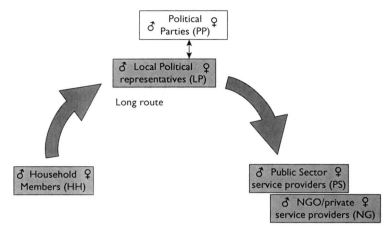

Source: Adapted from World Bank (2003).

SC/ST leaders are more likely than other leaders to be illiterate, although almost 16 percent of SC leaders and 21 percent of ST leaders report being functionally literate (see annex figure 6.A.2). Both groups are almost as likely as leaders of other backward classes (OBC) to have completed primary school. Box 6.1 provides case study evidence on the role of illiteracy as a potential obstacle for female gram panchayat presidents and members.

Almost 89 percent of council members are serving their first term; less than 17 percent have contested more than one election. Women and SC members are overrepresented among the new leaders, with almost 95 percent first-time legislators. The fact that less than 15 percent of ST and OBC leaders and 17 percent of male legislators served more than one term suggests that political history is not significant, even among groups that have historically held positions of power. Only a small proportion of council members come from families that held or once held elected positions in any of the panchayati raj institutions: 8 percent of male representatives, 7 percent of representatives from SCs, 4 percent of representatives from STs and OBCs, and 2 percent of female representatives reported having family members who held or once held elected positions.

The data also suggest that elections are fairly competitive: just 22 percent of members ever ran unopposed, and less than 2 percent ran unopposed more than once. Moreover, the study provides no evidence to support the oft-repeated concern that a potential deficit of political candidates from marginalized groups could reduce political competition. In fact, the study suggests the opposite to be true: SC/ST and female representatives are less likely ever to have been elected unopposed than male representatives or representatives from OBCs. There are no significant differences between SCs and OBCs in this

Box 6.1 Is Illiteracy an Obstacle to Women's Participation in Local Politics in India?

Illiteracy has been discussed as an important obstacle to women's participation in local politics in India. Datta (1998) notes that women with low levels of literacy find it impossible to participate in decision-making processes that are heavily dependent on written work and the legal language of agendas, minutes, and schedules. Jayal (2006, p. 24) observes that "without exception, every single piece of survey research on this question cites the recognition of women representatives that they would have been better able to contribute to the proceedings and activities of the panchayats had they had the advantage of schooling."

Evidence from the case studies suggests that the importance of illiteracy depends on a number of context-specific factors. In the A–B1 gram panchayat, in Bihar, for example, the female president was illiterate and could not effectively participate in the selection of beneficiaries for various development programs implemented by the gram panchayat. The president, a woman who belonged to a scheduled caste, did not have a political background or a family history of political leadership. This gave scope for others, such as the gram panchayat secretary and village elites, to take advantage of the situation and indulge in corrupt practices. The fact that beneficiaries were not selected in a gram sabha (village) meeting contributed to the problem.

In the A2–A1 gram panchayat in Karnataka, the team could observe that the gram sabha was functioning well; the gram panchayat secretary himself was proactive in promoting the participation of women. A female member of the block panchayat participated in the meeting, providing support to the gram panchayat president. As every beneficiary was discussed in the meeting, the negative effects of illiteracy could be minimized. Moreover, as one ex-president of a gram panchayat emphasized, many important tasks do not require literacy: "I do not know how to read or write, so I signed wherever I was asked to sign. I know I was an uneducated panchayat member, but I tried to do the best I could with whatever was possible to do with my hands, until (the matter) was in my hands. I didn't abdicate responsibility into someone else's hands. It is not necessary to be educated to see if the drainage is clean; I can see that for myself."

Source: Authors.

regard: almost one-fifth of each of these groups had been elected unopposed once. ST candidates are more likely than any other caste groups to have been elected unopposed, and they are more likely to have served more than one term as gram panchayat member.

The majority of council members are active in local organizations (see annex figure 6.A.3). SC members are most active: almost 70 percent either belong to a local organization or have a family member who belongs to one.

OBC council members follow close behind, with ST members reporting lower albeit still substantial participation (56 percent). Women are slightly less likely than men to belong to a local organization (65 percent of female and 68 percent of male legislators are members of a local organization).

Priorities of Political Representatives

This section analyzes the data that measure political representatives' perceptions of local investment priorities. It also examines the actions they initiated to address the problems.

Provision of drinking water is a major investment priority, with 46 percent of council members reporting it as their top priority (see annex table 6.A.1). Sanitation/drainage also ranks prominently, with almost 14 percent reporting it as the top priority and 30 percent ranking it second. Health and roads are also key priority areas. Council members from different caste groups seem to share these overall priorities, with 40–50 percent from each group listing drinking water as a top area for action and 13–18 percent reporting sanitation/drainage to be a key problem (see annex table 6.A.2).

There are no substantial differences between the perceptions of men and women; about 45 percent of men and 48 percent of women perceive water as the key priority on election (table 6.1). Sanitation/drainage and health figure prominently among the priority areas for action.

Representatives' Relationships with Households

This section deals with the accountability relationships between households and political representatives. As discussed in chapter 2, these mechanisms can

Table 6.1 Most Important Investment Priority of Gram Panchayat Members, by Gender

Priority	Male (n = 143)	Female (n = 129)
Water	44.1	47.6
Sanitation/drainage	13.3	15.1
Health	11.2	10.3
Housing	9.8	10.3
Roads	9.1	4.8
Electricity	6.3	4.0
Education	1.4	1.6
Street lights	1.4	3.2
Transport	1.4	2.4
Livelihood opportunities	1.4	0.0
Irrigation	0.7	0.0
Illicit liquor	0.0	0.8

Source: ISEC-IFPRI Survey 2006.

take a variety of forms, including voting, lobbying, and meetings at which representatives have to justify their actions.

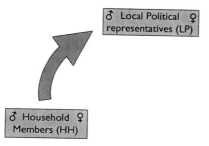

Voting and Political Party Membership

More than 90 percent of both male and female respondents report voting. Formal political party membership does not seem to be a major "accountability link" in India, however, as just 6.8 percent of male and 5.7 percent of female respondents indicate that they belong to a political party. The percentage is somewhat higher (10 percent) among STs and general castes (all castes not classified as ST or OBC).

Participation in Meetings

In Karnataka, three types of local meetings provide a platform for citizens to interact with their elected representatives: *gram sabha* (village assembly meetings), the *jamabandhi* (public audit meetings), and the general body meeting of gram panchayat councils. The gram sabha is the institutional platform that stimulates the political participation of citizens and decides on the distribution of public goods within villages at least four times a year (see Besley and others 2004).[1] The jamabandhi program is the annual public audit of the financial records and registers of the gram panchayat. Introduced in 2001, it is implemented by officials at the block level, who are requested to disseminate the results to the village constituents. Village constituents use the results to evaluate the functioning of the gram panchayat in terms of its effectiveness and use of funds.[2] In addition to the gram sabha and jamabandhi meetings, one can also consider the general body meeting of gram panchayats. Initiated to discuss resource planning at the village level, the meeting is mandated to take place at least once a month. These meetings are not open to the general public; they are forums in which local political representatives interact among themselves.

The majority of gram panchayats meet twice a year, falling short of the mandate to meet four times a year (see annex figure 6.A.4). This finding is in line with other evidence on the irregularity of gram sabha meetings and thus to the potential ineffectiveness of gram sabhas as an institutional mechanism for promoting participation in the planning and implementation of development programs (see, for example, Srivastava 2006, for Uttar Pradesh). Gram panchayat general body meetings are held 6–9 times a year—less frequently than the mandated 12 times a year. The meetings appear to be summoned when need arises. Almost all gram panchayats implement the obligatory annual jamabandhi meeting. Across all types of meetings, there is no significant difference in the number of meetings in gram panchayats with female and male gram panchayat presidents.

Women are less likely to attend gram sabha and jamabhandi meetings than men,[3] although women who do attend do so as often as men, attending an average 1.2 gram sabha meetings a year (figure 6.2). The main issues discussed at meetings are drinking water, road infrastructure, beneficiary selection, housing, and drainage (see annex figure 6.A.5).

There are no significant gender differences in the propensity of women and men to attend gram panchayat general body meetings. The absence of gender differences is attributable to the fact that these meetings are open only to elected council members, who are required to attend.

Participation in gram sabha meetings is positively associated with political party membership and with membership in village associations (table 6.2). Women, but not members of SC/ST, are less likely to attend meetings than

Figure 6.2   Attendance Rates at Different Types of Community Meetings in Karnataka

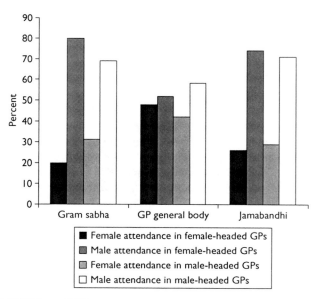

■ Female attendance in female-headed GPs
▨ Male attendance in female-headed GPs
▨ Female attendance in male-headed GPs
☐ Male attendance in male-headed GPs

Source: ISEC-IFPRI Survey 2006.
Note: Sample observation sizes were as follows: In female-headed GPs, 21 for gram sabha and general body meetings and 17 for jamabandhi meetings; in male-headed GPs, 46 for gram sabha meetings, 47 for general body meetings, and 44 for jamabandhi meetings.

Table 6.2 Factors Associated with Participation in Gram Sabha Meetings in Karnataka

Variable	Probit result
Membership in a political party	0.122**
	(0.053)
Membership in at least one village association	0.091***
	(0.034)
Member of SC/ST	−0.032
	(0.038)
Female gender	−0.252***
	(0.041)
Landless household	0.005
	(0.038)
Income	−0.002***
	(0.001)
Literacy	0.132***
	(0.036)
Number of observations	918

Source: Authors, based on Birner, Shekher, and Palaniswamy 2007 and data from the ISEC-IFPRI Survey 2006.
Note: Standard errors are in parentheses.
***Significant at the 1% level; **significant at the 5% level.

others. Wealthier households tend to participate less, although literacy increases the likelihood of participation.

Most household respondents present at gram sabha meetings attend only one meeting, although most gram panchayats organized at least two gram sabha meetings a year. Households that are dissatisfied with gram sabha meetings criticize the inadequate availability of information about the meeting, the lack of information about its agenda, and the inconvenience of the location. The gender of the gram panchayat president does not influence satisfaction with the gram sabha meetings.

Interaction with Political Representatives and Officials

Both female and male household respondents predominantly contact officials at the lowest government tier to address service delivery problems. Women are less likely than men to interact with gram panchayat and block panchayat presidents, gram panchayat secretaries, male gram panchayat members, block panchayat and district panchayat members, district officials, and members of the legislative assembly (see annex figure 6.A.6). The fact that household members rarely contact government staff at the block level (where the professionals responsible for service provision are located) suggests that the long route of accountability is more attractive or accessible than the short route. In fact, the importance of local politicians as problem solvers can be seen as an indicator of the importance of the long route of accountability. Both male and female household respondents are more likely to contact male rather than female gram panchayat members. This result could be driven by the smaller share of female gram panchayat members or by behavioral and institutional factors that cause female gram panchayat members to be perceived as less effective in addressing service delivery problems.

Households interacted more than twice a year with all parties and almost five times a year with ex–gram panchayat and block panchayat members (figure 6.3). Female household members do not interact with most officials, except female gram panchayat members and ex–gram panchayat members.

The most frequent reasons why household members contact officials is to discuss drainage, drinking water, and housing (see annex figure 6.A.7). Agricultural extension and livestock services never featured as a reason. The most important reason for interacting with the gram panchayat bill collector appears to be road infrastructure development. The gram panchayat president is contacted primarily to discuss issues related to drinking water.

The results of a probit model show that households in which at least one member participates in a village organization are more likely to contact an official concerning drainage or drinking water than households that do not (table 6.3). Political activism, measured by membership in a political party or

Figure 6.3   Average Annual Number of Meetings between Households and Officials and Percentage of Women in Karnataka Who Interacted with Officials in Past Year

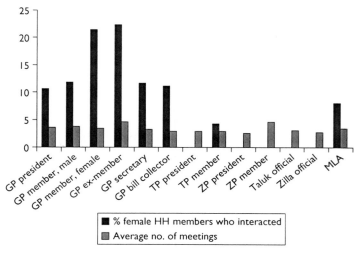

Source: ISEC-IFPRI Survey 2006.
Note: GP = gram panchayat; TP = taluk/block panchayat; ZP = zilla/district panchayat; MLA = member of the legislative assembly (n = 966).

Table 6.3   Factors Associated with Contacting an Official Concerning Drainage or Drinking Water in Karnataka

Variable	Probit result
Politically active	0.030
	(0.037)
Member of village group	0.070***
	(0.024)
SC/ST	−0.034
	(0.029)
Female gender	−0.017
	(0.028)
Landless household	−0.045
	(0.029)
Household income	−0.000
	(0.000)
Literacy of household head	0.008
	(0.027)
Number of observations	924

Source: Authors, based on Birner, Shekher, and Palaniswamy 2007 and the data from ISEC-IFPRI Survey 2006.
Note: Standard errors are in parentheses.
***Significant at the 1% level.

contributions to political campaigns, is not associated with the propensity to contact an official. Neither SC/ST status nor literacy significantly affects the likelihood of contacting an official.

Participation in meetings and contacting of public officials does not necessarily result in better service provision outcomes: local power structures may undermine the effectiveness of such efforts. In Bihar, the use of physical violence is a serious obstacle in this respect (box 6.2).

Effectiveness of Political Representatives in Providing Services

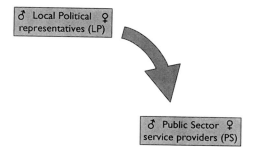

This section deals with the "second leg" of the long route of accountability. It examines the role local political representatives can play in influencing

Box 6.2 Violence as an Obstacle to the Long Route of Accountability in Bihar

Violence can undermine the effectiveness of contacting elected leaders and public officials as a means to improve local governance and public service provision, as the case of Bihar shows. In A–A1, a woman explained in a self-help group meeting that complaints against the corrupt gram panchayat president could not be made, because the president's husband was always involved, and he was accompanied by six armed bodyguards. If any complaints were made to visiting officials against the president, her husband would threaten them and their families with violence. Women recounted cases in which the husbands of women who had complained were kidnapped and beaten up. Even their daughters were molested. The household of one woman who complained was branded as violating the village rules, and no food or wage labor was offered to its members. This type of violence and excommunication made even the most vocal female member of the self-help group remain silent and meek in public gatherings.

Source: Bihar case study 2008.

service providers or working together with service providers to deliver public services.

In India, the ability of local political representatives to pursue activities depends on the different schemes available and on the functionaries and funds they can rely on. Programs are funded using different resources, including funds raised by the gram panchaysts themselves (taxes, penalties, fines), statutory development grants, the Twelfth Finance Commission grant, and funds that come under the Sampoorna Grameen Rozgar Yojana (SGRY) scheme (see annex figure 6.A.8). The SGRY program, which aims to create wage employment and durable community infrastructure in rural India, is the largest and only universal decentralized program of public goods provision implemented through the panchayati raj institutions in Karnataka. The funds provided under this program represent 27–35 percent of the total finances received by the gram panchayats in the sample.

The availability of financial resources does not differ between male- and female-headed gram panchayats. However, differences prevail in the availability of resources from the different schemes across time. For almost all financial schemes, the observed time effects in the income and expenditure flows of male- and female-headed gram panchayats are statistically significant.

Effect of Gender and Caste of Local Politicians on Resource Allocation

Using data from the 2006 household and gram panchayat survey, Palaniswamy and Krishnan (2008) evaluate how local power structures influence the functioning of two institutions—a formula-based system of intergovernmental fiscal transfers to the gram panchayat and a council-based voting system at the level of the gram panchayat—that shape the allocation of local public resources in Karnataka. Although a set of rules defines the operation of both institutions, these rules are set in an institutional environment in which the bargaining power of disadvantaged and elite social groups and that of female and male gram panchayat members differs.

Their study exploits the policy of mandated representation in the gram panchayats to identify the effects of relative bargaining power and power hierarchies. Public resource allocation is identified through the fiscal resources received by the gram panchayat and its constituent villages. As indicated in chapter 3, this policy mandates the reservation of seats for women and for people from SCs, STs, and OBCs.[4]

Results based on the allocation of financial resources from the SGRY program suggest that the design of political institutions matters. Although the formula-bound allocation of fiscal grants to the village councils was successfully implemented, the within-council allocation governed by a legislative voting process reveals severe targeting failures. The results suggest that these targeting failures reflect elements of elite capture and that female council members are not uniformly disadvantaged in bargaining for public resources. Specifically, female council members belonging to SCs receive significantly fewer resources than other women, than men from SCs, and than other disadvantaged social groups (tables 6.4 and 6.5).

Table 6.4 reports the results on the effect of village bargaining power on village-level SGRY expenditures. The average effect of being represented by an SC or ST reserved councilor is negative and significant, indicating that the villages represented by SC or ST councilors receive fewer resources; the average effect of being represented by a female reserved councilor is not significant, although the sign is negative (column 1). When variables that may be correlated with superior bargaining power are included (column 2), the only variable significantly correlated with greater SGRY expenditure is the dummy variable, indicating that the village is represented by a council member from an OBC dominant caste. This suggests that SC/ST council members elected from reserved seats may perform worse than other council members. However, they perform worse only when compared with councilors who do not belong to the dominant castes. Notably, the sign on the dummy variable that measures the effect of being represented by a female council member is positive, although it is not significant. This suggests that female members perform no differently from men when the comparison group excludes councilors who belong to the OBC dominant castes.

Interaction terms are used for female council members elected to reserved seats in order to separate the effects of caste and gender (table 6.5). In the first specification, the average effect of SC/ST council members on village SGRY expenditures is negative. Female council members from an SC or

Table 6.4 Village Bargaining Power and SGRY Expenditures

Variable	(1)	(2)
Village represented by SC reserved member	−48,407.03*	−9,110.52
	(29,035.31)	(36,644.50)
Village represented by ST reserved member	−12,8662.73**	−7,9206.00
	(5,7620.55)	(63,739.22)
Village represented by member of OBC "A"	−4,2620.30	−18,184.40
	(3,6421.34)	(45,329.10)
Village represented by member of OBC "B"	−3,3006.90	−42,818.07
	(46,956.26)	(55,569.55)
Village represented by female reserved member	−22,302.41	16,475.78
	(26,946.73)	(42,166.14)
Village population	4.15	4.33
	(6.97)	(6.78)
Village SC population	−60.16	−67.49
	(69.36)	(73.45)
Village ST population	−3.54	−25.62
	(35.40)	(53.28)
Village represented by member of OBC dominant caste		5,5245.62
		(34,213.14)
Village represented by member elected unopposed		3,9205.15
		(44,430.47)
Land owned by village representative		200.63
		(829.50)
SC/ST hamlet dummy		47,400.80
		(39,264.21)
Number of observations	199	196
R^2	0.69	0.73

Source: Palaniswamy and Krishnan 2008.
Note: Robust standard errors in parentheses, clustered at the gram panchayat level. Regressions include a constant term, a gram panchayat president dummy, and a dummy for whether the village is reserved for an SC/ST gram panchayat president.
**Significant at the 5% level; *significant at the 10% level.

disadvantaged caste, including an ST, perform worse than other council members, including councilors who do not belong to the OBC dominant castes (column 2). Female council members from an ST or OBC do not perform significantly worse than councilors from nondominant castes. This suggests that female council members have differential bargaining abilities and that these abilities depend on their caste identities.

The role played by their husbands has been posited to influence the effectiveness of female gram panchayat members. The qualitative case studies suggest that there is a considerable variation regarding their effect (box 6.3).

Table 6.5 Identity and Gender of Village Representative and Village SGRY Expenditures

Variable	(1)	(2)
Village represented by SC member	−57,690.82*	26,202.53
	(29,970.56)	(35,529.49)
Village represented by ST member	−304,839.20**	−266,548.38**
	(128,919.78)	(114,460.21)
Village represented by member of OBC "A"	−65,806.51*	1,261.89
	(38,349.42)	(41,678.14)
Village represented by member of OBC "B"	−50,265.23	−100,795.50**
	(36,558.48)	(47,100.31)
Village represented by SC female (interaction)	−201,552.95	−215,331.52*
	(129,845.99)	(110,009.46)
Village represented by ST female (interaction)	−13,113.20	34,303.27
	(39,147.61)	(59,185.85)
Village represented by OBC female (interaction)	14,887.47	39,282.56
	(30,140.01)	(35,160.68)
Village population	2.88	1.33
	(5.88)	(5.26)
Village SC population	−52.68	−52.66
	(57.74)	(51.45)
Village ST population	2.78	−1.64
	(38.42)	(62.86)
Village represented by member of OBC dominant caste		127,972.51***
		(46,071.67)
Number of observations	199	196
R^2	0.71	0.76

Source: Palaniswamy and Krishnan 2008.

Note: Robust standard errors in parentheses, clustered at the GP level; Regressions include constant term, GP president village and GP president reserved for SC/ST dummies; column 2 includes village represented by member elected unopposed, land owned by village representative, and SC/ST hamlet. Both specifications include gram panchayat dummies; neither includes district dummies.

***Significant at the 1% level; **significant at the 5% level; *significant at the 10% level.

Interaction of Local Politicians with the Public Administration and with State and National Politicians

Elected officials at higher levels of local government and at the state level are the main channels through which council members address problems of rural service provision (table 6.6).[5] Half of members were also able to meet the executive officer at the block level. Less than 5 percent contact the district panchayat executive officer (see Birner, Shekher, and Palaniswamy 2007 for details).

Thirty-eight percent of gram panchayat council members found that the officials they contacted to solve rural service provision problems were effective

Box 6.3 Are Female Panchayat Presidents Merely Tokens for Their Husbands?

The case studies in Bihar indicate that the role of the husbands of gram panchayat presidents can range across a wide spectrum. At the one end of the spectrum are husbands who effectively manage the affairs on behalf of their wives. In the A-A1 gram panchayat in Bihar, for example, the husband of the female gram panchayat president was a dominant person. His wife was illiterate, belonged to an SC, and did not show much interest in her position. Moreover, she had refused to run for office because she had eight children and was pregnant. Her husband used his family's membership in the *paswans* (the dominant caste among the local SCs) to manipulate the local power structure and secure the gram panchayat presidency for his wife. In reality, he functioned as the gram panchayat president.

At the other end of the spectrum, husbands can be very supportive without interfering in their wives' responsibilities as elected representatives. The husbands of the female president of B-district panchayat in Bihar and the female block panchayat president in the A-district of Karnataka played very facilitating roles, helping their wives discharge their responsibilities without making their presence felt.

Source: Bihar case study 2008.

Table 6.6 Contacts of Gram Panchayat Council Members (percentages)

Official met	Ever	Occasionally	Sometimes	Frequently
GP president (n = 218)	80.1	3.2	14.7	82.1
Other GP member (n = 165)	60.7	1.8	10.3	87.9
GP secretary (n = 249)	91.5	4.8	15.3	79.9
TP members/president (n = 179)	65.8	15.6	35.2	49.2
TP executive officer (n = 137)	50.4	20.4	45.3	34.3
TP other officer (n = 24)	8.8	25.0	20.8	54.2
ZP members/president (n = 153)	56.3	21.6	36.0	42.5
ZP executive officer (n = 37)	13.6	35.1	35.1	29.7
Other district official (n = 13)	4.8	53.9	23.1	23.1
Member of legislative assembly (n = 176)	64.7	32.4	49.4	18.2
Member of parliament (n = 40)	14.7	47.5	42.5	10.0
Traditional panchayat member (n = 35)	12.9	2.9	20.0	77.1
Other (n = 24)	8.8	33.3	62.5	4.2

Source: ISEC-IFPRI Survey 2006.
Note: GP = gram panchayat; TP = taluk/block panchayat; ZP = zilla/district panchayat. Columns 2-4 (occasionally, sometimes, frequently) are breakdowns of column 1 (ever). The entries in columns 2-4 may not sum to 100 due to rounding.

in resolving these problems. Gender, caste, holding of a reserved seat, land ownership, and political history were not significantly associated with satisfaction with the contacted officials (table 6.7). Unexpectedly, literacy was negatively associated with being satisfied, which may indicate that literate council members are more critical of the actions the contacted officials undertook. Council members who held seats reserved for SC/ST were less likely to contact a member of parliament or the state legislative assembly;

Variable	Action taken by contacted official considered successful by gram panchayat council member	Likelihood of contacting member of parliament or state legislative assembly
Female gender	0.053	−0.138
	(0.136)	(0.381)
Member of SC/ST	−0.019	0.124
	(0.089)	(0.326)
Gram panchayat president	0.019	0.060
	(0.072)	(0.137)
Seat reserved for SC/ST	−0.070	−0.608*
	(0.120)	(0.339)
Seat reserved for women	−0.130	0.226
	(0.135)	(0.286)
Land ownership (acres)	−0.004	0.047***
	(0.003)	(0.015)
Political history (family member of gram panchayat representative held elected office before)	0.069	−0.504
	(0.141)	(0.497)
Literate, not completed primary school[a]	0.001	
	(0.117)	
Literate, completed primary school	−0.202**	0.338*
	(0.088)	(0.188)
Secondary education	0.028	0.133
	(0.090)	(0.261)
Number of observations	272	60

Table 6.7 Factors Associated with Gram Panchayat Council Members' Effectiveness and Likelihood of Contacting Member of Parliament or the State Legislative Assembly

Source: Authors, based on Birner, Shekher, and Palaniswamy 2007 and data from ISEC-IFPRI Survey 2006.

Note: Standard errors are in parentheses.

a. No illiterate council member contacted a member of parliament or the state legislative assembly.

***Significant at the 1% level; **significant at the 5% level; *significant at the 10% level.

Box 6.4 Dealing with the Bureaucracy: Strategies of Female Politicians

The case of a female block panchayat president in the A2-A block in Karnataka illustrates the challenges female representatives face in dealing with public officials. Asked about the biggest challenge women face in leadership positions, she responded, "It's the attitude of the bureaucrats." She explained that she had benefited from training that focused on showing panchayat members how to question bureaucrats. As she explained, she learned how to push for answers when a bureaucrat says "the funds have not come." She said that it is necessary to ask "How is it possible that the funds have not come?" However, as she pointed out, "as a man, you can speak with authority to them [the bureaucrats], you can speak with a loud and authoritative voice, then they listen to you. As a woman, you can't do that."

When asked what other means female presidents have at their disposal, she related the following event: The block panchayat council members were very dissatisfied with the previous head of the block, who misused development funds. The block panchayat president, together with her fellow panchayat council members, took action to have him replaced. They organized a silent demonstration in the form of a "sit-in" in front of his office. This was culturally acceptable for women to do, and it attracted considerable media attention. As a consequence, the executive officer was replaced.

Source: Karnataka case study 2008.

---

literate council members and members from the land-owning class were more likely to do so.

When asked to cite the factors that may cause the interaction with higher-level officials to be ineffective or unsatisfactory, council members referred to the lack of a timely response, the release of insufficient grants, the inadequate or insufficient number of new capital and infrastructure installments (such as drainage systems, borewells, and street lights), and the absence of any action taken (despite assurances that action would be taken).

The study indicates that female panchayat members face challenges in contacting public officials, because established gender roles make it difficult for them to exercise authority. They sometimes develop innovative strategies to deal with this problem (box 6.4).

GHANA

The Ghana case study was conducted in two districts of the savannah zone, S-1 and S-2. S-1 was headed by a female district chief executive, S-2 by a male chief executive.

Representatives' Relationship to Households

This section deals with the relationship between political representatives and households, the first leg in the long route of accountability (see figure 2.1). It is based on the household survey, the survey of districts assembly members, and the qualitative case studies.

Interaction between Households and Representatives

Households in the three agroecological zones interact more frequently with unit committees and assembly members than with district assembly staff (table 6.8). At the household level, male-headed and female-headed households and female spouses use the unit committee members and assembly person more often to communicate concerns or needs. This is not surprising as these two elected representatives live in households in the community and are thus the first point of contact when there is a problem.

Political party functionaries are also contacted frequently. Both major political parties in Ghana have membership structures that reach down below the district level, which may be why political party members are accessible. In all three agroecological zones, male-headed households interact more with the political party functionaries than female-headed households and female spouses. In the transition zone, there are more interactions with male- and female-headed households and female spouses than in the forest and savannah zones.

Table 6.8 **Percentage of Household Heads and Spouses Contacting Various Elected Representatives in Ghana, by Zone and Gender**

Zone/contact person	Male household heads	Female household heads	Female spouses
Forest zone	(*n* = 259)	(*n* = 120)	(*n* = 163)
Unit committee member	53	26	28
Assemblyman/woman	43	23	22
District assembly personnel	10	4	2
Political party functionary	24	9	9
Transition zone	(*n* = 303)	(*n* = 66)	(*n* = 189)
Unit committee member	59	33	41
Assemblyman/woman	59	41	41
District assembly personnel	20	11	7
Political party functionary	39	20	21
Savannah zone	(*n* = 341)	(*n* = 30)	(*n* = 149)
Unit committee member	42	27	34
Assemblyman/woman	48	27	37
District assembly personnel	9	13	3
Political party functionary	23	10	12

Source: ISSR-IPFPRI Survey 2008.

The case study findings from S-1 and S-2 indicate that the unit committees appear to be a forum within which less educated women participate in district assembly affairs. This finding may indicate that the role of the unit committees has increased over time, as the earlier literature generally considered the subdistrict structures to be dysfunctional (NCG and Dege Consult 2007). Members of the district assembly and the unit committees perform different roles, which correspond to the gender dynamics prevalent in rural society. The case study observations suggest that the unit committee member serves as a focal person within the community to elicit information on needs and priorities and to motivate self-help. The assembly member channels this information to the district government. Often the sole point of contact between a community and external actors, the assembly member lobbies to bring the resources funneled into the district by the national government or NGOs to meet the priorities of the community. Whereas unit committee members work predominantly with their peers, functioning within their indigenous social structure, assembly members intermediate between the local community context and the district assembly. In the S-1 and S-2 districts, where 75–95 percent of women are illiterate and only a small percentage attended the formal schools where English, the prevailing language, is taught, many of the women in the qualitative gender case study considered serving as an assembly member to be out of their reach. The extreme time demands on rural women's lives make the time-consuming yet unpaid position patently unattractive. For these reasons, women were not interested in serving on the assembly.

Serving on a unit committee would appear to be more feasible for women, but the informality with which unit committees are constituted precludes them from participating in even this realm. Unit committee positions are elective if more than 10 people nominate themselves for the committee (the first elections were held in 1998). Frequently, however, communities forgo this election, and opinion leaders chose 10 people to sit on the committee, if such a committee meets at all. Often most community members do not know the process by which the committee is chosen. In these cases, it is not likely that women will be selected to join the committee.

Voting

Voter turnout in the presidential elections in the six districts surveyed increased considerably between 2000 and 2004, rising from 60 percent to 85 percent (table 6.9). Generally, voter turnout was higher in the selected districts in the savannah zone than in the forest and transition zones.

The survey conducted for this study shows even higher voter turnout for all categories of elections and all types of respondents (table 6.10). These figures have to be interpreted with care, as overreporting is common in ex post questions about voting. Still, as official figures also show a turnout of more than

Table 6.9 Voter Turnout in the 2000 and 2004 Presidential Elections, by Survey District in Ghana (percent)

Zone/district	2000	2004
Forest zone		
F-1	58	85
F-2	62	86
Transition zone		
T-1	54	86
T-2	55	81
Savannah zone		
S-1	65	85
S-2	67	89

Source: Web site of the Electoral Commission of Ghana (http://www.ec.gov.gh/).

Table 6.10 Self-Reported Voter Turnout in Surveyed Districts in Ghana, by Zone and Office (percent)

Type of election	Male household heads ($n = 236$)	Female household heads ($n = 120$)	Female spouses ($n = 163$)
Forest zone			
District assembly	96	94	89
Unit committee	95	91	85
Member of parliament	97	95	94
President	97	95	94
Transition zone	($n = 316$)	($n = 69$)	($n = 218$)
District assembly	98	98	95
Unit committee	97	98	95
Member of parliament	98	98	96
President	98	98	96
Savannah zone	($n = 346$)	($n = 33$)	($n = 184$)
District assembly	98	93	95
Unit committee	95	91	93
Member of parliament	99	93	94
President	99	93	94

Source: ISSER-IFPRI Survey 2008.

80 percent, one can conclude that participation in the form of voting is very high in all three regions.

Effectiveness of Political Representatives in Providing Services

The effectiveness of political representatives in providing services depends on a variety of factors, discussed in this section. These include membership in subcommittees of the district assembly, the ability to raise resources and implement projects, relationships with other actors, and support from NGOs and external agencies.

Membership in Subcommittees

The survey covered 114 district assembly members, 10 of whom were female (table 6.11). (As the number of interviewed female district assembly members was low, reflecting their small share of all members, the figures in table 6.11 are only indicative.) No female member was on the executive committee, the committee that governs the district with the district chief executive. (The executive committee is formed by the heads of the subcommittees, none of whom were female.) As the district assembly meetings are not held frequently, the subcommittees are important for actual decision making. According to qualitative information, the assembly mostly approves what has been developed by the subcommittees, the district chief executive, and the district administration. Female district assembly members appear to play a larger role in the Water and Sanitation Subcommittee, which does not seem attractive to male district assembly members.

Implementation of Projects

From the viewpoint of political representatives in Ghana, providing public services is typically synonymous with securing "development projects" for their communities. This section discusses the factors that influence the effectiveness of assembly members in securing these projects.

Factors that influence the effectiveness of assembly members. The case study tried to establish whether women are as effective as men in securing development projects for their areas. The sample was skewed toward first-term

Table 6.11 Gender Composition of District Assembly Committees (percentage of all members)

Committee	Male (n = 104)	Female (n = 10)
Executive committee	26	0
Subcommittees		
Social services	29	29
Water and sanitation	3	14
Agricultural production	21	14
Works	14	14
Development planning	12	14
Finance/administration	19	14
Social justice	18	14
Civic	13	0

Source: ISSER-IFPRI Survey 2008.

Note: Districts assembly members can participate in more than one subcommittee.

female representatives, as there was only one second-term female representative. Although two of the three women in S-1 and S-2 districts had secured fewer projects than some of the men interviewed (one assemblywoman had secured grinding mills for women's groups in her area with the help of the female district chief executive; the other had cleaned up a sanitation crisis in her community), this could be attributed more to their lack of experience and other factors (box 6.5).

The effectiveness of district assembly members also depends on the extent to which their priorities match those of households. In the forest and the savannah zones, both households and assembly members cited insufficient drinking water as the major problem (assembly members in the transition zone ranked the problem of roads higher than households did). In the savannah zone, assembly

---

Box 6.5   District Assembly Members as "Glorified Beggars"

As one interviewed female assembly member put it, assembly members are like "glorified beggars." This expression captures the mismatch—articulated in many interviews—between the high expectations of constituents and the limited influence that assembly members actually have on the public administration. If the role of assembly members is to act as delegates for their communities and to lobby influential actors to bring resources home, then the ability to lobby would seem to matter greatly to their performance and thus their long-term electoral success, assuming that citizens vote based on performance. The case study evidence suggests that three factors influence the ability of district assembly members to lobby: social networks, transportation/mobility, and experience and knowledge of the assembly system. One question of importance to gender studies is whether female assembly members have equitable access to the factors that determine their success. The qualitative field research identified the following dynamics.

Both men and women in the assembly draw on extensive networks of relationships to support their work, at both the community and district levels. They draw on relationships built on family ties; shared ethnic, religious, professional, and educational backgrounds; and other factors. The study could not show that women who are already in leadership positions are excluded from any particularly important networks. In particular, women seem to be no more or less likely to be tied into the district-level party machinery than men. Some men and women were secretive about their party affiliations, and some were public about them. Further analysis is needed to fully explicate such linkages and their impact on women's performance.

Transportation almost certainly puts women at a disadvantage. Women often need accompaniment to travel long distances or at night, when many

(continued)

assembly members handle their assembly work. Mobility challenges means that they are less able to show up at the assembly as often as men (which seems to be an important strategy for learning about opportunities and reminding staff of their requests). Mobility challenges also mean that women may not be able to visit communities in which they are not resident, which affects their relationships with their constituents. This may affect assembly members in the savannah zone in particular, where few district assembly members reside in their constituency.

Time in the assembly seems to be one of the biggest factors predicting the success of an assembly member. Although this seems gender neutral at face value, women are only slowly entering local government activities in Ghana and thus have less experience within the system to draw on. Presumably, this will change as women's tenure in local governance grows. However, there may be gender-specific factors, such as time constraints caused by family obligations, that dissuade women from having as long a tenure in the assembly as men.

Source: Ghana case studies 2008.

members paid close attention to sanitation, which received little attention by households (unlike in the transition zone). None of the female household heads ranked it as a concern. This discrepancy may reflect different levels of awareness, as a number of water and sanitation projects in that zone may have aimed to build awareness specifically among assembly members.

Perceptions of the role and effectiveness of female assembly members. Gender training was widespread among district assembly members: 73 percent of male and 80 percent of female assembly members had received training with a gender component (table 6.12). All female district assembly members felt they had the same advantages as male assembly members. Eighty percent of male assembly members agreed with their female counterparts on this question, and the difference between men and women was not statistically significant.

Among male district assembly members who believed that their female counterparts did not have the same advantages, one cited the outspokenness of men in assembly deliberations as the reason for this; another said of female assembly members, "Most are not popular." No statistical difference could be determined between men and women on the question of whether male and female district assembly members had the same responsibilities toward women: 4 of the 6 female respondents and 54 percent of the 46 male respondents believed that promoting the interests of women was equally the responsibility of all assembly members. Men were slightly more likely than women (96 percent versus 80 percent) to believe that female assembly members were very effective or somewhat effective in promoting the interests of women, a

Table 6.12 Training and Perceptions of Assembly Members Regarding Gender Issues (percent)

Question	Male	Female
Have you received training with a gender component?	73 ($n = 58$)	80 ($n = 10$)
Did you find the training useful? (percentage of those who received training with gender component)	55 ($n = 42$)	63 ($n = 8$)
Do female district assembly members have the same advantages as male members?	80 ($n = 49$)	100 ($n = 5$)
Do both male and female district assembly members have the same responsibilities toward women?	($n = 46$)	($n = 6$)
Female members have special responsibility	46	33
All members have equal responsibility	54	67
How effective are female district assembly members in promoting the interests of women?	($n = 42$)	($n = 5$)
Very effective	67	40
Somewhat effective	29	40
Not very effective	2	20
Not at all effective	2	0

Source: ISSER-IFPRI Survey 2008.

result that had marginal statistical significance. Among those who believed that women were not effective in promoting women's interests, one woman cited women's inability to speak up as the reason for this. A male assembly member suggested that women had not organized into effective groups. Another male respondent felt that women "are not time conscious."

Gender differences in project implementation. The case study provides evidence on the role of district assembly members in implementing projects. As securing a project through lobbying and monitoring its implementation takes enormous effort and follow-through (and serving on the assembly is a voluntary position), assembly members appear to initially prioritize one or two projects. Although the projects chosen may come about through a confluence of factors external to the assembly member, the case study evidence suggests that the first projects chosen often seem to reflect a priority of the representative, perhaps a motivating force for seeking office in the first place. Given this prioritization, the female assembly members in the case study appeared to pursue what could be considered "women's goods" more or more quickly than did the assemblymen. One worked first on securing grinding mills for four of her communities, on getting boreholes drilled for domestic water supply, and on securing credit for women's groups. Another worked on improving the public toilets in her area. The third convinced women in her district to form women's group and organized the rural enterprise officer to offer training on income-generating activities. At the same time, the female assembly members seek more general community services, such as small dams and reservoirs, schools, and health centers.

Two male assembly members were teachers; they chose to work on school-focused projects first, including teachers' accommodation, a vocational school, and a junior-secondary school. This could suggest that representatives choose projects that align with their own preferences, which are shaped by their experiences and characteristics, including gender and occupation, rather than choosing projects requested by any particular political constituency.

Male advocates for women are also often found in these conservative gender environments. Because literacy rates are much lower among women in these two districts than among men, a younger, relatively better-educated, literate male acted as a secretary to a women's group in many communities, keeping their records and helping them fill out applications for credit. A similar pattern appeared in the S-2 district assembly, where because no woman was available, the acting planning officer assumed the responsibilities of the gender desk officer. These young men often said that they identify with women because they identify with their mothers. "Women in this society are really suffering," commented one. When asked why he had become an advocate for women, one respondent replied, "Here we practice [an] extended family system, so all the women in the group are my mothers. That is why I deem it necessary to help them. Sometimes you see women in other communities organizing themselves, and you feel that women in your community should also have functional groups."

Relations with Actors at Different Levels

There is a wide range of interactions and information flows between the district assembly member and other actors involved in local governance and rural service provision (table 6.13). Because the number of female district assembly members was small, differences in the percentages have to be interpreted with care. Still, it seems that female district assembly members have

Table 6.13 Interactions of Male and Female District Assembly Members in Ghana with Other Actors

| | | Percent | |
| | | Male | Female |
Actor	Frequency	(n = 104)	(n = 10)
District chief executive	Never	0	0
	Sporadic	42	50
	Frequent	58	50
Member of parliament	Never	15	30
	Sporadic	61	60
	Frequent	24	10
			(continued)

Table 6.13 (Continued)

Actor	Frequency	Percent	
		Male (*n* = 104)	Female (*n* = 10)
Presiding member of the district assembly	Never	4	20
	Sporadic	42	40
	Frequent	54	40
Appointed members of the district assembly	Never	1	0
	Sporadic	46	50
	Frequent	53	50
Other assembly members	Never	3	0
	Sporadic	35	70
	Frequent	62	30
Official from line ministers	Never	8	10
	Sporadic	56	40
	Frequent	36	50
District assembly official	Never	2	10
	Sporadic	42	30
	Frequent	57	60
Chiefs	Never	6	10
	Sporadic	43	50
	Frequent	51	40
NGOs in your district	Never	34	50
	Sporadic	50	40
	Frequent	16	10
Farmer-based organization member	Never	44	70
	Sporadic	43	20
	Frequent	12	10
Water and sanitation committee member	Never	25	40
	Sporadic	42	30
	Frequent	32	30
Agricultural extension agent	Never	18	70
	Sporadic	52	20
	Frequent	30	10
Unit committee member	Never	5	10
	Sporadic	36	40
	Frequent	59	50
Member of your community	Sporadic	42	30
	Frequent	58	70
Political party functionary	Never	15	0
	Sporadic	49	33
	Frequent	36	67

Source: ISSER-IFPRI Survey 2008.

Note: "Sporadic" indicates less than once a month; "frequent" indicates several times a month. Missing values are not displayed in the table. The average response rate for the questions displayed in the table was 97 percent for male respondents and 77 percent for female respondents.

almost equal access to the district chief executive; they interact less frequently with members of parliament and with other assembly members. Seventy percent of the female district assembly members never interacted with extension officers. Interaction between male or female assembly members and farmer-based organizations and NGOs was also low. One-third of the male and female assembly members indicated that they interact frequently with the water and sanitation committees.

The only type of actor with whom female assembly members interact more frequently than their male counterparts is political party functionaries. This suggests that the role of political parties highlighted in the literature review in chapter 2 may also play a role here. The case study provides some evidence on the role of political parties in local governance. In 2006, the Northern Sector Awareness on Action Centre (NORSAAC), a local advocacy NGO, lobbied the district chief executives to make sure that half of their appointees (that is, half of the 30 percent appointed members to the assembly) were female. They also provided them with a list to prove that there were capable candidates in their district. The district chief executives protested when the women were not of their party. Even when there was no excuse on technical or capacity grounds, the district chief executives favored the appointment of their party members to the assembly. This finding resonates with the criticism in the literature that party politics play an important role in the local government system in Ghana, even though it is designed to be nonpartisan (NCG and Dege Consult 2007).

Securing financial resources from different actors. Half of male assembly members but only 27 percent of female members were able to secure funding from the assembly's resources (table 6.14). The female members relied more on other resources, which may have included donor agencies. They also made use of a larger share of the grant that members of parliaments can spend in their constituencies. Although almost 10 percent of the male assembly members could access funds of the central government, none of the female members was able to leverage this source of funds.

Table 6.14 Major Source of Funds for Development Used by Male and Female District Assembly Members in Ghana (percent)

Source of funds	Male assembly members (*n* = 104)	Female assembly members (*n* = 10)
District assembly	50	30
District Assembly Common Fund	18	20
Central government	9	0
NGO	8	10
Member of parliament grant	5	10
Other	10	30

Source: ISSER-IFPRI Survey 2008.

GENDER AND GOVERNANCE IN RURAL SERVICES

Role of international organizations and advocacy NGOs. NORSAAC was funded by the international development organization ActionAid, with the objective of supporting women contest district assembly seats in the 2006 elections. In the six months before the local government elections, NORSAAC met with the gender desk officers in 10 of the districts in the Northern Region and asked them to select women who could attend training sessions in Tamale. More than 100 women were trained on the district assembly concept, public speaking and advocacy, campaign strategies, and other relevant topics; two-thirds of the trainees contested district assembly seats. Those who contested were given further support in the form of campaign posters and paid radio spots. NORSAAC did not distribute cash (small sums of money may have been made available to female contenders through the Ministry of Women and Children's Affairs). Of the 67 women trainees who ran for election, 23 won seats, 8 of which were in study district S-1. Thus, the training efforts by the NGO likely explain the comparatively high share of female assembly members in this district.

The women in the S-1 district also had the support of a committed activist, who offered moral support and helped target resources. The gender desk officer (the officer at the district level whose task it is to mainstream gender into district affairs) traveled to nearly every community in the district to solicit women's participation and convince community opinion leaders to support women's candidacies. NORSAAC paid some of her transport costs. She then connected the women with resources such as cash and skills training (from NORSAAC and from the Ministry of Women's and Children's Affairs) to stand for the elections. She visited women in their communities before the election to provide moral support, which seemed to mean a lot to women running for elections in remote communities. She also monitored voting, which went smoothly.

The female district chief executive in S-1 district also likely supported female candidates in the district. She supported the endeavor of the gender desk officer with fuel money from the District Assembly Common Fund. She also made it possible for her to use the motorbike provided by the District Capacity Building Project (DISCAP), funded by the Canadian International Development Agency. The district chief executive also traveled to communities in which women were running for election to unofficially campaign for them. She recounts that she would secretly promise goods, such as grinding mills, to female constituents if they would vote for the women representatives. This practice lies in contrast to that reported by the district chief executive in district S-2, who said he avoided campaigning for any particular assembly candidate because he would have to work with all the winners when they went to the assembly and he would not have wanted to create any rancor by throwing his weight "behind the wrong horse."

Perhaps the S-1 district chief executive felt that gender was a more important issue than political party considerations in supporting certain candidates. Probably, however, she did not give as strong support to women who were staunch members of the other party. She later made the active gender desk officer an appointed assembly member so that it would have a stronger platform for her activities. This activism suggests that female leadership may attract other female leaders and that affirmative action in this position (were it to remain appointed) might be something to consider.

The case also throws some light on the role of international development agencies. DISCAP did more than just provide transport. It piloted the gender desk approach in northern Ghana. Subsequently, the minister of the Ministry of Women and Children's Affairs pledged to regularize this position. In its project completion report, the project listed the following under its achievements: "In the 2006 local elections, the number of women elected to district assemblies, as well as the number of women holding executive positions in assemblies, both doubled compared to the previous local elections in 2002" (CIDA and MLGRDE 2007, p. 12). The extent to which this result can be attributed to DISCAP is unclear, but international support for local activism likely influenced this outcome.

ETHIOPIA

This section presents the results relating to the long route of accountability in Ethiopia. It is based on both the household survey and case study findings.

Representatives' Relationship to Households

This section discusses the interface between rural residents and local political representatives. it also examines resources—such as access to information and social capital and the extent to which residents are able to participate in the political process—that may better enable them to exercise their voice.

Knowledge and Access to Information

For rural residents to be able to hold local governments and service providers accountable for the quality of public services in their area, they must have general information about local and national matters, provided through the media or telecommunication devices. The use of media sources and telecommunication tools is highly constrained in Ethiopia, particularly among women (figure 6.4). For example, only slightly more than half of men and slightly more than a quarter of women had listened to a radio in the previous 12 months, and just 13 percent of men and 6 percent of women had watched TV (the figures for newspapers were half these rates). The number of respondents who had used the remaining forms of media was small.

Accessing these sources of information and communication requires complementary assets and endowments (private physical assets such as radios and mobile phones and public services and infrastructure such as landline access).

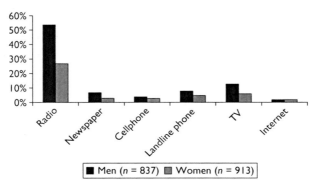

Source: EEPRI-IFPRI Survey 2009.

Literacy is needed to read newspapers; financial resources are required to pay
for services such as phone centers. All of these assets were in short supply in the
study area. Furthermore, even where farmers have access to such low-cost
media as radios, most stations that reach rural areas are controlled by the government or the Ethiopian People's Revolutionary Democratic Front (EPRDF)
(U.S. State Department 2009).

Participation in Meetings

The research team observed several meetings in kebeles with local and district
officials. In Tigray-K and a neighboring kebele, the meetings were very well
attended, although district government officials did most of the talking. Participation in civic affairs is well institutionalized in the Tigray region, and citizens are willing to air grievances at such meetings.

In contrast, the team attended a meeting to discuss the annual development
plan in Amhara-K3. Although kebele leaders went door to door trying to
round up participants, very few residents attended. Interestingly, later the same
day the team attended a worship service for the feast of St. Michael at a church
in the same kebele. Although the church was well off the main road (unlike the
meeting area in the kebele center) and accessible only by footpath up a steep
mountainside, hundreds of people were present, including most of the local
political leaders. Evidently, residents felt that the assembly (which consisted of
a public reading of the district's plan) offered no benefit, whereas the church
service offered a meal and perhaps spiritual sustenance to a community of
devout Orthodox Christians. Participation has a cost: farmers' time and labor
are not free; they will not attend meetings if they do not perceive a benefit to
doing so. The reading of an already established plan offers few benefits in the
middle of harvest time. Even in less busy times, farmers may prefer to do other

things, such as meet with neighbors to discuss farming issues, exchange seeds, or work at crafts that can generate supplemental income.

Officials in both Amhara-D3 and Oromia-D say that low rates of participation in meetings demonstrate that participation is no longer coerced, as in the past, when local governments fined citizens for failing to show up. Officials do not analyze why citizens do not find participation beneficial and seek to ameliorate the situation.

Voting

The most explicit form of holding service providers accountable through the long route is through voting in political elections (see figure 1.1). Voter turnout in the study area was very high (table 6.15), and although there was a substantial gender gap, women report very high rates of participation in elections, particularly in local elections. The vast majority (nine-tenths) of male respondents and three-quarters of female respondents reported having voted some time in their life in elections at the lowest level, the kebele. Some 65 percent of men and more than half of women reported that they had voted in federal elections in their lifetime.

Placing these results within Ethiopia's political historical context points to the limitation of drawing strong conclusions about the free exercise of voice—and the effective use of the long route of accountability—from high participation in elections. Relatively competitive elections are a necessary but insufficient condition for the basic narrative of the long route to hold, and for participation in elections to be a measure of the extent of citizens' exercise of voice. An additional condition for the long route to function well is that political participation through elections be voluntary. As the literature on Ethiopian electoral practice suggests, neither condition appears to hold (Pausewang, Tronvoll, and Aalen 2002; Lefort 2007; Aalen and Tronvoll 2008).

EPRDF–affiliated and associated parties secured virtually all of the seats at stake in the 2008 kebele and district council elections. The government

Table 6.15 Percentage of Respondents in Ethiopia Who Ever Voted or Attended a Local Meeting, by Gender

Election/meeting	Male (n = 843)	Female (n = 918)	Statistical significance of difference
Kebele election	91	76	***
District election	89	74	***
Regional election	65	51	***
Federal election	65	51	**
Meeting organized by the kebele council	24	5	***
Meeting organized at the district level	12	3	***

Source: EEPRI-IFPRI Survey 2009.
***Significant at the 1% level; **significant at the 5% level.

disqualified many opposition party and independent candidates (Aalen and Tronvoll 2008). In Tigray-D and Amhara-D3, party and government officials told the team that the party consulted local residents before putting candidate slates together. Given that the contest was essentially a one-party race, party officials said that it was important for individual office seekers to be those EPRDF party members who also have community support. This observation indicates that at least in some regions, the party makes some effort to create accountability at the local level, even though the de facto electoral system does not require this strategy.

The local wings of the party organized around demographic groups, in particular women and youth, were active. Female leaders in both Tigray-K and Amhara-K3 viewed the local party women's league as creating space in which women could meet and discuss issues and problems among themselves.

Several factors appear to be related to political and community participation (table 6.16). The gender of the respondent emerges as a strong indicator of the likelihood of both participation in elections and attendance at community meetings, even after controlling for other factors. These other factors, especially the literacy status of the respondent, the wealth status, whether the respondent is a head of household (for participation in community meetings), and even household size are strong indicators of these forms of participation, with people who are more educated, wealthier, heads of households, and living in larger households more likely to vote or attend community meetings.

The extent of such participation also varies by location. Afar-D is the area in which individuals participate the least by far in political and community activities. This is consistent with other findings pointing to low engagement with and access to local services and events. (In many cases, given the institutional underdevelopment in this area, "low engagement" may reflect the absence of these activities.) Interestingly, the greatest likelihood of respondents participating in elections and in community meetings is in Amhara-D2 and in SNNP-D, not in Tigray-D, where one could have expected vibrant local engagement of citizens in light of Tigray's legacy of such engagement and the qualitative findings discussed above.

Interaction with Political Representatives

Holding a position of leadership in the community—heading or holding a lead position in the local funeral society (*iddir*), leading the women's association or the youth association, serving in the kebele council, and so on—may allow an individual to have a stronger voice within the community on decisions about services and infrastructure in which community members participate. It is therefore of interest to assess the extent to which women and men hold such positions or have relatives in such positions through whom they can exercise their voice.

In the study area, only a very small fraction of women (4 percent) held or had ever held a village/community lead position (table 6.17). In contrast,

Table 6.16 Factors Associated with Voting in Local Elections and Attending Community Meetings in Ethiopia

Variable	Ever voted in local (district and kebele) elections		Number of types of local community meetings attended	
Gender (1 = male)	0.614*** (0.13)	0.582*** (0.122)	0.263** (0.121)	0.333*** (0.127)
Education (1 = literate)	0.408*** (0.116)	0.450*** (0.109)	0.461*** (0.087)	0.507*** (0.091)
Respondent status (1 = head, 0 = spouse)	0.074 (0.125)	−0.002 (0.115)	0.771*** (0.121)	0.646*** (0.126)
Wealth (number of consumer asset types owned)	0.051** (0.023)	0.085*** (0.02)	0.114*** (0.018)	0.103*** (0.018)
Household size (number of household members)	0.060*** (0.017)	0.033* (0.015)	0.060*** (0.012)	0.018 (0.012)
Working-age women (percent of household members)	−0.008 (0.01)	−0.004 (0.009)	−0.030*** (0.007)	−0.026*** (0.008)
Working-age men (percent of household members)	−0.011 (0.01)	−0.006 (0.009)	−0.034*** (0.007)	−0.030*** (0.008)
Female dependents (percent of household members)	−0.013 (0.01)	−0.009 (0.009)	−0.033*** (0.007)	−0.029*** (0.007)
Male dependents (percent of household members)	−0.010 (0.009)	−0.008 (0.009)	−0.033*** (0.007)	−0.031*** (0.007)
Afar-D	−0.636*** (0.155)		−1.296*** (0.166)	
Amhara-D2	1.211*** (0.218)		0.368*** (0.146)	

Variable	(1)	(2)	(3)	(4)
Benesh G-D	0.214 (0.151)		-0.562*** (0.139)	
Gambella-D	0.200 (0.144)		0.200 (0.141)	
Oromia-D	0.069 (0.154)		-0.572*** (0.143)	
SNNP-D	0.920*** (0.172)		0.755*** (0.136)	
Tigray-D	0.474*** (0.156)		0.220 (0.144)	
Constant	0.870 (0.945)	0.778 (0.878)	3.593*** (0.699)	3.471*** (0.74)
Number of observations	1,732		1,766	
Likelihood ratio chi-square test	276.04***	151.46***		
F-statistic			38.52***	36.35***
Adjusted R^2			0.254	0.152

Source: Authors.

Note: Standard errors are in parentheses. Amhara-D3 is the excluded district.
***Significant at the 1% level; **significant at the 5% level.

Table 6.17 Social Capital and Local Leadership in Ethiopia, by Gender (percentage of respondents)

Indicator	Male (n = 843)	Female (n = 918)	Statistical significance of difference
Extent of leadership role of respondents and their relatives			
Hold or have ever held official or traditional lead position	31	4	***
Any living relatives (not including spouses) that hold or have ever held official or traditional lead position	27	19	**
Gender of relative who has lead position (percent female)		2	n.a.
Spoke personally to the following local leader within the last year			
Religious leader of this village	71	58	***
Extension agent	49	30	***
Kebele chair	69	41	***
Community elder	63	49	***
Head of iddir (funeral society)	26	12	***
Head of agricultural cooperative	15	7	***
Water committee member	12	5	***
District council member	15	3	***
Kebele council member	26	8	***
Local party leader	17	7	***

Source: EEPRI-IFPRI Survey 2009.

Note: n.a. = Not applicable.

***Significant at the 1% level; **significant at the 5% level.

nearly one-third of male respondents held or had held some local position. Moreover, only 2 percent of relatives who held or had held a leadership position were women.

Being in a position of local leadership oneself or having a relative in such a position may lead more directly to an enhanced ability to exercise voice relative to regular residents on matters pertaining to the community's development. Being well acquainted and socially connected to people in senior local positions could contribute indirectly. Women have consistently and substantially fewer personal interactions with such individuals. Women have fewer interactions than men with religious leaders and community elders, and the gender gap is even wider with respect to local political leaders (see table 6.17). Interestingly, women also have much less contact with leaders of the agricultural cooperative and the water committee.

A number of institutions exist to foster the accountability of kebele and district government to citizens. These institutions vary in effectiveness. Farmers in Amhara-K1 informed the team that they looked to the kebele chair to resolve grievances. The chair is an elected member of the kebele council, which appoints the chair to office. In Tigray-K, the council replaced the chair as a result of poor performance.

Since the 2008 elections, kebele councils have had standing committees to address development issues, security questions, and gender equality. These committees were too new to evaluate.

Oromia-K residents complained to the team about the lack of services received from the district government. Representatives on the district council were not able to get the district government to pay greater attention to the community's needs. District officials in Oromia-D felt that their hands were tied by priority setting and budget limitations imposed by the regional government, but kebele leaders and residents told the team that they saw a breach in the social contract instead. They pointed out that residents had provided labor to improve the roads between the district capital and their community but had not received the requested services.

Kebele councils in Tigray-K and Amhara-K3 meet monthly and also work with local representatives to the district council, who attend kebele council meetings. District council speakers in Tigray-D and Amhara-D3 make periodic visits to kebeles and provide support to the kebele councils. District councils frequently discuss development issues, including agricultural development and drinking water. The district council's running committees seem to provide checks and balances over the district government, but the influence of council representatives is limited.

Effectiveness of Political Representatives in Providing Services

This section presents the study's findings on the relationship between local political authorities and higher-tier government bodies and party functionaries. It also discusses how local political representatives interact with user organizations, such as agricultural cooperatives.

Representatives' Relationship with Regional and National Governments

Financial support and information flows are two important mechanisms through which regional and national governments can influence the effectiveness of local political representatives. Financial support from the national and regional level to districts is formula driven. Although district governments discuss plans and allocation of budget resources with higher levels of government, guidance from above tends to trump bottom-up priorities and communications. The case study evidence suggests that district representatives on regional councils are not able to alter total resource levels, given reliance on formulas; the team received no information about how interactions between these representatives and district or kebele representatives might influence sectoral or territorial allocations of funds within districts or plan priorities.

Information tends to flow from the top down in Ethiopia. Although many institutional arrangements exist that could help make the information flow both ways, they will not play this role effectively as long as the command-and-control of policy making and implementation remain in place.

Representatives' Relationship with Political Parties

During the 2008 local elections, EPRDF party endorsement was virtually a requirement for winning office. Party leaders told the team that candidates had to be people who set a good development example, such as model farmers who send their children to school and otherwise participate in party-endorsed development activities (box 6.6). Party influence over political life was pervasive at all study sites. In Tigray-D and Amhara-D3, senior positions such as district

---

Box 6.6   The Nexus between the Ruling Party and Agricultural Activities in Tigray

Although the military dictatorship referred to as the Derg had been in power in Addis Ababa since 1974, it was not until the 1980s that large parts of the rural Tigray region came under control of the Tigray People's Liberation Front (TPLF), the movement that in 1991 became the core component of the ruling party EPRDF, after overthrowing the Derg. In the 1980s, the TPLF pursued a policy of strengthening Tigrayan farmers' livelihood base and promoting self-government of rural communities. This played a crucial role in increasing the loyalty farmers forged with the movement and in TPLF's ability to consolidate its legitimacy in the region.

The legacy of the political and economic alliance between farmers and the TPLF is complex. Some evidence suggests that the alliance remained in the postrevolutionary era. There are, however, reasons to question the idea that rural people in Tigray freely reward their government for development and self-governance with political support.

Local government officials and *tabia*-level "farmer-leaders" are in charge of stirring farmers' interest and stimulating their participation in development programs.[a] They adopt different strategies to do so, which in practice often intertwine. One strategy consists of pointing out to farmers the advantages of newly introduced technologies and agricultural techniques through extension and demonstration. Another rewards households that take part in development programs with privileged access to public resources, such as employment in the public work component of the government's Productive Safety Net Programme. Local government and farmer-leaders also try to win over farmers by capitalizing on the TPLF's historical legitimacy, won through its struggle against the Derg. They frequently do so by extrapolating feelings of hatred against the Derg to poverty and underdevelopment, which they represent as farmers' current enemies to be defeated.

(continued)

Box 6.6 (Continued)

Local party leaders motivate party members, such as tabia council members and other farmer-leaders, to take part in the programs and to set an example for others. For tabia council members, "representing the people" means setting an example. As one local administrator said to a farmer-leader, "I saw your pond looks bad. You have to take responsibility and make sure that at least your own ponds are fine. To lead the people, you have to show them."

For ordinary farmers, the TPLF–development nexus creates opportunities for upward social and political mobility. Indeed, the fact that on average TPLF members are more active participants in development programs is not exclusively the result of the mobilization strategies described above. The local party leadership also invites already successful and innovating farmers to join the TPLF. For obvious reasons, most farmers accept the invitation. Strengthening the TPLF ranks with innovative farmers increases the chance that future development interventions quickly gain a foothold.

In the agricultural development realm, the local institutional machinery, including the local party apparatus, is mobilized only in order to implement the government's agenda, which is channeled from the highest tiers of government on down. Room for using the local structures to take advantage of local knowledge on what does and does not work is severely restricted. This is illustrated by a village leader called on to lead by example: "If I had a good catchment near my land, I would have dug a pond before, but what is the use of a pond if it is impossible for water to enter it? Subdistrict administrators visited me in my house. I tried to convince them of the impossibility of a pond on my land, but they did not accept this. One day at a meeting in the district, my case was brought up again. I was so tired of it that I decided to dig a pond anyway."

It could be argued that the EPRDF, with the TPLF at its core, has reduced opportunities for rural people to foster and develop. In general, despite Ethiopia's transformation into a federal state and the decentralization processes in progress, power devolution to regional and local government levels remains inadequate, even in Tigray with its pre–1991 history of local empowerment under the then-rebel movement TPLF.

Source: Segers and others 2008.

a. A tabia is analogous to a kebele in other parts of the country. The term *farmer-leaders* refers to tabia leaders who have livelihoods similar to those of typical rural residents. Such leaders include heads of community women's and youth associations, tabia council members, and others.

and kebele council leadership posts frequently go to veterans of the anti-Derg struggle and the war with Eritrea. Veterans also dominate in cooperative and party leadership positions. In Oromia-D, in contrast, former Derg soldiers occupy some key leadership jobs.

Party influence is pervasive at all levels of government and in most civil society organizations in Ethiopia. In keeping with the Leninist character of the EPRDF, party decision making is extremely top down and party discipline strictly enforced. As a party official in Amhara-D3 informed the team, "The party is the father of the community." The party's self-image is one of benevolent authoritarianism.

Representatives' Relationship with User Organizations

Cooperatives in Ethiopia have an identity as user associations and organizations that are linked to government through both their genesis and their key role in channeling government-provided inputs and services to farmers. Their genesis informs this link to government primarily through the way in which cooperatives are created: one of the main tasks of the government's cooperative promotion agencies at all levels is to help create, set up, and advise agricultural cooperatives in order to meet the government's goal of bringing cooperatives' services to 70 percent of society by having one cooperative in each kebele of the country by 2010 (Federal Cooperative Agency 2006).

The strong government-led effort behind the creation and strengthening of cooperatives has given these organizations access to local governments. It also provides the potential for cooperatives to function as effective mediators between farmers and government. The study households reported cooperatives in their community to have been involved in government meetings at the kebele and district level at which local officials discuss the local government's agenda for agriculture in the community (table 6.18). Households stated that cooperatives were present at district-level meetings more often than at kebele meetings. Their more frequent presence may reflect the fact that district-level decisions have greater effects on people's lives and that kebele plans are usually derived from the plans of a higher tier.

The potential role of cooperatives as interlocutors between residents and local government is brought out by the finding that cooperatives engage their members in government plans through discussions at membership meetings. Cooperatives are more often said to be present during district meetings than kebele meetings. In line with this, the interactions between cooperative managers and cooperative members are more often about the district government's agricultural agenda than the kebele government's. The fact that cooperative leaders engage with members about the government's agenda is promising for the role that cooperatives could play as mediators between the state and farmers. What remains unanswered is whether the interactions upward (the involvement in agricultural planning meetings of the government) and downward (the discussion of these plans with members) serve only as a conduit of information to farmers about state mandates and targets or whether these interactions have the potential to channel concerns and priorities of farmers up to government.

Table 6.18 Residents' Perception of Influence of Cooperatives on Local Government in Ethiopia (percentage of respondents agreeing with statement)

Statement	Percent (n = 250)
Cooperative leaders were involved in meetings on the kebele government's agricultural plans	30
Cooperative leaders were involved in meetings on the district government's agricultural plans	48
The cooperative conducted a discussion among members on the kebele government's agricultural plans	33
The cooperative conducted a discussion among members on the district government's agricultural plans	50
Perception of influence of cooperative on kebele government's priorities	
High	12
Some	17
Little	9
No	31
Don't know	32
Perception of influence of cooperative on district government's priorities	
High	7
Some	18
Little	3
No	28
Don't know	44

Source: EEPRI-IFPRI Survey 2009.

Cooperative leaders in both Tigray-D and Amhara-D3 reported that the government has a significant influence on the cooperatives' agenda. These leaders had their own ideas about how best to serve their members but felt constrained to follow the part established by the government.

The literature on agricultural cooperatives in Ethiopia under the current regime is extremely sparse, and almost no research has been conducted on the interaction among cooperatives, the state as manifested through local government, and farmers.[6] In particular, little is known about the direction and nature of influence, accountability, and pressure among these three actors. The households in this study reported very mixed responses about their perception of their cooperatives' influence on kebele and district government, and interviews with cooperative leaders suggest that the government holds the trump cards in these interactions. Nevertheless, 29 percent of respondents believe cooperatives have influence on the priorities of the kebele governments, and 25 percent think they have some influence on district governments. These perceptions point to a certain degree of influence that cooperatives can exercise over government, notwithstanding the constraints cooperative leaders perceive in their interactions with the authorities.

Representatives' Relationship with Service Providers

The case studies suggest that the kebele councils and administrations play no role in budgeting; in Amhara-K3 and Oromia-K, their role in planning was not much more than symbolic. There are kebele representatives on district councils who can attempt to win additional resources for their communities. In Tigray-K, these representatives work closely with the kebele council to raise local issues in the district council. However, as budget ceilings are fixed above the district level, any effort to bolster one's own allocation means engaging in a zero-sum game with neighboring kebeles. District budget officials in Tigray-D, Amhara-D3, and Oromia-D told the team that they try to develop spending plans that allocate resources fairly across kebeles, particularly with regard to scarce capital spending projects. In Oromia-D, officials said that they regularly lobby the regional government for additional resources. In Tigray-D and Oromia-D, a five-year strategic plan shapes annual planning and budgeting.

District councils have standing committees that oversee service provision. These bodies receive reports from the relevant sectoral offices, pose questions to officials, and report to the full council. Since the 2008 elections, the kebele councils have expanded in size and now have a parallel set of standing committees, including women's affairs committees in Tigray-D and Amhara-D3. Extension agents work closely with kebele cabinets and village leaders in Tigray-K; inclusion of the extension team leader in the kebele cabinet is national policy. Kebele councils and cabinets also oversee water committees. As water committees are usually composed of citizen volunteers, however, kebeles remain dependent on district governments and donor agencies for financial resources, capacity development, and spare parts.

ANNEX

The Long Route of Accountability

This annex provides information on gram panchayat members and activities in India.

Figure 6.A.1   Occupation of Gram Panchayat Members

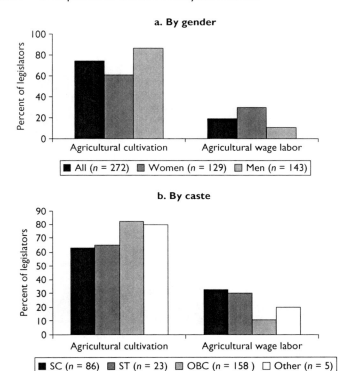

a. By gender

■ All (*n* = 272)   ▨ Women (*n* = 129)   ▨ Men (*n* = 143)

b. By caste

■ SC (*n* = 86)   ▨ ST (*n* = 23)   ▨ OBC (*n* = 158)   □ Other (*n* = 5)

Source: ISEC-IFPRI Survey 2006.

Figure 6.A.2   Literacy and Education of Gram Panchayat Members

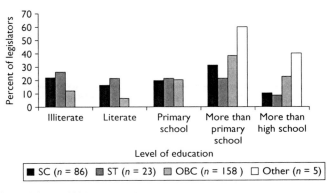

■ SC (*n* = 86)   ▨ ST (*n* = 23)   ▨ OBC (*n* = 158)   □ Other (*n* = 5)

Source: ISEC-IFPRI Survey 2006.

Figure 6.A.3   Membership of Gram Panchayat Members in Local
                Organizations, by Caste

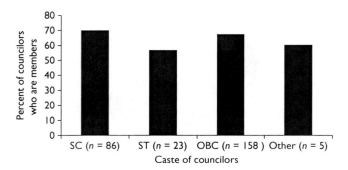

Source: ISEC-IFPRI Survey 2006.
Note: Survey question was: "Are you or family members members of any local organization?"

Table 6.A.1	Investment Priorities of Gram Panchayat (percent)		
Problem	**First priority** (*n* = 272)	**Second priority** (*n* = 272)	**Third priority** (*n* = 272)
Water	45.7	9.7	5.6
Sanitation/drainage	14.1	30.1	14.9
Health	10.8	6.7	5.6
Housing	10.0	10.0	26.0
Roads	7.1	19.0	15.6
Electricity	5.2	7.8	8.2
Street lights	2.2	7.4	10.8
Transport	1.9	6.3	6.3
Education	1.5	1.9	2.2
Livelihood opportunities	0.7	0	1.9
Irrigation	0.4	0.4	1.5
Illicit liquor	0.4	0.4	1.5
Other	0.0	0.4	0.0

Source: ISEC-IFPRI Survey 2006.

Table 6.A.2	Investment Priorities of Gram Panchayat Members, by Caste (percent)				
Top-ranked investment	SC (n = 86)	ST (n = 23)	OBC (n = 158)	Other (n = 5)	Total (n = 272)
Water	43.5	39.1	48.7	20	45.7
Sanitation/drainage	12.9	17.4	14.7	0	14.1
Housing	10.6	17.4	9.0	0	10.0
Health	10.6	4.4	11.5	20	10.8
Roads	8.2	8.7	5.8	20	7.1
Electricity	4.7	8.7	5.1	0	5.2
Transport	3.5	0.0	1.3	0	1.9
Livelihood opportunities	2.4	0.0	0.0	0	0.7
Street lights	2.4	4.4	0.6	40	2.2
Education	1.2	0.0	1.9	0	1.5
Illicit Liquor	0.0	0.0	0.6	0	0.4
Irrigation	0.0	0.0	0.6	0	0.4

Source: ISEC-IFPRI Survey 2006.

Note: SC = scheduled caste; ST = scheduled tribe; OBC = other backward caste.

Figure 6.A.4   Average Number of Meetings of Gram Sabha, Gram Panchayat, and Jamabandhi, by Gender of President

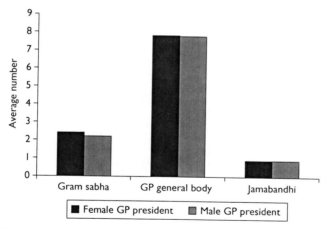

Source: ISEC-IFPRI Survey 2006.

Note: Sample observation sizes: For both GP general body and gram sabha meetings, $n = 28$ for female GP presidents and $n = 49$ for male GP presidents. For Jamabandhi meetings $n = 25$ and $n = 49$, respectively.

Figure 6.A.5   Perceptions of Issues Discussed at Gram Sabha Meetings, by
                Gender of Household Head

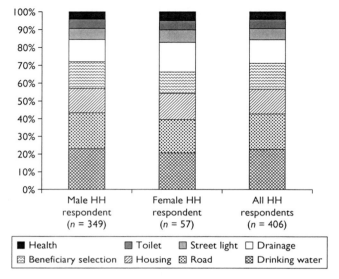

Source: ISEC-IFPRI Survey 2006.

Figure 6.A.6   Household Interaction with Panchayat Members and Officials,
                by Gender of Household Head

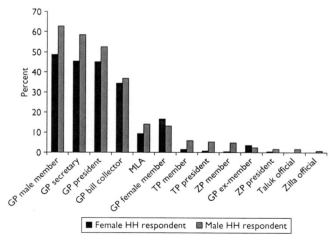

Source: ISEC-IFPRI Survey 2006.
Note: GP = gram panchayat; TP = taluk panchayat; ZP = zilla panchayat; MLA = member of
legislative assembly. The number of observations differs between male- and female-headed households and across the different partners of interaction. The maximum number of observations was
452 for male-headed households and 120 for female-headed households.

Figure 6.A.7   Reason for Interaction with Panchayat Members and Officials

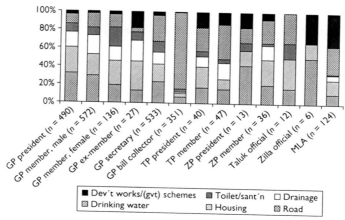

Source: ISEC-IFPRI Survey 2006.
Note: GP = gram panchayat; TP = taluk panchayat; ZP = zilla panchayat; MLA = member of legislative assembly.

Figure 6.A.8   Activities Undertaken under Devolved Schemes, as Reported by Male and Female Gram Panchayat Presidents

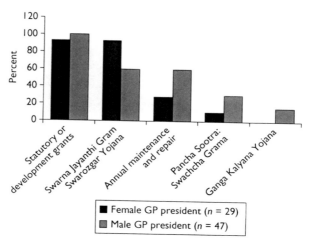

Source: ISEC-IFPRI Survey 2006.
Note: Figures show percentage of presidents who report action in each area.

NOTES

1. Until 2001, gram sabhas were required to meet at least twice a year.
2. In a study of Karnataka, Sivanna and Babu (2002) show that the jamabandhi program does not ensure transparency and accountability in local governance, given the poor quality of the accounting books and the failure of the audit-implementing parties to disseminate the results.
3. This evidence is consistent with other evidence in the literature. See Alsop, Krishna, and Sjoblom (2000) for a study in Rajasthan and Madhya Pradesh that identifies the political and socioeconomic factors behind the participation of local citizens in gram panchayat activities.
4. People from OBCs are a heterogeneous social group. Reservation for this group is divided into two subcategories: one for politically dominant groups (OBC "B"), the other for OBC castes that are not politically dominant (OBC "A").
5. Because council members in female- and male-headed gram panchyats do not differ in their contacts according to Kruskal-Wallis test statistics, separate results for male- and female-headed GPs are not reported.
6. The very few peer-reviewed journal articles that focus on cooperatives in post–1991 Ethiopia include Staal, Delgado, and Nicholson (1997); Bernard, Taffesse, and Gabre-Madhin (2008); Francesconi and Ruben (2008); Bernard and Spielman (2009); and Spielman, Cohen, and Mogues (forthcoming).

CHAPTER SEVEN

Comparing the Three Countries

his chapter summarizes and compares the findings from the three countries. It then uses the framework developed in chapter 2 to analyze differences in the accountability relations in the three countries, based on the empirical findings presented in chapters 5 and 6.

SYNOPSIS AND DISCUSSION OF MAIN FINDINGS

Tables 7.1 and 7.2 summarize the study's main findings. These findings are based on both the surveys and the qualitative case studies conducted for this study. As the sampling strategy was guided by the goal of analyzing accountability links between households, service providers, and elected representatives, the samples are not statistically representative at the national or regional level. However, the sampling strategies aimed to avoid bias, and the sample sizes are considerable (966 households in Karnataka, India; 1,168 households in Ghana; and 1,072 households in Ethiopia).

Agricultural Extension

This section summarizes the findings regarding agricultural extension. It compares the findings from the three countries, paying specific attention to the gender dimension of providing agricultural extension.

Table 7.1 Summary of Findings on Agricultural Extension

Indicator	India	Ghana	Ethiopia
Service provision outcome			
Access	Moderate gender gap: 29 percent of male-headed households and 18 percent of female-headed households (with land) met with extension agent; 85 percent of contacts were individual visits, 15 percent group visits. Among households with livestock, 72 percent of male-headed and 79 percent of female-headed households received livestock service.	Very limited access, especially for women; 11–12 percent of male-headed and 0–2 percent of female-headed households (with land) received agricultural extension visits. Among households with livestock, 5–34 percent of male-headed and 0–24 percent of female-headed households received livestock service. Less than 2 percent of female spouses in male-headed households received agricultural extension visits, 0–15 percent received livestock-related visits; 10–15 percent of male-headed and 0–6 percent of female-headed households received group visits; 17–24 percent of male-headed and 0–6 percent of female-headed households attended community meetings related to agriculture or livestock.	Moderate access for men and women but large variation across regions: 27 percent of men and 20 percent of women received agricultural extension agent visits at home or on the farm, ranging from 2 percent in surveyed districts in Afar to 54 percent in Tigray; 28 percent of men and 11 percent of women participated in community meetings on agriculture; 5.0 percent of men and 1.0 percent of women visited demonstration plots, 0.9 percent of men and 0.4 percent of women visited a farmer training center, and 1.1 percent of men and 0.9 percent of women visited demonstration homes.
Satisfaction	Households receiving attention mostly satisfied; limited access is perceived to be main problem.	Households receiving services very satisfied (90 percent very satisfied with public sector extension, 72 percent very satisfied with NGO). Results are not consistent with agricultural activities; only 15 percent of male household heads, 7 percent of female household heads, and 5 percent of female spouses tried anything new to them in past 2 years.	95 percent of men visited by an extension or other expert reported being very satisfied, 5 percent reported being somewhat satisfied. Results are not consistent with agricultural activities: only 8 percent of farmers tried anything new to them in past two years.

Service providers			
Role of providers	Public sector main provider; NGOs and private sector not active providers of agricultural extension in study areas; private animal health providers without specific training operate in community.	Public sector main provider; access to extension by NGOs limited to community meetings; NGOs hire public sector extension agents.	NGOs offer training to extension agents and other district-level civil servants (for example, on gender); NGOs do not provide extension to households in study area; farmers informally exchange knowledge, seeds, and practices.
Main public sector institution in charge	Departments of agriculture and animal husbandry	Ministry of Food and Agriculture	Regional Bureaus of Agriculture and Federal Ministry of Agriculture and Rural Development
Funding	Various centrally and state-sponsored schemes, such as the Food Security Mission and Scheme to promote ATMA	Specific programs in certain districts only; general funds available to extension agents are limited.	District governments pay extension agents' salaries.
Level of government of front-line service providers	Block level (ATMA to be formed at district level, with ATMA structure at block level)	District level (District Agricultural Development Unit)	Kebele level (although providers are hired by and report to district government); policy to have minimum team of three extension agents at each kebele fulfilled in some kebeles and not others.
Line of accountability for staff	Department of Agriculture	Ministry of Food and Agriculture; planned to change under local government service	District-level agricultural line ministry (WoARD)
Institutional unit in charge of women/gender	No specific institutional unit in the Department of Agriculture in Karnataka; at national level, Gender Resource Center in Agriculture in the Department of Agriculture and Cooperation	Women in Agricultural Development (WIAD) Directorate in Ministry of Food and Agriculture, represented at district level.	Gender desks and gender focal points at woreda level; liaison with woreda offices of women's affairs. At kebele level, there is a women's affairs position in the cabinet.

(continued)

Table 7.1 (Continued)

Indicator	India	Ghana	Ethiopia
Female front-line staff	No female agricultural extension workers, 10 percent female veterinary assistants in surveyed blocks in Karnataka.	One WIAD officer mandated per district; 15 percent of surveyed extension agents are women.	4–16 percent of staff in case study were women, including an average 9 percent female kebele-level extension agents; in one case study district, 24 percent of district-based staff were women.
Main problems identified by front-line staff	Lack of manpower and political interference; discontent with salaries and pay scales, lack of opportunities for promotion.	Lack of transport and lack of funds; dissatisfaction with salaries and work conditions; about half of staff disagree with policies they have to implement.	Varies by region but includes dissatisfaction with career opportunities and chances for further studies; dissatisfaction with remoteness of some deployments; lack of support from superiors to provide more demand-driven services.

Links between service providers, households, and community organizations (short route of accountability)

	India	Ghana	Ethiopia
Main approach to extension	Extension agents provide subsidized inputs for new technologies under various schemes; efforts to link farmers to markets under ATMA.	Extension agents establish demonstration plots and visit groups and individuals, give farm-specific advice, and provide access to group-based credit.	Extension agents mainly distribute nonsubsidized technology packages.
Discretion of field staff/service providers	Medium (need to implement schemes)	High; no effective targets	Very low; hard quotas regarding the number of packages farmers have to adopt; discouraged from adapting packages to meet local demand.

Role of user organizations	Strategy to form farmers interest groups under ATMA, but low capacity to support group formation; cooperatives not inclusive (no farmers cooperatives and only 11 percent of dairy cooperatives had female chairs); some efforts to link agricultural services to women's self-help groups.	Strategy to form FBOs, but coverage is limited; existing groups focus on credit; men more likely than women to belong to FBOs.	Farmer cooperatives have wide coverage, do not provide extension directly but are closely tied to "package approach"; cooperatives dominated by government and party influence; cooperative governing bodies are expected to include some women.
Targeting of beneficiaries	Concentration on "leading farmers"; some schemes have provisions for members of SC/ST groups or households living below poverty line.	Extension agents have to report number of male and female farmers met; concentration on "award-winning" farmers.	Concentration on "model farmers," who are expected to work with "followers"; incentive to work with farmers who can be signed up for packages.
Targets related to women	Concentration on male heads of household; guidelines to involve women under ATMA-funded activities (30 percent funds targeted to women).	Extension agents report number of female farmers met; WIAD with dedicated staff in each district.	Cultural perception that "women do not farm" limits attention to women; EPRDF party philosophy promotes gender equity; local women's associations, party women's leagues, and women's affairs officials work with extension agents to involve women in extension ("women's development package").
Role of political representatives (long route)			
Involvement of political representatives	Block panchayat partly involved in beneficiary selection; almost no involvement of gram panchayat; not foreseen under ATMA.	Decentralized in principle, but district assembly and district chief executive not involved; may change if composite budget and Local Government Services are implemented.	High level of integration: extension team leader serves as agricultural portfolio holder in kebele cabinet; no political competition for election of local councilors.

(continued)

Table 7.1 (Continued)

Indicator	India	Ghana	Ethiopia
Household preference for different routes of accountability			
Complaints	Less than 10 percent of households complain about extension or livestock services; all complaints are directed to gram or block panchayat politicians or members of legislative assembly.	Low incidence of complaints; complaints directed to Ministry of Food and Agriculture district office or district assembly member.	Farmers contact kebele council/chair (formal procedure); grievance committees for specific programs also receive complaints.

Source: Authors.

Note: Figures on access to extension refer to year preceding the survey, which was administered in 2006 in Karnataka, in 2008 in Ghana, and in 2009 in Ethiopia.

Access to Agricultural Extension

Access of households to extension differs widely across the three study countries. Ethiopia, the country with the lowest GDP in the study, achieved the best outcome for women in terms of access to agricultural extension: 20 percent of the women covered in the sample received agricultural extension visits at home or on the farm. Twenty-seven percent of the men in the sample had access to agricultural extension visits, the same percentage as in Karnataka, India. Access varied widely across regions, however, ranging from 2 percent in Afar to 54 percent in Tigray. Moreover, a high level of access does not necessarily indicate utilization or good-quality service. As a result of the top-down approach and the focus on getting model farmers to adopt fixed technology packages, extension tends to neglect poor farmers, particularly women. Ethiopia's extension system is not client oriented, and its system is rather unresponsive to user demand. The national goal is that women should account for 50 percent of extension users, but the team found many barriers to women's participation in extension programs, including cultural norms and the inappropriateness of the "women's development package" for female household heads.

Access to extension is lowest in Ghana, where about 12 percent of male-headed households received individual visits of agricultural extension officers and 10–15 percent attended group meetings organized by agricultural extension officers. There was some variation across agroecological zones. Access to livestock services was greatest in the savannah zone, where livestock is most important: 34 percent of male-headed households with livestock in this zone reported individual visits from a livestock officer.

Despite the predominant role of women in agriculture in Ghana, just 2 percent of female household heads in the transition zone and none of the female household heads in the forest and savannah zones. Across the three zones, less than 2 percent of female spouses in male-headed households received agricultural extension visits. Access to livestock extension was better: 24 percent of female-headed households and 5 percent of female spouses in the transition zone received visits by livestock officers. However, neither group was visited in the forest zone. In the savannah zone, 15 percent of both female-headed households and female spouses were visited.

Access to extension through group meetings and community meetings was not much better for female-headed households (2 percent in the forest zone and 4–6 percent in the transition zone; no such services were provided in the savannah zone). Female spouses in male-headed households had somewhat better access to both group and community meetings on agricultural and livestock issues (5–9 percent), indicating that spouses may either have more time to make use of these opportunities or accompany their husbands.

Access to agricultural extension was also limited in Karnataka, India (although it was higher than the national average for India of 6 percent). Among households with land, 29 percent of male-headed households and

18 percent of female-headed households met with extension agents during the year before the survey. Access to livestock services was rather high: 72 percent of male-headed households with livestock and 79 percent of female-headed households received such services.

Limited Role of Alternative Modes of Extension

Individual visits by public sector extension agents, which can be referred to as the "traditional model," remain the predominant mode of providing extension in all three countries. The traditional model dominates despite efforts to promote group- and community-based extension and to encourage the active participation of other extension providers. In India, 85 percent of extension contacts were individual visits. In Ghana, the percentage of farmers who accessed extension services through group visits and community meetings was slightly higher than for individual visits, but extension agents dedicated almost half of their field interactions with farmers to individual visits. In Ethiopia, community meetings organized by extension officers and individual visits by extension agents each reached about 26 percent of male farmers, but female farmers apparently found community meetings less accessible, as only 11 percent received extension in this form.

NGOs were not active in providing extension in the surveyed districts of Karnataka; they also played only a limited role in Ghana and Ethiopia. In Ghana, only one farmer had received a visit from an NGO extension provider in the year preceding the survey. NGOs organized 14 percent of the community-based meetings that were held on agricultural and livestock-related issues. In the surveyed districts of Ethiopia, the extension role of NGOs was limited to the training of extension agents and other district-level staff; it did not involve direct interaction with farmers. Private sector enterprises did not provide extension services per se in the surveyed regions of any of the three countries, although farmers who bought inputs from private input dealers received advice related to those inputs.

High Level of Farmer Satisfaction

Across the three countries, reported farmer satisfaction with extension services was high. In Karnataka, most of the farmers who received extension services were satisfied. The main complaint voiced was that the extension agent did not visit their village at all or frequently enough. In Ghana, 90 percent of farmers receiving government extension were very satisfied with the service, and only 4 percent were somewhat or very dissatisfied. Almost all extension recipients in Ethiopia expressed satisfaction with the service.

These high satisfaction rates may be linked to some reluctance to express dissatisfaction, as respondents in both Ghana and Ethiopia also reported satisfaction with drinking water, which they had identified as their major problem.

In Ethiopia, extension service focuses on high-value agricultural production. Better-off and educated farmers are the main recipients of extension packages, and performance awards. These farmers likely are quite satisfied with extension services. There are few such progressive farmers in most Ethiopian villages, and their practices have limited demonstration effects.

Lack of Involvement and Inclusiveness of Farmer-Based Organizations

Farmer-based organizations (FBOs) play a limited role in the provision of agricultural and veterinary extension services, despite ongoing efforts to promote them as a way to strengthen farmers' voice and access with regard to agricultural and veterinary extension services. The case study evidence from Karnataka and Bihar indicates that the extension staff does not have sufficient capacity to promote the formation of the farmers interest groups foreseen under the Agricultural Technology Management Agency (ATMA) model. The main farmers organizations that already exist, farmers cooperatives and dairy cooperative societies, play a role mainly in facilitating access to subsidized inputs. In the case of the dairy cooperatives, they also play an important role in providing livestock services, such as artificial insemination. The Bihar case study suggests that there is little coordination between the services provided by the cooperatives and those provided by the government. The survey in Karnataka indicates that the leadership of the farmers and dairy cooperatives is not inclusive with regard to gender or caste. None of the surveyed farmers cooperatives and less than 11 percent of the dairy cooperatives had either female chairs or female secretaries, although 25 percent of the farmers cooperatives and 55 percent of the dairy cooperatives have a policy of reserving seats for women in their executive committees. Some 85 percent of the chairs of the farmers cooperatives and 96 percent of the chairs of the dairy cooperatives included in the survey belonged to the other backward class (OBC) category, which is politically dominant in Karnataka.

In Ghana, despite the policy of the Ministry of Agriculture to form village-based FBOs to improve access to agricultural extension services, these organizations have limited coverage. Various government programs provide subsidized credit using a group approach, which seems a major motivation to form these groups. The FBOs might therefore be best described as credit seekers. Controlling for other factors, women are less likely than men to join FBOs.

In Ethiopia, farmers cooperatives are the main type of FBO. Because they are in charge of providing inputs, they are closely linked to the "package approach" used by the Ethiopian extension system, even though they do not provide extension services themselves. Government guidelines stipulate that women should be represented in their governing bodies. Women sit on all committees of the cooperatives, although they generally do not serve as chairs. The cooperatives are dominated by state and party influence.

The Challenge of Demand-Driven Extension

The evidence from the three countries indicates that making agricultural extension demand driven remains a major challenge. The nature of the challenge differs across countries.

Lack of capacity in India. The lack of demand-driven extension in India seems to reflect the lack of overall capacity. Not having hired agricultural extension workers for more than a decade, the government has limited capacity for providing agricultural extension, and the private and nonprofit sector have not filled that gap—at least not at the time of the survey. The age profile of the extension agents interviewed in Karnataka reflects this hiring policy: of the surveyed extension agents, 71 percent were over 50, 27 percent were 40–50, and just 2 percent were 30–40. Each extension worker is estimated to be responsible for 7,000 farmers.

All extension agents noted that the lack of personnel is their major constraint, especially in view of the fact that the extension agents' main task was to implement a wide range of government programs, focused mainly on the provision of subsidized inputs. This situation leaves little room for responding to farmers' demand or providing new agricultural knowledge. This is reflected by the limited interaction of extension agents with agricultural research institutes: only 30 percent of agricultural extension agents had visited an agricultural research station or training center in the year before the survey.

These findings may not be unique to Karnataka. The 11th Plan for India points to the capacity constraint in the extension system (Government of India 2007b, p. 7): "With hindsight, it appears that the policy of restraining new hiring may have been excessive, as is evident from the age composition and high vacancies among extension staff."

Agricultural extension workers and veterinary assistants identify political interference in their work as another main constraint. This may be linked to the fact that the distribution of subsidized inputs is one of the extension agents' main tasks, a task inherently prone to elite capture.

Lack of focus on outcomes in Ghana. In Ghana, the extension agent– to–farmer ratio (estimated at 1:1,500) is more favorable than in India, although vacancies in the more remote areas are common (GSSP 2009). In districts where agricultural extension agents do not have to implement specific programs, there seems little direction as to what kind of goals they should achieve. They seem to be able to respond to farmers' individual demands, but they do not seem to be focused on reaching overall goals for the sector. Many extension agents indicate that they can set goals themselves, that their targets refer largely to the numbers of farmers they visit or the numbers of demonstration plots they establish, not to outcome goals such as an increases in production. This situation prevails even though the district agricultural offices set production goals.

GENDER AND GOVERNANCE IN RURAL SERVICES

Only one of 70 extension agents interviewed mentioned an increase in agricultural production or productivity as the biggest success in his or her career; helping individual farmers win an award was the biggest success for a quarter of the male and half of the female extension agents interviewed. This seems to suggest a strong orientation on making individual farmers successful, which may contribute to the fact that fewer farmers in Ghana have access to extension, even though the farmer–to–extension agent ratio is better. The percentage of extension agents who believe that credit is the main constraint in production is larger than the percentage of farmers who see credit as their main constraint. This perception difference may also contribute to the fact that extension agents often promote technologies that require no specific inputs, such as planting maize in rows, and are less prepared to address other agronomic constraints farmers face.

In the absence of specific (government) programs, extension agents have limited funds to provide extension services; most consider access to transport their main problem. As in India, the linkages between research and extension seem weak. The number of agricultural extension workers who met with agricultural researchers in the year before the survey ranged from 7 percent in the transition zone to 38 percent in the savannah zone.

Overreliance on a package approach in Ethiopia. In Ethiopia, staff capacity is generally not a problem, as a result of the policy of placing three agricultural extension agents in each kebele. The remarkably high access rates also reflect this policy. The top-down nature of public service delivery in Ethiopia makes it difficult to tailor agricultural extension to farmers' demands, however. Farmers in Ethiopia had more access to extension services than those in India or Ghana, but almost none of the extension visits resulted from farmers demanding or requesting some specific advice or information. The incentives of the extension agents are set in such a way that they try to maximize farmers' willingness to adopt the (unsubsidized) technology packages. Extension agents are discouraged from adapting the packages to local needs. Even where they want to tailor their advice to the diverse context, situation, and needs of different households and to take local knowledge into account, pressure from the district agriculture office to persuade a given quota of farmers to adopt standardized technology packages and the fact that opportunities for promotion and training depend strongly on meeting such quotas discourage extension workers from pursuing activities characterized by a demand-oriented focus.

The packages themselves have become less rigid in recent years, with a menu of options now available to farmers. However, the quota system for evaluating extension agents remains in effect. The top-down orientation of delivery starts from the higher tiers of government and runs all the way down to the local level. In principle, front-line extension agents work directly with farmers, supervisors coach and ensure their strong performance, and subject matter specialists provide technical backup. In practice, these actors form a chain of command, the main purpose of which is to make farmers adopt the standard-ized agricultural packages. Little room is provided for the flow of feedback from farmers to extension agents and up to the district agricultural office.

The posting of agents to the kebeles attunes them to local needs and desires. These agents are well positioned to play an important role in facilitating bottom-up information flow if their incentives are altered to encourage them to do so.

The training of extension personnel also reflects the supply orientation of the extension service. Preservice training focuses heavily on technical issues, nearly to the exclusion of aspects such as community organization and inter-action and gender concerns, topics that would contribute to the ability of front-line service providers to manage community members' concerns and feedback and to use this feedback to better tailor services to farmers' needs. Extension workers did receive in-service training on these topics, among others, from NGOs.

Increasing Women's Access to Extension

Strategies to increase women's access to agricultural extension suffer from the general problems faced by the extension system. They also suffer from the per-ception bias regarding women in agriculture, which grossly underestimates the role they play.

The three countries differ considerably with respect to the strategies they have adopted to promote women's access to agricultural extension. In India, these efforts are confined to the ATMA model of extension reform, whose guidelines indicate that 30 percent of the funding provided under the program should reach female farmers. Other provisions ensure female participation in ATMA's governing bodies. Pilot testing of ATMA focused on activities in which women were most heavily involved (for example, livestock and horticulture) in order to be able to convince the administration to adopt a gender focus at all (Swanson, personal communication, January 2009). The countrywide imple-mentation of ATMA was still in an early stage during the time the field research for this study was conducted; the study could therefore not assess the extent to which these provisions had been implemented or the effect they had had. Case study evidence indicates that extension workers try to increase the participation of women in extension activities under ATMA. Such efforts involve their own challenges, such as selecting women who can effectively benefit from the activities rather than just "getting the numbers right." Efforts are underway in India to link extension activities with women's self-help groups or their federations.

Apart from the ATMA-related activities and efforts to link extension with self-help groups, India had fewer provisions to address gender issues in agri-cultural extension than the other two countries studied. It is the only one of the three countries that had no female staff among the agricultural extension agents in the surveyed regions or special institutional provisions within the extension service, such as gender focal points. The qualitative field research indicates that the perception bias regarding women's role in agriculture limits the attention given to expanding extension services to women. Although the national policy framework for agricultural extension fully acknowledges the role of women in agriculture (Birner and Anderson 2007), within the agricultural administration the topic often does not receive priority, because of the perception that women are not involved in agricultural decision making. Moreover, there is a lack of female staff among agricultural extension workers, a problem that is related to the policy of not having hired field staff for many years.

The lack of strategies to promote gender equity among public administration or service providers in India presents a remarkable contrast with the strategies targeting political representatives. Still, the main reason why women have limited access to agricultural extension services is not the lack of strategies that make the service more responsive to the needs of women. It is rather the overall deterioration of the public sector extension system. The few agricultural extension agents who are still left in the system are required to spend most of their time implementing subsidized input programs that are subject to considerable political interference rather than disseminating or delivering knowledge. This deterioration of the system disproportionally affects women, as they are not considered a target group of the activities in which the few remaining extension agents are engaged. Nonpublic actors have not stepped in (at least not in the surveyed areas at the time of the study).

Ghana is the most advanced of the three countries in terms of institutionalizing attention to gender in the public agricultural extension system. At the national level, one of its seven directorates is Women in Agricultural Development (WIAD), and there is one designated senior officer in charge of WIAD in each district agricultural office. Supported by the District Capacity Building Project (DISCAP) project, the Ministry of Women and Children's Affairs is establishing gender desks in each district assembly.

The field research suggests that the perception bias regarding women's role in agriculture is less pronounced in Ghana than in the other two countries. Women are widely recognized to be farmers in their own right. Ghana also has the highest percentage of female extension staff in the surveyed areas (15 percent). Although still low in light of the prominent role of women in agriculture, the figure compares favorably with the complete lack of female extension staff in India and the 9 percent figure in Ethiopia. The achievements in institutionalizing attention to gender in the public administration system have not improved female farmers' access to extension services in Ghana, however; access to agricultural extension by women remains very low.

Investigation of the question of why female access to extension services is so low despite the government's far-reaching efforts to increase access requires further research. The findings in this report indicate that the answer may lie in the general problems faced by the extension service sector. If the system had a stronger focus on increasing agricultural productivity, extension agents would have more incentives to focus on women, considering their important role in agricultural production. Extension agents' tendency to work with award-winning farmers may discourage them from working with female farmers, whom they may perceive as less likely to win awards. It may also be the case that the institutionalization of gender issues in the agricultural administration has been driven by international development agencies, which provide almost 80 percent of agricultural funding (not including salaries) in Ghana (GSSP 2009). If this is the case, buy-in by the administrative and political leadership may not be not sufficient to ensure that efforts to mainstream gender in the public administration are translated into actual outcomes for women.[1]

Ethiopia also pursues the strategy of mainstreaming gender through the "gender machinery" in the public administration. There are woreda (district) Offices of Women's Affairs as well as gender desks or gender focal points within each line department at the woreda level, including in the Woreda (District) Office of Agriculture and Rural Development (WoARD), the office in charge of agricultural and rural development. There is also a women's affairs position in the kebele cabinet.

Despite this machinery, women's access to extension services is low relative to that of men. Significantly fewer women than men attend community meetings organized by extension agents, and substantially fewer women visit demonstration homes and plots. The percentage of women who report that an extension agent visited their home is closer to that reported by men (20 versus 27 percent), but this does not reveal whether the woman actually came into contact with the agent during the visit or whether the extension officer proffered his or her advice to the man in the household. Qualitative fieldwork found that extension agents targeted men even when the advice concerned activities primarily undertaken by women (such as poultry keeping).

Compared with women in Ghana, Ethiopian women have better access to extension because their communities have greater access to extension. The creation of a "women's package" indicates that agricultural officials are trying to improve their services to women. Extension agents are trying to find ways around cultural taboos to work with more women (for example, by collaborating with local women's associations). The rapid expansion of the extension service has created many more opportunities for women to work as crop, livestock, and natural resources management specialists rather than only as home economists.

Despite these efforts, gender-differentiated treatment in extension persists in Ethiopia. A recurring theme in the study was the cultural perception that "women don't farm," even where the range of agricultural activities in which women engage is well known. The perception of men as "farmers" and women as "farm wives" means that men are assumed to pass on professional advice to their wives. The somewhat different realms of agriculture that women and men engage in go largely unrecognized. Moreover, when the wife is not present during the contact with the extension agent, she loses the opportunity to follow up with questions addressed to the extension agent.

The standardization of extension and input packages discussed above also affects women in particular ways; the "women's packages" largely address agricultural activities that farm wives traditionally undertake. The larger set of activities undertaken by female household heads (usually widows and divorced women) remain largely ignored in the design of extension packages for women.

Making Extension More Gender Sensitive by Linking It with Women's Groups

Given the limited access of women to agricultural and veterinary extension services in India, efforts to link agricultural and veterinary advisory services to women's self-help groups are promising. This model builds on the investment made by other agencies and programs to support the formation of women's self-help groups, an activity for which the existing extension service does not have sufficient capacity. Women's self-help groups also seem more inclusive in terms of caste than farmers or dairy cooperatives: 16 percent of the surveyed women's self-help groups in Karnataka had a chair from a scheduled caste or tribe. Agricultural staff in charge of extension in Karnataka frequently interact with women's self-help groups, which is a promising sign. Case study evidence from Bihar also indicates that it is a useful strategy to link extension services for both crops and livestock to women's self-help groups formed under different programs, such as the World Bank's rural livelihood projects. However, if the capacity of the extension service itself is too limited in terms of staff and financial resources to achieve reasonable coverage, this strategy will not in itself be sufficient for improving service provision. Moreover, one needs to take care not to overload women's self-help groups with too many functions.

Linking extension services to women's self-help groups may also hold promise in Ghana and Ethiopia. In Ghana, the extension service forms FBOs with only female members to improve women's access to extension services. The outreach of this strategy still seems to be limited. The survey indicates that few such groups have been formed, possibly because of weak outreach.

In Ethiopia, women are organized in various forums associated with the political party system. Women's associations and the women's league of the party are possible entry points for strengthening service delivery to women. Party philosophy and government policy strongly support gender equality while recognizing the barriers posed by centuries of patriarchal culture. Women's associations and women's wings of political parties not created by external agencies such as donors are present through the country at the lowest administrative unit. These groups are particularly active in facilitating women's access to the extension agent and in gently pushing some of the cultural frontiers by discussing gender equality and women's abilities. However, the literature suggests that the overt government and party affiliation of women's groups and their use for political mobilization for the ruling party has led to hesitancy on the part of female rural residents in some parts of the country to actively participate (World Bank 2001). This dual role may constitute a check on these institutions' success rate if trust in their gender awareness work is undermined by their political undertakings.

The Limited Role of the Long Route of Accountability

All three countries faced considerable challenges in making the short route of accountability work for agricultural extension, especially for women. The long route of accountability also plays only a limited role in all three countries. In India and Ghana, farmers appear to want to use the long route. It largely fails, because the agricultural extension system is subject to administrative rather than political decentralization. Phrased differently, extension is a "deconcentrated" rather than a "devolved" service. As a consequence, political representatives can exercise little influence on agricultural extension services, which makes the long route of accountability ineffective. In Ethiopia, where agricultural extension has been decentralized administratively and politically, the effectiveness of the long route of accountability is limited by the nature of the country's political system.

The deconcentrated nature of agricultural extension in India and Ghana. Agricultural extension agents are located at the block level in India. The agents' line of accountability remains within the Department of Agriculture. The elected block panchayat members are to some extent involved in providing agricultural extension services. However, their role seems largely confined to the selection of beneficiaries of subsidized input programs, such as subsidized tractors. The survey and the case studies indicate that the gram panchayats play no substantial role in agricultural extension. They do not even seem to be involved in selecting beneficiaries for agricultural extension programs or in any planning activities for agricultural or livestock extension.

The ATMA reform model does not envisage a particular role for the elected representatives of the gram panchayats, the block panchayats, or the district panchayats. The design of ATMA follows the short route of accountability; ATMA envisages increasing farmers' voice through the creation of farmer interest groups and their representation in ATMA's governing bodies.

The rationale of working through FBOs rather than through the panchayati raj system may be justified on the grounds that not all citizens whom the panchayat council members represent are farmers or livestock keepers. Given the difficulties of creating FBOs and making them inclusive with regard to both gender and caste, this strategy should be reconsidered. Although the panchayati raj system is not free from the problem of elite capture, it has more enforceable provisions for ensuring the representation of both women and members of SC/ST groups than FBOs do. India's reservation policy works only because it can rely on the entire machinery of the state for its implementation. Decisions on which seats to reserve in panchayat councils are frequently challenged in court. State election commissions have to fend off considerable political pressure to implement the reservation policy in an impartial manner. Implementing quota policies for FBOs may be difficult without a similar institutional backup mechanism. This may explain why none of the surveyed farmers cooperatives and only 11 percent of the dairy cooperatives had a female chair, despite the fact that many of them had a provision to include female members in their executive committees. In view of the difficulties of making the short route of accountability functioning and inclusive, it seems worth placing more emphasis on the long route and increasing the authority of the panchayati raj system with regard to agricultural programs. The fact that users of extension services may prefer this route is also indicated by the fact that the few (male and female) farmers who actually complained about agricultural extension all approached either elected gram or block panchayat council members or members of the legislative assembly. This may indicate that in rural areas, elected representatives are more accessible than the actors along the supposedly short route of accountability.

The situation in Ghana is similar to that in India, in the sense that the council of political representatives, the district assembly, has little authority over the agricultural extension system (or any agricultural program). Agriculture has been decentralized to the district level, but it remains a deconcentrated rather than a decentralized service. The directors of the district agricultural offices have more authority and discretion than they did before the system was decentralized, but the lines of accountability for both staff and funds remain within the Ministry of Food and Agriculture. The case studies suggest that neither the assembly nor the district chief executive have full information about the budget of the district agricultural offices. The plans of the agricultural offices are supposed to be integrated into the district development planning process, but this provision seems to be implemented partially, at best. Better integration will probably be possible once the composite budget and Local Government Service are implemented. Both provisions have been discussed for a long time, however; whether they will become a reality remains to be seen.

District assembly members are more accessible to rural people than ministry staff is: only 4 percent of all households interviewed had ever visited a Ministry of Food and Agriculture district office, the only place where they could launch complaints regarding agricultural extension if the agricultural extension agent does not visit them. The district assembly member seems to be the most accessible person—often the only person—rural people can access as their link to the government in Ghana, where the "reach" of the state is not very deep. In India, at least one government agent, the gram panchayat secretary, is located in each cluster of villages. In Ethiopia, as discussed below, the reach of the state goes even farther than in India.

These observations point to a more general problem. In countries in which the reach of the state is not deep and the coverage of user organizations limited, the short route of accountability is not really short, because actors are just too far away to be reached. The so-called long route of accountability seems shorter for rural people. However, as discussed below, this route is ineffective at improving service provision if only the first leg of the route (from citizens to their political representatives) works.

There are thus important reasons for strengthening the long route of accountability for agricultural extension. If, however, funding for agricultural extension is fully devolved to local governments, the provision of service may decline.[2] The survey results suggest that agriculture-related services are not a household priority as long as the needs for other basic services, especially water, are not met.[3] Hence, there is a need to craft an institutional design that uses the potential of the long route to improve the effectiveness of agricultural extension services while at the same time avoiding the under-provision of this service.

Lack of political competition in Ethiopia. The situation is quite different in Ethiopia, where the reach of the state is extraordinarily deep. Decentralization has enabled the state to reach down to the level of groupings of 30–50 households. The kebele, with an average population of about 5,000, is the lowest formal administrative unit at which deliberative, executive, and judicial bodies manage local affairs. But the existence of a formalized state structure at this level has made possible the organization of households into *mengistawi budin* (government teams), which, through their leaders, coordinate the implementation of government development programs, ensure labor and other contributions from households for government initiatives, and in some cases work closely with and even evaluate the performance of front-line extension workers. The deep reach of the state also manifests itself in the ability of the government to dramatically expand public services that constitute a priority area in its policy framework. Agricultural extension delivery is one such priority area.

Hence, unlike in Ghana and India, the short route of accountability is more accessible for rural households in Ethiopia, at least in terms of physical proximity. The challenge in Ethiopia is to make agricultural extension more responsive to the needs of farmers, including female farmers. Could the long route of accountability be used more effectively to achieve this goal? There is some evidence that farmers use this route, contacting the kebele council or chairpersons to lodge complaints. The political constellation in Ethiopia limits the effectiveness of this route, however. The first leg of the long route, which implies accountability of political representatives to the citizens they represent, has never functioned in Ethiopia through the avenue of political competition.

Ethiopia has the formal structure of a representative democracy: there are elected representatives, a political machinery suggesting a multiparty system, periodic elections at every tier of government, and constitutionally stipulated political rights to exercise voice. Yet this machinery does not lead to de facto political competition, because the political voice of both citizens and potential competitors to the ruling party has been consistently suppressed, resulting in the ruling party's domination of federal, regional, and local governments irrespective of residents' political preferences (see references in chapter 4). Hence, efforts to use the long route of accountability to make extension more demand driven would have to address mechanisms that work within the ruling party. This issue is discussed below.

Drinking Water

The governance challenges involved in the provision of drinking water differ from those of providing agricultural extension in several ways, as noted in chapter 1. First, providing drinking water facilities is less prone to elite capture by individuals than agricultural extension because it is a community infrastructure. Capture can nevertheless occur regarding the selection of villages in which facilities are to be constructed and the location of facilities within the village. The main strategy for addressing gender concerns is to increase access. As women are usually in charge of fetching water, they are the ones who will directly benefit from the increase in access to safe drinking water. Second, the construction and maintenance of drinking water facilities can be standardized to a much larger extent than agricultural extension because they involve less specificity and thus require less scope for discretion. Third, the maintenance of drinking water facilities can be delegated to communities themselves. Agricultural extension is quite different in this respect because it has a "bridging function" in the agricultural innovation system—extension agents are supposed to constantly provide new knowledge that communities do not have, and they are supposed to constantly channel farmers' concerns back into the agricultural research system. In the case of drinking water, no such constant bridging function is required.

The provision of drinking water involves its own challenges. The construction of infrastructure facilities, when contracted out to the private sector, offers considerable scope for corruption. Moreover, providing drinking water facilities is not sufficient to encourage people to use them, especially if the policy is to charge fees. Provision of drinking water therefore has to be accompanied by education and the creation of public awareness, which is a task that is similar to extension.

Access to Drinking Water

India is the most advanced of the three countries in terms of access to drinking water: 88 percent of households surveyed in Karnataka use safe drinking water sources, and 97 percent have a water source within 1 kilometer, with an average distance of just 0.03 kilometers. In Ghana, access differs considerably across agroecological zones: safe drinking water is accessible to 69 percent of households in the forest zone, 52 percent in the transition zone, and 60 percent

Table 7.2 Summary of Findings on Drinking Water Supply

	India	Ghana	Ethiopia
Service provision outcome			
Access to water	88 percent of households use safe drinking water sources; 97 percent of households have a water source within 1 kilometer (average distance is 0.03 kilometers).	Depending on agroecological zone, 52–69 percent of households use safe drinking water sources; average time needed to get water is 19–31 minutes.	32 percent of households use safe drinking water sources; average time to get to safe water sources during dry season is 127 minutes to a river, lake, spring, or pond and 119 minutes to a well with a pump.
Satisfaction with drinking water	90 percent of male and female respondents are satisfied with drinking water; more than 40 percent are not at all satisfied with drainage.	88–93 percent of households are satisfied with boreholes/wells; satisfaction rates with unsafe water sources are also high.	44 percent of households are very satisfied and 27 percent are somewhat satisfied with quantity; 36 percent are very satisfied and 16 percent are somewhat satisfied with quality during the dry season; considerable dissatisfaction with governance of water systems.
Service providers			
Role of providers	Department of Rural Development and Panchayati Raj in charge; responsibility devolved to gram panchayats; NGOs not active in survey areas.	Community Water and Sanitation Agency main public sector agency; responsibility devolved to district assemblies; NGOs contracted for community facilitation; NGOs also provide drinking water independently.	Construction and major rehabilitation of facilities managed by district water desks/offices, which are backstopped by Regional Water Bureaus; water desks are under WoARD; trend is toward elevating them to technical offices independent of WoARD.

Role of community-based organizations	Gram panchayat, which hires watermen, in charge; World Bank Water and Sanitation Project promoted village water and sanitation committees as part of gram panchayat.	WATSANs are supposed to mobilize initial contribution, collect fees, and ensure maintenance; just 14–27 percent of villages have one.	Establishment of water committees that manage one water facility (often multiple water committees in one kebele); committees register users, mobilize labor contributions, collect fees, ensure maintenance.
Funding	Multiple schemes and programs channeled through Department of Rural Development and Panchayati Raj to gram panchayats.	Multiple projects, mostly donor funded; communities expected to provide 5–10 percent of funding. NGO funding also important.	District water desk provides some funds for construction. However, since districts rarely have capital budgets, Regional Water Bureaus often also fund facility construction. Off-budget donor and NGO funding also important. Communities expected to provide labor and sometimes financial contributions.
Level of government of front-line service providers	Block level: junior engineers in charge of technical aspects of drinking water facilities.	District assembly: Community Water and Sanitation Team (CWST), formed by district assembly staff.	District water desk located at district level; water committees at kebele or subkebele level.
Line of accountability for staff	Junior engineers within the Department of Rural Development and Panchayati Raj; waterman to gram panchayat; water and sanitation committee supposedly to users or gram panchayat council members.	CWST accountable to district assembly, NGO staff to NGO management and, if contracted, the district assemblies; WATSANs supposed to be accountable to users.	Water committees accountable to users and district water desk (although the district water desk is not a formal reporting relationship, as committees are not part of government).
Institutional unit in charge of women/gender	Rule requires that women make up 30 percent of members of water and sanitation committees (apparently not fully implemented).	Gender focal point at district assembly; guideline that CWSTs and WATSANs should have female members.	Women represented on all water committees but generally do not lead them; in one study site, rule that all water committee chairs must be women.

(continued)

Table 7.2 (Continued)

	India	Ghana	Ethiopia
Female front-line staff	2 percent women among surveyed junior engineers.	Usually one of three CWST members female; 16 percent of interviewed NGO staff female.	Water technicians overwhelmingly male; water committees include women.
Main problems identified by front-line staff	Political interference in infrastructure provision; general positive attitudes of senior staff regarding decentralization of drinking water provision (perception that it has speeded up provision of facilities).	Difficulties ensuring sustainability of WATSANs; expectations of WATSAN executive committee members to be remunerated for their time, especially when they collect water fees.	Hard to get users to pay even minimal fees when unprotected sources available; much dissatisfaction about different community contributions (labor and money) for each water system; no training provided to water committees in community organization or gender.

Links between service providers, households, and community-organizations (short route of accountability)

	India	Ghana	Ethiopia
Main approach to provide drinking water	Gram panchayats in charge of organizing construction, with technical support from junior engineer; management by gram panchayat with waterman or water and sanitation committee where existing.	Communities must request facilities and provide 5–10 percent of funding (see above); NGOs involved in community facilitation; where WATSANs exist, they are responsible for maintenance.	Water committees made up of community members in charge of maintenance; construction of infrastructure organized by water desk at woreda level.
Discretion of field staff/service providers	Gram panchayat has full discretion in determining location of facilities, hiring waterman, setting water fees, and managing facilities.	WATSANs have significant discretion over collection of water fees and organization of maintenance; district assemblies follow guidelines from Community Water and Sanitation Agency, which follows National Water Policy.	Water committees have significant discretion to design system of water use, collect user fees; district water desk receives guidelines and policies from Regional Water Bureaus, which follow national policy formulated by Ministry of Water Resources.

Targeting of beneficiaries	Decision at gram panchayat level (village meetings); programs may have guidelines (such as funding earmarked for SC/ST communities).	Guidelines of Community Water and Sanitation Agency; decision making by district assembly.	Systems village based; goal to increase coverage and serve more villages; districts highly involved in decision making.
User contribution/fees	43 percent of households paid water tax in 2005/06; no contributions to construction in terms of labor or funds.	Depending on agroecological zone, 53–83 percent of households pay for water from borehole with pump, 46–98 percent pay for public standpipes; payment rates highest in savannah zone.	Water committees supposed to collect fees; actual collection difficult, because many refuse to pay, especially if unprotected sources are available.
Role of political representatives (long route)			
Involvement of political representatives	Gram panchayat in charge; role delegated to them, so they become the service providers.	District assembly members represent their constituencies in getting access to water; they are also main contact for complaints (see below); evidence that unit committees are also involved in management of facilities.	Kebele cabinet member is responsible for drinking water; kebele council oversees service provision. District water desk is a technical agency; head not in cabinet. Economic Affairs Committee of District Council carries out oversight.
Household preference for different routes of accountability			
Complaints	42 percent of users who are dissatisfied or experience problems contact gram panchayat president or members; 13 percent contract gram panchayat secretary; 38 percent do not contact anyone.	11 percent of male and 8 percent of female household heads complain when dissatisfied; 12 percent of male and 6 percent of female household heads who complain approach WATSAN; 55 percent of male and 37 percent of female household heads approach district assembly member.	Drinking water governance issues raised in kebele-level meetings and elsewhere. No users' congresses in study area.

Source: Authors.

in the savannah zone. The average time needed to get to the water source and fetch water is 19–31 minutes, depending on the agroecological zone. Access to safe drinking water in Ethiopia is low: just 32 percent of the surveyed households use safe drinking water sources, and 3 percent use wells without pumps (classified as safe if protected). The average time to get to the most frequently used water sources during dry season ranges from 127 minutes (for rivers, lakes, springs, or ponds) to 119 minutes (for wells with pump).[4]

Importance of and Reported Satisfaction with Drinking Water

Using the methodology typically applied in citizens' report card surveys, the surveys aimed to find out how satisfied citizens were with the drinking water services. In India, the majority of respondents (90 percent), both male and female, were satisfied. This is not surprising given the extensive access to safe drinking water. They were less satisfied with sanitation issues: more than 40 percent were not at all satisfied with drainage.

Reported satisfaction rates for drinking water were also high in Ghana, despite much lower rates of access. Satisfaction with boreholes or wells with pumps, the main source of safe drinking water in rural areas, ranged from 84 percent to 99 percent. Households also indicated high satisfaction rates with unsafe water sources, such as streams and rivers: among households in the forest zone, 82 percent were satisfied with the water quality in rivers, lakes, and springs, which are not considered safe sources. In the savannah and transition zones, more than half of all households were satisfied with the quality of these sources. In Ethiopia, 71 percent of households were very or somewhat satisfied with the quantity and 52 percent with the quality of drinking water (dry season), even though access was very limited.

In both Ghana and Ethiopia, a significant share of households identified water as their main concern. Among both male and female household heads in Ghana's savannah zone, 45 percent rated water as their first priority area. In Ethiopia, 34 percent of female respondents considered drinking water to be their main problem, a larger percentage than for any other identified service or infrastructure type. However, as discussed below, few respondents expressed discontent with the governance of water systems. The share of households that took any action, such as contacting political representatives or public officials to complain, was also low in all three countries.

Several factors may explain the apparent inconsistency between the problem ratings on the one hand and the satisfaction ratings and disinclination to complain on the other. First, awareness about the health advantages of using safe drinking water sources seems limited, as indicated by the high satisfaction rates with the quality of unsafe drinking water sources. Second, respondents may feel uncomfortable giving answers that might be seen as critical of the government. (Given the nature of the political system in Ethiopia, one might expect this problem to be more prevalent there than in the other two countries.) Third, households may not take action because they may feel that doing so will have little effect and is therefore not worth the (opportunity) costs involved. As a result of some level of nonexcludability in drinking water supply, there is also a collective action type problem in filing complaints against this service.

One member of parliament in Ghana, who was interviewed in 2008, explained another reason, which seems to be relevant in the other countries as well: politicians typically portray infrastructure such as drinking water facilities as a "personal gift" that they benevolently provide to the community. This is reflected in the language they use: "I gave you this borewell." The constituencies also perceive such infrastructure to be a personal gift, especially if they have low expectation levels. A gift cannot be challenged or criticized. This problem is obviously linked to a clientelistic system of service provision. If citizens perceive community infrastructure for safe drinking water as a basic right and support it with their own resources through contributions and taxes, they might be more willing to express dissatisfaction and lodge complaints.

Decentralization of Drinking Water Provision

In both India and Ghana, the provision of drinking water has been decentralized to a larger extent than agricultural extension. In Karnataka, drinking water supply is one of the few functions that have been effectively devolved to the gram panchayat level. The gram panchayats are in charge of managing the resources available for drinking water provision under different programs. They are also in charge of hiring the "waterman," the person in charge of looking after the water facilities. The gram panchayats collect a water tax (only half of surveyed households paid it). In line with this decentralization policy, the technical capacity for supporting the gram panchayats is no longer located in any particular line department; it has been integrated into the Department of Rural Development and Panchayati Raj.

Water supply has been devolved to the district assemblies in Ghana. There is no longer a line department in charge of this service. The Ghana Community Water and Sanitation Agency is located at the regional level and has mainly facilitating and supervising functions. The district assembly designates three of its staff member to form a District Water and Sanitation Team (DWST). NGOs are contracted for community facilitation, as the DWST does not have sufficient personnel to fulfill this function. NGOs also provide drinking water independently. The elected and appointed district assembly members are expected to guide and control decisions on investments for drinking water supply.

In Ethiopia, the construction and major rehabilitation of drinking water facilities is managed by district water desks, which are backstopped by the Regional Water Bureaus, a set-up similar to that in Ghana. Water desks are administrative units under the WoARD. One can observe a trend to make them independent from WoARD.

More than agricultural extension, drinking water lends itself to management by local government councils rather than specific community-based organizations, because every citizen needs access to safe drinking water. Yet it has been a major strategy in all three countries to promote specific community-based organizations. In India, the rationale for this strategy is not immediately obvious, as, unlike in Ghana, each gram panchayat has a functioning local council, which is supported by a government employee (the gram panchayat secretary).

In view of this situation, the considerations for agricultural extension apply to drinking water. It may be more promising to rely on elected representatives (the long route of accountability) than specific user groups, because the machinery of the state ensures that the panchayati raj institutions are socially inclusive and follow the reservation guidelines. As in the case of agricultural extension, households seem to prefer to approach their elected representatives rather than the user group functionaries. Among respondents who decided to approach someone to address problems regarding drinking water, 68 percent contacted either the gram panchayat president, a gram panchayat member, or an elected member at the block or district panchayat. The others approached the gram panchayat secretary or the waterman. No one in the sample approached a water and sanitation committee, casting some doubt on this strategy. One approach for harnessing the potential of water and sanitation committees despite these challenges is to link them to the gram panchayat council, as discussed in chapter 8.

In Ghana, where district assembly members have more limited capacity than the panchayat councils, water and sanitation committees (WATSANs) have been promoted to manage drinking water facilities. It is not clear why forming WATSANs makes more sense than strengthening the unit committees to take over this task. The WATSANs do not function as a universal mechanism for managing rural drinking water supply, even though the Ghanaian water policy stipulates that this should be the case.

About 14–27 percent of villages in Ghana have a WATSAN, depending on the agroecological zone. Of the 49 WATSAN chairs and secretaries interviewed, 20 percent were women. About a fifth of chairs were chosen in competitive elections; another fifth were appointed by the chief or administrative authority. WATSANs are in charge of maintenance; they rarely have a say in the provision of physical infrastructure.

As in India, few citizens (about 10 percent) complain if they are dissatisfied with the provision of drinking water. Among male-headed households who complained, only 12 percent approached a WATSAN. Among female-headed households, the share was 6 percent. The others approached the district assembly or unit committee members, indicating that, as in the case of extension, citizens find this "long" route of accountability more accessible.

In Ethiopia, water committees have been established, each of which is supposed to manage one water facility. There are often multiple water committees in one kebele, as well as committees that serve users across kebele lines. Committees register users, mobilize labor contributions, collect fees, and ensure maintenance. Making them inclusive seems as challenging in Ethiopia as in the other countries. Although bringing water to the household is undertaken predominantly by women (and their children), at all but one site the water committee leaders were men (women were members of the committees).

The water committees do not seem to be effective in counteracting the top-down nature of service provision. In some cases, the functioning of water facilities was compromised if the organization that constructed the facility did not take into account the community's knowledge of water sources in determining where to locate the facility. Such phenomena prevailed no matter whether the government, NGOs, or the private sector was responsible for the construction of drinking water facilities.

ROUTES OF ACCOUNTABILITY IN COMPARISON

This section applies the framework presented in chapter 2 (see figure 2.1) to compare the accountability mechanisms identified in the three countries. Special attention is paid to strategies for improving gender equity, which have been classified with reference to the framework (box 2.2).

India

The long route of accountability, which links service providers and households through their elected representatives (link HH–LP–PS), is particularly strong in India (figure 7.1). Gram panchayat members have more authority to implement development projects than do their counterparts in Ghana, because they have gained control over the resources for drinking water supply (as well as for a number of other development schemes not discussed in this report, such as the National Rural Employment Guarantee Scheme). In Ghana authority is assigned to a higher level of local government—the district assembly, which typically covers more than 80,000 people—making direct participation more difficult. Gram panchayat members are elected in a competitive political process.

India has put in place reservation policies that ensure the inclusion of women and disadvantaged groups at all levels of the panchayat system. It also has effective institutional mechanisms in place, in the form of the State Election Commission and the courts, which ensure that the reservation policies are implemented. Indian states also invest in developing the capacity of elected local representatives through state-level training institutes, further strengthening this route of accountability. The case study suggests that Karnataka is a

Figure 7.1   Main Routes of Accountability in India

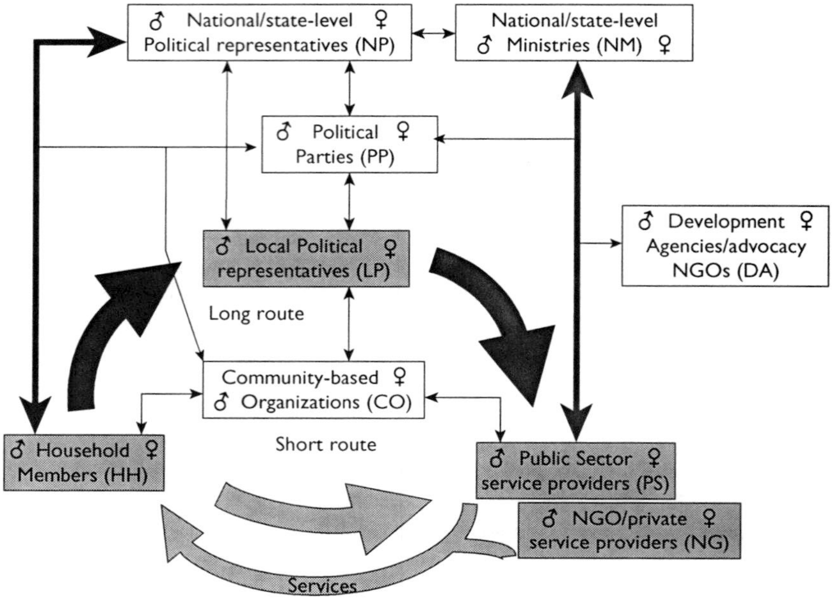

Source: Authors.

model in this regard, as the training provided aims at empowering elected representatives to hold the public administration accountable (see box 6.4).[5]

This route of accountability is used effectively to provide drinking water; it is not used effectively to provide agricultural and livestock services. Households still approach their political representatives at the local or state level (HH–LP or HH–NP), but in this case, the second leg of the long route of accountability (LP–PS) is less effective, because these services are deconcentrated rather than devolved, as discussed above. There is still strong upward accountability (PS–NM) in these services, because staff members remain accountable within the public administration and mainly implement schemes decided at the state or national level (NM).

A matter of concern is the fact that very few institutions within the public administration (along the route NM–PS–HH) aim to make agricultural service provision more responsive to gender needs. The emphasis on gender inclusiveness in the long route of accountability and its virtual absence within the short route is a remarkable feature of the local governance system in India. In view of the strength of the long route of accountability—which is more accessible and thus not really a long route—efforts to create an alternative short route by creating service-specific community organizations (HH–CO–PS) have had limited success, as the water and sanitation committees and FBOs under ATMA show. The desirability of such institutions can be questioned, considering the problems of making them inclusive in the absence of dedicated enforcement mechanisms for strategies, such as gender quotas. Relying on women's self-help groups that have already been formed under other programs seems a promising strategy for reaching women.

The inclusiveness of the gram panchayat system is ensured by reservation policies and by efforts to build the capacity of its members. The representation of women and members of SC/ST groups does not necessarily translate into better policy outcomes for women, however. The design of programs matters. If the allocation of resources within the gram panchayat is left entirely to the bargaining power of its council members, villages represented by female members of SC/ST groups may well lose out. Special provisions in program design are required to address this challenge.

The reservation policy for women does not apply to members of the state legislative assemblies (NP in the figure). Despite decentralization, members of legislative assemblies remain powerful actors at the local level. They are involved in local politics; have their own funding, which they can spend at the local level; and have influence over the public administration. The fact that members of the public administration consider political interference as a main obstacle to fulfilling their mission indicates that this influence may be clientelistic (see box 1.1). This suggests that members of legislative assemblies may misuse their power over the public administration (the second leg in the long route of accountability) for political gains, most likely linked to party politics. They may also pressure the public administration to perform better (a positive use of this leg). Their actual role is an empirical question, a topic for further research.

Ghana

Decentralization in Ghana created an important institution through which rural citizens can gain better access to the government: the district assembly. In rural areas, the assembly member is virtually the only link, other than the local chief, by which rural people can access state institutions. This indicates a strong link from household to local political representatives (figure 7.2). Unlike in India and Ethiopia, the level at which the public administration "ends" is the district, an entity with more than 80,000 people. People trust their assembly members, contact them frequently, and are able to hold them accountable. Accountability is created not only by competitive elections but also through close community relations. Assembly members seem to be motivated in different ways, ranging from intrinsic or religious-based motivations to political ambitions (using their position as a stepping stone to higher positions in the political system). The linkages between district assembly members and political parties (LP–PP) are strong despite the non-partisan nature of the system. The main problem assembly members face is

Figure 7.2   Main Routes of Accountability in Ghana

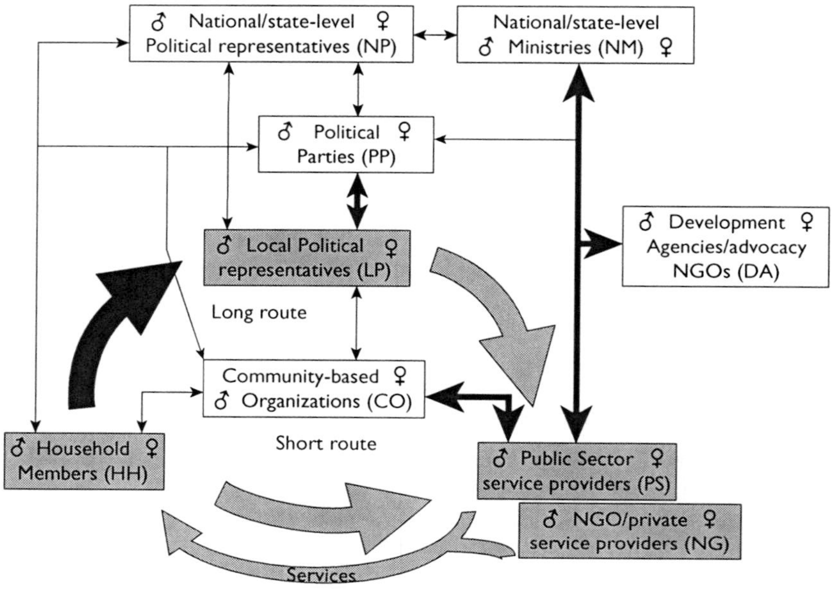

Source: Authors.

that the second leg of the accountability link (LP–PS) is not particularly well developed. Unlike gram panchayat members, who have de facto control over resources and program implementation, district assembly members are limited to lobbying the public administration.

Despite the strong link between households and their elected politicians (HH–LP), international development agencies seemed to have pushed for short-route mechanisms, especially WATSANs in the case of drinking water and FBOs in the case of agricultural extension. This influence is exercised both directly, through projects at the district level (DA–PS), and indirectly, by influencing government policies (DA–NM). Development agencies have also promoted NGOs, especially in the case of drinking water supply. The extent to which NGOs are ultimately accountable to households remains unclear. As in India, this short route through community-based organizations involves its own challenges: the effort it takes to create such institutions in a sustainable way and to make them inclusive is often underestimated. It may also be the case that efforts to create links from PS through COs and NGs undermine efforts to strengthen the missing PS–CO link. This topic has received little attention in the donor discourse in Ghana, where concern seems to focus on the fact that the district chief executive is appointed rather than elected. Yet even under an appointed district chief executive, there is ample room for improving local

GENDER AND GOVERNANCE IN RURAL SERVICES

governance by strengthening the position of the district assembly members and the emerging subdistrict structures, especially the unit committees. As noted, the case study indicates that the unit committees seem to be a platform that is particularly accessible for women.

One challenge of the local governance system in Ghana is the limited role of strategies to improve gender equity that target the long route of accountability, an interesting contrast with the case of India. In the absence of a reservation policy, few women get elected as district assembly members. NGOs can play a role in increasing their number, as the case study shows. There is also a strategy in place to increase the number of female district assembly members through a quota for women among appointed members, but this avenue seems to have been partly compromised by party politics. In contrast to India, strategies to make service provision more gender sensitive that target the public administration play a dominant role in Ghana, especially in the form of the women's machinery. There is also some evidence that these strategies are promoted by international development agencies (links DA–PS and DA–NM). These strategies have not resulted in better service provision outcomes for women, especially in the case of agricultural extension.

Ethiopia

The Ethiopian Peoples Revolutionary Democratic Front (EPRDF) occupies a central place in the routes of accountability in Ethiopia. The party has a strong influence on elected representatives at the local and national levels (PP–LP and PP–NP), public sector service providers (PP–PS and PP–NM), and community-based organizations (PP–CO) (figure 7.3). The party dominates all politically elected bodies. It also influences many positions not formally appointed through the governing party, such as leadership positions of formally nongovernmental institutions (for example, local women's associations and agricultural cooperatives), which are filled by members of the party. The statement made by one local party official interviewed in this study that the party is the "father of the community" summarizes the self-image of the party as a benevolent authority.

In Tigray-D and Amhara-D3, senior positions at the local level—such as leadership positions within the kebele council, cooperatives, and the local party structure itself—are occupied by party members who are veterans of the war against the previous military regime or the more recent war with Eritrea. Party officials consider it the role of party members to stand out as development role models, in terms of both their own economic performance and their willingness to implement the governments' programs, such as by adopting government agricultural packages or by making sure that their children attend school.

Accountability between the party and households (PP–HH) seems to be the missing link in the accountability network. Of course, even in a one-party system, the authorities respond to citizens' grievances when their discontent

Figure 7.3 Main Routes of Accountability in Ethiopia

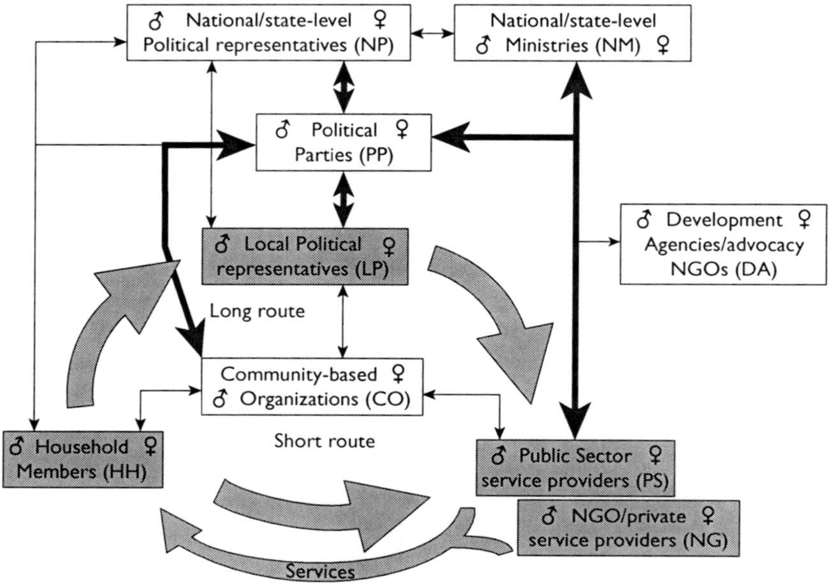

Source: Authors.

may threaten the party's hold on power. The extensive "good governance" reforms following the 2005 elections illustrate this in Ethiopia. The establishment of reasonably effective grievance committees for the productive safety net program, efforts to expand representation in kebele councils, the support given to these councils by the district council speaker's office, and the establishment of additional oversight committees at the kebele level are all efforts to enhance accountability mechanisms. But the strong lines of accountability remain those that lead upward. Top-down modes of decision making and political reliance on democratic centralism mean that downward accountability in Ethiopia is weak.

In Ethiopia, neither the short route nor the long route of accountability ensure that residents' needs and priorities for public goods are met by the state; the powerful forces of upward accountability determine the nature and quality of service delivery. Upward accountability has some advantages. The fact that extension providers in Ethiopia reach a larger share of farmers, both male and female, may reflect not only the favorable agent-to-farmer ratio but also the strong discipline among the extension agents that induces them to meet their package targets. Also contributing to the success of agricultural extension is the high priority placed on this service by the political leadership of the country and party. The standardized system reduces the challenge of supervising and monitoring extension agents, which is one of the inherent challenges of providing this service. Efforts to promote the Green Revolution in India and the training and visit extension system used this approach. Agricultural development in China and Vietnam also thrived under a similar top-down system of a one-party state. Yet there is an important difference between the Green Revolution regions in these countries and Ethiopia: the Green Revolution regions have rather uniform irrigated agricultural systems. A top-down package approach works well in such environments. African agriculture is characterized by agroecological diversity. This is especially true in Ethiopia, where different agroecologies often exist within a single district. Technologies do not "travel far" in this part of the world. Pardey and others (2007) find that only Australia is similar to Africa in the need to tailor technologies to very specific situations. Therefore, for technical reasons alone, a more demand-driven approach is essential to develop agriculture in Ethiopia (for a summary of the substantial body of literature on the value of participatory approaches, see Cohen, Rocchigiani, and Garrett 2008).

A standardized approach might work better in providing infrastructure for drinking water than in providing extension services. However, a major challenge of providing drinking water is creating awareness about the advantages of safe drinking water and encouraging communities to work collectively to maintain drinking water facilities. Although this task is less challenging than providing agricultural extension, it still requires discretion on the part of the facilitator, for which a top-down approach is less suitable than a demand-driven approach. Considering the low access of the population to safe drinking water in Ethiopia, especially compared with agricultural extension, the main problem seems to be that the need for access to safe drinking water has not become a political priority, possibly because of the weak accountability linking actors in the system to households.

NOTES

1. The research team identified a tendency among development partners to consider the institutionalization of gender strategies or increased awareness of the gender concept as main achievements, paying less attention to actual outcomes. For example, a review of the gender desks in district assemblies by one donor agency highlighted a better understanding of the concept of gender as a major achievement. The review did not discuss any outcomes, such as access of male and female citizens to services provided by district assemblies, that might have been achieved as a consequence of institutionalizing the gender desks.
2. Findings from Bolivia, for example, indicate that funding to agriculture declined after decentralization (World Bank 2007e).
3. The low demand for agricultural extension is related to the market failures of extension discussed in chapter 1.
4. The households covered in the Ethiopia survey may have better access than the national average. In 2004, the last year for which data are available from the World

Development Indicators database, only 11 percent of the rural households in Ethiopia had safe drinking water. Information collected during the study indicated an average of 18 percent.

5. A visit to the Abdul Nazir Sab State Institute for Rural Development in Mysore supported this observation. The institute uses a range of training methods to reach a large number of elected gram panchayat members (such as satellite-assisted training), taking illiteracy among the trainees into account (for example, by using media such as short movies).

CHAPTER EIGHT

Implications for Policy and Research

The opportunities and challenges of making rural service provision more responsive to the needs of women differ significantly across countries and across services. They depend on the political system, the system of local governance, the way in which a particular service is organized, and the role of women regarding that service. Efforts to improve the gender responsiveness of rural service provision thus have to be context specific, based on a sound analysis of opportunities and constraints. Transferring best practices from one country to another may have limited success because opportunities, challenges, and entry points for interventions differ considerably.

This chapter presents both cross-cutting and country-specific recommendations for policy design and research. The first part of the chapter presents cross-cutting insights. The second part of the chapter presents recommendations for each of the three study countries.

CROSS-CUTTING INSIGHTS FOR POLICY DESIGN AND RESEARCH

This section discusses two cross-cutting issues for policy design and research. The first is the need to develop analytical tools for understanding why and to what extent rural services fail women. The second is the need to consider alternative strategies to the widespread approach of forming service-specific user associations to improve service provision.

Understanding Why Rural Services Fail Women

Rural services can fail women for very different reasons. This failure is often linked to general problems associated with providing the service (table 8.1). In such cases, introducing gender-related strategies will have limited effect. It is therefore important to undertake a general assessment of the problems with the service as a first step and to link gender-related efforts to general reform efforts regarding the service.

Gender-specific problems can also account for the poor provision of service to women. The widespread perception bias regarding the actual role of women in agriculture can contribute to the low priority afforded provision of better services to women. In Ethiopia, women are not considered to be farmers, despite the many farming activities they perform; in India women are perceived as "providing only labor" rather than making farming-related decisions. This bias persists despite ample evidence that documents the role of women in agriculture. Innovative strategies are needed to address this perception bias.

Using Qualitative and Quantitative Tools to Help Identify Problems and Opportunities

The accountability framework developed in the 2004 *World Development Report* provides a useful basis for diagnosing problems and identifying opportunities in rural service provision. The framework, which is flexible enough to be expanded, classifies strategies for making service provision more gender sensitive by identifying the actors and the accountability linkages the strategies target.

Surveys that collect gender-disaggregated data from different actors in the local governance system (rural households, political representatives, service providers, and community-based organizations) can provide insights regarding the bottlenecks to and opportunities for improving rural service provision and making rural services more responsive to gender needs. Based on the experience

Table 8.1   General Problems in Providing Rural Services

Problem	Example
Lack of staff and resources	Agricultural extension in India
Capture of the service by the better-off	Agricultural extension in India
Lack of appropriate management to make the service effective and focused on outcomes	Agricultural extension in Ghana
Service provision methods and staff incentives that discourage responsiveness to users	Package agricultural extension approach in Ethiopia
Lack of political priority to provide the service	Drinking water in Ethiopia
Users' lack of awareness and knowledge about the relevance of the service for their well-being	Drinking water in some regions in Ghana

Source: Authors.

of this study, it will be possible to develop standardized survey instruments, which include only those survey questions that provided useful diagnostic indicators.

The study suggests that surveys are best accompanied by qualitative case studies, which provide inside knowledge on questions surveys cannot answer. Where time and resources do not allow surveys to be carried out, qualitative case studies can provide important insights. The case study methods applied, especially the influence-network mapping and the process-influence mapping tools (not discussed in this report), appear promising for future research.

Collecting Gender-Disaggregated Access Data and Interpreting Satisfaction Indicators

Access to services is one of the most important diagnostic indicators. To capture the full gender dimension, services that can be supplied individually, such as agricultural extension, should be measured separately for male-headed households, female-headed households, and female spouses in male-headed households.

The need to obtain gender-disaggregated data on access to services has long been emphasized; for essential services, such as health and education, such indicators exist. In contrast, there is a dearth of such indicators for agriculture-related services, such as extension. The surveys conducted for this study included questions on a range of agriculture-related services, such as credit, land administration, and marketing services. Reports on these topics will be prepared as future outputs of this research project. A set of gender-disaggregated agricultural and rural governance indicators will also be developed on this basis.

The findings of this study cast some doubt on the reliability of satisfaction indicators, which are now widely used in citizen report card studies. In all three sampled countries, household members expressed high satisfaction rates, even for services that they identified as their main area of concern and services to which they had little access. The reasons may be manifold: lack of knowledge (about the advantages of improved drinking water, for example); low expectation rates; reluctance to criticize government service providers; perceptions that services are gifts from benevolent politicians that cannot be questioned; and so on. Understanding why satisfaction indicators are unreliable requires further research. In the meantime, such data should be interpreted with care.

Developing Alternatives to Service-Specific User Associations

International development agencies seem to place high hopes on fostering community-based user organizations, such as water and sanitation committees and farmer-based organizations (FBOs), as a way of improving rural service provision. There are good reasons for choosing this strategy: if they are not coopted by this system, community-based organizations can help circumvent a clientelistic political system, empower the rural poor with respect to both politicians and the public administration, and create healthy checks and balances in the local governance system; they may also yield other benefits, such as economies of scale. They seem particularly suitable for services, such as agricultural extension, that are not relevant for the entire population.

These benefits notwithstanding, organizations promoting this strategy may have underestimated the effort it takes to build sustainable local institutions and make them inclusive with regard to women and marginalized groups. Attention needs to be paid to the relationships between user organizations, as the short route of accountability, and local political representatives, who constitute the long route of accountability.

For services that need to be provided to the entire village population, such as drinking water supply, investing in local councils, such as the unit committees in Ghana, may be a useful alternative to developing specialized committees. Where public funds for institution building are limited and people's opportunity costs of time are high, it may make sense to invest in the democratic institutions of a decentralized state rather than in parallel structures (see Manor 2004). In contrast, if services are to be provided only to specific groups, such as households owning dairy cattle, the formation of user groups is likely to have a comparative advantage, especially if such groups can become the vehicle for a range of services (such as feed supply, credit, breeding services, and milk marketing in the case of dairy cattle).

It would be useful to determine which people or institutions rural people approach when they have problems and how effective their contacts are in addressing the problems. The study presents some evidence that rural people often approach elected representatives, because they are more accessible than other officials. For men and women in rural areas, the long route of accountability often represents the shortest route—or the only accessible route—especially in countries in which other state institutions (specifically the public administration) do not reach very deep.

COUNTRY-SPECIFIC RECOMMENDATIONS

A set of policy recommendations was derived for each country. Each set addresses the country-specific challenges identified in this study.

India

This section presents recommendations for India. It first presents strategies for the country's general decentralization policy. It then offers recommendations for agricultural extension, livestock services, drinking water provision, and sanitation.

General Decentralization Policy

Decentralization policy in India has led to a more far-reaching empowerment of local political representatives than was observed in Ghana or Ethiopia. Gram panchayat members have been empowered to manage several rural development programs, including public works and infrastructure provision. With the reservation of seats for women in the panchayati raj institutions, India has the most far-reaching policy of involving women in local governance of the three countries.

The study identified some challenges that require attention, namely, elite capture of the intervillage allocation of public resources, capacity constraints in managing programs at the gram panchayat level, and constraints for female household members in attending gram sabha meetings. The following approaches appear promising in addressing these problems.

Preventing elite capture. The formula-bound allocation of fiscal grants to the gram panchayats was successfully implemented, but the allocation of funds to the villages within the gram panchayats turned out to be subject to severe targeting failures, as the analysis by Palaniswamy and Krishnan (2008) under this project shows. This allocation is the outcome of a bargaining process by the gram panchayat members, the result of which appears to reflect elite capture. Female gram panchayat members who belong to scheduled castes receive significantly fewer resources than either other women or men from a scheduled caste or similarly disadvantaged social groups.

To address this problem, policy makers could apply a formula for distributing grants to villages—a strategy that worked well at the gram panchayat level. The challenge is devising a mechanism for implementing the formula. One option would be to use mechanisms currently in place for other programs, such as monitoring by block officials and gram panchayat secretaries. It may also be useful to create awareness about the problem by training gram panchayat members, improve transparency about intervillage distribution of funds through more stringent reporting in gram sabha or jamabandhi (public audit) meetings, and increase the attendance of women from scheduled castes and tribes at these meetings (see below).

Increasing administrative support at the gram panchayat level. The gram panchayat secretaries play an important role in providing administrative support to the gram panchayat members in implementing various programs. These secretaries are overburdened with the large number of programs that have been decentralized to the gram panchayat level. It is therefore essential to increase the administrative capacity at this level by hiring additional staff (a strategy that the government of Karnataka recently started to use). Female gram panchayat members may be more comfortable interacting with female administrative staff. New staff could be trained to assist illiterate gram panchayat members. Good candidates for these posts would be women with experience with gender-related sectors or programs. Gender mainstreaming could be part of the training all new staff receive.

Making it easier for women to attend gram sabha meetings. Confirming earlier studies, this study shows that women are less likely than men to attend gram sabha meetings. To address this problem, attention should be paid to holding meetings at times of the day that are convenient for women. Information about the meetings and the agenda of the meetings should also be improved. The gram panchayat secretaries can play a role in reaching this goal. The training programs for gram panchayat members could sensitize them about the importance of announcing gram sabha meetings in advance, communicating their agenda, and finding appropriate locations that encourage women to attend.

Agricultural Extension and Livestock Services

India's agricultural extension system has deteriorated, largely as a result of the policy of not hiring staff. The limited resources available tend to serve better-off farmers, a problem that disadvantages female-headed households with agricultural land. This elite capture is underlined by agents' complaints of political interference as an important obstacle to their ability to perform their duties.

As the survey of extension agents indicates, merit-based promotion is not used as a mechanism to create accountability. In addition, the current extension system no longer functions as a bridge between agricultural research and farmers. The implementation of Agricultural Technology Management Agency (ATMA) has considerable potential to make agricultural extension more demand driven and responsive to women's needs. Case study evidence indicates, however, that it faces considerable challenges, as the investment needed to form functioning farmers' interest groups has been underestimated. To some extent, implementation of ATMA is perceived only as another subsidized input program. Several approaches appear promising in addressing these problems.

Dealing with the staff shortage problem. Addressing the staff shortage problem is not sufficient in view of the other challenges identified by the study, but no other strategy will succeed without addressing this problem. There are different ways of increasing the number of agricultural extension agents; simply hiring more staff under the civil service system may not be the preferred option. Hiring staff on a contract basis for specific programs is one option, currently used by the government of Karnataka. This option provides more flexibility in adjusting staff strength and skills to changing needs over time. Contracting NGOs that work in the agricultural sector, contracting private sector companies that can provide extension services, and establishing public-private partnerships are other options.

Before a strategy for increasing agricultural extension staff is adopted, a thorough analysis should be conducted of the human resources (numbers, qualifications, skill sets) required to improve agricultural extension. This exercise should have a long-term perspective that takes into account the future challenges of agricultural development (such as adapting to climate change and meeting trade requirements); the availability of modern information and communication technologies; and a vision for the roles that the public, private, and nonprofit sectors will play in the future. The answers may well depend on the specific conditions and priorities of each state.

Whatever strategy is chosen, it is essential to pay special attention to the skills (and infrastructure) required to provide better services to female farmers. In view of the positive experience in other countries (Ghana, in particular), the strategy of hiring female extension agents to better serve female farmers deserves special attention. It may also be useful to learn from the positive experience with female extension agents and farmers' field schools for women's groups in other states of India (Parmesh Shah, World Bank, personal communication 2009).

The standing committees on agriculture and industry in the district panchayats could also play a proactive role in mobilizing public awareness for the inclusion of gender issues in plans and policies of decentralized bodies and government departments. They could also play an important role in the monitoring and evaluation of efforts to make agricultural service provision more gender responsive. Paying attention to the representation of women in the membership and leadership of these committees may increase their effectiveness in this regard. It may also enhance gender mainstreaming if these committees pay special attention to subsectors in which women are particularly active, such as dairy production and horticulture.

Addressing management challenges in the public sector. To improve the working environment of agricultural extension staff that continue to be employed by the public sector, efforts are required to resolve the management challenges identified by the study, particularly political interference and the low prevalence of merit-based promotion. Both problems are deeply entrenched in the public administration more generally and cannot be resolved in isolation within the agricultural departments.

Current reform approaches seem to ignore these problems rather than try to identify how they can be tackled within the current political and administrative system. The hiring of new staff outside the civil service system may offer new opportunities for merit-based promotion and other incentive systems, such as merit-based wage compensation. Adequate salary structures within the public service still remain important to avoid demoralizing public sector staff, however.

The problem of political interference could be reduced by strengthening the role of agricultural extension staff in improving the knowledge and skill base of the farming population rather than using extension agents mainly to implement subsidized input programs. Reforming the subsidy system involves political challenges; doing so would reduce the opportunities for politicians to interfere with the work of extension agents.

The extent to which a right-to-information approach can be used to reduce political pressure and elite capture should also be explored. Such an approach would require increasing the transparency about availability and target groups of agricultural programs. The media (local radio) and advocacy NGOs, which can assist disadvantaged and female farmers in filing right-to-information requests, could play a role in this respect.

Reestablishing the function of agricultural extension as a bridge between agricultural research and farmers/markets. The low level of interaction between agricultural extension agents and agricultural researchers points to a serious problem. Under the training and visit system, extension agents and researchers were required to meet every two weeks. A more promising alternative is to use a more demand-driven approach. Extension agents could be required to visit with agricultural researchers more frequently than they currently do to meet farmers' knowledge demands if participatory planning approaches for the introduction of new technologies, commodities, and farming practices are implemented, as piloted under ATMA. The establishment of governing structures that involve both agricultural researchers and extension agents, as foreseen under ATMA, is another promising approach for improving the bridging function of agricultural extension.

Forming functioning FBOs. Case study evidence collected under this project indicates that the challenge of forming farmer interest groups, as foreseen under the ATMA model, has been underestimated. Extension agents, who could facilitate group formation, are limited in numbers and do not necessarily have the skills required to form and supervise groups. Moreover, they are used to working mainly with better-off farmers.

If the strategy of forming farmers interest groups is to be pursued, qualified facilitators for group formation should be hired and group representatives should be trained. The sizable investments made in rural livelihood projects (supported by the World Bank, DFID, IFAD, and others) can serve as a benchmark.

Special attention needs to be paid to making farmers groups inclusive in terms of gender and caste. Currently, farmers and dairy cooperatives have very few female members—and even fewer women in leadership positions—even where affirmative action policies are in place. One way of addressing this problem is to form groups made up exclusively of female farmers.

Although the best strategy for improving rural service provision will always depend on the specific situation, it may be promising to link agricultural service provision to existing groups. This is already happening in the case of dairy cooperatives, which provide their own livestock services. Women's self-help groups can also play a role. Using women's self-help groups for the provision of agricultural services is viable only if there is a match between the type of service and the economic opportunities and interests of the group members, however. Care must be taken not to overload women's self-help groups with too many functions.

Federations of community-based organizations at a higher level may be the best entry point. Experiments such as those conducted by the State Poverty Eradication Commission Kudumbashree in Kerala (http://www.kudumbashree .org/) and the community-managed resource centers organized by the NGO MYRADA (Mysore Resettlement Development Agency) in Karnataka (http:// www.myrada.org/) are interesting examples for the design of such approaches. Agricultural producer companies, an institutional alternative to state-dominated cooperatives introduced through a legal change in the early 2000s, are also an interesting option as user organizations for agricultural extension services.

Group-based approaches not only require investment in formation, they also demand farmers' time, which can be a particular constraint for female farmers. Therefore, alternatives to group-based approaches should be considered. One option that deserves particular attention are Internet kiosks (places in villages that provide public access to computers). An example is the e-*choupals* (Internet kiosks) run by the Indian Tobacco Company, through which farmers can sell their produce online and access agriculture-related information. Cell phone–based approaches can also be used to provide extension services. They are suitable for providing market-related information or answering farmers' questions. Such approaches must be tailored to the capacity and extension needs of different groups of farmers, including female farmers and households with marginal land holdings.

Water Supply and Sanitation

Karnataka has achieved widespread access to safe drinking water. Rural water supply is fully devolved to the gram panchayat level; water and sanitation committees have been introduced in an effort to strengthen the short route of accountability. Drainage, as one aspect of sanitation, however, has remained a challenge. The following sections present recommendations to address the problems identified in the study.

Increasing the involvement of women in water and sanitation committees and strengthening their accountability within the panchayati raj system. This project did not aim to conduct an impact evaluation of the water and sanitation committees. The study findings indicate, however, potential challenges regarding the accountability and inclusiveness of these committees, as discussed in chapter 7.

Two strategies could be used to address these challenges. First, to ensure the accountability of the water and sanitation committee within the gram panchayat system, the gram panchayat member who represents the village or ward in which the committee is located could be an ex officio member of the committee. The water and sanitation committee may be formally constituted as a subcommittee of the gram panchayat, a strategy already being pursued in Karnataka. Committee members could also be required to report in gram sabha or ward sabha meetings to improve accountability.

Second, a quota system could be used to increase the representation of women in leadership positions of the water and sanitation committees. As water supply has been devolved to the gram panchayat, it seems reasonable to request that the water and sanitation committees have at least the same rule of 33 percent representation of women among both members and chairs. (This rule has already been promoted under the Second Karnataka Rural Water and Sanitation project). Implementing the quota system may be a challenge, because women's representation in leadership positions is currently low, even though affirmative action policies are already in place in almost half of the cases. It may be useful to sensitize gram panchayat members and the gram panchayat secretaries to ensure the implementation of a quota system in these committees. Likewise, the block officials involved in drinking water supply could be instructed to pay more attention to this issue.

Focusing more attention on drainage. The study indicates that satisfaction levels with drainage were rather low. Although satisfaction data have to be interpreted with care this finding indicates that a shift in attention to drainage might be justified. Strategies to achieve this goal may include increased allocation of funding for sanitation, including drainage, and awareness creation among panchayat council members as well as front-line professionals.

Including gender issues in training of front-line professionals. According to survey results, gender aspects are not included as part of training programs for the front-line professionals in charge of water and sanitation (junior engineers), almost all of whom are male. Analyzing the content of the training programs that junior engineers receive, identifying areas in which a focus on gender is appropriate, and adjusting training programs and material accordingly would be useful. Gender-sensitive areas include interaction of junior engineers with gram panchayats and water and sanitation committees, maintenance of drinking water facilities and the recharge of groundwater, and the need for separate toilets for girls at school.

Increasing the share of female front-line professionals. Efforts could be made to increase the share of junior engineers when hiring new staff. Implementing such an approach should not be difficult in Karnataka, where the large number of engineering colleges turn out significant numbers of female graduates. It seems reasonable to assume that rural women would feel more comfortable approaching female junior engineers and that female engineers may have a better understanding of women-specific needs.

Ghana

This section presents recommendations for Ghana. It first presents recommended strategies for the country's general decentralization policy. It then offers recommendations for agricultural extension and drinking water provision.

General Decentralization Policy

Ghana's decentralization policy was successful in bringing government closer to the people. District assembly members—described by one respondent as "doorstep politicians"—are highly accessible to their community members. They receive almost no remuneration even though they often work full time in fulfilling their duties.

The role the district assembly members can play with respect to the district administration and the district chief executive and his executive committee is limited, however. District assembly members describe themselves as a "glorified beggars," because they have to "beg" the district administration and other governmental and nongovernmental agencies to implement projects. Although the district assembly ultimately votes on the budget, assembly members do not control resources and programs as gram panchayat members do in India. Moreover, in the absence of a reservation policy, the number of female district assembly members is low. A variety of strategies can be considered to address these challenges.

Empowering district assembly members. Several approaches could be used to empower district assembly members:

- Increasing the share of discretionary district-level resources that are not earmarked for or tied to specific programs would broaden the role district assembly members can play with respect to the district administration.
- Providing assembly members with dedicated office space at the district assembly and increasing their travel allowances would facilitate closer interaction with the district administration. Paying them salaries is also an option, although the effects of such a strategy need to be carefully assessed. (It could reduce the possibility of attracting intrinsically motivated candidates.) Although the resource requirements for realizing these suggestions are significant, these options should at least be taken into account in policy debates over how to strengthen the local government system.
- Providing more training to district assembly members, with the aim of improving their capacity to deal effectively with the district administration, could strengthen their role, too.

Increasing the share of female district assembly members. The following strategies may be considered to reach this goal:

- Cross-country evidence indicates that instituting a quota or reservation system would be the most effective way of increasing the share of female district assembly members (Horowitz 2009). Doing so requires a sovereign political decision that only the Ghanaian people and their political representatives can make.

- Formally recognizing the partisan nature of the local government system might allow political parties to take more deliberate steps in promoting female candidates, for example, through party quotas. Whether the parties would pursue such strategies is, of course, their decision. The parties need to address the challenges they may confront during the implementation of party quotas, such as identifying and encouraging sufficient numbers of suitable female candidates.
- The main strategy that can be used within the current political system is encouraging and supporting female candidates and female district assembly members. Possible approaches include mentoring and providing special funds to female district assembly candidates and members, training male and female district assembly members on gender mainstreaming, and providing special training for female members. Such efforts are already being pursued by the Institute of Local Government Studies, but unlike in India, the institute has no secured budget for this purpose; funding for such training has to be raised on a case-by-case basis. Advocacy NGOs and other advocates such as activist female district chief executives who support female candidates can play an important role in supporting female candidates and members.

Increasing gender equity in political representation can be considered a goal in its own right. It is not necessarily a sufficient strategy to achieve better outcomes for women. As the case of India shows, female political representatives may achieve worse outcomes for women, depending on local power structures and program design. Therefore, additional efforts are necessary to attain better outcomes for women.

Strengthening district gender focal points. Piloted by the District Capacity Building Project (DISCAP), gender focal points have been promoted as gender machinery at the district level. Staff members who serve as these focal points face some challenges. In particular, they usually still have obligations under the department to which they belong or have to double up as other staff members of the assembly.

To make the focal point strategy work, focal point staff need to have a working environment suitable for their task, which includes relieving them of other obligations. Providing systematic training to focal point staff and strengthening their relationships with the district assembly members may also help increase their effectiveness.

The role the gender focal point person can play also depends on the department he or she comes from and its standing in the local government system. Choosing the department strategically can help increase the effectiveness of this function.

Strengthening the subdistrict structure (area councils and unit committees). The study indicates that area councils and unit committees already play a more pronounced role than is currently assumed; further strengthening their role and building their capacity would be useful. If they can play a more pronounced role in current efforts to use participatory planning approaches and to monitor and evaluate development activities while collaborating with the district assembly members, the long route of accountability could be strengthened considerably. Unit committees and area councils will be effective as an element in the chain that links rural citizens to the service providers, however, only if the role of the district assembly members is also strengthened. The district administration also needs to engage regularly with the unit committees and area councils to strengthen their functions. For increasing the representation of women in area councils and unit committees, the considerations presented above for the case of district assembly members also apply.

Agricultural Extension

Farmers' access to agricultural extension in Ghana is limited, despite an extension-agent-to-farmer ratio that is comparatively favorable. Access by female-headed households is particularly minimal, despite the prominent role women play in agriculture and the specific efforts Ghana has undertaken to support women in agriculture, especially by creating a gender-specific "machinery" within the agricultural administration in the form of Women in Agricultural Development (WIAD) units. A variety of strategies could be considered to address these challenges.

Improving management. Extension agents lack sufficient resources for transportation and for implementing extension activities such as demonstration plots. Efforts to increase resource availability should be accompanied by changes in the management of agricultural extension staff. Extension agents have considerable potential: they are committed to the task of introducing new technologies and they have generally positive attitudes about male as well as female farmers and to their work. This potential is not full realized, however, because they receive limited direction about what they should focus on, have limited interaction with agricultural researchers, and seem to have limited awareness that agronomic problems are major constraints to increased production for some of their clients. In addition, they seem to concentrate on working with potentially award-winning farmers rather than working toward increasing agricultural productivity more broadly in their districts.

To address these problems, the following strategies may be pursued:

- To improve the focus on agricultural productivity and other outcome-related targets, it would be useful to explicitly make such targets part of the extension agents' agenda. Emphasis is currently placed on the number of male and female farmers extension agents meet. One cannot hold extension providers fully accountable for yield increases or improved market access of their clients, as these outcomes also depend on other factors. But moving such outcome goals higher on the agenda of the extension agents seems justified. The Ministry of Food and Agriculture could introduce awards for communities and districts that were most successful in increasing agricultural productivity at the community/district level rather than rewarding only individual farmers.

- Tighter focus on the linkages between extension and agricultural research also seems justified. The research-extension linkage committees (RELCs) at the district level are supposed to fulfill this function, but this strategy does not seem to be sufficient. Increasing farmers' demand for new knowledge by, for example, strengthening participatory extension planning and technology development approaches may be a useful strategy for creating more incentives for extension agents to channel this demand to the research system.
- In view of the small percentage of farmers who try new technologies, it seems useful to devise incentive systems that reward extension agents for the number of male and female farmers who adopt new technologies. Generating this information is a challenge. The possibility of including a module in surveys that are conducted regularly at the district level, such as the Core Welfare Indicators Questionnaire, could be explored.

A range of efforts to reform the Ministry of Food and Agriculture have been tried in the past, with support from various donor organizations. It might be useful to review past reform experiences and to adopt a reform approach such as Appreciative Inquiry. Rather than viewing the organization as a problem that has be resolved (usually by restructuring using external consultants), Appreciate Inquiry uses the values of an organization as a starting point for reform and relies on internal change agents (Cooperrider and others 2008).

Increasing access of female farmers. The following strategies can be considered to increase access of female farmers to extension services:

- Determine the factors that prevent women from accessing agricultural extension provided at community-based meetings, so that problems can be addressed (by, for example, organizing meetings at times and locations that make them more accessible for female heads of agricultural households). It would also be useful to identify the extent to which WIAD has tried to address these problems and the implementation problems WIAD officers may have faced in doing so.
- Increase the proportion of female extension agents.
- Reward extension agents for outreach to female farmers in performance reviews.

Preparing extension agents for Local Government Service. One of the changes planned to strengthen the local government system is the introduction of a Local Government Service as a separate category of public officials outside the current civil service. It is planned to include agricultural extension in this new service. It would be useful to use this opportunity to increase accountability and to pilot-test approaches through which extension agents, district assembly members, and district assembly staff can work together under this new system. In this context, efforts to better link the planning approaches of the District Agricultural Development Units and the district assemblies could also be strengthened. The experiences of the integrated planning approach piloted by the German Agency for Development Cooperation (GTZ) should be examined.

Reconsidering the role of FBOs. FBOs have been promoted as a major strategy to deliver agricultural extension services more effectively. Despite the considerable investments in forming FBOs, coverage remains limited, suggesting sustainability problems. Moreover, FBOs seem more attractive to male than to female farmers. Several strategies could address these challenges:

- The formation of FBOs seems to be partly linked to government programs that provide access to agricultural credit or other types of benefits. To make FBOs more sustainable and expand their life beyond these programs, they could be encouraged to engage in activities that benefit their members beyond government programs and beyond serving as a vehicle for extension services. Examples include joint agricultural marketing, agroprocessing, joint purchasing of agricultural inputs, and joint use of agricultural machinery. It would be useful to explore the experience with development interventions that have pursued this strategy.
- To increase the engagement of women in FBOs, it seems useful to analyze the problems they face in joining these organizations. The formation of FBOs made up only of women seems a promising approach to meeting women farmers' needs.
- In view of the challenges involved in FBO development, it may be useful to consider alternative strategies to increasing access to agricultural extension. As in India, such approaches may involve the use of information and communication technologies, such as cell phones. More evidence is required to assess the extent to which and how these approaches can be tailored to the needs of women. Using radio more extensively for agricultural extension also seems a promising approach for reaching female farmers (albeit not with farm-specific advice).

Drinking Water Supply

Ghana has made impressive progress in increasing access to safe drinking water; the share of rural households that pay for drinking water is large. The formation of Water and Sanitation Committees (WATSANs) has been a central element in the strategies used by the government and donors to improve access to drinking water in rural areas.

This approach faces some challenges. Considering the efforts made by the government and donor agencies to promote WATSANs, coverage seems limited (14–27 percent of the surveyed communities had WATSANs). Moreover, WATSANs play only a limited role in the construction of drinking water facilities, such as the choice of contractors, even though they have to contribute funds for construction. The following strategies could be used to address these challenges:

Understanding the reasons for the limited coverage of WATSANs. Qualitative case study evidence points to sustainability issues. Some WATSAN members lose interest in performing voluntary tasks without any remuneration while the WATSANs collect funds.

Strengthening the role of the WATSANs in the local accountability system. Although the WATSANs are in charge of water and sanitation, rural citizens contact their district assembly member or their unit committee member rather than a WATSAN member if they experience problems with drinking water supply. This is not necessarily a problem, as it may indicate that the short route and the long route of accountability are used in a synergistic way. However, it may indicate a lack of trust in the capacity of the WATSANs to resolve problems. In just 20 percent of WATSANs are executive members elected by members; in half the cases, they are appointed at a community meeting or through other means. WATSANs do not function as membership organizations with regular membership meetings; instead, the executive members perform all tasks. This may restrict their accountability, because it limits the need of executive members to provide feedback to members. It would be useful to consider how accountability can be created within these organizations and with respect to the populations they serve. Making them subcommittees of the unit committees is one approach, as members of unit committees are elected, and almost half of the surveyed WATSAN respondents were already unit committee or area council members. This indicates that such an approach should be feasible, although more evidence is required regarding the accountability relations between the two types of organizations.

Strengthening unit committees. Because drinking water is needed by the entire population rather than specific groups, the unit committees could perform the tasks of the WATSANs. At the same time, unit committees could provide other rural services. Turning unit committees into multipurpose committees that also play a formal role in the local government system could be considered as an alternative to the formation of specialized user organizations for services that everyone needs.

Ethiopia

This section presents recommendations for Ethiopia. It first presents recommended strategies for the country's general decentralization policy. It then offers recommendations for agricultural extension and drinking water provision.

General Decentralization Policy

To ensure that decentralization support is effective, it is important to first identify which local agencies are key to the quality and quantity of a particular service, so that support can prioritize strengthening these agencies. Since the introduction of local-level decentralization in Ethiopia, local governments have become important public bodies in the implementation of government development policy in general and the provision of public services in particular. The district tier of government has gained salience because it is low enough to be (geographically) accessible to residents but aggregates a sufficiently large number of communities to have formal structures, offices, and agencies in place to provide the public administration needed to implement policy. Within the district government, the district cabinet is one of the most important bodies in influencing the quality and quantity of public services such as agricultural extension and, to a lesser extent, drinking water supply. The following strategies can be considered to use the potential of local governments more effectively to improve rural service provision.

Strengthening the organizations charged with building the capacity of the relevant local agencies. The decentralization process in general, and the capacity needed to provide services at the local level in particular, have received substantial external assistance in recent years, most prominently through the Public Sector Capacity Building Program (PSCAP) support project (see the annex to chapter 3). PSCAP works only through the federal and regional governments, not directly through the district governments. However, regional governments operate various programs to strengthen the key public sector bodies at the local level. Among these are regional training institutes, such as the Amhara Management Institute and the Oromia Management Commission, which provide training to district cabinet members. Creation of such organizations is an important step toward institutionalizing district government training and scaling back reliance on fragmented ad hoc training through consultants.

Supporting region-level organizations that strengthen the capacity of the key players and decision makers at the local level, such as the district cabinets. It is not clear that the resources currently provided by the regional training institutes through the regional Bureaus of Capacity Building are sufficient or used in the most effective way. Limited attention is paid to evaluation and impact of the training activities undertaken by these institutes. Moreover, only the Amhara and Oromia regions have such institutes, forcing district officials from other regions to travel to receive training.

Paying more attention to gender dimensions in the delivery of public services to enhance the development effect of such assistance. This study highlights the development impact of implementing policies on public service provision in a way that speaks to the productive contribution of women as well as men in rural areas. It focuses on documenting and assessing the extent of attention given in agricultural extension and water supply to women's and men's access to these services. The findings on both issues may be useful in introducing gender dimensions in the training modules used by the regional training institutions targeting local governments.

Conducting research and gaining greater understanding of the processes within the ruling party that ultimately affect the quality of public services. Processes and mechanisms within the ruling party could be important drivers of policy design and policy implementation in agricultural extension and water supply. Intraparty processes are germane to the criteria and factors affecting who ultimately holds political offices in local government and what incentives these local political officials face with respect to their engagement in public service provision. These processes are also likely to be very important factors affecting who takes on civil servant positions at the kebele and district levels, what incentives they face, and what accountability mechanisms exist between the political and the public administration realms at the local level.

Better understanding the processes that operate within the party that affect local political and civil service systems and the interface between the two. Party dynamics are not a realm into which external development assistance can directly enter. Nevertheless, research shedding light on these processes would likely go a long way toward identifying the driving forces, incentives, and accountability systems that influence how public services for men and women are delivered. This understanding would also make more clear the opportunities and constraints that exist for planned interventions seeking to improve the extension and water sectors.

Increasing the effectiveness of support for decentralized service delivery by taking political reality into consideration when considering how to target support. In policy work on decentralization and the gender aspects of local service delivery in Ethiopia, it is important to carefully consider alternative interventions. For example, rank and file members of the local council play only a limited role in influencing decisions on which and how services are delivered to residents; executive bodies are much more influential local players. Resources committed to deepening decentralization and empowering residents by focusing on training and capacity building of local councils may therefore not achieve the desired results. Worse yet, by helping "formalize" but not strengthen weak institutions, committing such resources may help advance an image of empowered and functional institutions that may not correspond with reality. Financial support for the decentralization process ought to be provided so that the main goal of the support has a higher chance of being met. This can be accomplished by accounting for the political realities on the ground that affect which institutions are weak and which institutions are strong and can be built upon.

Agricultural Extension

The study identified that the main challenges of extension include lack of discretion of extension agents, and unequal extension coverage. Ethiopia was more successful than Ghana in reaching female farmers, but some gender gaps remain. The following strategies appear promising to address these challenges.

Giving extension agents greater discretion. The lack of flexibility of the agricultural packages extension agents are supposed to promote contrasts with the diversity of agriculture in Ethiopia. When given the chance, extension agents are often willing to adapt the packages to make them relevant to the farmers they work with. The incentives inherent in policies and the local public administration structure discourage such adaptation of packages, however. Agricultural extension agents could be given greater discretion and more space to experiment with farmers with potentially more appropriate technology and input packages than those they are obliged to promote. Progress has been made in diversifying farmers' packages, which now offer packages for women (spouses of household heads) and pastoralists. However, even the more diversified menu cannot substitute for microlevel adaptation, a process that would make new inputs and practices more credible to farmers. This is particularly important with regard to extension agents' work with women (both household heads and spouses of heads), which is less frequent than with men. Both female farmers and extension agents need to have the opportunity to experiment with input combinations and other advice on agricultural practices.

Extending coverage where it is currently very limited, including to pastoral areas. Extension coverage varies widely across Ethiopia. In a district in the Afar region, a pastoral area, only 2 percent of respondents come into contact with an extension agent; the highest rate of contact was 54 percent, at a study site in the Tigray region. Reducing these stark differences is important because access to agricultural extension is critical in all regions of the country to promote agricultural development. The federal government is already supporting regions with little extension access to increase coverage, but additional efforts seem justified to reach this goal.

Identifying innovative ways to bridge the gender gap in access to extension services. The gender gap in access to extension services can be reduced in a variety of ways. One is to use women's associations as a bridge between extension workers and women farmers, as suggested in chapter 7. External assistance to expand this and other approaches to bringing women's access to extension advice more in line with that of men could include better and more detailed documentation on how and through which mechanisms women's associations are successful in bringing extension advice to their members. Lessons learned could then be taken into account in expanding this approach, possibly through a project in a small number of rural districts. Such a project could then lead to a more widely applicable policy after further lessons are learned on what works and what doesn't in this approach.

Drinking Water Supply

The study identified a range of problems in drinking water supply, including limited access to safe drinking water and deficits in the capacity and exclusiveness of water committees (chapter 7). The following strategies can be used to address these problems.

Increasing the limited coverage of safe drinking water. Access to safe drinking water is very limited in Ethiopia, especially in contrast to the other two countries analyzed. Both men and women identified problems with access to and quality of drinking water as top concerns. External support could help to improve the coverage of drinking water. Different instruments of assistance—policy lending and investment instruments, for example—could be considered and weighed against each other to determine the mix of external assistance most likely to expand coverage within the context of the government's drinking water policy. It would be useful for the government to consider the level of priority it gives this sector in light of the potentially important productivity effects of reducing the amount of time women spend fetching water (rather than in agricultural activities) and the improvements in health better access to safe drinking water would yield.

Training water committees on community relations. One important reason for the lack of adequate drinking water facilities in rural areas is the poor governance of facilities by water committees. Water committees are often trained only in technical issues related to water facilities. Training on managing community relations, raising awareness of the need to maintain water infrastructure, and other "soft" skills is very limited. Donor assistance could help expand this form of capacity building. As training of water communities is commonly undertaken (or commissioned) by district water desks or regional water bureaus, an assessment could first be made regarding how well versed these trainers are with community relations topics relating to water user groups. Targeting the public sector agencies tasked with training water committees may be a more efficient way to support this issue.

Ensuring that a maintenance system is in place. Service providers responsible for the construction of water facilities—regional water bureaus, district water desks, and NGOs—should plan for how the facilities will be maintained after construction. Service providers at times think through the process only until the completion of construction. Building infrastructure is a waste of resources if facilities fall into disrepair because of inadequate maintenance systems.

Drawing on local knowledge and local considerations in selecting sites. Another reason why facilities fail to produce sufficient water has been the failure of local governments and NGOs to adequately consider information from local residents in the selection of sites. Both geological expertise by service providers and local knowledge of the community can be drawn on to reduce mistakes in site selection. More consideration needs to be given to nontechnical community concerns, such as loss of land for some community members and compensation for such loss. Such issues can affect support of the community behind the project and thus affect subsequent willingness to contribute to maintaining the facility.

Drawing attention to gender issues in accessing and managing water sources. In some research sites, the local government has focused attention on the burden of fetching water, displaying posters, for example, that appeal to men to contribute to this task. Efforts to change cultural norms that create gender-imbalanced burdens could be considered more widely and assessed for their ability to effect changes in behavior. Other local policies, such as mandating that all water committee chairs be women, could also be considered for their usefulness and feasibility in scaling up, taking into consideration the cultural acceptability of such policies in each area.

CONCLUDING REMARKS: WHAT CREATES POLITICAL INCENTIVES TO IMPROVE OUTCOMES FOR WOMEN?

The accountability linkages for rural service provision differ widely across countries. They are affected by a country's political system, its approach to decentralization in service provision, and its culture. Understanding these linkages is essential for identifying entry points to make rural service provision more responsive to gender needs.

This study throws light on various aspects of these linkages, but essential questions remain. Which mechanisms in the local governance system create political incentives for producing better outcomes for the rural population in general and rural women in particular? How do these mechanisms differ across political systems? Which mechanisms work within a (de facto) one-party system? Which mechanisms work in two-party and multiparty systems that are subject to political competition but plagued with clientelism and elite capture? Future research, including research using the data collected for this project, will have to address these questions.

The political reforms of the past decade, with their emphasis on decentralization and empowerment, have opened new opportunities for improving the provision of agricultural and rural services to those that have benefited least from them in the past—the rural poor and rural women. The author team hopes that this report will help increase interest in and action on these opportunities.

REFERENCES

Aalen, L. 2002. *Ethnic Federalism in a Dominant Party State: The Ethiopia Experience 1991–2000.* Bergen, Norway: Chr. Michelsen Institute.

Aalen, L., and K. Tronvoll. 2008. "The 2008 Ethiopian Local Elections: The Return of Electoral Authoritarianism." *African Affairs* 108 (430): 111–20.

ActionAid Ghana. 2002. *Local Governance Performance: Case Study of Five Districts of Ghana.* Accra: Action Aid Ghana.

AfDB (African Development Bank). 2004. "Ethiopia: Multi-Sector Country Gender Profile: Agriculture and Rural Development North East and South Region (ONAR)." AfDB, Abidjan, Côte d'Ivoire.

Agarwal, Arun, and Nicolas Perrin. 2009. "Comparative Study of Rural Institutions for Improving Governance and Development: Afghanistan, Ethiopia, India, Vietnam, and Yemen." Social Development Working Paper 114, World Bank, Washington, DC.

Agarwal, B. 1994. *A Field of One's Own: Gender and Land Rights in South Asia.* Cambridge, U.K.: Cambridge University Press.

Ahuja, M. L. 2005. *General Elections in India: Electoral Politics, Electoral Reforms and Political Parties.* New Delhi: Icon Publications.

Allah-Mensah, B. 2003. "Gender and Local Governance in Ghana: The Case of the 2002 District Level Elections." In *Local Government in Ghana: Grassroots Participation in the 2002 Local Government Elections,* ed. Nicholas Amponsah and Kwame Boafo-Arthur, 19–48. Department of Political Science, University of Legon/Ibis, Ghana.

Alsop, R. J., A. Krishna, and D. Sjoblom. 2000. "Are Gram Panchayats Inclusive? Report of a Study Conducted in Rajasthan and Madhya Pradesh." South Asia Social Development Unit, World Bank, Washington, DC.

Anderson, J. R. 2008. "Agricultural Advisory Services." Background paper for the *World Development Report 2008,* World Bank, Washington, DC.

Asante, F. 2006. "Decentralization in Ghana: An Annotated Bibliography." International Food Policy Research Institute, Accra.

Aziz, Abdul, N. Sivanna, M. Devendra Babu, Madhushree Sekher, and C. Charles Nelson. 2002. *Decentralized Governance and Planning: A Comparative Study in Three South Indian States*. New Delhi: Macmillan Publishers.

Ban, R., and V. Rao. 2008a. "Is Deliberation Equitable? Evidence from Transcripts of Village Meetings in South India." Development Research Group, Poverty Team, World Bank, Washington, DC.

————. 2008b. "Tokenism or Agency? The Impact of Women's Reservations on Panchayats in South India." *Economic Development and Cultural Change* 56 (3): 510–30.

Bardhan, P., D. Mookherjee, and M. P. Torrado. 2005. "Impact of Reservations of *Panchayat* Pradhans on Targeting in West Bengal." Working Paper 104, Bureau for Research and Economic Analysis of Development (BREAD), Duke University, Durham, NC.

————. 2008. "Powerful Women: Does Exposure Reduce Bias?" Working Paper 175, Center for International Development, Harvard University, Cambridge, MA.

Beaman, L., R. Chattopadhyay, E. Duflo, R. Pande, and P. Topalova. 2008. "Powerful Women: Does Exposure Reduce Prejudice?" Working Paper 2008-0092, Weatherhead Center for International Affairs, Harvard University, Cambridge, MA.

Berhanu, G., D. Hoekstra, and A. Tegegne. 2006. "Commercialization of Ethiopian Agriculture: Extension Service from Input Supplier to Knowledge Broker and Facilitator." IPMS (Improving Productivity and Market Success) of Ethiopian Farmers Project Working Paper 1, International Livestock Research Institute, Nairobi.

Bernard, T., and D. Spielman. 2009. "Reaching the Rural Poor through Rural Producer Organisations? A Study of Agricultural Marketing Cooperatives in Ethiopia." *Food Policy* 34 (1): 60–69.

Bernard, T., A. S. Taffesse, and E. Gabre-Madhin. 2008. "Impact of Cooperatives on Smallholders' Commercialization Behavior: Evidence from Ethiopia." *Agricultural Economics* 39 (2): 147–61.

Besley, T., R. Pande, L. Rahman, and V. Rao. 2004. "The Politics of Public Good Provision: Evidence from Indian Local Governments." *Journal of the European Economics Association* 2 (2–3): 416–26.

Besley, T., R. Pande, and V. Rao. 2005a. "Participatory Democracy in Action: Survey Evidence from South India." *Journal of the European Economics Association* 3 (2–3): 648–57.

————. 2005b. "Political Selection and the Quality of Government: Evidence from South India." Discussion Paper 5201, Centre for Economic Policy Research, London.

Bhavani, R. R. 2009. "Do Electoral Quotas Work after They Are Withdrawn? Evidence from a Natural Experiment in India." *American Political Science Review* 103 (1): 23–35.

Birner, R. 2007. "Improving Governance to Eradicate Hunger and Poverty." 2020 Focus Brief on the World's Poor and Hungry People, International Food Policy Research Institute, Washington, DC.

Birner, R., and J. R. Anderson. 2007. "How to Make Agricultural Extension Demand-Driven? The Case of India's Agricultural Extension Policy." Discussion Paper 00729, International Food Policy Research Institute, Washington, DC.

Birner, R., M. Sekher, and N. Palaniswamy. 2007. "How Can Decentralization Lead to Better Rural Service Provision? Theoretical Considerations and Empirical Evidence from Karnataka, India." Paper presented at the annual conference of "Verein für Socialpolitik: Research Committee Development Economics," University of Göttingen, Germany, June 29–30.

Birner, R., and J. von Braun. 2007. "Decentralization and Public Service Provision: A Framework for Pro-Poor Institutional Design." Paper presented at a conference on "Effectiveness of Decentralized Service Delivery," Moncalieri, Italy, September 3–4.

Bishop-Sambrook, C. 2004. *Gender Analysis: An Overview of Gender Issues in the Agricultural Sector of Ethiopia.* IPMS (Improving Productivity and Market Success) Gender Analysis and Strategy Paper, Addis Ababa.

Buchy, M., and F. Basaznew. 2005. "Gender-Blind Organisations Deliver Gender-Biased Services: The Case of Awasa Bureau of Agriculture in Southern Ethiopia." *Gender, Technology and Development* 9 (2): 235–51.

Chattopadhyay, R., and E. Duflo. 2004. "Women as Policy Makers: Evidence from a Randomized Policy Experiment in India." *Econometrica* 72 (5): 1409–43.

CIDA (Canadian International Development Agency), and MLGRDE (Ministry of Local Government, Rural Development, and Environment). 2007. *District Capacity Building Project (DISCAP) Project Completion Report.* Report prepared by E. T. Jackson and Associates Ltd., Ottawa (CIDA) and Accra (MLGRDE).

Cohen, M. J., M. Rocchigiani, and J. L. Garrett. 2008. "Empowering Communities through Food-Based Programmes: Ethiopia Case Study." Discussion Paper, World Food Programme, Rome.

Cooperrider, D. L., Whitney, D., and Stavros, J. M. 2008. *Appreciative Inquiry Handbook: For Leaders of Change.* San Francisco, CA: Berrett-Koehler Publishers.

Crewett, W., A. Bogale, and B. Korf. 2008. "Land Tenure in Ethiopia: Continuity and Change, Shifting Rulers, and the Quest for State Control." CAPRi Working Paper 91, CGIAR Systemwide Program on Collective Action and Property Rights, Consultative Group on Agricultural Research, Washington, DC.

Cusack, K. 2007. "Gender Mainstreaming at the District Level in Ghana: An Assessment." Canadian International Development Agency, Accra.

Datta, B. 1998. *And Who Will Make the Chapatis? A Study of All-Women Panchayats in Maharashtra.* Calcutta: Stree.

Demessie, S., E. Kebede, and A. Shimeles. 2005. *Ethiopia Strategic Country Gender Assessment.* World Bank, Washington, DC.

Dercon, Stefan, Daniel O. Gillian, John Hoddinott, and Tassew Woldehanna. 2007. "The Impact of Roads and Agricultural Extension on Consumption Growth and Poverty in Fifteen Ethiopian Villages." Working Paper 260, Centre for the Study of African Economies, Department of Economics, University of Oxford, Oxford, U.K.

Deshpande, R. S., Brajesh Jha, S. M. Jharwal, Vijay Paul Sharma, and R. P. S. Malik, eds. 2008. *Glimpses of Indian Agriculture: Macro and Micro Aspects.* New Delhi: Academic Foundation.

Dollar, D., R. Fisman, and R. Gatti. 2001. "Are Women Really the 'Fairer' Sex? Corruption and Women in Government." *Journal of Economic Behavior and Organization* 46 (4): 423–29.

Dom, C., and M. Mussa. 2006a. *Review of Implementation of the Decentralisation Policy: A Sample Survey in Four Sentinel Weredas of Tigray Region.* Report for the Embassy of Ireland and the Regional Government of Tigray, prepared by Mokoro Limited, Oxford, U.K.

———. 2006b. *Review of Implementation of the Decentralisation Policy: A Sample Survey in Six Weredas of Amhara Region.* Report for the Embassy of Sweden and Amhara National Regional State, prepared by Mokoro Limited, Oxford, U.K.

Duflo, E., G. Fischer, and R. Chattopadhyay. 2005. "Efficiency and Rent Seeking in Local Government: Evidence from Randomized Policy Experiments in India." Department of Economics, Massachusetts Institute of Technology, Cambridge, MA. http://www .imf.org/external/np/res/seminars/2005/weak/edpa.pdf.

EEA (Ethiopian Economic Association) and EEPRI (Ethiopian Economic Policy Research Institute). 2006. *Evaluation of the Ethiopian Agricultural Extension with Particular Emphasis on the Participatory Demonstration and Training Extension System (PADETES).* Addis Ababa: EEA and EEPRI.

Engel, Stefanie, Maria Iskandarani, and Maria del Pilar Useche. 2005. "Improved Water Supply in the Ghanaian Volta Basin: Who Uses It and Who Participates in Community Decision-Making?" EPT Discussion Paper 129, International Food Policy Research Institute, Washington, DC.

EPRDF (Ethiopian Peoples Revolutionary Democratic Front). 2006. Statute. http://www.eprdf.org.et/Eprdffiles/Basicdoc/Basicdocuments_files/statute.htm.

Fafchamps, M., and A. Quisumbing. 2005. "Marriage, Bequest and Assortative Matching in Rural Ethiopia." *Economic Development and Cultural Change* 53 (2): 347–80.

Federal Cooperative Agency. 2006. *Five-Year Development Plan.* Addis Ababa: Government of Ethiopia.

Fekade, K. 2000. "Existing Political Parties in Ethiopia." Paper presented to the Gender Forum session on women and politics, Addis Ababa, April 20.

Foster, A., and M. Rosenzweig. 2004. "Democratization, Decentralization and the Distribution of Local Public Goods in a Poor Rural Economy." Working Paper 01-056, Penn Institute for Economic Research Philadelphia. http://ssrn.com/abstract=300421.

Francesconi, G. N. 2009. *Cooperation for Competition: Linking Ethiopian Farmers to Markets.* Wageningen, Netherlands: Wageningen Academic Publishers.

Francesconi, G. N., and R. Ruben. 2008. "The Life Cycle of Agricultural Cooperatives: Implications for Management and Governance in Ethiopia." *Journal of Rural Cooperation* 36 (2): 115–30.

Gain, T. S. Raji. 2004. "Economic Empowerment of Rural Women: A Few Successful Interventions." In *Women in Agricultural Development,* ed. Indu Grover and Deepak Grover, 313–21. Udaipur, India: Agrotech Publishing Academy.

Gebre-Egziabher, T., and K. Berhanu. 2007. "A Literature Review of Decentralization in Ethiopia." In *Decentralization in Ethiopia,* ed. T. Assefa and T. Gebre-Egziabher. Addis Ababa: Forum for Social Studies.

Ghatak, M., and M. Ghatak. 2002. "Recent Reforms in the *Panchayat* System in West Bengal: Toward Greater Participatory Governance?" *Economic and Political Weekly* 37 (1): 45–58.

Government of Ethiopia. 2000. *Ethiopia National Action Plan.* Addis Ababa: Government of Ethiopia. http://www.un.org/womenwatch/daw/country/national/ethiopia .htm.

———. 2004. *A National Report on Progress Made in the Implementation Platform for Action (Beijing + 10).* Addis Ababa: Prime Minister's Office, Women's Affairs Sub-Sector.

Government of Ethiopia, and World Bank 1998. *Implementing the Ethiopian National Policy for Women: Institutional and Regulatory Issues.* Washington, DC: World Bank.

Government of India. 1997. *Women in India: A Statistical Profile.* Department of Women and Child Development, New Delhi: Government of India.

Government of India. 2003. *Report of Standing Committee on Urban and Rural Development.* 46th Report. New Delhi: Ministry of Rural Development, Lok Sabha Secretariat.

———. 2007a. *Annual Report 2006–2007.* New Delhi: Ministry of Agriculture. http://agricoop.nic.in/AnnualReport06-07/OVERVIEW.pdf.

————. 2007b. *Eleventh Five-Year Plan.* New Delhi: National Planning Commission.

Government of Karnataka. 1993. *The Karnataka Panchayati Raj Act 1993.* http://rdpr
.kar.nic.in.

Grover, Indu, and Deepak Grover, eds. 2004. *Women in Agricultural Development.*
Udaipur, India: Agrotech Publishing Academy.

GSSP (Ghana Strategy Support Program). 2009. "Public Expenditure and Institutional
Review: Ghana's Ministry of Food and Agriculture." IFPRI-GSSP Working Paper, International Food Policy Research Institute and Ghana Strategy Support Program, Accra.

GTZ (Gesellschaft für Technische Zusammenarbeit) 2007. *Ghana: Local Governance and
Poverty Reduction Support Programme—Program Description.* Eschborn, Germany.

Gulati, Leela. 1995. "Rural Families and Household Economies in Asia and the Pacific:
India." Paper in the "Report of the Regional Expert Consultation Meeting," Food and
Agriculture Organization, Bangkok, November 7–10.

Gupta, Shaibal. 2002. "Subaltern Resurgence: A Reconnaisance of Panchayat Elections
in Bihar." Crisis States Programme Working Paper 8, Development Studies Institute,
London School of Economics, London.

Horowitz, L. 2009. *Getting Better Government for Women: A Literature Review.* Agriculture and Rural Development Department Discussion Paper 43, World Bank,
Washington, DC.

IFAD (International Fund for Agricultural Development). 2005. *IFAD's Performance
and Impact in Decentralising Environments: Experiences from Ethiopia, Tanzania and
Uganda.* Report 1641. Rome: IFAD.

IFPRI (International Food Policy Research Institute). 2000. *Women: The Key to Food
Security: Looking into the Household.* Washington, DC: IFPRI.

————. 2005. *Women: Still the Key to Food and Nutrition Security.* Report 33. Washington, DC: IFPRI.

IIPS (International Institute of Population Sciences) and Macro-International. 2007.
National Family Health Survey (NFHS III), 2005–2006. Mumbai: IIPS.

ISEC (Institute for Social and Economic Change) and IFPRI (International Food Policy
Research Institute). 2006. "Making Decentralization and Local Governance Work
for the Rural Poor: An Interim Report on Case Study of Two-Gram Panchayats in
Karnataka." Bangalore, India: ISEC and IFPRI.

Issaka, F. 1994. "Women and Decision-Making in Local Government." Paper presented
at a seminar on "African Women and Governance: Towards Action for Women's
Participation in Decision-Making," Entebbe, Uganda, July 24–30.

Jain, S. P. 2007. "Integration of Rural Women with Agriculture and Rural Development."
In *The Indian State and the Women's Problematic: Running with the Hare and Hunt-
ing with the Hounds,* ed. R. B. S. Verma, H. S. Verma, and Nadeem Hasnain, 334–78.
New Delhi: Serials Publications.

Jayal, N. G. 2006. "Engendering Local Democracy: The Impact of Quotas for Women in
India's Panchayats." *Democratization* 13 (1): 15–35.

Kaufmann, D., A. Kraay, and M. Mastruzzi. 2008. "Governance Matters VII: Aggregate
and Individual Governance Indicators 1996–2007." Policy Research Working Paper
4654, World Bank, Washington, DC.

Keefer, P. 2005. "Democratization and Clientelism: Why Are Young Democracies Badly
Governed?" Policy Research Working Paper 3594, World Bank, Washington, DC.

Keefer, P., and Khemani, S. 2005. "Democracy, Public Expenditures, and the Poor:
Understanding Political Incentives for Providing Public Services. *World Bank
Research Observer,* 2 (1): 1–27.

Kumar, S. 2000. "Study on the Motion of No-Confidence Against Women Sarpanch in Tuljapur Block of Osmanabad District." In *Gender and Governance in India Workshop Compendium*, 1–4. Mumbai: Tata Institute of Social Sciences.

Ladha, J. K., K. S. Fischer, M. Hossain, P. R. Hobbs, and B. Hardy. 2000. *Improving the Productivity and Sustainability of Rice-Wheat Systems of the Indo-Gangetic Plains: A Synthesis of NARS–IRRI Partnership Research*. Discussion Paper 20, International Rice Research Institute, Los Baños, Philippines.

Lefort, R. 2007. "Powers—Mengist—and Peasants in Rural Ethiopia: The May 2005 Elections." *Journal of Modern African Studies* 45 (2): 253–73.

Leino, Jessica. Forthcoming. "Ladies First? Gender and the Community Management of Water Infrastructure in Kenya." Graduate Student and Research Fellow Working Paper 30, Center for International Development, Harvard University, Cambridge, MA.

Lemma, M. 2007. *The Agricultural Knowledge System in Tigray, Ethiopia: Recent History and Actual Effectiveness*. Weikersheim, Germany: Margraff Publishers.

Lenin, V. I. 1902 (reprinted 1969). *What Is to Be Done? Burning Questions of Our Movement*. New York: International Publishers.

Malena, C., C. Daddieh, and K. Odei-Tettey. 2007. *Building the Demand-Side of Good Governance: Enhancing Conditions for Social Accountability in Ghana*. Washington, DC: World Bank.

Manor, J. 2004. "'User Committees': A Potentially Destructive New Trend in Democratic Decentralisation?" *European Journal of Development Research* 16 (1):192–213.

Mason, A., and E. King. 2001. *Engendering Development: Through Gender Equality in Rights, Resources, and Voice*. Washington, DC: World Bank.

Meinzen-Dick, R., and A. Knox. 2001. "Collective Action, Property Rights, and Devolution of Natural Resource Management: A Conceptual Framework." In *Collective Action, Property Rights, and Devolution of Natural Resource Management: Exchange of Knowledge and Implications for Policy*, ed. R. Meinzen-Dick, A. Knox, and M. DiGregorio, 441–73. Eurasburg: System-wide Program on Collective Action and Property Rights (CAPRi), International Center for Living Aquatic Resources Management (ICLARM), German Foundation for International Development/Centre for Food, Rural Development and Environment (ZEL/DSE).

MLGRDE (Ministry of Local Government, Rural Development, and Environment). 2007. *Operational Manual for the Implementation and Administration of the District Development Fund*. Accra: MLGRDE.

MoFA (Ministry of Food and Agriculture). 2007. *Food and Agriculture Sector Development Policy (FASDEP II)*. Accra: MoFA.

MOPED (Ministry of Planning and Economic Development). 1993. *An Economic Development Strategy for Ethiopia: A Comprehensive Guide and a Development Strategy for the Future*. Addis Ababa: MOPED.

Morris, Michael L., and Cheryl R. Doss. 1999. "How Does Gender Affect the Adoption of Agricultural Innovations? The Case of Improved Maize Technology in Ghana." Paper presented at the annual meeting of the American Agricultural Economics Association, Nashville, August 8–11.

MoWA (Ministry of Women's Affairs). 2006. *National Action Plan for Gender Equality (NAP-GE) 2006–2010*. Addis Ababa: MoWA.

MoWR (Ministry of Water Resources). 2004. *Ethiopian Water Resources Management Policy*. Addis Ababa: MoWR.

Muir, A. 2004. "Building Capacity in Ethiopia to Strengthen the Participation of Citizens' Associations in Development: A Study of the Organisational Associations of

Citizens." Paper prepared by the International NGO Training and Research Centre (INTRAC), Oxford, U.K., for the World Bank. http://siteresources.worldbank.org/INTUNITFESSD/Resources/AssociationallifeVolumeImainreport.pdf.

Munshi, K., and M. Rosenzweig. 2008. "The Efficacy of Parochial Politics: Caste, Commitment, and Competence in Indian Local Governments." Working Paper 182, Bureau for Research and Economic Analysis of Development (BREAD), Duke University, Durham, NC.

NCG (Nordic Consulting Group) and Dege Consult. 2007. *Joint Government of Ghana and Development Partner Decentralization Policy Review*. Accra: NCE and Dege Consult.

NRCWA (National Research Center for Women in Agriculture). 2004. *Annual Report 2003–04*. Bhubaneswar, India: NRCWA.

North, D. C., J. J. Wallis, and B. R. Weingast. 2009. *Violence and Social Orders: A Conceptual Framework for Interpreting Recorded Human History*. New York: Cambridge University Press.

NSSO (National Sample Survey Organisation). 2005. *Situation Assessment Survey of Farmers: Access to Modern Technology for Farming—National Sample Survey, 59th Round (January–December 2003)*. Report 499(59/33/2). New Delhi: Ministry of Statistics and Programme Implementation.

Ofei-Aboagye, E. 2000. "Promoting the Participation of Women in Local Governance and Development: The Case of Ghana." Paper prepared for a seminar on "European Support for Democratic Decentralization and Municipal Development: A Contribution to Local Development and Poverty Reduction," Maastricht, Netherlands, June 14–15.

———. 2004. "Promoting Gender Sensitivity in Local Governance in Ghana." *Development in Practice* 14 (6): 735–60.

Oi, J. C. 1991. *State and Peasant in Contemporary China: The Political Economy of Village Government*. Berkeley: University of California Press.

Olson, M. 1965. *The Logic of Collective Action*. Cambridge, MA: Harvard University Press.

Palaniswamy, N., and N. Krishnan. 2008. "Local Politics, Political Institutions and Public Resource Allocation." Discussion Paper 834, International Food Policy and Research Institute, Washington, DC.

Panth, A. N., and S. K. Puri. 2006. "A Step Towards Strengthening of Panchayat Raj in Bihar." Bihar Panchayat Sashaktiakaran Abhiyan (BPSA), PACS-Bihar, Patn, India.

Pardey, P., J. James, J. Alston, S. Wood, B. Koo, E. Binenbaum, E., T. Hurley, and P. Glewwe. 2007. "Science, Technology and Skills." Background paper to the *World Development Report 2008* commissioned by the CGIAR Science Council and prepared by the International Science and Technology Practice and Policy (InSTePP) Center, University of Minnesota, Department of Applied Economics, St. Paul, MN.

Paul, Samuel, Suresh Balakrishnan, Gopakumar K. Thampi, Sita Sekhar, and M. Vivekananda. 2006. *Who Benefits from India's Public Services? A People's Audit of Five Basic Services*. New Delhi: Academic Foundation.

Pausewang, S., K. Tronvoll, and L. Aalen. 2003. *Ethiopia Since the Derg: A Decade of Democratic Pretension and Performance*. London: Zed.

Pritchett, L., and M. Woolcock. 2004. "Solutions When the Solution Is the Problem: Arraying the Disarray in Development." *World Development* 32 (2): 191–212.

Quisumbing, A., L. Brown., H. S. Feldstein, L. Haddad, and C. Pena. 1995. *Women: The Key to Food Security*. Food Policy Report 21, International Food Policy Research Institute, Washington, DC.

Quisumbing, Agnes R., Keijira Otsuka, with S. Suyanto, J. B. Aidoo, and E. Payongayong. 2001. "Land, Trees, and Women: Evolution of Land Tenure Institutions in Western

Ghana and Sumatra." Research Report 121, International Food Policy Research Institute, Washington, DC.

Raabe, Katharina. 2008. "Reforming the Agricultural Extension System in India: What Do We Know about What Works Where and Why?" Discussion Paper 775, International Food Policy and Research Institute, Washington, DC.

Raabe, K., M. Sekher, and R. Birner. 2009. "The Effects of Political Reservations for Women on Local Governance and Rural Service Provision: Survey Evidence from Karnataka." IFPRI Discussion Paper 878, International Food Policy Research Institute, Washington, DC. http://www.ifpri.org/pubs/dp/IFPRIDP00878.pdf.

Rao, Brinda. 1996. *Dry Wells and "Deserted" Women: Gender, Ecology and Agency in Rural India*. New Delhi: Indian Social Institute.

Rao, Govinda M., H. K. Amar Nath, and B. P. Vani. 2004. "Fiscal Decentralization in Karnataka." In *Fiscal Decentralization to Rural Governments in India*, ed. Geeta Sethi, 43–106. New Delhi: Oxford University Press.

Reddy, M. N., and B. Swanson. 2006. "Strategy for Up-Scaling the ATMA Model in India." *Annual Conference Proceedings of the Association for International Agricultural and Extension Education* 22: 561–69.

Rondinelli, D. A. 1981. "Government Decentralization in Comparative Perspective." *International Review of Administrative Science* 47 (2): 133–45.

Segers, K., J. Dessein, S. Hagberg, P. Develtere, M. Haile, and J. Deckers. 2008. "Be Like Bees: The Politics of Mobilising Farmers for Development in Tigray, Ethiopia." *African Affairs* 108 (430): 91–109.

Sen, A. 1990a. "Gender and Cooperative Conflicts." In *Persistent Inequalities*, ed. I. Tinker, 123–50. New York: Oxford University Press.

———. 1990b. "More than 100 Million Women Are Missing." *New York Review of Books* 37 (20). http://www.nybooks.com/articles/3408.

Sharma, Rita. 2004. "Technology Dissemination for Women in Agriculture." In *Women in Agricultural Development*, ed. Indu Grover and Deepak Grover, 322–30. Udaipur, India: Agrotech Publishing Academy.

Shoba, A. 1999. "Does Land Ownership Make a Difference? Women's Role in Agriculture in Kerala, India." In *Women, Land and Agriculture*, ed. Caroline Sweetman 19–27. Oxford, U.K.: Oxfam.

Singh, J. P., B. E. Swanson, and K. M. Singh. 2006. "Developing a Decentralized, Market-Driven Extension System in India: The ATMA Model." In *Changing Roles of Agricultural Extension in Asian Nation*, ed. A.W. Van den Ban and R. K. Samanta, 203–23. Delhi: B. R. Publishing.

Sivanna, N. 2002. "Process and Performance of Panchayats." In *Decentralised Goverance and Planning: A Comparative Study in Three South Indian States*, ed. Abdul Aziz, N. Sivanna, M. Devendra Babu, Madhushree Sekher, and C. Charles Nelson, 141–97. New Delhi: Macmillan.

Sivanna, N., and D. Babu. 2002. "Panchayati Jamabandhi in Karnataka: An Evaluation Study." Working Paper 142, Institute for Social and Economic Change, Bangalore, India.

Spielman, D., M. Cohen, and T. Mogues. Forthcoming. "Local Governance Systems and Smallholder Cooperatives in Ethiopia." *International Journal of Agricultural Resources, Governance and Ecology*.

Spring, A., and B. Groelsema. 2004. *Enhancing Civil Society Organizations and Women's Participation in Ethiopia: A Program Design for Civil Society and Women's Empowerment*. Management Systems International, Washington, DC.

Srivastava, R. S. 2006. "Panchayats, Bureaucracy, and Poverty Alleviation in Uttar Pradesh." In *Governance in India: Decentralization, and Beyond*, ed. Niraja Gopal Jayal, Amit Prakash, and Pradeep Kumar Sharma, 125–48. Oxford, U.K.: Oxford University Press.

Staal, S., C. Delgado, and C. Nicholson. 1997. "Smallholder Dairying under Transactions Costs in East Africa." *World Development* 25 (5): 779–94.

Sulaiman, R. V. 2003. *Innovations in Agricultural Extension in India*. Sustainable Development Department, Food and Agriculture Organization, Rome. http://www.fao.org/sd/2003/KN0603_en.html.

Swamy, A., S. Knack, Y. Lee, and O. Azfar. 2001. "Gender and Corruption." *Journal of Development Economics* 64 (1): 25–55.

Swarnalatha, Arya. 2007. "Women and Watershed Development in India: Issues and Strategies." *Indian Journal of Gender Studies* 14 (2): 199–230.

Sweetman, Caroline, ed. 1999. *Women, Land and Agriculture*. Oxford, U.K.: Oxfam.

UNIFEM (UN Development Fund for Women). 2009. *Progress of the World's Women 2008/09—Gender and Accountability: Who Answers to Women?* New York: UNIFEM.

U.S. Department of State. 2009. *2008 Human Rights Reports: Ethiopia*. Bureau of Democracy, Human Rights and Labor, Washington, DC. http://www.state.gov/g/drl/rls/hrrpt/2008/af/119001.htm.

van de Walle, N. 2001. *African Economies and the Politics of Permanent Crisis*. New York: Cambridge University Press.

Vaughan, S., and K. Tronvoll. 2003. *The Culture of Power in Contemporary Ethiopian Political Life*. SIDA Studies 10, Swedish International Development Cooperation Agency, Stockholm.

Vecchio, Nerina, and Karthik C. Roy. 1998. *Poverty, Female Headed Households and Sustainable Development*. Westport, CT: Greenwood Press.

Whitney, D., and M. J. Stavros. 2008. *Appreciative Inquiry Handbook: For Leaders of Change*. San Francisco: Berrett-Koehler Publishers.

Work, R. 2002. "Overview of Decentralisation Worldwide: A Stepping Stone to Improved Governance and Human Development." Paper presented at the Second International Conference on "Decentralisation Federalism: The Future of Decentralizing States?" Manila, July 25–27.

World Bank. 2001. *Ethiopia Wereda Studies, Volume I: The Main Phase*. Draft, Africa Region, Country Department 6, World Bank, Washington, DC. Site sources.worldbank.org/ETHIOPIAEXTN/Resources/main_phase.doc.

———. 2002. *Capacity Building for Decentralized Service Delivery Project*. Project Appraisal Document for a Credit to the Federal Democratic Republic of Ethiopia. Washington, DC: Africa Regional Office, Ethiopia and Sudan Country Department, Water and Urban 1, World Bank.

———. 2003. *World Development Report 2004: Making Services Work for Poor People*. Washington, DC: World Bank.

———. 2004. *Public Sector Capacity Building Programme Support Project*. Project Appraisal Document for a Credit to the Federal Democratic Republic of Ethiopia. Washington, DC: Africa Region, Country Department 2, Public Sector Reform and Capacity Building Unit, World Bank.

———. 2005. *Implementation Completion Report on a Credit and a Loan to India for the National Agricultural Technology Project*. Report 34385, Washington, DC: South Asia Region, Agriculture and Rural Development Unit, World Bank.

————. 2006. *Protection of Basic Services Project*. Project Appraisal Document for a Credit to the Federal Democratic Republic of Ethiopia. Washington, DC: Africa Region, Country Department 6, Human Development III, World Bank.

————. 2007a. *Ghana: Community-Based Rural Development Project*. Project Appraisal Document, Africa Regional Office, World Bank, Washington, DC.

————. 2007b. *India: Rural Governments and Service Delivery*. Report 38901-IN, South Asia Region, Agriculture and Rural Development Unit, World Bank, Washington, DC.

————. 2007c. "Local Government Discretion and Accountability: A Local Governance Framework." Social Development Working Paper 40153, World Bank, Washington, DC.

————. 2007d. *Strengthening World Bank Group Engagement on Governance and Anti-Corruption*. Washington, DC: World Bank.

————. 2007e. *World Development Report 2008: Agriculture for Development*. Washington, DC: World Bank.

World Bank, FAO (Food and Agriculture Organization), and IFAD (International Fund for Agricultural Development). 2008. *Gender in Agriculture Sourcebook*. Washington, DC: World Bank. http://go.worldbank.org/5Z9QPCC7L0.

Yilmaz, S., and V. Venugopal. 2009. "Obstacles to Decentralisation in Ethiopia: Political Controls versus Discretion and Accountability." Paper presented to conference on "Obstacles to Decentralisation: Lessons from Selected Countries," Georgia State University, Atlanta, September 21–23.

INDEX

Boxes, figures, notes, and tables are indicated by *b, f, n,* and *t,* respectively.

short route of accountability in, 162–86. *See also* more specific subheadings, *this entry*
community-based organizations, role of, 183–86, 184–85*t*
household access to and satisfaction with services, 162–72
long and short routes compared, 281–83, 282*f*
service provider performance, 172–83
specific needs of, xviii
strategies for promoting gender equity in, 60–61, 87, 88–90*t*
user organizations. *See also* subhead "community-based organizations," *this entry*
agricultural extension programs, provision of, 166–67
coordination with other sectors, lack of, 182
political representatives, relationship between cooperatives and, 242–44, 243*t*
voting in, 234–35, 234*t*, 236–37*t*
Ethiopian Economic Policy Research Institute (EEPRI), 13, 99

farmer-based organizations (FBOs)
agricultural extension programs and, 259, 266–67
Ethiopian agricultural cooperatives in, 183–84, 184*t*, 185*f*, 259
in Ghana. *See under* Ghana
in India, 120, 259, 266–67, 292–93
knowledge gaps regarding, 9
policy recommendations regarding, xxxiv–xxxv, xxxviii–xxxix
service failures of, 4*b*
food crisis of 2008, 1, 6
front-line professionals, 11*b*, 18. *See also* service providers

GDI. *See* Gender-related Development Index

gender and governance in rural services, xvii–xviii, xxv–xlii, 1–15
accountability, xxvii–xxviii. *See also* accountability
agricultural extension programs, xxviii–xxxi. *See also* agricultural extension programs
clientelism, problem of, 8*b*. *See also* clientelism
comparative data for three study countries, 251–84. *See also* comparative accountability relations in India, Ghana, and Ethiopia
conceptual framework, 17–34. *See also* conceptual framework
decentralization, 6. *See also* decentralization
definitions pertinent to, 10–12*b*
democratization, 6, 8*b*, 27
drinking water, xxxi–xxxii. *See also* drinking water
empirical findings, xxviii–xxxii
future research in, xlii, 31–32, 32–33*b*
importance of serving rural poor and women, 4–6
institutionalization or awareness of gender versus outcomes, 283*n*1
knowledge gaps regarding, 9, 31–32, 32–33*b*
literature review, 23–31
market, state, NGO, and community failures in, xxv, 1–4, 2–4*b*
methodology of study, xxvii–xxviii, 93–103. *See also* methodology
objectives of study, xxvi–xxvii, 14
policy recommendations, xxxii–xlii, 285–305. *See also* policy recommendations
political incentives to improve, 305
understanding why and how rural services fail women, 286*t*
value of governance reforms, 6–7
Gender and Governance in Rural Services Project, 12–13

gender budgeting, 20–21, 44, 61
gender equity, promoting. *See* strategies
    for promoting gender equity
Gender, Institutions, and Development
    Index (GIDI), 39t, 40
Gender-related Development Index
    (GDI), 39t, 40
German Development Agency (GTZ),
    69–76, 78t, 84, 298
Getting Good Government for Women:
    A Literature Review
    (Horowitz 2009), 23
Ghana, 49–55, 77–84
    agricultural extension programs,
        53–55
    access to, xxviii–xxix, 298
    comparative findings on. *See*
        under comparative
        accountability relations
        in India, Ghana, and Ethiopia
    deconcentrated nature of, 266–68
    FBOs. *See* subhead "FBOs,"
        this entry
    household access to and
        satisfaction with services,
        132–36, 133–36t, 143t,
        194–96t
    Local Government Service,
        preparing extension agents
        for, 298–99
    outcomes, lack of focus on, xxx,
        260–61
    policy recommendations for,
        xxxvii–xxxix, 297–99
    provision of, 54–55
    RELCs, 54
    as research opportunities, 298
    role of women in Ghanian
        agriculture, 53–54
    route of accountability in, xxxi
    service provider performance,
        142–53, 149–55t
    WIAD directorate, xxx–xxxi,
        53, 54, 98
    agricultural indicators, 35–36, 37t
    community-based organizations, role
        of, 156–62, 158–62t,
        198–200t

comparative data for three study
    countries. *See* comparative
    accountability relations in
    India, Ghana, and Ethiopia
decentralization, 50–52
    challenges of, 51–52b
    international government agency
        initiatives, 84
    literature review, 77–81
    policy recommendations for,
        xxxvi–xxxvii, 295–97
DISCAP, xxxvii, 52b, 84, 231, 232,
    263, 296
drinking water, xxxi–xxxii, 55
    complaints and responses,
        160, 161t
    construction or rehabilitation
        of facility, community
        contributions to,
        160–61, 200t
    CWSA, 55, 156, 160
    decentralization of, 275–76
    DWSTs, 55
    household access to and
        satisfaction with services,
        136–39, 137t, 138t, 144–48t,
        197t
    literature review, 81
    National Community Water
        and Sanitation
        Program, 55
    payments for, 161–62, 162t,
        200t
    policy recommendations for,
        xxxix, 299–300
    service provider performance,
        153–56
    WATSANs, xxxix, 55, 98, 156,
        158–60, 159–61t,
        276, 300
economic indicators, 35–36, 36t
education and training
    enrollment and literacy rates,
        37–40, 38–39t
    illiteracy as bar to participation in
        local politics, 222
    political representatives, gender
        training for, 226, 227t

FBOs in
　　extension agents meeting with, 142
　　factors associated with membership
　　　　in, 157, 158*t*, 259
　　methodology of study and, 98
　　policy recommendations,
　　　　xxxviii–xxxix, 299
　　role of, 54–55, 156–57, 259
gender and social indicators, 37–40,
　　38–39*t*
governance indicators, 36–37, 37*t*
household access to and satisfaction
　　with services
　　agricultural extension programs,
　　　　132–36, 133–36*t*, 143*t*,
　　　　194–96*t*
　　basic characteristics of
　　　　households, 194*t*
　　drinking water, 136–39, 137*t*, 138*t*,
　　　　144–48*t*, 197*t*
　　factors associated with, 139–42,
　　　　141*t*, 143–48*t*
　　priorities for service provision,
　　　　139, 140*t*
international government agency
　　initiatives in, 81–84
long route of accountability in,
　　220–32, 279–81, 280*f*. *See also*
　　subhead "political
　　representatives," *this entry*
methodology of study in, 97–99, 98*t*
NORSAAC, 230, 231
policy recommendations for,
　　xxxvi–xxxix, 294–300
　　agricultural extension programs,
　　　　xxxvii–xxxix, 297–99
　　decentralization policy,
　　　　xxxvi–xxxvii, 295–97
　　drinking water, xxxix, 299–300
political parties, 49
political representatives
　　development projects, securing,
　　　　224–28, 225–26*b*, 227*t*
　　empowering and strengthening,
　　　　295–97
　　female officials, increasing, 295–96
　　gender training for, 226, 227*t*

as "glorified beggars," 225–26*b*
households, interactions with,
　　221–23, 221*t*, 223*t*
illiteracy as bar to participation in
　　local politics, 222
international organizations and
　　NGOs, interactions with,
　　231–32
other political/public officials,
　　interactions with, 228–29*t*,
　　228–30
resource allocations, securing,
　　230*t*
service providers and, 223–32,
　　224*t*, 225–26*b*, 227–30*t*
short versus long route of
　　accountability compared,
　　279–81, 280*f*
subcommittee membership, 224*t*
political system, 49–52
qualitative case studies in, 99
quantitative data collection in,
　　97–98, 98*t*
service provider performance,
　　142–56
　　agricultural extension agents,
　　　　142–53, 149–55*t*
　　drinking water, 153–56
　　farmers' constraints, perceptions
　　　　of, 152–53, 154–55*t*
　　interactions with other actors,
　　　　151–52, 152*t*
　　mission orientation and
　　　　constraints, 149–51, 150–51*t*
　　political representatives and,
　　　　223–32, 224*t*, 225–26*b*,
　　　　227–30*t*
　　profile and capacity of front-line
　　　　professionals, 142–49, 149*t*
　　work environment, perceptions of,
　　　　152, 153*t*
short route of accountability in,
　　132–62. *See also* more specific
　　subheadings, *this entry*
community-based organizations,
　　role of, 156–62, 158–62*t*,
　　198–200*t*

in Ethiopia, 87, 91*b,* 183
in Ghana, 81–84
in India, 69–76, 78–80*t*
International Union of Local
    Authorities Declaration on
    Women (1998), 77
ISEC. *See* Institute for Social and
    Economic Change
ISSER. *See* Institute of Statistical Social
    and Economic Research

jamabandhi program, India, xxxiii,
    209–10, 210*f,* 247*f,*
    250*n*2, 289

Karnataka, India. *See* India
kebeles (local political subdivisions in
    Ghana), 49–52. *See also*
    Ghana
knowledge gaps, 9, 31–32, 32–33*b*

Latin America and Caribbean,
    promoting gender equity in,
    26
livestock services in India. *See*
    subheading "veterinary
    services," under India
long route of accountability, 207–xxxi
    in agricultural extension programs,
        xxxi, 266–69
    in conceptual framework, xxvii*f,*
        xxviii
    defined, 8, 11*b*
    diagram of, 206*f*
    in Ethiopia, 232–44, 281–83, 282*f.*
        See also subhead "political
        representatives," under
        Ethiopia
    in Ghana, 220–32, 279–81, 280*f.*
        See also subhead "political
        representatives," under
        Ghana
    in India, 205–20, 244–49, 277–79,
        278*f. See also* subhead
        "political representatives,"
        under India
    short and long routes compared,
        277–83, 278*f,* 280*f,* 282*f*

Mahila Abhivrudhi Yojane scheme,
    Karnataka, India, 44
Managing Environmental Resources to
    Enable Transitions (MERET)
    project, Ethiopia, 64
market failure, xxv, 1, 2*b*
MDGs. *See* Millennium Development
    Goals
mengistawi budin (government teams)
    in Ethiopia, 41*f,* 57, 92*n*6,
        178, 181, 268
MERET. *See* Managing Environmental
    Resources to Enable Transi-
    tions project, Ethiopia
methodology, xxvii–xxviii, 93–103. *See*
    also conceptual framework;
    qualitative case studies;
    quantitative data collection
    in Ethiopia, 99–102, 101–3*t*
    in Ghana, 97–99, 98*t*
    in India, 93–97, 94*t,* 96*t,* 102–3*t*
Millennium Development Goals
    (MDGs), xvii, 5, 6
mortality rates, 38*t*

National Community Water and
    Sanitation Program, Ghana, 55
National Policy on Women (NPW),
    Ethiopia, 60–61, 86
Net-Map, 97, 102, 103*n*1
New Partnership for African
    Development, 6
NGOs. *See* nongovernmental
    organizations
Nigeria, women in local government
    in, 29
nongovernment organizations (NGOs)
    in conceptual framework, 18*f,* 20
    Ethiopia
        agricultural extension programs
            in, 166–67
        service provider interactions in,
            182–83
    Ghana's drinking water supply
        and, 156
    service failures of, xxv, 1, 3–4*b,* 4
    strategies for promoting gender
        equity in, 29

NORSAAC. *See* Northern Sector Awareness on Action Centre, Ghana

North, Douglass, 8*b*

Northern Sector Awareness on Action Centre (NORSAAC), Ghana, 230, 231

NPW. *See* National Policy on Women, Ethiopia

other backward caste (OBC) groups. *See* special caste/special tribe/other backward caste (SC/ST/OBC) groups in India

PBS. *See* Protection of Basic Services Project, Ethiopia

Philippines, gender strategies in, 27, 31

policy recommendations, xxxii–xlii, 285–305. *See also under* Ethiopia; Ghana; India
  alternatives to user associations, developing, 287–88
  cross-cutting strategies for promoting gender equity, 25*b*, 31, 286–88
  for FBOs, xxxiv–xxxv, xxxviii–xxxix
  gender-disaggregated data, collecting and using, 286–87
  qualitative and quantitative tools, using, 286–87
  satisfaction indicators, developing, 287
  understanding why and how rural services fail women, 286*t*

political incentives to improve gender and governance in rural services, 305

political parties
  accountability, improving, 21, 22*b*
  in conceptual framework, 20
  in Ethiopia, 56, 240–41*b*, 240–42
  in Ghana, 49
  in India, 40, 209
  role of, 6, 9
  strategies for promoting gender equity, 25*b*, 28–31

political representatives. *See also under* Ethiopia; Ghana; India

accountability, improving, 22*b*. *See also* long route of accountability
  in conceptual framework, 18–19
  corruption, bribery, and female politicians, 30–31
  defined, 11*b*
  future research questions, 33*b*
  husbands of female politicians in India, 214*b*, 216, 218*b*
  reservation policies in India, 66–68
  strategies for promoting gender equity, 24–25*b*, 28–31

privatization, effectiveness of, 28

Protection of Basic Services Project (PBS), Ethiopia, 87

Public Sector Capacity Building Program Support Project (PSCAP), Ethiopia, 87, 91*b*, 301

qualitative case studies
  in Ethiopia, 101–03*t*
  in Ghana, 99
  in India, 95–97, 102–03*t*
  policy recommendations, use in developing, 286–87

quantitative data collection
  in Ethiopia, 99–101, 101*t*
  in Ghana, 97–98, 98*t*
  in India, 93–95, 94*t*, 96*t*
  policy recommendations, use in developing, 286–87

Research and Extension Linkage Committees (RELCs), Ghana, 54

research opportunities, agricultural extension programs as, 292, 298

reservation policies in India, 66–68

rural services. *See* gender and governance in rural services

Sampoorna Grameen Rozgar Yojana (SGRY) scheme, India, 43, 94, 214, 215, 216*t*, 217*t*

LaVergne, TN USA
27 July 2010
191100LV00009B/40/P